A Communicative
Grammar of English

A Communicative Grammar of English

Geoffrey Leech
Jan Svartvik

Based on *A Grammar of Contemporary English*
by Randolph Quirk, Sidney Greenbaum,
Geoffrey Leech, Jan Svartvik

Longman

LONGMAN GROUP LIMITED
London

*Associated companies, branches and representatives
throughout the world*

© Longman Group Ltd. 1975

First published 1975

ISBN 0 582 55238 9

Printed in Great Britain by William Clowes & Sons, Limited
London, Beccles and Colchester

Acknowledgements

We gratefully acknowledge the help and advice of a number of friends and scholars in the preparation of this book. R A Close in particular deserves our thanks for giving us the benefit of his long and varied experience in English language teaching in cogent and detailed comments on the book in manuscript. A similar vote of thanks goes to Christopher Candlin, whose expertise in applied linguistics was of great value in the revision of Part Three. Two American readers, Faith Ann Johansson and William Pepicello, have earned our gratitude for hunting down 'unAmerican' influences in the draft, as well as for more general comments. We thank our co-authors of *A Grammar of Contemporary English* for their blessing on this enterprise, as well as for the more practical benefit of their advice and interest. We also thank Delia Halnon, Peter Clifford and Gordon Walsh of Longman for their care, expertise, and friendly guidance in bringing this book to press.

GL and JS

Contents

8   Contents

Preface

To the student

A Communicative Grammar of English is a new kind of grammar. In writing it, we have assumed that studying grammar, for the overseas student, makes most sense if one starts with the question 'How can I use grammar to communicate?'. Thus the main part of the book is devoted to the USES of grammar, rather than to grammatical STRUCTURE.

The book is intended primarily for the fairly advanced student, for example the first-year university student. If you are such a student you will have studied English grammar in one form or another already, but here we offer you a new perspective on the subject, which relates grammatical structure systematically to meanings, uses and situations. In this way we hope you will improve and extend the range of your communicative skill in the language. The book also supplies the essential information about grammatical forms and structures which you will need, and can therefore be used as a general reference book or sourcebook on English grammar.

The plan of the whole book is as follows:

Part One   Varieties of English
Here we explain briefly different kinds or varieties of English, such as ⟨informal English⟩, ⟨written English⟩ and ⟨American English⟩. We make extensive use of such labels in the other parts of the book, because it is important, for communication, to know in what contexts a particular form of language will be used. Part One ends with a list of references to variety labels, which enables you to follow up the range of grammatical constructions and uses associated with a given variety, such as ⟨informal English⟩.

Part Two   Intonation
Much of the book deals with spoken English, and effective communication in speech depends to a great extent on intonation. So in this part, we introduce the most important features of English intonation, together with the intonation symbols which are used in Part Three.

Part Three   Grammar in use
This is the central part of the book which you will want to use most. In it the different types of meaning and different ways of organising meaning are discussed in systematic order.

Part Four   Grammatical compendium
This part is a reference guide to English grammatical forms and structures, arranged in alphabetical order. It is a necessary complement to Part Three, in that it explains the grammatical terms used there.

There is a comprehensive index at the end of the book which will give you convenient access to the information contained in the various parts.

To the teacher

A Communicative Grammar of English is a fresh departure in grammar writing in that it employs a communicative rather than a structural approach. There are several reasons for emphasising the communication aspects of learning English grammar. Here, let us consider just two.

The type of student we have had in mind when writing this book is fairly advanced, for example a first-year student at a university or training college. Usually, he already has grounding in the grammar of the language after several years of school English. Yet his proficiency in actually using the language may be disappointing. This, we believe, may be partly attributed to 'grammar fatigue'. The student may therefore benefit from looking at grammar from another angle, where grammatical structures are systematically related to meanings, uses and situations.

The conventional method of presenting English grammar in terms of structure also has a certain drawback in itself. For example, in such a grammar notions of time may be dealt with in as many as four different places: under the tense of the verb, under time adverbs, under prepositional phrases denoting time and under temporal conjunctions and clauses. The student who is primarily interested in making use of the language rather than in learning about its structure (and this is true for the majority of foreign students) is not likely to find such an arrangement particularly helpful. The organisation of *A Communicative Grammar of English*, the central part of which deals with grammar in use, makes it possible to bring similar notions, such as those involving time, together in one place.

The book consists of four parts:

Part One   Varieties of English
Where English gives us a choice of grammatical structures for a particular purpose, the different grammatical structures available are often not equivalent, since they belong to different 'styles' or 'varieties'. We believe that the appropriate choice is as important as it is difficult for the type of student we have in mind. Throughout the book, therefore, we make use of 'variety labels' such as ⟨formal⟩, ⟨informal⟩, ⟨written⟩, ⟨spoken⟩. Part One describes what these variety labels mean, and supplies a detailed list of their uses in the rest of the book.

Part Two   Intonation
Intonation is clearly important in a communicative treatment stressing spoken English. In Part Two our object is to provide the student with the basic informa-

tion about English intonation that he needs in order to understand the intonation marking used in Part Three.

Part Three   Grammar in use

Communication is not a simple process. It is helpful, for our purpose, to think of four circles, each including the other, representing the different types of meaning and different ways of organising meaning. The four circles in the figure correspond to Sections A–D in Part Three.

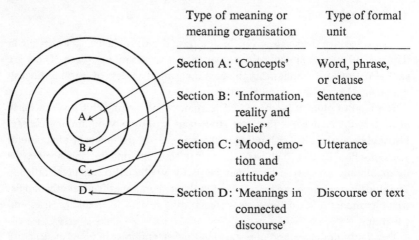

Type of meaning or meaning organisation	Type of formal unit
Section A: 'Concepts'	Word, phrase, or clause
Section B: 'Information, reality and belief'	Sentence
Section C: 'Mood, emotion and attitude'	Utterance
Section D: 'Meanings in connected discourse'	Discourse or text

The right-hand column, stating the 'types of formal unit' associated with each section, should not be interpreted too strictly: it is useful to see the relation between the different layers of meaning and a hierarchy of grammatical units, but there is much overlap of categories, and other factors must be allowed for. For example, intonation has an important role in the expression of meaning in Sections B, C and D.

Section A: Concepts

The first circle is that of notional or conceptual meaning. Here we find the basic meaning categories of grammar: categories like 'number', 'definite meaning', 'amount', 'time', 'manner', 'degree'. Such categories identify aspects of our experience of the world. The structural units dealt with here are smaller than the sentence: *ie* words, phrases or clauses.

Section B: Information, reality and belief

The second circle represents logical communication. Here we make use of the categories of Section A to make judgements about truth and falsehood, and to give and elicit information about the world. Such categories as 'statements, questions and responses', 'affirmation and denial', 'possibility' and 'certainty' belong here. The formal unit we are chiefly concerned with is the sentence.

Section C: Mood, emotion and attitude

The third circle involves yet another dimension of communication: the attitudes and behaviour of speaker and hearer. At the speaker's end, language can express attitudes and emotions; at the receiving end, language can control or influence the actions and attitudes of the hearer. This 'controlling' aspect of communication is performed through such speech acts as commanding, suggesting, advising, threatening, promising. Speech acts like these belong to what is often called the 'pragmatic' or 'interactional' aspect of communication. The logical meaning of sentences (Section B) is made use of, but is extended, or perhaps even 'distorted' to perform a different type of function. A question, for example, is logically designed to elicit information on a particular point; but it can be adapted 'pragmatically' for the purpose of making an offer:

> *Would you like some cake?*

or making a suggestion:

> *Why don't you come with me?*

or expressing a strong feeling:

> *Wasn't it a marvellous play?*

The unit of language we are dealing with here is the UTTERANCE, which may or may not correspond to a sentence in length.

Section D: Meanings in connected discourse

The fourth circle comprises the organisational aspect of communication. The question here is 'How shall we arrange our thoughts', *ie* in what order shall we put them, and how shall we bind them together, in order to communicate them in the most appropriate way? Grammar is flexible enough to offer a considerable choice in such matters. This may be called the 'textual' or 'discourse' aspect of communication, because it concerns the composition of a whole text or discourse, not just the way we construct a single sentence.

The four circles of the diagram represent a rational progression from the most limited and detailed sphere of meaning to the most inclusive. This design underlies Part Three, but we have not stuck to it too rigidly. To have done so would often have meant inconvenient repetitions of material in different chapters. In dealing with emotive meaning (Section C), for example, we have moved directly from the EXPRESSION of emotion to the DESCRIPTION of emotion, since the two are often interrelated, even though it might be argued that the description of emotion belongs more properly to notional meaning (Section A). The overriding consideration, in arranging the material in sections, is that of dealing with related communicative choices together.

Part Four   Grammatical compendium

Of the two main parts of the book, Part Three 'Grammar in use' is central and Part Four 'Grammatical compendium' is complementary to it: we need to know both the communicative choices offered by grammar (Part Three), and also the structural grammatical choices through which communication must be channelled (Part Four). The two sets of choices are, however, largely independent, and so are best dealt with separately. The entries in Part Four are arranged alphabetically.

Index

With a new arrangement, as in this grammar, it is essential to have numerous cross-references and a comprehensive index. We have aimed to provide both.

Relation to other work

This book is based on Randolph Quirk, Sidney Greenbaum, Geoffrey Leech and Jan Svartvik, *A Grammar of Contemporary English* (Longman, 1972). However, it cannot be regarded purely as a condensed version of that larger work since its arrangement is totally different, and it contains additional material (especially in Part Three). On the other hand, the structural or formal aspect of grammar is less comprehensively treated here than in *A Grammar of Contemporary English* and also in Randolph Quirk and Sidney Greenbaum, *A University Grammar of English* (Longman, 1973). We have therefore added to each entry in Part Four a reference to the most relevant sections of *A Grammar of Contemporary English*, so that, if required, a more detailed treatment of the topic can be consulted in that book. We have attempted to simplify grammatical terminology and classifications as far as possible, so that the terms and categories treated in Part Four do not in every case correspond to the same terms in *A Grammar of Contemporary English*.

It would be tedious to attempt to acknowledge, except in the most general terms, the debts we owe to linguistic research. As influences on Part Three, mention must be made of recent developments in the study of semantics, pragmatics and discourse, and of the 'functional' approach to language as exemplified in M A K Halliday's *Explorations in the Functions of Language* (Arnold, 1973). A parallel development in language teaching method has been the orientation towards 'communicative' teaching in the work of D A Wilkins and others (see, for example, C N Candlin [ed.], *The Communicative Teaching of English* [Longman, 1975]).

Lancaster and Lund, May 1974

GL and JS

Symbols

(Intonation symbols are discussed in 31–43.)

*	An asterisk signifies that what follows it is 'not good English', *ie* an unacceptable usage:
	*the car of John
( )	Optional items:
	but he didn't (do so)
/ or { }	Choice of items:

    Did anybody/somebody phone?

$$\text{the film} \begin{cases} \text{which we like best} \\ \text{that we like best} \\ \text{we like best} \end{cases}$$

The two methods of representing alternatives can be combined:

$$\begin{cases} \text{all} \\ \text{both} \end{cases} \begin{cases} \text{the/these books} \\ \text{books} \end{cases}$$

This means that the following six combinations can occur:

    all the books
    all these books
    all books
    both the books
    both these books
    both books

[ ]	Bracketed numerals appear after examples when required for cross-reference:
	As in sentence [5], . . .
⟨ ⟩	Variety labels (*see* 1):
	⟨formal⟩, ⟨AmE⟩, *etc.* [On ⟨GA⟩, ⟨RP⟩, *see* p. 17]
see	Cross-references:
	(*see* 408) means 'see Section 408 in this grammar'.
	(*GCE*: 14.2) means 'see *A Grammar of Contemporary English*, Section 14.2'.
/ /	Slants enclose phonemic transcriptions: *see* p. 17.
‖	The double bar separates RP and GA pronunciations: *see* p. 17.

Key to phonetic symbols

Vowels and diphthongs

iː	as in b*ea*d	ɔː	as in c*augh*t ⟨RP⟩
ɪ	as in b*i*d	ʊ	as in p*u*ll
e	as in b*e*d	uː	as in p*oo*l
æ	as in b*a*d	ʌ	as in c*u*t
ɑː	as in c*a*lm	ɜː	as in b*ir*d ⟨RP⟩
ɒ	as in c*o*t ⟨RP⟩	ə	as in cupb*oar*d ⟨RP⟩
eɪ	as in f*ai*l	ɪə	as in p*eer* ⟨RP⟩
oʊ	as in f*oa*l	eə	as in p*air* ⟨RP⟩
aɪ	as in f*i*le		
aʊ	as in f*ow*l		
ɔɪ	as in f*oi*l		

Consonants

p	as in *p*ig	h	as in *h*ot
b	as in *b*ig	m	as in su*m*
t	as in *t*wo	n	as in su*n*
d	as in *d*o	ŋ	as in su*ng*
k	as in *c*ome, *k*ing	l	as in *l*ot
g	as in *g*um	r	as in *r*ot
tʃ	as in *ch*eap	w	as in *w*et
dʒ	as in *j*eep, bri*dge*	j	as in *y*et
f	as in *f*ew		
v	as in *v*iew		
θ	as in *th*ing		
ð	as in *th*en		
s	as in i*ce*, *s*ay		
z	as in e*y*es, *y*oo		
ʃ	as in pre*ss*ure, *sh*ow		
ʒ	as in plea*s*ure		

Note on phonetic symbols

Phonetic symbols are used only occasionally in this text, mainly where they are needed to illustrate a grammatical distinction or rule. We have tried to use a system of transcription which is not biased towards a particular kind of speech, but this is not easy since British and American English (the two national varieties with which we are chiefly concerned) differ more obviously in pronunciation than in any other respect. To simplify matters, we consider only one accent from each national variety: *Received Pronunciation*, or RP, which is common among educated speakers in England (though not elsewhere in Britain); and *General American* pronunciation, or GA, which is used in the central and northern areas of the United States and in parts of Canada. The differences between these accents may be summarised under the following headings:

a *Different sounds are used for the same phoneme.* In other words, a phoneme (or 'distinctive sound', enclosed within slants / /) that is linguistically the same may be phonetically different in RP and GA. Very many differences fall into this category. For example:

/ɪ/, as in *bid*, is often more central in GA than in RP.

/e/, as in *bed*, is usually more open in GA than in RP.

/æ/, as in *bad*, is usually longer and more close in GA than in RP.

/ɔ:/, as in *cause*, is usually more open in GA than in RP.

/oʊ/, as in *go*, has a more central and unrounded first element in RP than in GA (which is why many British books show the vowel as /əʊ/; in GA the first element is closer to [o]).

/t/ and /d/ between vowels, as in *latter* and *ladder*, are often the same in GA (with the tongue flapped against the roof of the mouth).

/r/ is retroflex in GA but not in RP.

There are many other differences of this type, which for our present purposes we ignore.

b *RP and GA have a different number of phonemes.* Where RP has the four phonemes /æ/, /ɑ:/, /ɒ/ and /ɔ:/, GA has only three, /æ/, /ɑ/ and /ɔ:/. There is considerable variation in words with these vowels. For example:

RP has /æ/ in *hat, man*; /ɑ:/ in *path, laugh, calm, father*; /ɒ/ in *got, log, cross, long*; /ɔ:/ in *law, cause*.

GA has /æ/ in *hat, man, path, laugh*; /ɑ/ in *calm, father, got, log*; /ɔ:/ in *cross, long, law, cause*.

In this text, we use the double bar ‖ to separate RP and GA pronunciations where necessary: the form before the double bar is RP, while that following is GA. For example:

got /gɒt‖gɑt/, *long* /lɒŋ‖lɔ:ŋ/

In other cases we represent RP and GA by a single transcription:

hat /hæt/, *law* /lɔ:/.

c *A sound used in one accent may be omitted in the other.* For example, RP does not pronounce a written *r* before a consonant:

farm /fɑ:m‖fɑrm/, *cord* /kɔ:d‖kɔrd/, *burn* /bɜ:n‖bɜrn/

At the end of a word, /r/ is pronounced in RP if the next word begins with a vowel but not otherwise, whereas it is always pronounced in GA. To show this, a small raised /ʳ/ is used:

far /fɑ:ʳ/, *store* /stɔ:ʳ/, *sir* /sɜ:ʳ/

On the other hand, before a written 'long' *u* RP inserts /j/ after certain consonants while GA does not:

tube /tjuːb‖tuːb/, *assume* /əˈsjuːm‖əˈsuːm/

d *Different phonemes may be used in the same word.* There are no regular principles for this type of variation, which is found only with individual words. For example:

ate /et‖eɪt/, *clerk* /klɑːk‖klɜrk/, *shone* /ʃɒn‖ʃoʊn/

Part One

Varieties of English

1

To use a language properly, we of course have to know the grammatical structures of the language and their meanings. (These are the subjects of Parts Three and Four of this book.) But we also have to know what forms of language are appropriate for given situations, and for this purpose, you will find in both those parts (as in many dictionaries) instances of 'variety labels' such as ⟨AmE⟩ (for American English), ⟨BrE⟩ (for British English), ⟨RP⟩ (for Received Pronunciation), ⟨GA⟩ (for General American), ⟨formal⟩, ⟨informal⟩, ⟨polite⟩, ⟨familiar⟩. These labels are reminders that the English language is, in a sense, not a single language, but many languages, each of which belongs to a particular geographical area or to a particular kind of situation. The English used in the United States is somewhat different from the English used in Great Britain; the English used in formal written communications is in some ways different from the English used in informal conversation. Obviously, in a general book of this kind we must ignore many of the less important differences. The purpose of Part One is to explain briefly what is meant by the variety labels that you will meet, and to illustrate the varieties of English they refer to. If you wish to follow up a particular variety in detail you may do so by means of the entries for variety labels in the list at the end of this Part (*see* 23–30).

The 'common core'

2

Luckily for the learner, many of the features of English are found in all, or nearly all varieties. We say that general features of this kind belong to the 'common core' of the language. Take, for instance, the three words *children, offspring*, and *kids. Children* is a 'common core' term; *offspring* is rather formal (and used of animals as well as human beings); *kids* is informal and familiar. It is safest, when in doubt, to use the 'common core' term; thus *children* is the word you would want to use most often. But part of 'knowing English' is knowing in what circumstances it would be possible to use *offspring* or *kids* instead of *children*. Let us take another illustration, this time from grammar:

Feeling tired, John went to bed early.	[1]
John went to bed early because he felt tired.	[2]
John felt tired, so he went to bed early.	[3]

Sentence [2] is a 'common core' construction. It could (for example) be used in both speech and writing. [1] is rather formal in construction, typical of written exposition; [3] is informal, and is likely to occur in a relaxed conversation.

In this book you can assume that features of English which are given no variety label belong to the 'common core'.

Geographical and national varieties ⟨BrE⟩ ⟨AmE⟩ (*see* 29–30)

3

English is spoken as a native language by nearly three hundred million people: in the United States of America, Canada, Britain, Ireland, Australia, the Caribbean, and many other places. But since the varieties of English used in the United States and in Britain are the most important in terms of population and influence, the only national varieties we shall distinguish in this book are American English ⟨AmE⟩ and British English ⟨BrE⟩. In general, what we say in this book applies equally to ⟨AmE⟩ and ⟨BrE⟩. The grammatical differences between the two varieties (in comparison with differences of pronunciation and vocabulary) are not very great.

Here are some brief examples of how ⟨AmE⟩ and ⟨BrE⟩ can differ.

4

(A)   ⟨AmE⟩ has two past participle forms of *get*: *gotten* and *got*, whereas ⟨BrE⟩ has only one: *got* (*see* 604). (The past tense form is *got* in both varieties.) For example:

⟨AmE⟩: Have you *gotten/got* the tickets for the match?
⟨BrE⟩: Have you *got* the tickets for the match?

5

(B)   There is also a difference in the repeated subject after *one* (*see* 692). In ⟨AmE⟩ we can say:

One cannot succeed unless *he* tries hard.

In ⟨BrE⟩ we have to say:

One cannot succeed unless *one* tries hard.

6

(C)   The normal complement after *different* is *than* in ⟨AmE⟩ but *from* (or sometimes *to*) in ⟨BrE⟩.

⟨AmE⟩: Their house is different *than* ours.
⟨BrE⟩: Their house is different *from* ours.

7

(D)   The use of the subjunctive after verbs like *demand, require, insist, suggest, etc*, is more common in ⟨AmE⟩ than ⟨BrE⟩, where the construction is restricted to rather formal contexts (*see* 823):

They suggested that Smith *be* dropped from the team.
⟨chiefly AmE⟩
They suggested that Smith *should be* dropped from the team.
⟨AmE⟩ and ⟨BrE⟩

Within each English-speaking country there are many differences of regional dialect (for example, between the English spoken in New England and in the

Southern States of the U.S.A.). These differences rarely affect grammatical usage in written English or in educated spoken English, so we shall ignore them in this text.

In representing pronunciation, we shall distinguish where necessary between General American ⟨GA⟩ and Received Pronunciation ⟨RP⟩, two varieties of pronunciation associated with ⟨AmE⟩ and ⟨BrE⟩ respectively. See the Note on phonetic symbols, p. 17.

Written and spoken English ⟨written⟩ ⟨spoken⟩ (see 23–24)

8

The English of speech tends to be different from the English of writing in some fairly obvious ways. For example, in writing we usually have time to plan our message, to think about it carefully while writing, and to revise it afterwards if necessary. In speech (unless it is, say, a lecture prepared in advance), we have no time to do this, but must shape our message as we go:

> Well I've just come back from New York where it was pretty clear
> that . this was a general trend with young people there . and er I um
> I'm worried though because you see . it seems that . you're kind of
> putting the whole blame on the family instead of on the conditions a
> family's being forced to live in these days . look . if you took er I
> mean monkeys are very good parents aren't they . rhesus monkeys
> and so on . they look after their young marvellously—now you put
> them together you crowd them . and they're extremely bad
> parents . . .

Often we use in speech words and phrases like *well*, *you see*, and *kind of* which add little information, but tell us something of the speaker's attitude to his audience and to what he is saying. We also often hesitate, or fill in gaps with 'hesitation fillers' like *er* /ɜːʳ/ and *um* /əm/ while we think of what next to say. We may fail to complete a sentence, or lose track of our sentence and mix up one grammatical construction with another. All these features do not normally occur in writing.

9

In general, the grammar of spoken sentences is simpler and less strictly constructed than the grammar of written sentences. It is difficult to divide a spoken conversation into separate sentences, and the connections between one clause and another are less clear because the speaker relies more on the hearer's understanding of context (see 259–63) and on his ability to interrupt if he fails to understand. But in 'getting across' his message, the speaker is able to rely on features of intonation which tell us a great deal that cannot be given in written punctuation.

In this book we treat written and spoken English as of equal importance. But sometimes, when we give intonation marks (see 31–43) or present examples of dialogue, it will be clear that we are thinking of spoken English.

Formal and informal English ⟨formal⟩ ⟨informal⟩ (see 25–26)

10

Formal language is the type of language we use publicly for some serious purpose, for example, in official reports, business letters and regulations. Formal

English is nearly always written. Exceptionally it is used in speech, for example in formal public speeches.

Informal language (*ie* colloquial language) is the language of private conversation, of personal letters, *etc*. It is the first type of language that a native-speaking child becomes familiar with. Because it is generally easier to understand than formal English, it is often used nowadays in public communication of a popular kind: for example, advertisements and popular newspapers mainly employ a colloquial or informal style.

11

There are various degrees of formality, as these examples show:

When his dad died, Pete had to get another job.   [4]
After his father's death, Peter had to change his job.   [5]
On the decease of his father, Mr Brown was obliged to seek
alternative employment.   [6]

These sentences mean *roughly* the same thing, but would occur in different situations. Sentence [4] could be part of a casual conversation between friends of Peter Brown. [5] is of fairly neutral ('common core') style. [6] is very formal, in fact stilted, and would only occur in a written report.

12

In English there are many differences of vocabulary between formal and informal language. Much of the vocabulary of formal English is of French, Latin, and Greek origin; and we can often 'translate' these terms into informal language by replacing them by words or phrases of Anglo-Saxon origin: compare *commence, continue, conclude* ⟨formal⟩ with *begin, keep (up), end*:

The meeting will { commence at 4 p.m.   ⟨formal⟩
{ begin at 4 o'clock.

The government is { continuing its struggle against inflation.
{   ⟨formal⟩
{ keeping up its fight against inflation.
{   ⟨rather informal⟩

The concert concluded with a performance of Beethoven's 5th symphony. ⟨formal⟩

They ended the concert with Beethoven's 5th. ⟨informal⟩

Many phrasal and prepositional verbs (*see* 696–703) are characteristic of informal style:

⟨FORMAL⟩ OR COMMON CORE WORD	⟨INFORMAL⟩ EQUIVALENT
discover	*find out*
explode	*blow up*
encounter	*come across*
invent	*make up*
enter	*go in (to)*
tolerate	*put up with*
investigate	*look into*
surrender	*give in*

But there is not always a direct 'translation' between formal and informal English. This may be because an informal term has emotive qualities not present in formal language, or because formal language often insists on greater preciseness. The informal word *job*, for instance, has no formal equivalent: instead, we have to choose a more precise and restricted term, according to the context: *employment*, *post* (*esp* ⟨BrE⟩), *position*, *appointment*, *profession*, *vocation*, etc.

13

There are also some grammatical differences between formal and informal English: for example, the use of *who* and *whom*, and the placing of a preposition at the beginning or at the end of a clause (*see* 579, 791):

$$=\begin{cases} \text{She longed for a friend } in\ whom \text{ she could confide. } \langle\text{formal}\rangle \\ \text{She longed for a friend } (who) \text{ she could confide } in. \langle\text{informal}\rangle \end{cases}$$

$$=\begin{cases} In\ what \text{ country was he born? } \langle\text{formal}\rangle \\ What \text{ country was he born } in? \langle\text{informal}\rangle \end{cases}$$

Impersonal style ⟨impersonal⟩

14

Formal written language often goes with an impersonal style; *ie* one in which the speaker does not refer directly to himself or his readers, but avoids the pronouns *I*, *you*, *we*. Some of the common features of impersonal language are passives (*see* 676–82), sentences beginning with introductory *it* (*see* 584–7), and abstract nouns (*see* 54–6). Each of these features is illustrated in:

> *Announcement from the librarian*
> It has been noted with concern that the stock of books in the library has been declining alarmingly. Students are asked to remind themselves of the rules for the borrowing and return of books, and to bear in mind the needs of other students. Penalties for overdue books will in the future be strictly enforced.

The author of this notice could have written a more informal and less impersonal message on these lines:

> The number of books in the library has been going down. Please make sure you know the rules for borrowing, and don't forget that the library is for *everyone's* convenience. So from now on, we're going to enforce the rules strictly. *You have been warned!*

Polite and familiar language ⟨polite⟩ ⟨familiar⟩ (*see* 27–28)

15

Our language tends to be more polite when we are talking to a person we do not know well, or a person senior to ourselves in terms of age or social position.

The opposite of 'polite' is 'familiar'. When we know someone well or intimately, we tend to drop polite forms of language. For example, instead of using the polite vocative *Mr Brown*, we use a first name (*Peter*) or a short name (*Pete*) or even a nickname (*Shortie*). English has no special familiar pronouns, like some languages (*eg* French *tu*, German *du*), but familiarity can be shown in other ways. Compare, for example, these requests (*see* 347 Note 9):

> Shut the door, will you? ⟨familiar⟩

Would you please shut the do͞or? ⟨polite⟩

I wonder if you would mind shutting the do͞or? ⟨more polite⟩

Words like *please* and *kindly* have the sole function of indicating politeness. One can also be familiar in referring to a third person:

Pete's old woman hit the roof when he came home with that
   doll from the disco. ⟨very familiar⟩   [7]

Peter's wife was very angry when he came home with the girl
   from the discotheque. ⟨common core⟩   [8]

We might judge [7] to be ⟨impolite⟩ in that it fails to show proper respect to Peter's wife and the girl. In other words, impoliteness is normally a question of being familiar in the wrong circumstances.

16

Sentence [7] is also an example of slang. Slang is language which is very familiar in style, and is usually restricted to the members of a particular social group, for example 'teenage slang', 'army slang', 'theatre slang'. Slang is not usually fully understood by people outside a particular social group, and so has a value of showing the intimacy and solidarity of its members. Because of its restricted use, we shall not be concerned with slang in this book.

Tactful and tentative language ⟨tactful⟩ ⟨tentative⟩

17

Politeness is connected with tact or diplomacy. To be tactful is to avoid causing offence or distress to someone. Sometimes tact means disguising or covering up the truth. In the following sentences, *gone* and *passed away* are ways of avoiding mentioning the unpleasant fact of Peter's father's death:

Peter's father has gone at last.

Peter's father has passed away at last.

Here is a tactful imperative, said by Mr Brown to his new typist, Miss Smith:

Would you like to type this letter for me?

It may be Miss Smith's job to do what Mr Brown tells her to do. But by disguising his order in the form of a question about Miss Smith's wishes, he may win her co-operation more readily.

18

A request, suggestion, *etc* can be made more tactful by making it more tentative. Compare:

I suggest that we postpone the meeting until tomorrow.

May I suggest that we postpone the meeting until tomorrow?
   ⟨tactful⟩

Could I suggest that we postpone the meeting until tomorrow?
   ⟨tentative, more tactful⟩

In other cases tentativeness is not connected with tact, but is simply an indication of the speaker's reluctance to commit himself on a given question. For example, *might* is a more tentative way of expressing possibility than *may*:

Someone may have made a mistake.

Someone might have made a mistake. ⟨tentative⟩

Literary, elevated or rhetorical language ⟨literary⟩ ⟨elevated⟩ ⟨rhetorical⟩
19
Some features of English of limited use have a 'literary' or 'elevated' tone: they belong mainly to the literary language of the past, but can still be used by a writer or public speaker of today if he wants to impress us or move us by the solemnity or seriousness of what he has to say. An example of such elevated language comes from the Inaugural Speech of President Kennedy (1961):

> Let the word go forth from this time and place, to friend and foe
> alike, that the torch has passed to a new generation of
> Americans . . .

This contains the old-fashioned (archaic) words *forth* and *foe*, and also begins with an elevated *let*-construction (*see* 521).

In addition to the variety labels ⟨literary⟩ and ⟨elevated⟩, we sometimes use the related label ⟨rhetorical⟩. This signifies a stylised use of language, whether in speech or writing, which is consciously chosen for an emphatic or emotive effect. A good example of this is the so-called 'rhetorical question', which is meant to be interpreted as an emphatic statement:

> Is it any wonder that politicians are mistrusted? (='It is no
> wonder that . . .')

Although we often meet them in the literature of earlier periods, literary, elevated and rhetorical forms of language are not particularly common in the everyday language of today, and we shall only need to refer to them occasionally in this book.

Levels of usage
20
Apart from the national varieties ⟨AmE⟩ and ⟨BrE⟩, the different types of English we have discussed belong to different 'levels of usage'. We might attempt to place them on a scale running from 'elevated English' at one extreme to 'slang' at the other extreme. But it is probably better, in the main, to think of three pairs of contrasting levels:

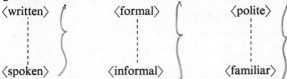

| ⟨written⟩ | ⟨formal⟩ | ⟨polite⟩ |
| ⟨spoken⟩ | ⟨informal⟩ | ⟨familiar⟩ |

This diagram represents only the most important levels of usage, and ignores the more restricted variety labels, such as ⟨impersonal⟩ and ⟨elevated⟩. The features at the top of the diagram tend to go together, and likewise those at the bottom. But this need not be the case. For example, it is possible to express oneself politely in spoken English, and it is possible to express oneself informally in written English.

21
In Parts Three and Four, we make liberal use of labels for levels of usage, because we feel it is important to give you as full guidance as possible on the 'appropriate use' of English grammatical forms and structures. Some other speakers of English might disagree with some of our uses of these labels. This is because the

feeling for 'levels of usage' is very much a subjective matter, depending on the intuitions of individuals who use the language. For example, an older English speaker might regard as 'familiar' a form of language which might not seem so to a younger English speaker. We would like you to use these labels for guidance in your own use of the language, rather than to consider them as descriptive of general standards of 'appropriateness'.

Again, we emphasise that examples and constructions which are not marked by variety labels may be considered to belong to the common core of English.

Selective list of variety references
22

For those who wish to explore the characteristics of different varieties of English in more detail, we now give a list of references to variety labels in the rest of this book. For this purpose, we limit ourselves to the eight most important variety labels, and to a selection of the more important references to these labels. References are to sections.

23
⟨*Written*⟩
Listing and adding: *firstly, to conclude, etc* 370
Explanation: *ie, eg, viz* 373
Participial and verbless clauses: *Cleared, the site will be very valuable* 388, 407–9
Pieces of information set off by punctuation 411
Main and subsidiary information: focus, weight, topic, *etc* 422–4, 427
Cleft sentences: *It's more time that we need* 434–7
Concord: *Neither of them has . . .* 540
Genitive 570–2
A personal pronoun substituting for a following noun phrase 686
Spelling changes: *lady/ladies, etc* 808–21

24
⟨*Spoken*⟩
Pieces of information set off by tone units 36, 411–13, 479 (sentence adverbials), 490 (apposition), 522 (comment clauses)
Rising intonation in questions 41, 249, 800
Making a new start: *Now, what was the other thing . . .?* 368
Use of coordination 377
Unlinked clauses 389
Subject-verb inversion: *Here's the milkman* 431
Auxiliary verbs: contracted forms 497, 630
Comment clauses in end-position: *He's a pacifist, you see* 522
Genitive 570–2

25
⟨*Formal*⟩
Amount words: *many people* 58, 60, *a majority* (*minority*) *of* 58
First person pronouns, *we* (for *I*): *As we showed . . .* 85
Pronouns with indefinite reference: *One never knows what may happen* 86
Choice of *this* and *that* 89

Introductory *there*: *There are two patients* . . . 591

Uncontracted forms: *He is not* . . . 630

Nominal *-ing* clauses: *I am surprised at John's/his making that mistake* 650

Relative pronouns: *the girl to whom he spoke* 791–4

Subordination signalled by inversion: *Had I known,* . . . 828

26

⟨*Informal*⟩

Species nouns: *most kinds of cats, these kind of dogs* 52

Amount words: *a lot of (lots of) people* 58, 60, 566

Pronouns with indefinite reference: *You never know* . . ., *They say* . . . 86

Time-when, omitting the preposition: *I saw her the day after her birthday* 144

Duration: *for ages* 156

Place: *Over here is where I put the books* 161, *You don't see many trams about* 180, 190

Manner, means and instrument: *What did he write it with?* 192, *She cooks turkey the way I like* 193–4

Result: *I took no notice of him so he* . . . 202, 380

Negative purpose: *He left early in case he* . . . 203

Contrast: *though* 212

Condition, contrast: *all the same* 214, *anyway* 216

Degree: *a lot, a bit, etc* 219–21

Comparison: *Is he that tall?* 232

Addition: *too, as well* 238

Wh-questions: *Who did you send books to, and why?* 252

Short questions: *Who with?* 255

Hypothetical meaning: *If I was younger* . . ., *I wish I was dead* 285–6, 825

Appearance: *He looks as if he's ill* 305

Negative intensifiers: *a bit* 317

Permission: *Is it all right if* . . .? 340

Obligation: *I've got to* 341–2, *You'd better* 343

Greetings of introduction: *Hello* 358

Beginning and ending letters: *Dear George, Love from Janet,* 360

Regrets: *I'm sorry I was unable* . . . 361

Changing the subject: *by the way* 369

Reinforcement: *in any case, anyway* 371

Positive condition: *You'll feel better, then* 381

Negative condition: *Put your overcoat on, or* . . . 382

Alternatives: *or else* 385

Unlinked clauses 389

Substitutes: —'*Who wants to play?*'—'*Me*' 398, *do that* (instead of *do so*) 400, *You can borrow my pen, if you want* 403

Emphatic topic: *Joe his name is* 427

Subject-verb inversion: *Here comes the bus* 431

Demonstrative+*wh*-clause: *This is how you start the engine* 438

Adverbs with adjective form: *He was dead drunk* 461, *He spoke loud and clear* 463

Commands: *Somebody let me out* 521

Comment clauses: *He's a pacifist, you see* 522

Comparison: *taller than me* 528, 687

Concord: *Neither of them have . . . , Has anybody brought their camera?* 540

Interrogative and relative pronouns: *Who is he marrying?, He couldn't remember which shelf he kept it on* 581, 642, 791–4

Introductory *there*: *There's two patients . . .* 591

Nominal *that*-clauses with *that* omitted: *I knew he was wrong* 640

Nominal *-ing* clauses: *I'm surprised at John/him making that mistake* 650

Passives: the *get*-passive (*he got hurt*) 680

Phrasal verbs: *catch on, etc* 696–8

Finite clause as postmodifier: *I like the way she does her hair* 728

27

⟨*Polite*⟩

Intonation: rising tone 42

Future: *When will you be visiting us again?* 134

Questions: *Please could I . . .?* 253, 255

Permission: *May we smoke in here?* 340

Politer commands: *This way, please* 347

Polite requests: *Would you be so kind as to . . .?* 349

Refusing invitations: *That's very kind of you but . . .* 351

Beginning and ending conversations: *Good evening* 358

Accepting offers: *Yes, please* 363

28

⟨*Familiar*⟩

Pointer words: *. . . when this girl came up to me . . .* 90

Short questions: *Where to?* 255

Echo questions: *Sorry, what was his job?* 257

Omission of information: *See you later* 261

Emotive emphasis in speech: *Do be quiet!, He's an absolute saint, Has she grown!, etc* 308–20

Answers to requests: *OK* 348

Invitations: *Come in and sit down* 351

Beginning and ending conversations, greetings, *etc*: *See you, Hi, How's things?* 358–9

Good wishes, *etc*: *Cheers!* 362

Offers: *Have some more coffee* 363

Vocatives: *daddy, you guys, etc* 364

Omission of the definite article: *Dad will soon be home* 756

Quantifiers: *That's some car you have there* 768

29

⟨*AmE*⟩

Pronouns with indefinite reference: *One should always look after one's/his/your money* 86

The past for the present perfect: *Did you eat yet?* 115

Time-when: *on the weekend* 143, *I'll see you Saturday* 144

Duration: *from June through December* 153

The use of *about* and *around* 180

Requests for repetition: *Excuse me?* 258

The subjunctive: *Congress decided that the present law continue* . . . 291, 823

Certainty or logical necessity: *You have to be joking!* 297

Ending letters: *Sincerely yours*, 360

Getting attention: *I beg your pardon!* 365

Restrictive apposition with omitted determiner: *Art critic Paul Jones* 490

Articles: *go to the university* 495

Auxiliary verbs: *I don't have any books* 499, *ain't* 500

Concord with group nouns: *The audience was* . . . 536

Irregular verbs: *learned* 597, *dreamed* 600, *gotten*, *shined* 604, *spit* 607, *dove, ate* /eɪt/ 616

Times and dates: *at a quarter of six, at ten minutes after six* 668, *on May 5th* 669

Spelling: *travel/traveling* 819

30

⟨*BrE*⟩

Pronouns with indefinite reference: *One should always look after one's money* 86

Time-when: *at the weekend* 143

Negative purpose: *in case he should* . . . 203

Requests for repetition: *Sorry?* 258

Certainty or logical necessity: *Need there be* . . . ? 298, 342

Describing emotions: *I was furious with John* 321

Insistence: *I shan't give in!* 339

Prohibition: *You oughtn't to waste* . . . 344

Farewells: *Cheerio!* 358

Ending letters: *Yours sincerely*, 360

Apologies: *Excuse me* 361

Do as a substitute 399

Articles: *go to university* 495

Auxiliary verbs: *I haven't any books* 499, 672, *Aren't I?* 500, *shan't, mayn't* 501, *Used he to smoke?* 502, *daren't, needn't* 503

Concord: group nouns (*The audience were* . . .) 536

Irregular verbs: *learnt* 597, *dreamt* 600, *got* 604, *ate* /et/ 616

Dates: *on 5 May* 669

Spelling: *travel/travelling* 819

Subordinating conjunctions: *whilst* 830

Part Two

Part Two

Intonation

31

You will need some knowledge of English intonation patterns if you are to understand English grammar. This is because features of intonation are important for signalling grammatical distinctions such as that between statements and questions. Here we concentrate on explaining those features of stress and intonation which play a significant role in grammar, and which therefore need to be discussed and symbolised in Part Three. The features we have to explain are:

Stress	(symbolised by: ')
Nucleus	(symbolised by <u>underlining</u>)
Tone unit	(tone unit boundaries are marked by |)
Tones	*a* falling tone (symbolised `)
	b rising tone (symbolised ´)
	c fall-rise tone (symbolised ᵛ or `´)

Stress

32

The rhythm of English is based on stress. In connected speech, we feel the rhythm of the language in the sequence of STRESSED syllables. Between one stressed syllable and another there may occur one or more UNSTRESSED syllables. The stressed syllables in these examples are preceded by ', and the unstressed syllables are unmarked:

> We've de'cided to 'go to the In'dustrial Exhi'bition.
>
> Can you 'tell me the ex'act 'time it 'opens?

This means that the syllables in capitals below are stressed:

> We've deCIDed to GO to the inDUStrial exhiBItion.
>
> Can you TELL me the exACT TIME it OPens?

33

The normal rules for placing stress are as follows:

(A) The syllables which are stressed are:

    a   one-syllable words of major word-classes (*see* 884–6), *ie* nouns (*time*), verbs (*go*), adjectives (*black*), adverbs (*well*).

    b   the accented syllables of words of more than one syllable of major word classes, *eg* de'CIDed, ex'ACT, 'OPens.

(B) The syllables which are unstressed are:

    a words of minor word-classes (*see* 884–6), *eg* prepositions (*to*), pronouns (*it*), articles (*the*).

    b the unaccented syllables of words of more than one syllable, *eg* de'cid*ed*, *ex*'act, 'op*ens*.

There is no easily-learned rule as to which syllable of a word of more than one syllable is accented. As we see above, accent varies from word to word, so that the first syllable of 'op*ens* is accented, but the second syllable of *ex*'act; the second syllable of *in*'dustrial, but the third syllable of exhi'bition. The placing of stress is also variable according to sentence context, emphasis, speed of utterance, *etc*, and so the rules above are not without exceptions.

34

One point to notice is that a prepositional adverb (*see* 746) belongs to a major word-class, and is therefore stressed, whereas a one-syllable preposition (*see* 744) is usually unstressed. Contrast:

    This 'bed has 'not been 'slept in. (*in* = preposition)

    The 'injured 'man was 'carried 'in. (*in* = prepositional adverb)

The same contrast is sometimes seen between the particle of a prepositional verb (*see* 699) and the particle of a phrasal verb (*see* 696–8):

    He's re'lying on our 'help. (*rely on* = prepositional verb)

    He's 'putting 'on a 'new 'play. (*put on* = phrasal verb)

But the particle may also be unstressed:

    'Make up 'your mind!

In the examples in this book, stress will be marked only where it is necessary for the point illustrated.

Nucleus

35

Not all stressed syllables are of equal importance. Some stressed syllables have greater prominence than others, and form the NUCLEUS, or focal point, of an intonation pattern. For normal purposes, we may describe a nucleus as a strongly stressed syllable which marks a major change of pitch direction, *ie* where the pitch goes up or down. The change of pitch on the nucleus is indicated by an arrow in these and other examples:

In both these examples, the nucleus marks a decisive fall in pitch towards the end of the sentence. (The step-up in pitch on the first stress [-*ly*- and *bed*] is something which will not concern us in our analysis.) As a nucleus is always stressed, there is no need to put a stress mark before it. Often in our examples, we simply indicate the nucleus without indicating the other stressed syllables:

    He's relying on our <u>help</u>.

    This bed has not been <u>slept</u> in.

Tone unit

36

The basic unit of intonation in English is the TONE UNIT. A tone unit, for our purposes, will be considered as a stretch of speech which contains ONE nucleus, and which may contain other stressed syllables, normally preceding the nucleus. The boundaries of a tone unit are marked by the symbol |:

|He's relying on our help.|

|This bed has not been slept in.|

In these examples, the tone unit has the length of a whole sentence. But a sentence often contains more than one tone unit. The number of tone units depends on the length of the sentence, and the degree of emphasis given to various parts of it. The second example above could be pronounced with two tone units:

|This bed | has not been slept in.|

The additional nucleus on *this* here expresses an emphasis on '*this* bed' in contrast to other beds. The following sentence might be pronounced with either two or three tone units, as indicated:

|Last August | we went to stay with our cousins in Mexico.|

|Last August | we went to stay with our cousins | in Mexico.|

In general, we include tone unit boundaries in our examples only where they serve an illustrative purpose; more usually, we omit them.

Tones

37

By TONE, we mean the type of pitch-change which takes place on the nucleus. The three most important tones in English, and the only ones we need distinguish here, are the FALLING tone (`), the RISING tone (´), and the FALL-RISE tone (ˇ or `´):

|Here's a cup of tea for you.|

|Can you tell me the exact time it opens?|

|I can't allow you to do that.|

|The Johnsons | are buying a freezer | so they tell me.|

These can be more precisely represented:

38

The tone of a nucleus determines the pitch of the rest of the tone unit following it. Thus after a falling tone, the rest of the tone unit is at a low pitch. After a rising tone, the rest of the tone unit moves in an upward pitch direction. *Compare:*

(He studies chemistry,) | but he's not really ˋinterested in it |

but he's not really ˎinterested in it |

(So you study chemistry.) | Are you really ´interested in it? |

Are you really interested in it?

39

The fall-rise tone, as its name suggests, consists of a fall in pitch followed by a rise. If the nucleus is the last syllable of the tone unit, the fall and rise both take place on one syllable—the nuclear syllable. Otherwise, the rise occurs in the remainder of the tone unit. *Compare:*

I know he made a mistake

but it wasn't his fault |

but he said he was sorry |

but he didn't mean to do it |

We symbolise these three as follows:

|It wasn't his ˅fault.|

|He said he was ˅sorry.|

|He didn't ˋmean to do´ it.|

Where the rise of the fall-rise extends to a stressed syllable after the nucleus, as in the last example, we signal the fall-rise tone by placing a fall on the nucleus and a rise on the later stressed syllable. This will make it easier for you to follow the intonation contour when you read the examples.

The meanings of tones

40

The meanings of the tones are difficult to specify in general terms. Roughly speaking, the FALLING tone expresses 'certainty', 'completeness', 'independence'. Thus a straightforward statement normally ends with a falling tone, since it asserts a fact of which the speaker is certain. It has an air of finality:

|It's five o'ˋclock.| |Here is the ˋnews.|

41

A RISING tone, on the other hand, expresses 'uncertainty' or 'incompleteness' or 'dependence'. A *yes-no* question (*see* 778) usually has a rising tone, as the speaker is uncertain of the truth of what he is asking about:

|Are you léaving?| |Can I hélp you?|

Parenthetical and subsidiary information in a statement is also often spoken with a rising tone, because this information is incomplete, being dependent for its full understanding on the main assertion:

|If you lìke, | we can go for a pícnic | láter.|

42

Encouraging or ⟨polite⟩ denials, commands, invitations, greetings, farewells, *etc* are generally spoken with a rising tone:

(A) |Are you búsy?| (B) |Nó.| ('Please interrupt me if you
                                         wish')

|'Do sit dówn.|

Here the finality of the falling tone would sound ⟨impolite⟩.

The type of rising tone heard in a *yes-no* question is normally higher than in other cases, and so we may distinguish it by the special term QUESTION INTONATION. We do not distinguish it, however, from other rising tones in our notation.

43

A FALL-RISE tone, as we might expect, combines the falling tone's meaning of 'assertion, certainty' with the rising tone's meaning 'dependence, incompleteness'. At the end of a sentence, it often conveys a feeling of reservation; that is, it asserts something, and at the same time suggests that there is something else to be said:

|That's not mỳ sígnature.| ('it must be somebody else's')

(A) |Do you like póp-music?| (B) |Sŏmetimes,| ('but not in
                                               general')

(A) |Are you búsy?| (B) |Not rĕally.| ('Well, I am, but
                                               not so busy that I can't talk to
                                               you')

At the beginning or in the middle of a sentence, it is a more forceful alternative to the rising tone, expressing the assertion of one point, together with the implication that another point is to follow:

|Mòst of the tíme | we stayed on the bèach.|

|People who work in ŏffices | ought to take plenty of èxercise.|

Part Three

Part Three

Grammar in use

Section A: Concepts

Referring to objects, substances and materials

44

It is through nouns and noun phrases that grammar organises the way we refer to objects. We begin with CONCRETE NOUNS, or nouns referring to objects and substances with physical existence. (We shall use the word 'object' to refer generally to things, animals, people, *etc*.) Our first topic will be count and mass concrete nouns, and the various constructions in which they are linked by *of*.

Singular and plural: one and many
45

Count nouns refer in the singular to one object, and in the plural to more than one object:

Singular   *Plural*

*   * *   * *   * *
                      *   * *   * * *
                                                  * *

a star
one star   two stars   three stars   seven stars *etc*
a single star

Groups of objects
46

We may refer to objects as belonging to a group or set:

a $\begin{Bmatrix} \text{group} \\ \text{number} \end{Bmatrix}$ of stars   a small group of stars   a large group of stars

Group nouns
47
Nouns like *group*, which refer to a set of objects, are called GROUP NOUNS. Group nouns, like other nouns, may be singular or plural: *one group of stars, three groups of stars etc.*

Often a special group noun is used with certain kinds of objects:

an *army* (of soldiers)	a *crew* (of sailors)
a *crowd* (of people)	a *gang* (of thieves, bandits, *etc*)
a *herd* (of cattle)	a *pack* (of cards)
a *flock* (of sheep)	a *constellation* (of stars)

Many group nouns refer to a group of people having a special relationship with one another, or brought together for a particular reason: *tribe, family, committee, club, audience, government, administration, team, etc*. With these nouns, there is a choice of whether to use a singular or plural verb, depending on whether you mean the group as a unit, or the sum of its members (*see* 537):

The audience is/are enjoying the show.   [1]

The government never $\left\{ \begin{array}{l} \text{makes up its mind} \\ \text{make up their minds} \end{array} \right\}$ in a hurry.   [2]

Notice also the difference here between *its mind* (singular) and *their minds* (plural).

Note
People is normally not a group noun, but the plural of *person* (*see* 657).

Partition: part and whole
48
Parts of objects can be referred to by PART NOUNS like *part* (contrasted with *whole*), *half, a quarter, two-thirds, etc*; also by UNIT NOUNS like *piece, slice*:

| the (whole) cake | a slice of the cake | half (of) the cake | (a) quarter of the cake |

part of the cake

Mass nouns
49
Mass nouns (sometimes called 'non-count' nouns) typically refer to substances, whether liquid or solid: *oil, water, butter, wood, leather, iron, rock, glass, etc* (*see* 654). Mass nouns are always singular: it makes no sense to 'count' the quantity of a mass substance which is not naturally divisible into separate objects. You can say:

$\left\{ \begin{array}{l} \text{There's some milk in the refrigerator.} \\ \text{There are two bottles of milk in the refrigerator.} \end{array} \right.$

but not:
$\left\{ \begin{array}{l} \text{*There are some milks in the refrigerator.} \\ \text{*There are two milks in the refrigerator. (see 53)} \end{array} \right.$

Some mass nouns, we might argue, should 'really' be count, because the 'substance' is divisible into separate things: *furniture* consists of *pieces of furniture*, *grass* of separate *blades of grass*, *hair* of separate *strands of hair* (or *hairs*), *wheat* of separate *grains of wheat*. But PSYCHOLOGICALLY we think of such things as indivisible when we use a mass noun.

On mass nouns 'becoming' count nouns (*two sugars*, *several martinis*, *etc*), *see* 53.

Division of objects and substances
Unit nouns
50
As with single objects, masses can be subdivided by the use of nouns like *part*:
> Part of the butter has melted.

In addition, there are many countable UNIT NOUNS, as we shall call them, which can be used to subdivide notionally a mass into separate 'pieces'. *Piece* and *bit* ⟨informal⟩ are general-purpose unit nouns, which can be combined with most mass nouns:
> a piece of bread   a piece of paper   a piece of land

There are also unit nouns which typically go with a particular mass noun:

a blade of grass	a sheet of paper
a block of ice	a speck of dust
a pile of rubbish	a bar of chocolate
a lump of sugar	a load of hay

As with part nouns, unit nouns are linked to the other noun by *of*.

Nouns of measure
51
One way to divide a mass into separate 'pieces' is to measure it off into length, weight, *etc*:

LENGTH	a foot of water	AREA	an acre of land
	a yard of cloth		
WEIGHT	an ounce of tobacco	VOLUME	a pint of beer
	a pound of butter		a quart of milk
	a ton of coal		a gallon of oil

Species nouns
52
Here is another type of division: nouns like *type, kind, sort, species, class, variety* can divide a mass or a set of objects into 'types' or 'species':
> Teak is a *type* of wood.
> A Ford is a *make* of car.
> A tiger is a *species* of mammal.

You can use either the singular or plural of a count noun following a plural species noun:

> I like most kinds of $\begin{cases} \text{cat.} \\ \text{cats. ⟨more informal⟩} \end{cases}$

We usually premodify the species noun rather than the noun which follows:
> a Japanese make of car (*not* *a make of Japanese car)

a delicious kind of bread

a strange species of mammal

Notice that the second noun, when count, usually has no indefinite article: *a strange kind of mammal* rather than *a strange kind of a mammal*.

In ⟨informal⟩ English, there is a mixed construction in which the determiner (if any) and the verb are plural, although the species noun is singular:

These kind of dogs are easy to train. ⟨informal⟩

This kind of dog is easy to train. ⟨more formal⟩

Nouns which can be both count and mass
53

Quite a number of nouns can be both count and mass (*see* 654). *Wood*, for instance, is count when it refers to a collection of trees (=a forest), and mass when it refers to the material of which trees are composed:

We went for a walk in the *woods*.

In America many of the houses are made of *wood*.

Many food nouns are count when they refer to the article in its 'whole' state, but are mass when they refer to the food in the mass, *eg* as eaten at table:

She baked *a cake*.	Would you like (*some*) *cake*?
We grow our own *carrots*.	A good stew must contain *carrot*.
I bought *a dozen eggs*.	There's *some egg* left on the plate.

So also *a cheese/cheese, a potato/potato, etc.*

On the other hand, in many cases English has a separate count noun and a separate mass noun referring to the same area of meaning:

COUNT	MASS
a pig	pork
a leaf	foliage
a loaf	bread
a meal	food
a job ⟨informal⟩	work
a vehicle	traffic

Sometimes words which are usually mass nouns are 'converted' into count unit nouns or count species nouns:

May I have two *sugars* in my coffee? (=two lumps of sugar)

Some of the best *tobaccos* are grown in Turkey. (=kinds of tobacco)

Occasionally the opposite happens: count nouns are 'converted' into mass nouns after a noun of measure: *a few square feet of floor; an inch of cigarette.*

Abstractions

54

Abstract nouns are nouns which refer to states, events, feelings, *etc.* Just like concrete nouns, they combine with part nouns, unit nouns, species nouns, and measure nouns, and can be either count or mass, even though these notions cannot be understood in a physical sense.

In general, abstract nouns can more easily be both 'count' and 'mass' than concrete nouns.

Nouns referring to events and occasions (*talk, knock, shot, meeting, etc*) are usually count:

> I had *a talk* with Jim.
>
> There was *a loud knock* at the door.
>
> The committee had *three meetings*.

But *talk* (with other nouns like *sound, thought*) can also be a mass noun:

> I dislike *idle talk*.
>
> Modern planes fly faster than *sound*.
>
> He was deep in *thought*.

Other abstract nouns tend to be mass nouns: *honesty, happiness, information, progress, etc*:

> *Happiness* is often a product of *honesty* and hard *work*.
>
> His speech was followed by loud *applause*.
>
> I have some *homework* to finish.
>
> He is engaged in scientific *research*.

55

Notice that the following nouns are mass nouns in English, but not in some other languages: *anger, behaviour, chess, conduct, courage, dancing, harm, moonlight, parking, poetry, safety, shopping, smoking, sunshine, violence*.

But again, many such nouns (*eg experience, difficulty, trouble*) can be either count or mass (with some difference of meaning):

> ⎰ We had little *difficulty* convincing him.
> ⎱ *but:* He is having financial *difficulties*.
>
> ⎰ He is a policeman of many years' *experience*.
> ⎱ *but:* Tell me about your *experiences* abroad.
>
> ⎰ I have some *work* to do this evening.
> ⎱ *but:* They played two *works* by an unknown French composer.

Some abstract nouns which are normally mass can become singular count nouns when their meaning is limited by specific reference to a person, *etc*:

> He has had *a* good *education*.
>
> She plays Mozart with *a* rare *grace* and *delicacy* of touch. ⟨rather formal⟩

56

Partition of abstract nouns is illustrated by:

> Part of his *education* was at Cambridge.

Division is illustrated in these phrases:

UNIT NOUNS	a (good) game of chess	a (sudden) fit of anger
	a (sudden) burst of applause	an (interesting) item of news
	an (excellent) piece of research	a (long) spell of hard work
	a (fine) piece of work	a (useful) bit of advice ⟨informal⟩
MEASURE NOUNS	three months of hard work	
	(*also* three months' hard work) (*see* 96)	

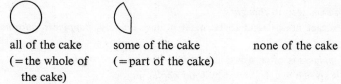

SPECIES NOUNS	an (exciting) type of dance	a (strange) kind of behaviour

Amount or quantity

Amount words (or quantifiers) (*see* 765–76)

57

Amount words like *all*, *some* and *none* can be applied to both count and mass nouns:

(A) APPLIED TO SINGULAR COUNT NOUNS, they are equivalent to part nouns

all of the cake   some of the cake   none of the cake
(=the whole of   (=part of the cake)
the cake)

(B) APPLIED TO PLURAL NOUNS

all (of) the stars   some of the stars   none of the stars

(C) APPLIED TO MASS NOUNS

all of the land   some of the land   none of the land

Note these relations of meaning between *all*, *some* and *none*:

> {*Some* of the stars were *in*visible.
> {=*Not all* (of) the stars were visible.
> {*None* of the stars were visible.
> {=*All* (of) the stars were *in*visible.

58

Other amount words specify more precisely the meaning 'some':

	WITH COUNT NOUNS	WITH MASS NOUNS
A LARGE AMOUNT	*many* ⟨formal⟩ (But *see* 60) *a lot* ⟨informal⟩ *a large number*	*much* ⟨formal⟩ (But *see* 60) *a lot* ⟨informal⟩ *a great deal*
A SMALL AMOUNT	*a few* *a small number*	*a little*
NOT A LARGE AMOUNT	*not many* *few*	*not much* *little*

Notice that *few* and *little* without *a* have a negative bias. Compare:

> *A few* (=a small number) of the students passed the examination.
> *Few* (=not many) of the students passed the examination.

The numbers *one, two, three, etc* and the fraction words *half, third, etc* are also amount words (where a definite total is being talked of): *Half of the milk was sour. Several*, another amount word, means 'slightly more than a few'. The comparative words *more, less*, and the superlative words *most, least*, are both count and mass (but *fewer* is generally preferred to *less* with count nouns.

A/the majority of and *a minority of* (both ⟨formal⟩), can be used with plural and group nouns:

The majority of the crew/passengers were rescued. (= Most of the crew . . .)

A minority of the committee/members were opposed to the motion.

(On concord with the verb in these and similar cases, *see* 535.)

Many and *much*
59

Many and *much* can be neutral words of amount, used, for example, in comparisons (*as many/much as*) and in questions (*how many/much?*). Compare the count and mass words in:

	COUNT		MASS
(A)	How *many* of the rolls have you eaten?	(A)	How *much* of the bread have you eaten?
	⎧ All of them		⎧ All of it
	⎪ Most of them		⎪ Most of it
	⎪ A lot of them		⎪ A lot of it
	⎪ Half of them		⎨ Half of it
(B)	⎨ Several of them	(B)	—
	⎪ A few of them		A little of it
	⎪ Three of them		—
	⎩ None of them		⎩ None of it

Indefinite use of amount words
60

Amount words have been illustrated above only where there is a definite 'total' or 'sphere' (represented by the circles in the diagrams) within which amounts are to be measured. Now we look at the general (indefinite) use of amount words, where the 'sphere' is unlimited. Here the amount word is used as a determiner (*see* 550), and *of* and *the* are omitted (except with *a lot of, a great deal of, a number of etc*):

COUNT	MASS
All crimes are avoidable.	*All* violence is avoidable.
(*ie* all of the crimes in the world)	
We did*n't* buy *many* things.	We did*n't* buy *much* food.
She knows *several* poets.	——
May I borrow *a few* dollars?	May I borrow *a little* money?
Most people enjoy parties.	*Most* advice is ignored.
There were *fewer* cars in those days.	There was *less* traffic in those days.

$$No \begin{Bmatrix} problem\ is \\ problems\ are \end{Bmatrix} insoluble. \qquad No \text{ work has been done today.}$$

In ⟨informal⟩ style, *a lot of* (or *lots of*) is preferred to *many* or *much* in positive statements:

> *Many* people derive *much* pleasure from attending music festivals.
> ⟨formal⟩
> Music festivals give *a lot of* fun to *lots of* people. ⟨informal⟩

But in questions and after negatives, (*very*) *many* and *much* are not restricted to ⟨formal⟩ English:

> He doesn't smoke *very much*.
> Do *many* people attend the meetings?

Words of general or inclusive meaning
61

All, both, every, each, and (sometimes) *any* are amount words of INCLUSIVE meaning.

With count nouns, *all* is used for quantities of more than two, and *both* for quantities of two only:

> The club is open to people of *both* sexes and *all* nationalities.

Every, each
62

Words like *every* and *each* can be called DISTRIBUTIVE, because they pick out the members of a set or group singly, rather than look at them all together. Apart from this difference, *every* has the same meaning as *all*:

> $\begin{cases} All \text{ good teachers study their subject(s) carefully.} & [1] \\ Every \text{ good teacher studies his subject carefully.} & [2] \end{cases}$

The 'distributive' meaning of *every* shows in the use of singular forms *teacher, studies, his* in [2].

63

Each is like *every* except that it can be used when the set has only two members. Thus *each* (unlike *all* and *every*) can sometimes replace *both*:

> She kissed *each/both* of her parents.

Note also the difference between:

> He gave a box of chocolates to all the girls.   [3]

> He gave a box of chocolates to $\begin{Bmatrix} each \\ every\ one \end{Bmatrix}$ of the girls.   [4]

[3] may mean that the girls shared one box of chocolates; [4] must mean that there were as many boxes of chocolates as girls. Like *every* in meaning are *everyone, everybody, everything,* and *everywhere*.

Any, either
64

The most common use of the determiners *any* and *either* is in negative sentences and questions (*see* 803–7), but here we consider them as distributive words.

Any can sometimes replace *all* and *every* in positive sentences:

> Any good teacher studies his subject carefully.   [5]

Here *any* has the same inclusive meaning as *all* and *every* in [1] and [2]. But *any* means something different in:

> You can paint the wall any colour you like.

Any colour means 'red *or* green *or* blue *or* . . .', while *every colour* means 'red *and* green *and* blue *and* . . .'. *Any* means 'it doesn't matter who/which/what . . .'.

65

When there are only two objects, *either* is used instead of *any*:

> You could ask either of my parents.
>> (=either my father or my mother)

66

Any can also be used with mass nouns and singular count nouns:

> Àny dog might bite a child if téased.

> Àny land is valuable theśe days.

As marked here, *any* often takes nuclear stress (*see* 35). Like *any* are *anyone*, *anybody*, *anything*, *anywhere*, *anyhow*, *anyway* and ⟨informal AmE⟩ *anyplace*.

> Anyone will tell you the way. (=Whoever you ask, he will . . .)

> He will eat anything. (=He will eat whatever you give him)

Scale of amount

67

We can order amount words roughly on a scale, moving from the inclusive words at the top, to the negative words at the bottom (*any* we place separately, because its main use, in negative and interrogative contexts, does not fit into the scale):

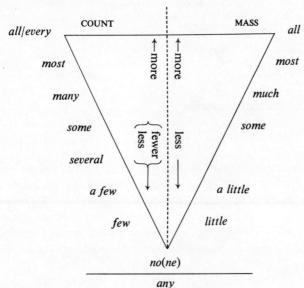

68

Positions on a scale of amount can be expressed not only through the words already discussed (which are determiners or pronouns) but by pronouns like *everybody*, *everything*, and by adverbs of frequency, duration, *etc.* We show some of the correspondences between different areas of meaning in the following table:

MASS	COUNT	PERSONAL	NON-PER-SONAL	FREQUENCY	DURATION	DEGREE
(*see 765–73*)	(*see 765–73*)	(*see 774–5*)	(*see 774–5*)	(*see 157*)	(*see 151–6*)	(*see 217–26*)
all	all every each	everyone everybody	every-thing	always	always for ever	absolutely entirely *etc*
much a lot (of)	many a lot (of)	—	—	often frequently	(for) a long time	very (very) much
some	some	someone somebody	some-thing	sometimes	(for) some time	rather somewhat quite
a little	a few	—	—	occasionally	(for) a while	a little a bit
little	few	—	—	rarely seldom	not . . . (for) long	scarcely hardly
no(ne)	no(ne)	no one nobody	noth-ing	never	—	not . . . at all
any	any	anyone anybody	any-thing	ever	—	at all

Definite and indefinite meaning

Uses of the definite article
69

When we use the definite article *the* we presume that both we and the hearer know what is being talked about. This is not the case when we use the indefinite article. Most of the words we have considered so far are indefinite; but if we want to express indefinite meaning without any added meaning of amount, *etc*, we use the indefinite article *a(n)* (with singular count nouns), or the zero indefinite article with mass nouns or plural count nouns (*see* 654): *Would you like a drink? Do you like chocolate?*

There are four circumstances in which definite meaning arises.

70

We use the definite article:

(A)   When identity has been established by an earlier mention (often with an indefinite article):

John bought a TV and *a radio,*   but he returned   *the radio.*

| FIRST | SECOND |
| MENTION | MENTION |

We call this the BACK-POINTING use of *the.*

71

(B)   When identity is established by the postmodification (*see* 719) that follows the noun:

John returned the radio *he bought yesterday.*

The wines $\begin{Bmatrix} \textit{of France} \\ \textit{which France produces} \end{Bmatrix}$ are the best in the world.

The discovery *of radium* marked the beginning *of a new era of medicine.*

This is the FORWARD-POINTING use of *the.*

72

(C)   When the object or group of objects is the only one that exists or has existed: *the stars, the earth, the world, the sea, the North Pole, the equator, the Reformation, the human race*:

The North Pole and the South Pole are equally distant from the equator.

This is the UNIQUE use of *the,* and it also arises where what is referred to is 'understood' to be unique in the context: *the sun, the moon, the kitchen, the town-hall, the Queen, the President, etc.* We could, if we wanted, make the definite meaning clear by postmodification (*the moon belonging to this earth, the kitchen of this house, the Queen of this country, etc*), but this would normally be unnecessary and laborious.

73

(D)   When reference is made to an institution shared by the community: *the radio, the television, the telephone, the paper(s) (ie newspaper(s)), the train, etc.*

What's in the paper(s) today?

He went to London on the train / by train.

Sometimes (*see* 495) the article may be omitted with this INSTITUTIONAL use:

What's on (the) television tonight?

Generic

74

A fifth use of the definite article which might be treated as a case of the UNIQUE use, is the GENERIC use, referring to what is general or typical for a whole class of objects. This is found with count nouns:

The tiger is a beautiful animal.   [1]

Here *the* indicates the uniqueness of the class of tigers, not of one individual member of the class. Thus [1] expresses essentially the same meaning as [2] and [3]:

Tigers are beautiful animals.   [2]

A tiger is a beautiful animal.   [3]

[2] is the general use of the plural indefinite form; [3] is the generic use of the indefinite singular. Thus when we are dealing with a whole class of objects, the differences between definite and indefinite, singular and plural, tend to lose their significance. There is, however, a slight difference in the fact that *the tiger* (generic) refers to the species as a whole, while *a tiger* (generic) refers to any member of the species. We can say:

> The tiger is in danger of becoming extinct.
>
> *but not:* *A tiger is in danger of becoming extinct.

75

Notice that the unstressed use of *some* /səm/ (*see* 553) cannot be used with nouns in the generic sense:

> I fried (some) eggs and bacon for breakfast.
>
> *but:* Eggs and bacon are good for you.

Specific versus generic meaning
76

In contrast to the GENERIC use of the definite article, all the other four uses (*see* 70–3) may be called SPECIFIC. For mass nouns, there is only one generic form, that with the zero article:

> Water is composed of hydrogen and oxygen.

The ways of expressing generic meaning can be summarised in the table:

	COUNT	MASS
GENERIC MEANING	the tiger a tiger tigers	water

As the table shows, the definite article with mass nouns, and also with plural nouns (with the exception of some nationality words, *see* 627–8) is always specific. The following examples illustrate generic meaning with *a* concrete mass nouns, *b* abstract mass nouns, and *c* plural nouns:

> *a* I like *wine, Venetian glass, Scandinavian wood*, . . .
>
> *b* I like *music, English literature, contemporary art*, . . .
>
> *c* I like *dogs, horses, classical languages*, . . .

In specific use, these nouns take the definite article:

	SPECIFIC USE	GENERIC USE
a	Pass *the butter*, please.	*Butter* is expensive nowadays.
b	*The acting* was poor, but we enjoyed *the music*.	I simply love *music* and *dancing*.
	Before you visit Spain, you ought to learn *the language*.	The scientific study of *language* is called linguistics.
c	Come and look at *the horses*!	*Horses* are my favourite animals.

77

Notice that English tends to treat mass and plural nouns as generic when they are pre-modified. But when they are postmodified, especially by an *of-* phrase, the article (or some other determiner) normally has to be present. This is especially the case with abstract mass nouns. *Compare:*

Chinese history	*the* history of China
American society	*the* society of the United States of America
early medieval architecture	*the* architecture of the early middle ages
animal behaviour	*the* behaviour of animals

The tendency is less marked with concrete mass nouns and plural nouns. We can omit *the* in

eighteenth-century furniture	(*the*) furniture of the eighteenth century
tropical birds	(*the*) birds of the tropics

Generic use of adjectives and group nouns
78
Adjectives are used with generic *the* to denote a class of people (*the poor, the unemployed, the young, the handicapped*), or to denote an abstract quality (*the absurd, the beautiful, the sublime*) (*see* 465–6). Some nationality adjectives (mostly those ending in *-ch* or *-sh*) are used in the same way to refer to a people collectively: *the Dutch, the English, the French, the Irish, the Welsh* (*see* 627–8). For generic meaning, we do not generally use *the* with a nationality word like *Welshman*. Note the difference between:

The Welsh are well known for their singing. ⎱	(GENERIC)
Welshmen are well known for their singing. ⎰	
The Welshmen I know sing well.	(SPECIFIC)

Note also generic group nouns like *the aristocracy, the public, the clergy, the administration, the Government*, which can be used with either a singular or a plural verb (*see* 47).

Other words of definite meaning
79
Apart from common nouns with *the*, the following words always or usually signal definite meaning:

PROPER NOUNS (*see* 755): *Susan, Chicago, Tuesday, Africa, etc.*
PERSONAL PRONOUNS (*see* 685): *he, she, it, they, you, etc.*
POINTER WORDS or DEMONSTRATIVES (*see* 548–9): *this, that, these, those, etc.*

We shall deal with these in turn, bearing in mind the types of definiteness already discussed (*see* 69–73).

Proper nouns
80
Proper nouns are understood to have unique reference, or at least unique reference in context: *Africa* refers to one particular continent, and *Susan* (in a given conversation) refers to one particular person. Usually no definite article comes before the singular proper noun (*see* 755–9).

81

But sometimes proper nouns change into common nouns. This happens, for example, when there is a possible confusion between two things of the same name, and in such a case *the* is used:

the Susan next door (not the Susan who works in your office)   [4]

the New York of story books (not the New York of reality)   [5]

In [5], as in many cases of proper nouns acting as common nouns, we distinguish not so much two things of the same name, but two aspects of the same thing. *The* is also sometimes used with premodifiers (*the young Shakespeare, the real Mr Kennedy*), but with place-names it is generally left out: *Ancient Greece, eighteenth-century London, upstate New York.*

In the same way proper nouns sometimes change to plural:

I know several Mr Wilsons (= 'people called "Mr Wilson"').

He was a friend of the Kennedys (= 'the family named "Kennedy"').

A proper noun may also sometimes follow the indefinite article:

The prize was given by a Dr Robertson.

This means 'a certain Dr Robertson' (a person you won't have heard of).

Third person pronouns
82

Third person pronouns (*he, she, it, they*) are usually definite because they point back to a previous mention. In a sense, they 'replace' an earlier noun phrase:

I phoned *the police* and asked *them*   (*ie* the police) what to do.

FIRST	SECOND
MENTION	MENTION

Concrete nouns are replaced by *he, she, it,* or *they* as follows:

he (*him, his, etc*) refers to a male person (or animal)

she (*her, etc*) refers to a female person (or animal)

it (*its, etc*) refers to an inanimate thing (or an animal)

they (*them, etc*) refers to anything plural.

83

He and *she* are used for animals when we think of them as having the personal qualities of human beings (*eg* family pets):

Have you given Rover *his* dog-biscuits?

It is otherwise used for animals, and sometimes for babies and very young children, especially when their sex is unknown or unimportant:

The dog was barking in *its* kennel.

The baby was crying in *its* $\begin{cases} \text{cot. } \langle\text{BrE}\rangle \\ \text{crib. } \langle\text{AmE}\rangle \end{cases}$

She is sometimes used for inanimate objects (especially ships) where we think of them as having animate qualities:

What a lovely ship! What is *she* called?

She can also be used of countries seen as political or cultural units, rather than as geographical units:

Last year *France* increased *her* exports by 10 per cent.

84

When a human noun is replaced by a pronoun and the sex is not known or specified, *he* is used rather than *she*:

A martyr is someone who gives up *his* life for *his* beliefs.

Mass nouns and singular abstract nouns are replaced by *it*:

I've washed my hair, and *it* won't keep tidy.

Virtue is *its* own reward.

First and second person pronouns

85

The first and second person pronouns have reference to the situation as follows:

I (*me, my etc*)	'the speaker'
we (*us, our, etc*)	'a group of people, including the speaker'
you (*your, etc*)	⌜'the hearer' (singular) ⎰'a group of people, including the hearer but excluding the speaker' (plural)

Sometimes a distinction is made between 'inclusive *we*', where *we* includes the hearer (= 'you and I'), and 'exclusive *we*', where it excludes the hearer:

Let's go to the dance tonight, shall *we*?   (INCLUSIVE)

We've enjoyed meeting you.   (EXCLUSIVE)

(said by Mr and Mrs Robertson to their guests)

Inclusive *we* (*us*) is often used by writers of books:

We noticed earlier, on page 200, that . . .

Let *us* now turn to another topic . . .

Note

[a] *We* is sometimes used to refer to the writer in ⟨formal⟩ writing, where *I* would be strictly appropriate: *As we showed in Chapter 2* . . .

[b] There is a playful, condescending use of *we* referring to the hearer; *eg* a doctor talking to a child patient: *How are we* (= 'you') *feeling today then?*

Indefinite use of pronouns: *one, you, they*

86

This is a convenient point to mention three pronouns with indefinite generic reference to people.

One (singular) is a rather ⟨formal and impersonal⟩ pronoun, meaning 'people in general, including you and me'. *You* is its ⟨informal⟩ equivalent:

One never knows what may happen. ⟨formal⟩

You never know what may happen. ⟨informal⟩

They can also be used indefinitely in ⟨informal⟩ English, but with a different meaning from *one* and *you*. It means roughly 'people (excluding you and me)':

They say it's going to rain tomorrow. (= 'People say . . .')

Note

In ⟨BrE⟩ and ⟨formal AmE⟩, *one* is used to point back to a previous use of *one*; in ⟨formal AmE⟩, *he* can also be used instead. In ⟨informal AmE⟩ *you* is used:

$$\textit{One} \text{ should always look after} \begin{cases} \textit{one's} \langle \text{BrE and formal AmE} \rangle \\ \textit{his} \langle \text{formal AmE} \rangle \\ \textit{your} \langle \text{informal AmE} \rangle \end{cases} \text{money.}$$

Pointer words

87

We use the term POINTER WORDS for words like the demonstratives *this* and *that*, which refer by *pointing* to something in the context. They can have three different uses.

88

(A) Pointer words can be BACK-POINTING (*ie* they can point to something mentioned earlier):

> I then tried to force the door open, but *this/that* was a mistake.

(B) Pointer words can be FORWARD-POINTING (*ie* they can point to something to be mentioned later):

> *This* is how you start a car: you make sure the gears are in neutral and that the handbrake is on, then turn the ignition key . . .

(C) Pointer words can be OUTWARD-POINTING (*ie* they can point to something in the context outside language):

> Would you like to sit in *this* chair (= 'the one by me') or in *that* one? (= 'the one away from me, over there')

This in such cases identifies something near the speaker (either physically, in terms of space or time, or psychologically). *That* identifies something not so near the speaker.

89

On this basis, we may separate two classes of pointer-words, those related to *this* (and having the 'near' meaning) and those related to *that* (and having the 'distant' meaning). Main members of each class are:

The *this* type:	*this* (singular)	*here* (= at this place)
	these (plural)	*now* (= at this time)
The *that* type:	*that* (singular)	*there* (= at that place)
	those (plural)	*then* (= at that time)
		(usually in the past)

This contrast of meaning is less clear in back-pointing and forward-pointing uses. *This* and *that* can replace each other with no difference of meaning in back-pointing, but *this* is commoner in ⟨formal⟩ English. For forward-pointing, only *this*, and the *this*-type words *these*, *here*, and *thus* can be used (but *see* 90):

> This is what I thought.   (FORWARD- or BACK-POINTING)
>
> That is what I thought.   (BACK-POINTING only)

Notice the opening and close of a radio news bulletin:

> *Here* is the news . . .   (FORWARD-POINTING)
>
> . . . And *that's* the end of the news. (BACK-POINTING)

90

Those is back-pointing when its meaning is defined by a postmodifier: *those who are lazy* (= 'people who are lazy') (*see* 549).

This and *that* in ⟨familiar⟩ use can 'point back' in a vague way to some shared knowledge of the speaker and hearer: *Have you seen this report about smoking?* (= 'a report I know about'), *It gives you that great feeling of clean air and open spaces* (= 'the feeling we all know about'). *This* can also be used ⟨familiarly⟩ to introduce something new in a narrative: *I was walking along the street when this girl came up to me . . .* (= 'a girl I'm going to tell you about').

Relations between ideas expressed by nouns

Relations expressed by *of*
91
We have talked of *of* used in phrases of partition, division, and amount:

      (a) part of the house   a kind of tree

      a group of stars   a lot of difficulty

Of is also used more generally as a means of indicating various relations between the meanings of two nouns:

the roof of the house	(the house has a roof; the roof is part of the house)
a friend of my father's (*see* 577)	(my father has a friend)
the courage of the firemen	(the firemen have courage; the firemen are courageous)
the envy of the world	(the world envies . . .)
the trial of the conspirators	(someone tries the conspirators)
the virtue of thrift	(thrift is a virtue)
a glass of water	(the glass has water in it; the glass contains water)
people of the Middle Ages	(people who lived in the Middle Ages)
the house of my dreams	(the house which I see in my dreams)
the College of Surgeons	(the College to which surgeons belong)

The 'have' relation
92
Both *of* and *with* can indicate a relation of 'having'. From the sentence 'NOUN$_1$ has NOUN$_2$' we can get:

    NOUN$_2$ of NOUN$_1$:   the roof of the house, the courage of the men

    NOUN$_1$ of NOUN$_2$:   men of (great) courage

    NOUN$_1$ with NOUN$_2$:   a house with a roof

In the 'NOUN$_1$ prep. NOUN$_2$' construction, *of* is used where NOUN$_2$ is abstract (*a performance of distinction, a man of wealth*) and *with* is used where NOUN$_2$ is concrete (*a woman with a large family, a man with money*).

The uses of the genitive
93
A genitive (ending *'s* or apostrophe only, *see* 570–2) can often be used with the same meaning as an *of*-phrase:

THE 'HAVE' RELATION ('Dr Brown has a son')

Dr Brown's son (definite)	⎧ a son of Dr Brown ⎨ a son of Dr Brown's (*see* 577) ⎩ (indefinite)
the earth's gravity	the gravity of the earth (more usual)

THE SUBJECT-VERB RELATION ('His parents consented')

his parents' consent	the consent of his parents
the train's departure	the departure of the train (more usual)

THE VERB-OBJECT RELATION ('They released the prisoner')

the prisoner's release	the release of the prisoner
a city's destruction	the destruction of a city (more usual)

THE SUBJECT-COMPLEMENT RELATION ('Everyone is happy')

everyone's happiness	the happiness of everyone
the country's beauty	the beauty of the country

94
In the following cases, the *of*-phrase is not used:

THE ORIGIN RELATION (The girl told a story, *etc*)

the girl's story (=a story that the girl told)

John's telegram (=a telegram from John, a telegram that John sent)

VARIOUS DESCRIPTIVE RELATIONS

a women's college (=a college for women)

a doctor's degree (=a doctoral degree)

Choice between an *of*-construction and the genitive
95
In general, the genitive is preferred for human nouns (*the girl's arrival*) and to a lesser extent for animal nouns (*horses' hooves*) and human group nouns (*the government's policy*). *Of* is used for mass nouns and abstract nouns (*a discovery of oil, the progress of science*). In general also, the genitive is preferred for the subject-verb relation, and *of* for the verb-object relation:

Livingstone's discovery (='Livingstone discovered something')

the discovery of Livingstone (=usually 'Somebody discovered Livingstone')

The subject function can also be indicated by a *by*-phrase. Hence the notion 'The army defeated the rebels' might be expressed in three ways:

the army's defeat of the rebels

the defeat of the rebels by the army

the rebels' defeat by the army

(But *the rebels' defeat of the army* has to mean that the rebels defeated the army!)

96

The *of*-construction is also preferred (especially in ⟨formal⟩ English) to the genitive where a long phrase follows the *of*. We can easily say:

the departure of the 4.30 train for Edinburgh

but not: *the 4.30 train for Edinburgh's departure (*see* 575)

Note two special cases of the genitive. Time nouns are frequently used in the
genitive, and also place nouns, when followed by a superlative:

this year's crop	the town's oldest pub (*or* the
two weeks' holiday	oldest pub in the town)
a moment's thought	Norway's greatest composer
today's menu (*or* the menu	the world's best chocolate (*or*
for today)	the best chocolate in the
	world)

Relations between people: *with, for, against*
97

With often means 'together with' or 'in company with':

I'm so glad you're coming *with us*.   [1]

Sheila was at the theatre *with her friends*.   [2]

Sentence [2] is not very different in meaning from

Sheila and her friends were at the theatre.

Without is the negative of *with* in this sense:

Sheila was ill, so we went to the theatre without her.

For conveys the idea of support (= in favour of), and like *with*, contrasts with
against:

Are you for or against the President?

With, in a situation of conflict or competition, means 'on the same side as':

Remember that every one of us is with you (= 'on your side')

Here *with* contrasts with *against* (= 'on the opposite side').

Are you with us or against us?

So also: *the fight against pollution, the campaign against inflation, etc.* However,
with conveys the idea of opposition between two people or groups in *fight with,
argue with, etc*: *He's always arguing with his sister.*

Ingredient, material: *with, of, out of, from*
98

With verbs of 'making', *with* indicates an ingredient, whereas *out of* or *of* indicates
the material of the whole thing:

A fruit cake is made *with* fruit, BUT a glass jug is made (*out*) *of* glass.

Made from indicates a substance from which something is derived:

Beer is made from hops.

Paper is made from wood-pulp.

Of alone is used in postmodifying phrases: *a ring of solid gold* (*ie* . . . made out of
solid gold), *a table of polished oak* (*ie* . . . consisting of polished oak). So also *a
solid-gold ring, a polished-oak table.*

Restrictive and non-restrictive meaning

99

Modifiers of a noun usually add meaning to the noun by helping to specify its meaning more exactly:

(A)	the children	(B)	the children *who live next door*
(A)	a king	(B)	a king *of Denmark*
(A)	buttered toast	(B)	*hot* buttered toast
(A)	the books	(B)	the *history* books

In each case, phrase (B) tells us more precisely than phrase (A) what the noun refers to. It NARROWS DOWN or RESTRICTS the meaning of the noun, by saying *what kind of* children, king, *etc* the speaker is talking of. This type of modifier may be called RESTRICTIVE.

100

There is also a NON-RESTRICTIVE type of modifier which does not limit the noun in this way. Compare:

Children *who learn eásily* |should start school as early as   [1]

   pòssible.| (RESTRICTIVE)

Chìldren, *who learn eásily* |should start school as early as   [2]

   pòssible.| (NON-RESTRICTIVE)

In [1], the relative clause is restrictive and tells us *what kind of* children ought to start school early. In [2], where the relative clause is non-restrictive, the speaker is talking about all children in general. This is signalled by a tone unit boundary (*see* 36) in ⟨speech⟩, or a comma in ⟨writing⟩, separating it from the preceding noun. The clause does not in any way limit the reference of *children*. The speaker tells us *a* that all children learn easily, and *b* that all children should start school early.

Non-restrictive adjectives
101

Adjectives, as well as relative clauses, can be non-restrictive. The clearest cases are adjectives modifying proper nouns: since a proper noun already has unique reference, it cannot be limited any further by the adjective (but *see* 81): *poor Bill, old Mrs Brown, the beautiful Highlands of Scotland*.

Non-restrictive adjectives are not necessarily marked, like non-restrictive relative clauses, by punctuation or intonation, and so ambiguities can occur:

The *patriotic* Americans have great respect for their country's
   constitution.   [3]

The *hungry* workers attacked the houses of their *rich*
   employers.   [4]

We might ask: Does [3] mean that 'all Americans have great respect' (non-restrictive)? Or does it mean that 'only some Americans (those who are patriotic, as opposed to those who are not) have great respect'? Does [4] refer to *all* the workers and *all* the employers, or just to the hungry workers (as opposed to those

with enough to eat), and to the rich employers (as opposed to the poor ones)?
These sentences could have either meaning.

Note

The ambiguity of [3] exists because *the Americans* can be either generic or not (*see* 627). We do not find the same ambiguity with (say) *the patriotic Irish*, because the noun *Irish* (as contrasted with *Irishmen*) must be generic.

102

Non-restrictive adjectives usually precede restrictive modifiers, and so the ordering of modifiers can make a difference to meaning:

his last great novel   [5]

his great last novel   [6]

In [5] *great* is restrictive, while in [6] *great* is non-restrictive. The meaning of [5] is therefore 'the last of his great novels', and the meaning of [6] is 'his last novel, which was great'.

Time, tense and aspect

103

We turn now to features of tense and aspect expressed by the verb phrase. Tense and aspect (*see* 880–3) relate the happening described by the verb to time in the past, present, or future.

States and events
104

Since tense relates the meaning of the verb to a time scale, we must first give some attention to the different kinds of meaning a verb may have. Broadly, verbs may refer either to an EVENT (*ie* a happening thought of as a single occurrence, with a definite beginning and end), or to a STATE (*ie* a state of affairs which continues over a period, and need not have a well-defined beginning and end).

Thus *be, live, stay, know, etc* may be considered STATE VERBS, and *get, come, leave, hit, etc* EVENT VERBS. This distinction is similar to the distinction between count and mass nouns, and (as we saw in 49 for count and mass), it is to some extent a conceptual rather than a real distinction. The same verb can change from one category to another, and the distinction is not always clear: *Did you remember his name?* could refer either to a state or to an event.

To be more accurate, then, we should talk of 'state uses of verbs' and 'event uses of verbs'; but it is convenient to keep to the simpler terms 'state verb' and 'event verb'.

105

The distinction between 'state' and 'event' gives rise to the following three basic kinds of verb meaning (illustrated in the past tense):

(1)	STATE	Napoleon was a Corsican.
(2)	SINGLE EVENT	Columbus discovered America.
(3)	SET OF REPEATED EVENTS (HABIT)	Paganini played the violin brilliantly.

The 'habit' meaning combines 'event' meaning with 'state' meaning: a habit is, in a sense, a state consisting of a series of events. We often specify 'state' meaning by adding an adverbial of duration: *Queen Victoria reigned for sixty-four years*. We specify 'habit' more precisely by adding an adverbial of frequency or an adverbial of duration: *He played the violin every day from the age of five*. (All three types of meaning can be clarified by an adverbial of time-when, *see* 140–50.)

To these three a further type of verbal meaning can be added, the TEMPORARY meaning expressed by the progressive aspect (*see* 122, 881–2): *She was cooking the dinner*.

Present time
106
The following are the main ways of referring to something which occurs at the present moment:

(A)   PRESENT STATE (the Simple Present Tense)

> I'*m* hungry.
>
> *Do* you *like* coffee?

The state may stretch indefinitely into the past and future, and so this use of the simple present tense applies also to general truths such as *The sun rises in the east*.

107

(B)   PRESENT EVENT (The Simple Present Tense)

> I *declare* the meeting closed.
>
> Bremner *passes* the ball to Lorimer.

This use is rather specialised, being limited to formal declarations, sports commentaries, demonstrations, *etc*. In most contexts, one rarely has the occasion to refer to an event begun and ended at the very moment of speech.

108

(C)   PRESENT 'HABIT' (The Simple Present Tense)

> He *works* in London (every day).
>
> I (often) *travel* abroad for my $\begin{cases} \text{holidays. } \langle \text{BrE} \rangle \\ \text{vacation. } \langle \text{AmE} \rangle \end{cases}$
>
> It *rains* a lot in this part of the world.

By 'habit' here, we mean a sequence of events.

109

(D)   TEMPORARY PRESENT (The Present Progressive)

> Look, it'*s raining*!
>
> The children *are sleeping* now.
>
> They *are living* in a rented house at the moment.

The meaning of the progressive aspect is 'limited duration'. Compare the meaning of the simple present in the parallel examples:

> It *rains* a lot in the Hebrides. (habit)
>
> Children usually *sleep* very soundly. (habit)
>
> They *live* in a large house. (permanently)

For single events, which in any case involve a limited time-span, the effect of the progressive is to emphasise the durational aspect of the event:

Nastase *serves*! (at this very moment)

Nastase *is serving*. (the service is a continuing activity)

With states the effect of the progressive is to put emphasis on the *limited* duration of the state of affairs:

They *live* in a rented house. (permanently)

They *are living* in a rented house. (temporarily)

110

(E)   TEMPORARY HABIT (The Present Progressive)

I'*m taking* dancing lessons this winter.

He'*s walking* to work while his car is being repaired.

This use combines the 'temporary' meaning of the progressive with the repetitive meaning of the habitual present.

111

Three rather less important ways of referring to the present may be added:

(F)   We can use the progressive aspect, when accompanied by *always* or a similar adverb, to convey not temporariness, but continuousness:

My children *are* always (=continually) *misbehaving*.

This use carries with it some feeling of disapproval.

(G)   Temporary and habitual meaning can be combined, in a different way from (E), to indicate a repetition of temporary happenings:

He'*s mowing* his lawn whenever I see him.

(H)   In special circumstances, the past tense can be used to refer to the present:

Did you *want* to speak to me? (=Do you want . . .)

I *wondered* whether you would help me. (=I wonder . . .)

Here the past tense is an indirect and more ⟨tactful⟩ substitute for the simple present tense (*see* 124(B)).

Past time

112

The present-time meanings (A) to (G) above are paralleled by similar past-time meanings: we have already illustrated some of these (*see* 105).

But there is a special problem of past-time reference in English: the question of how to choose between the use of the past tense and the use of the perfect aspect.

By a past-time happening, we mean a happening taking place in the past but not necessarily in the present time. The PAST TENSE is used when the past happening is related to a definite time in the past, which we may call 'THEN'.

In contrast, the PERFECT ASPECT is used for a past happening which is seen in relation to a later event or time. Thus the present perfect means 'past-time-related-to-present-time'. For example:

He *was* in prison for ten years. (='Now he's out')

He *has been* in prison for ten years. (='He's still there')

The past tense

113

The past tense refers to a DEFINITE time in the past, which may be identified by

a   a past time adverbial in the same sentence,

    b the preceding language context, *or*

    c the context outside language.

(On these aspects of definiteness, *see* 70–2.) Examples of the three types are:

    a Haydn *was born* in 1732.

    b Joan has become engaged; it *took* us completely by surprise. (Here
          the past tense *took* is used, because the event has already been
          identified in the first clause.)

    c *Did* the postman *bring* any letters? (Here we can use the past tense
          without language context, because it is understood that the post-
          man calls at a given time in the day.)

Note

  [*a*] A proper noun can, because of its definite meaning, provide the conditions
     for the past tense: *Caruso was a great singer.* (Here it is implied that
     Caruso is dead, or at least is no longer a practising singer.)

  [*b*] The past tense can sometimes be used when no definite time 'THEN' is easily
     apparent: *They told me you were ill.* Perhaps this is like *c* above, in that the
     speaker 'in his own mind' is thinking of a definite time.

114

The past tense also implies a gap between the time referred to and the present
moment:

    His sister *was* an invalid all her life (*ie* she's now dead).

    His sister *has been* an invalid all her life (*ie* she's still alive).

Adverbials referring to a past point or period of time normally go with the past
tense:

    The discovery *was made* in the sixteenth century, *etc.*

The present perfect

115

Four related uses of the present perfect may be noted:

(A) STATE LEADING UP TO THE PRESENT TIME

        That house *has been* empty for ages.   [1]

(B) INDEFINITE EVENT(S) IN A PERIOD LEADING UP TO THE PRESENT TIME

        Have you (ever) *been* to Florence?

        All my family *have had* measles (in the last year).

(C) HABIT IN A PERIOD LEADING UP TO THE PRESENT TIME

        He *has attended* lectures regularly (this term).

(D) PAST EVENT WITH RESULTS IN THE PRESENT TIME

        The taxi *has arrived.* (*ie* 'it's now here')

        Her doll *has been broken.* (*ie* 'it's still not mended')

      (*Compare:* Her doll was broken, but now it's mended.)

In these instances (except for (B)) the states, habits, or events may be understood
to continue at the present time; for example, to sentence [1] we could add '. . . and
it's still empty'.

Note

  [*a*] In sense (B), the present perfect often refers to the *recent* indefinite past:
     Have you eaten (yet)? I've studied your report (already). For such sentences,
     there is a tendency for ⟨AmE⟩ to prefer the past tense: *Did you eat yet?*

[b]   There is an idiomatic use of the past tense with *always*, *ever* and *never* to refer to a state or habit leading up to the present: *I always said* (= have said) *that he would end up in jail.*

The perfect progressive
116

The present perfect progressive (*have been V-ing*) has the same sort of meaning as the simple present perfect, except that the period leading up to the present has LIMITED DURATION:

I've been writing a letter to my nephew.

He *has been attending* lectures regularly.

The perfect progressive, like the simple perfect, can suggest that the results of the activity remain in the present: *You've been fighting!* (*ie* I can see that you have been fighting, because you have a black eye, torn clothes, *etc*). In such cases the activity has continued up to the *recent past*, not up to the present. Unlike the present perfect, the present perfect progressive with event verbs usually suggests an action continuing into the present:

I've read your book (= 'I've finished it').

I've been reading your book (normally = 'I'm still reading it').

The past perfect
117

The past perfect (simple or progressive) indicates 'past in the past'; that is, a time further in the past as seen from a definite viewpoint in the past:

The house *had been* empty for several months (when I bought it).

The goalkeeper *had injured* his leg, and couldn't play.

It *had been raining*, and the streets were still wet.

In meaning, the past perfect is neutral as regards the differences expressed by the past tense and present perfect. This means that if we put the events described in [2] and [3] further into the past, they both end up in the past perfect:

They tell me that $\begin{cases} \text{the parcel } \textit{arrived} \text{ on April 15th.} & \text{[2]} \\ \text{the parcel } \textit{has} \text{ already } \textit{arrived.} & \text{[3]} \end{cases}$

They told me that $\begin{cases} \text{the parcel } \textit{had arrived} \text{ on April 15th.} & \text{[2a]} \\ \text{the parcel } \textit{had} \text{ already } \textit{arrived.} & \text{[3a]} \end{cases}$

When describing one event following another in the past, we can show their relation by using the past perfect for the earlier event, or else we can use the past tense for both, and rely on the conjunction (*eg after*, *when*) to show which event took place earlier:

$\begin{cases} \text{After} \\ \text{When} \end{cases}$ the teacher $\begin{cases} \textit{left} \\ \textit{had left} \end{cases}$ the room, the children started talking.

All four of these sentences mean roughly the same, and indicate that the teacher left *before* the children started talking.

Perfect aspect in non-finite verbs
118

Non-finite verbs (*see* 877) have no tense, and so cannot express the difference between past tense and perfect aspect. Instead, the perfect aspect expresses general past meaning. In the three sentences below, each of the *as*-clauses can be replaced by the non-finite clause *Having written three chapters*:

> *As he wrote three chapters last month,* he's now taking a holiday.
> *As he has written three chapters already,* he's taking a holiday.
> *As he had written three chapters,* he decided to take a holiday.

The same is true for the perfect infinitive following a modal auxiliary:

> He *may have left* yesterday (*ie* Perhaps he *left* yesterday).
> He *may have left* already (*ie* Perhaps he *has left* already).

Adverbials in relation to the past and the present perfect
119

Some adverbials go with the past and others with the present perfect, for example:

THE PAST (point or period of time [which finished] in the past)

I *saw* him
- yesterday (evening).
- last night (last Monday).
- a week/month ago.
- in the morning.
- on Wednesday / in June / in 1974.
- at four o'clock.
- the other day.

THE PRESENT PERFECT (period leading up to present, or recent past time)

I *haven't seen* him
- since Tuesday/last week.
- since I met you.
- so far / up to now.
- lately.

EITHER THE PAST OR THE PRESENT PERFECT

I { *saw* / *have seen* } him
- today.
- this week/month/year.
- recently.

{ He always/never *forgot* / He's always/never *forgotten* } my wife's birthday.

State or habit in the past (*used to* and *would*)
120

Used to (*see* 502) expresses a state or habit in the past, as contrasted with the present:

> He *used to eat* out every day, but now he can't afford it.
> Iceland *used to belong* to Denmark (*ie* Iceland once belonged to Denmark).

Would (*see* 300) can also express a past habit, with the particular sense of 'characteristic, predictable behaviour':

> He *would wait* for her outside the office (every day).

Would is typical of narrative style, but *used to* is more characteristic of ⟨spoken⟩ English.

The simple present tense with past meaning

121

There are two special circumstances in which the simple present tense is used with past meaning:

(A) The 'historic present' is sometimes used in narrative, when we want to describe events vividly as if they are happening in our presence:

Then in *comes* the barman and *tries* to stop the fight.

(B) The present is used with verbs of communication, where more strictly the present perfect would be appropriate:

I *hear* you have changed your job.

They *tell* me you have changed your job. ⟨informal⟩

I *am informed* that your appointment has been terminated.
⟨formal⟩

The progressive aspect

122

The progressive aspect (*see* 109, 878–82) refers to activity IN PROGRESS, and therefore suggests not only that the activity is TEMPORARY (*ie* of limited duration), but that it NEED NOT BE COMPLETE. This element of meaning is most evident in the past tense or in the present perfect:

⎰ He *wrote* a novel several years ago (*ie* he finished it).
⎱ He *was writing* a novel several years ago (but I don't know whether
   he finished it).

⎰ I *have mended* the car this morning (*ie* the job's finished).
⎱ I *have been mending* the car this morning (but the job may not be
   finished).

Similarly, with verbs referring to a change of state, the progressive aspect indicates movement towards the change, rather than completion of the change itself:

The girl *was drowning* (but at the last moment I rescued her).

When linked to a non-progressive event verb, or to a point of time, the progressive normally indicates that at that point the activity or situation denoted by the verb is still in progress, *ie* has started but has not yet finished:

⎰ At eight o'clock   ⎱ they *were* (already) *eating* breakfast.
⎱ When I went downstairs ⎰

This means that the breakfast had started before 8 o'clock or the time that I went downstairs, and that it continued after that time.

Verbs taking and not taking the progressive

123

The verbs which most typically take the progressive aspect are verbs denoting ACTIVITIES (*walk, read, drink, write, work, etc*) or PROCESSES (*change, grow, widen, improve, etc*). Verbs denoting MOMENTARY events (*knock, jump, nod, kick, etc*), if used with the progressive, suggest repetition:

He *nodded* (one movement of the head).

He *was nodding* (repeated movements of the head).

124

State verbs often cannot be used with the progressive at all, because the notion of 'something in progress' cannot be easily applied to them. The verbs which normally do not take the progressive include:

(A) VERBS OF PERCEIVING *feel, hear, see, smell, taste.* To express continuing perception, we often use these verbs with *can* or *could*:

> I *can see* someone through the window, but I *can't hear* what
>   they're saying. (*not* *I am seeing . . .)

Verbs which have as their subject the thing perceived, such as *sound* and *look*, can also be included here:

> He *looks/sounds* as if he's enjoying himself. (*not* *He is looking . . .)

(B) VERBS REFERRING TO A STATE OF MIND OR FEELING *believe, adore, desire, detest, dislike, doubt, forget, hate, hope, imagine, know, like, love, mean, prefer, remember, suppose, understand, want, wish,* etc.

> I *forget* his name. (*not* *I am forgetting . . .)

The verbs *seem* and *appear* may also be included here:

> He *seems/appears* to be enjoying himself.

(C) VERBS REFERRING TO A RELATIONSHIP OR A STATE OF BEING *be, belong to, concern, consist of, contain, cost, depend on, deserve, equal, fit, have, involve, matter, owe, own, possess, remain, require, resemble, suffice,* etc.

> This carpet *belongs* to me. (*not* *. . . is belonging to me).

Notice that all these verbs are used without the progressive even when they refer to a temporary state:

> I*'m* hungry.
>
> I *forget* his name for the moment.

Note

The verb *have*, when it is a state verb, does not go with the progressive: *He has a good job* (*not* *He is having a good job*). But *have* can go with the progressive when it denotes a process or activity: *They were having dinner.*

125

Verbs of a fourth group, those referring to internal sensation (*hurt, feel, ache, etc*), can be used either with the progressive or the non-progressive with little difference of effect:

My back $\begin{cases} hurts. \\ is\ hurting. \end{cases}$ I $\begin{cases} felt \\ was\ feeling \end{cases}$ ill.

Exceptions

126

Although the types of verb (A), (B), and (C) above may be labelled 'non-progressive', there are special circumstances in which you hear them used with the progressive. In many circumstances, one may say that the state verb has been changed into an 'activity verb' (referring to an active form of behaviour). In place of *see* and *hear*, we have the equivalent activity verbs *look* (*at*) and *listen* (*to*):

> I*'m looking* at your drawings.
>
> He *was listening* to the news when I entered.

But for *smell, feel,* and *taste,* there is no special corresponding activity verb, so these verbs have to do duty for the state meaning and the activity meaning:

The doctor *is feeling* her pulse.   He says it *feels* normal.

We've *been tasting* the soup.   It *tastes* delicious.

In the same way, *think, imagine, remember, etc* can sometimes be used as 'mental activity' verbs:

I'*m thinking* about what you said.

The verb *be* can go with the progressive when the adjective or noun which follows it refers to a type of behaviour, or to the role a person is adopting: *He's (just) being awkward* (= 'causing difficulty'); *John is being a martyr* (= 'acting like a martyr').

127

Another exceptional case is the use of the progressive with *hope, want, etc* to express greater ⟨tentativeness⟩ and ⟨tact⟩. *Were you wanting to see me? We are hoping you will support us.*

Future time

128

There are five chief ways of expressing future time in the English verb phrase. The most important future constructions are those which use *will* (*shall*) and *be going to* (A and B below).

129

(A)   *Will/shall* (*see* 501)

Will (often reduced to '*ll*), or *shall* (with a first person subject) can express the neutral future of prediction:

Tomorrow's weather *will be* cold and cloudy.

It is particularly common in the main clause of a sentence with an *if*-clause or another conditional adverbial (*see* 208–16):

If you press this button, the door *will slide* back.

Wherever you go, you *will find* the local people friendly.

In that case, I'*ll have to* change my plan.

But with personal subjects, *will/shall* can also suggest an element of intention:

I'*ll meet* you at the station.

She'*ll make* a cup of coffee if you ask her.

130

(B)   *Be going to*

Be going to + INFINITIVE tends to indicate the future as a fulfilment of the present. This construction may refer to future resulting from a present intention:

What *are you going to do* today? I'*m going to stay* at home
    and write letters.

He'*s going to be* a doctor when he grows up.

It may also refer to the future resulting from other causative factors in the present:

I think I'*m going to faint* (*ie* I already feel ill).

It'*s going to rain* (*ie* I can already see black clouds gathering).

In sentences like these last two, *be going to* also carries the expectation that the event will happen SOON.

131

(C) PROGRESSIVE ASPECT

The present progressive is used for future events resulting from a present plan, programme, or arrangement:

We're *inviting* several people to a party.
Next they're *playing* a piece by Schubert.
We're *having* fish for dinner.

Like *be going to*, this construction (especially when there is no time adverbial) often suggests the NEAR future: *The Smiths are leaving* (=soon).

132

(D) SIMPLE PRESENT TENSE

The simple present tense is used for the future in certain types of subordinate clause, especially adverbial time clauses and conditional clauses:

$$\left.\begin{array}{l}\text{When}\\\text{Before}\\\text{If}\end{array}\right\}\text{ he } \textit{arrives}\text{, the band will play the National Anthem.}$$

Notice, however, that the verb in the MAIN clause has *will*. Some of the conjunctions which go with the present tense in this way are *after, as, before, once, until, when, as soon as, if, even if, unless, as long as, whatever, whoever*.

That-clauses following *hope, assume, suppose, etc* can also contain a verb in the present tense referring to the future:

$$\text{I hope the train } \left\{\begin{array}{l}\textit{isn't}\\\textit{won't be}\end{array}\right\} \text{ late.}$$

133

Apart from these cases, the simple present is used (but not too often) to refer to future events which are seen as absolutely certain, either *a* because they are determined in advance by calendar or timetable, or *b* because they are part of an unalterable plan:

Tomorrow *is* a Saturday.
The term *starts* at the beginning of October.
The match *takes place* on Thursday.
He *retires* next month.

In these sentences, we may say that the speaker treats the event as a fact, and puts aside the doubt one normally feels about the future:

$$\text{When } \left\{\begin{array}{l}\textit{do} \text{ we}\\\textit{will} \text{ we}\end{array}\right\} \textit{ get} \text{ there?}$$

134

(E) *Will/shall+* PROGRESSIVE ASPECT

Will (or *shall* or *'ll*) followed by the progressive can be used in a regular way to add the temporary meaning of the progressive to the future meaning of the *will* construction (*see* 129):

Don't call her at seven o'clock—she'*ll be eating* dinner.

But in addition, we can use the *will+* Progressive construction in a special way to refer to a future event which will take place 'as a matter of course':

When *will* you *be moving*?

The train *will be arriving* soon.

The construction is particularly useful for avoiding the suggestion of intention in the simple *will*-construction, and can therefore be more ⟨polite⟩.

When *will* you *visit* us again?   [4]

When *will* you *be visiting* us again?   [5]

Sentence [4] is most likely to be a question about the listener's intentions, while sentence [5] simply asks him to predict the time of his next visit.

Be to, be about to, be on the point/verge of
135
Some other ways of expressing future meaning are illustrated here:

The West German Chancellor *is to visit* France.

The chairman *is about to resign*.

He *was on the point/verge of leaving* the country when the telegram arrived.

Be + to-infinitive signifies an arrangement for the future (especially an official arrangement), while both *be about to* and *on the point/verge of* emphasise the nearness of a future event.

The future in the past
136
If we put the future constructions already mentioned (except the simple present) into the past tense, we arrive at a kind of 'future in the past' meaning (*ie* future seen from a viewpoint in the past). But such a meaning, as illustrated by *was going to* and *was about to*, usually carries the knowledge that the anticipated happening did not take place:

They *were* just *going to punish* him, when he escaped.

The priceless tapestry *was about to catch fire*, but the firemen saved it.

Was/were to and *would* are the only examples of constructions which refer to the fulfilled future in the past, but in this sense they are rare and rather ⟨literary⟩ in style:

After defeating Pompey's supporters, Caesar returned to Italy and proclaimed himself the permanent 'dictator' of Rome. He *was to pay* dearly for his ambition in due course: a year later one of his best friends, Marcus Brutus, *would lead* a successful plot to assassinate him.

However, for a series of events like this, the ordinary past tense can be used throughout: *returned, ... paid, ... led, etc.*

The past in the future
137
The past in the future is expressed by *will* + Perfect Infinitive:

Tomorrow Jean and Ken *will have been married* twenty years.

Summary
138
In conclusion, here is a table summarising some of the commonest meanings expressed through tense and aspect. The symbols used are explained on page 76.

Table: Tense and aspect

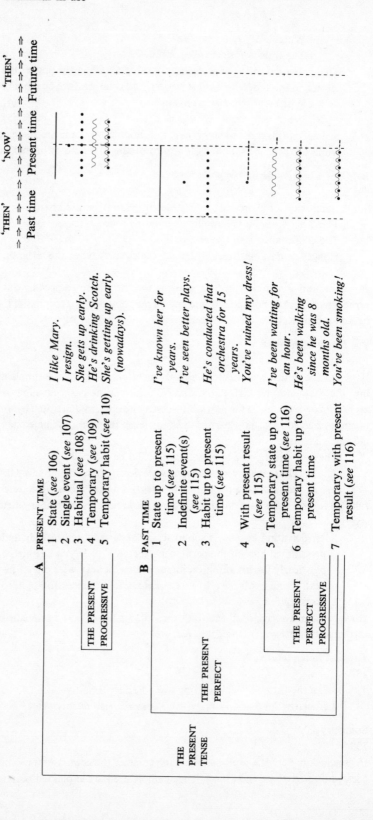

THE PRESENT TENSE

A   PRESENT TIME

1	State (*see* 106)	*I like Mary.*
2	Single event (*see* 107)	*I resign.*
3	Habitual (*see* 108)	*She gets up early.*

THE PRESENT PROGRESSIVE

4	Temporary (*see* 109)	*He's drinking Scotch.*
5	Temporary habit (*see* 110)	*She's getting up early (nowadays).*

B   PAST TIME

THE PRESENT PERFECT

1	State up to present time (*see* 115)	*I've known her for years.*
2	Indefinite event(s) (*see* 115)	*I've seen better plays.*
3	Habit up to present time (*see* 115)	*He's conducted that orchestra for 15 years.*
4	With present result (*see* 115)	*You've ruined my dress!*

THE PRESENT PERFECT PROGRESSIVE

5	Temporary state up to present time (*see* 116)	*I've been waiting for an hour.*
6	Temporary habit up to present time	*He's been walking since he was 8 months old.*
7	Temporary, with present result (*see* 116)	*You've been smoking!*

139

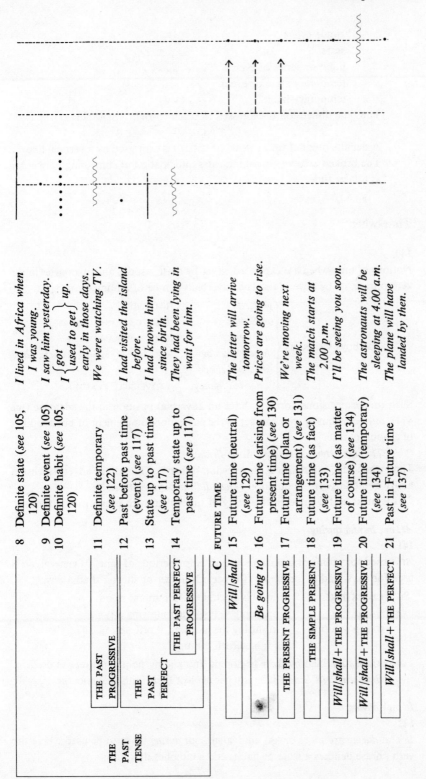

THE PAST TENSE	THE PAST PROGRESSIVE		8	Definite state (*see* 105, 120)	*I lived in Africa when I was young.*

8 Definite state (*see* 105, 120) — *I lived in Africa when I was young.*

9 Definite event (*see* 105) — *I saw him yesterday.*

10 Definite habit (*see* 105, 120) — *I got / used to get up early in those days.*

THE PAST PROGRESSIVE

11 Definite temporary (*see* 122) — *We were watching TV.*

THE PAST PERFECT

12 Past before past time (event) (*see* 117) — *I had visited the island before.*

13 State up to past time (*see* 117) — *I had known him since birth.*

THE PAST PERFECT PROGRESSIVE

14 Temporary state up to past time (*see* 117) — *They had been lying in wait for him.*

C FUTURE TIME

15 *Will/shall* — Future time (neutral) (*see* 129) — *The letter will arrive tomorrow.*

16 *Be going to* — Future time (arising from present time) (*see* 130) — *Prices are going to rise.*

17 THE PRESENT PROGRESSIVE — Future time (plan or arrangement) (*see* 131) — *We're moving next week.*

18 THE SIMPLE PRESENT — Future time (as fact) (*see* 133) — *The match starts at 2.00 p.m.*

19 *Will/shall* + THE PROGRESSIVE — Future time (as matter of course) (*see* 134) — *I'll be seeing you soon.*

20 *Will/shall* + THE PROGRESSIVE — Future time (temporary) (*see* 134) — *The astronauts will be sleeping at 4.00 a.m.*

21 *Will/shall* + THE PERFECT — Past in Future time (*see* 137) — *The plane will have landed by then.*

single event	.
state	————
habit or series of events	....
temporary state or event	⌄⌄⌄⌄⌄⌄
temporary habit	⌄⌄⌄⌄⌄⌄

The time dimension is expressed by a left-to-right arrow chain:

$$(\Rightarrow \Rightarrow \Rightarrow \Rightarrow \Rightarrow \Rightarrow).$$

A definite point of time ('NOW' or 'THEN') is expressed by a vertical line (|).
The broken arrow (– – –➤) indicates anticipation of something happening at a later time.

Time-when

140

Notions of time-when are expressed either by tense, aspect, and auxiliaries in the verb phrase, or by adverbials. The adverbials can be of a number of types:

	yesterday.	(ADVERB)
	on Saturday.	(PREPOSITIONAL PHRASE)
	last week.	(NOUN PHRASE)
The boys visited us	*three weeks ago.*	(NOUN PHRASE + *ago, back, etc*)
	whenever they	
	needed money.	(ADVERBIAL CLAUSE)

Such time expressions normally have an adverbial position in the sentence (*see* 474), but occasionally they can act as the subject or complement or postmodifier of a noun phrase.

The day after tomorrow will be *Friday.*

Time-when adverbials answer the question 'When?'. Thus all the adverbials listed above could answer the question *When did the boys visit you?*

It is most useful to begin the study of time-when with prepositional phrases.

At, on, in and *during*
141

At is used for points of time, and *on* and *in* for periods of time. In general, *on* is used for days, and *in* (or *during*) for periods longer or shorter than a day:

CLOCK TIME	at 10 o'clock, at 6.30 p.m., at noon
DAYS	on Sunday, (on) the following day
OTHER PERIODS	in/during the morning, April, spring, 1973, the nineteenth century

For periods identified by their beginning and ending points, *between* is used:

Between 1918 and 1939 many people lost their faith in democracy.

In and *during*
142

In and *during* are more or less equivalent, but *during* tends to be used where the verb phrase denotes a state or habit, and so implies duration:

He was injured *in the war*.

Many people suffered hardship *during the war*.

Only *during* can be used to mean 'in the course of' before nouns like *stay, visit, meal, etc*, referring to an event lasting some time:

We went to the zoo *during our stay* in Washington.

During the meal we talked about our plans.

Exceptions
143

At can be used for periods identified vaguely, as in *at that time, at breakfast time, at night*; also for short holiday periods (*at Christmas, at Easter*). In ⟨BrE⟩, *at the weekend* is used, but in ⟨AmE⟩ *on the weekend*. *On* is used before *morning, afternoon, evening*, and *night* when these periods are identified by the day of which they are a part: *on Monday evening, on the following evening*, but *in the evening*. (On the omission of the definite article in time expressions *see* 495.)

Note

By day and *by night* are idioms which can replace *during the day/night* with some activities such as travelling: *We travelled by night*.

Omitting the preposition
144

We almost always leave out the preposition before phrases beginning *last, next; this, that*; also before *today, yesterday, tomorrow*:

Did you go to the meeting *last Thursday*?

I'll mention it *next time* I see him.

Plums are more plentiful *this year*.

That day I had nothing important to do.

(The phrases *at this/that time, on this/that occasion* are however normal.) In ⟨informal⟩ English, we also usually leave out the preposition in phrases pointing to a time related indirectly to the present moment, or to a time before or after a definite time in the past or future:

I saw her $\begin{cases} \textit{the January before last.} \\ \textit{the day after her birthday.} \end{cases}$

The festival will be held $\begin{cases} \textit{the day after tomorrow.} \\ \textit{(in) the following spring.} \end{cases}$

The preposition is also sometimes omitted directly before days of the week:

I'll see you *Saturday*.

Sundays we go into the country.

This is especially common in ⟨informal AmE⟩.

Time relationships
145

Before and *after* (as prepositions, adverbs, and conjunctions) indicate relations between two times or events, as in

They were married *before the war*.

We ate *after I arrived*.

They have opposite meanings:

$=\begin{cases} \text{He arrived } after \text{ the play started.} \\ \text{The play started } before \text{ he arrived.} \end{cases}$

By refers to the time at which the result of an event is in existence:

> *By* Friday I was exhausted (*ie* I became exhausted before Friday, and I was still exhausted on Friday).

> Please send me the tickets *by next week* (*ie* I want to have the tickets not later than next week).

Already, *still*, *yet*, and *any more* are related in meaning to *by*-phrases. *Already* and *yet* require the perfect aspect when occurring with an event verb: *They have already left*; *They haven't left yet*. With state verbs and with the progressive aspect, they can occur with the present tense: *I know that already*; *He's not yet working*. Note the negative relation of these adverbs to *still* and *any more*:

> He *still* works here. = He hasn't stopped working here *yet*.

> He's *already* stopped working. = He isn't working *any more*.

We use *by now* often when we are not certain that the event has happened:

> He should have arrived *by now* ('. . . but I'm not sure').

Otherwise we prefer to use *already*:

> He has arrived *already*.

146

The preposition *in* (or *within* ⟨formal⟩) can have the meaning 'before the end of':

> He travelled round the world *in eighty days*.

> Phone me again *within a week*.

147

Here, for comparison, are some examples of time phrases with a particular noun, *night*:

> I woke up *in the* (*middle of the*) *night*. (*see* 141)

> (*On*) *Sunday night* we'll have a party. (*see* 141)

> Snow fell *during the night*. (*see* 142)

> Sometimes I can't sleep $\begin{cases} at \ night. \ (see \ 143) \\ nights. \end{cases}$

> $\left.\begin{array}{l} \text{We'll do Paris} \\ \text{We travelled} \end{array}\right\}$ *by night*. (*see* 143 Note)

> I'll be there *by Friday night*. (*see* 145)

> *For several nights* he had no sleep at all. (*see* 151)

> We stayed up *all night*. (*see* 152)

> Will you stay *overnight*? (*see* 153)

Measuring time

148

Ago following a noun phrase of time measure refers to a point of time in the past as measured from the present moment: 'We met *a year ago*'. For a similar measurement into the future, we use a measure phrase followed by *from now*, or *in* + measure phrase, or *in* + genitive measure phrase + *time*:

> I'll see you $\begin{cases} in \ three \ months. \\ three \ months \ from \ now. \\ in \ three \ months' \ time. \end{cases}$

In measuring forwards from a point of time in the past, only the first alternative is available:

He finished the job *in three months*. (*ie* from when he started it)

Before and *after*, and the adverbs *beforehand* and *afterwards*, *earlier* and *later*, can also follow a measure phrase:

I had met them *three months before(hand)*.

Ten years after his death, he suddenly became famous.

Time-when adverbs

149

There are two main groups of time-when adverbs (*see* 474):

(A)   *again, just* (= 'at this very moment'), *now, nowadays, then* (= 'at that time'), *today*, etc.

(B)   *afterwards, before(hand), first, formerly, just* (= 'a very short time ago/ before') *late(r), lately, next, previously, recently, since, soon, subsequently* ⟨formal⟩, *then* (= 'after that'), *ultimately* ⟨formal⟩, etc.

Group (A) identifies a point or period of time directly; Group (B) identifies a time indirectly, by reference to another point of time understood in the context.

Examples:

(A)   *Nowadays* people are difficult to please.

We're *just* leaving.

(B)   The guests have/had *just* left.

Have you been to the theatre *recently*?

He wrote last Christmas, but I haven't heard from him *since* (= 'since that time').

Time-when conjunctions

150

The main time-when conjunctions are *when, as, before, after* (*see* 145), *while* (*see* 154), *as soon as, once, now* (*that*):

When I last heard from him, he was living in Buenos Aires.

Buy your tickets *as soon as you can*.

Once you have taken the examination, you'll be able to relax.

Duration

151

Phrases of duration answer the question 'How long?'. *Compare:*

(A)   When did you stop there?   (B)   *In the summer.*

(A)   How long did you stop there?   (B)   *For the summer.*

The time-when phrase *in the summer* here indicates that the stop was INCLUDED in the summer period; the duration phrase *for the summer* indicates that the stop lasted AS LONG AS the summer period.

For with this meaning can also precede phrases of time measurement, *eg for a month, for several days, for two years.*

152

The preposition *for* is often left out, particularly before *all*:

I studied (*for*) *three years* in London.

The snowy weather lasted (*for*) *the whole winter*.

He's been gardening *all day* (*not* *for all day).

Note

For is generally not omitted when it comes first in the sentence: *For several years they lived in poverty;* or when it follows a negative: *I haven't seen him for eight years*.

153

Over can be used instead of *for* for short periods such as holidays:

We stayed with my parents *over* {
the holiday.
Christmas.
the weekend.
}

From . . . to are used to identify a period by its beginning and end: *from nine to five; from June to December.* In ⟨AmE⟩, *from . . . through* are used to make clear that the whole period includes the second period named; thus *from June through December* means '. . . up to and including December'. *Up to* normally specifies that the longer period does *not* include the period named:

He worked *up to Christmas* (*ie* but not over Christmas).

Until or *till* (*see* 155) can replace *to* in the construction *from . . . to . . .: from Monday till Friday.* But, with *from* absent, only: *We stayed until/till five.*

While, since and *until*

154

The conjunction *while* can mean either (a) 'duration' or (b) 'time-when', depending on the kind of verb meaning (*see* 104–5).

a   I stayed *while the meeting lasted* (*ie* for the duration of the meeting). (STATE VERB)

b   I arrived *while the meeting was in progress* (*ie* in the course of the meeting). (EVENT VERB)

Since also has these two functions:

a   He's lived here (*ever*) *since he was born* (*ie* for his whole life, from his birth up to now).

b   They've changed their car twice *since 1970* (*ie* between 1970 and now).

It is important to notice that *since* normally requires the perfective aspect in the verb of the main clause:

Since 1971, Britain *has had* decimal currency (*not* *Britain *has* decimal currency).

155

Until (or *till*) as preposition and conjunction has a meaning comparable to example *a* of *since* (the STATE VERB sense), except that it names the end-point rather than the beginning point of a period:

You're to stay in bed *until next Monday* (*ie* from now to next Monday).

In the negative, *until* can occur with event verbs, and is in practice equivalent to *before*:

$$=\begin{cases} \text{He didn't start to read } \textit{until he was ten.} \\ \text{He didn't start to read } \textit{before he was ten.} \end{cases}$$

Adverbs and idioms of duration
156
The following adverbs and idiomatic phrases indicate duration:

> *always, for ever* (both meaning 'for all time')
>
> *since* ('since then'), *recently, lately* (both meaning 'since a short time ago')
>
> *temporarily, for the moment, for a while* (all meaning 'for a short time')
>
> *for ages* ⟨informal⟩ ('for a long time').

Since, lately, and *recently* indicate either time-when or duration according to the type of verb meaning:

> They got married only *recently* (='a short time ago').
>
> He's *recently* been working at night (='since a short time ago').

Frequency

157
Expressions of FREQUENCY answer the question 'How many times?' or 'How often?'.

The upper and lower limits of frequency are expressed by *always* ('on every occasion') and *never* ('on no occasion'). Between these extremes, a rough indication of frequency (INDEFINITE FREQUENCY) can be given by:

most frequent ↑	*nearly always, almost always*
	usually, normally, generally, regularly (='on most occasions')
	often, frequently (='on many occasions')
	sometimes (='on some occasions')
	occasionally, now and then ⟨informal⟩ (='on a few occasions')
	rarely, seldom (='on few occasions')
least frequent	*hardly ever, scarcely ever* (='almost never')

(*Compare* 67–8.)

A more exact measurement of frequency (DEFINITE FREQUENCY) can be expressed in one of the following three ways:

(A)   *once a day, three times an hour, several times a week* (sometimes *per* ⟨formal, official⟩ is used instead of *a(n)* here: *once per day*)

(B)   *every day* (='once a day'), *every morning, every two years*

(C)   *daily* (='once a day'), *hourly, weekly, monthly, yearly.*

Daily, weekly etc can act as adjectives as well as adverbs:

$$\text{He visits me} \begin{cases} \textit{once a week.} \\ \textit{every week.} \\ \textit{weekly.} \end{cases} \qquad = \text{He pays me } \textit{a weekly} \text{ visit.}$$

We can also say *once every day*, *twice weekly*, etc. *Every other day*, *etc* means 'every two days'.

158

A further type of frequency expression involves the use of quantifiers like *some*, *any*, *most*, *many*:

> *Some days* I feel like giving up the job altogether.
>
> Come and see me *any time* you like.
>
> We play tennis *most weekends*.
>
> He's been to Russia *many times* as a reporter.

159

Frequency phrases generally have no preposition. One exception is phrases with the word *occasion(s)* ⟨rather formal⟩:

> *On several occasions* the President has refused to bow to the will of
>   Congress.

160

Frequency phrases sometimes lose much of their time meaning, and get a more abstract meaning, referring to INSTANCES rather than TIMES. *Always* and *sometimes* (for example) can be interpreted 'in every case', 'in some cases', rather than 'on every occasion', 'on some occasions':

> Children *often* ('in many cases') dislike tomatoes.
>
>   (roughly = 'Many children dislike tomatoes')
>
> Students *rarely* ('in few cases') used to fail the course.
>
>   (roughly = 'Few students used to fail the course')

Place, direction and distance

161

Expressions of place and direction are chiefly adverbials and postmodifiers. They answer the question *Where?*, so that all of the following could be answers to the question *Where did you leave the bicycle?*:

I left it	*(over) there.*	(ADVERB *see* 472, 480)
	in the street.	(PREPOSITIONAL PHRASE *see* 739, 743)
	two miles away.	(NOUN PHRASE + *away*, *back*, *etc*, *see* 651–3)
	where I found it.	(ADVERBIAL CLAUSE *see* 517)

Place expressions can also on occasion act as subject or complement of a sentence:

> *Over here* is *where I put the books*. ⟨informal⟩

You will see that the range of grammatical structures and functions for expressing place is similar to that for expressing time (*see* 140). You will also notice that some forms (*eg* the prepositions *at*, *from*, and *between*) have related meanings in the two fields.

Prepositions of place
162

Apart from the general adverbs *here*, *there*, *somewhere*, *anywhere*, *everywhere*, and *nowhere*, by far the most important words for indicating place are prepositions. The choice of preposition is often governed by the way we see an object, whether we see it

(A) as a point in space   (×)
(B) as a line   (———)
(C) as a surface   (⌐⊃)
(D) as an area   (▱)
(E) as a volume   (⬔)

The difference between 'surface' and 'area' will be explained below (*see* 165–6, 175).

We may distinguish '*at*-type' prepositions, which indicate a point (A); '*on*-type' prepositions, which indicate a line or a surface (B or C), and '*in*-type' prepositions, which indicate an area or a volume (D or E). Some prepositions (such as *across*) belong to more than one of these types.

At-type prepositions
163

(A) The place is seen as a POINT (*ie* a place which is identified quite generally, without being thought of in terms of length, width, or height):

to	*at*	*(away) from*	*away from*
→×	·×	×→	× ·
1	2	3	4

1 We went {to Stratford. / to the hotel. / to the door.

2 We stayed {at home. / at an inn. / at the entrance.

3 We came (*away*) {from the theatre. / from the house. / from the bus-stop.

4 We stayed {away from home. / away from England. / away from the village.

On-type prepositions
164

(B) The place is seen as a LINE, *ie* is a place thought of in terms of length, but not breadth or height (depth):

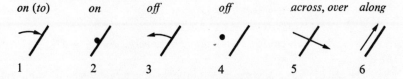

on (to)	*on*	*off*	*off*	*across, over*	*along*
1	2	3	4	5	6

1 The ball rolled *on to the goal-line*.
2 Memphis is a town *on the Mississippi*.
3 We turned *off the main road*.
4 Zanzibar is an island *off the coast of Africa*.
5 They drove *across the frontier*.
6 We walked *along the river bank*.

165

(C)   The place is seen as a SURFACE, *ie* is thought of in terms of length and width, but not height (or depth). (The surface need not be flat or horizontal.)

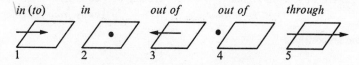

1   He fell *on* (*to*) *the floor.*
2   There's a green label *on the bottle.*
3   He took the picture *off the wall.*
4   That's a place *off the map.*
5   He took a walk *across the fields.*
6   He looked *through the window.*

The surface is often the *top* of some object (*on = on top of*): *He was lying on the bed*; *It fell off the table.*

Note

[*a*]   *On etc* is also used for public transport:

There were lots of passengers *on the bus/train/ship.*

We can also say *He travelled by bus. etc* (*see* 195–6)

[*b*]   Notice also *an apple on a tree, the ring on her finger* (where *on* = 'attached to').

***In*-type prepositions**

166

(D)   The place is seen as an AREA (usually an area of ground or territory enclosed by boundaries).

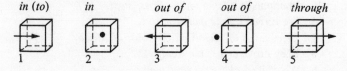

1   They crowded *into the streets.*
2   I have a house *in the city.*
3   They flew *out of the country.*
4   He stayed *out of the district.*
5   We went for a walk *through the park.*

167

(E)   The place is seen as a VOLUME, *ie* is thought of in terms of length, width, and height (or depth):

1   He ran *into the house.*
2   The food *in the cupboard.*
3   He climbed *out of the water.*
4   He was *out of the room.*
5   The wind blew *through the trees.*

168

Inside and *outside* are sometimes used instead of *in* (*to*) and *out of*:

We went/stayed *inside the building.*

He was listening *outside the room.*

Within is a slightly more ⟨formal⟩ word than *in*, and often indicates a location bounded by limits:

Many prisoners died *within the walls of the castle.*

He lives *within a stone's throw of the office.*

169

Some common transitive verbs such as *put, place, lay, stand* are followed by *on* and *in* rather than *on to* and *into*:

He put the cup *on the shelf.*

He placed the jewels *in a box.*

Also, *arrive* goes with *at, on,* or *in*: *The train arrives at/in Brussels at 7.15.*

Overlap between types of preposition

170

We can often use different prepositions with the same noun. But in such cases, the meaning will be slightly different.

My car is *at the cottage.*   (POINT, *ie* the cottage as a general location)

There is a new roof *on the cottage.* (SURFACE)

There are two beds *in the cottage.* (VOLUME)

Overlap between *at*-type and *in*-type prepositions

171

For towns and villages, either *at* or *in* is used, depending on point of view. *At Stratford* means we are seeing Stratford simply as a place on the map; *in Stratford* means we have a 'close up' view of the place as a town covering an area and containing streets, houses, *etc.* A very large town or city is generally treated as an area: *in New York. At New York* would only be used in a context of world-wide travel:

We stopped to refuel *at New York* on our way to Tokyo.

Parts of cities also require *in*: *in Chelsea* (part of London); *in Brooklyn* (part of New York).

172

For continents, countries, states, and other large areas we use *in*: *in Asia, in Ghana, in Virginia.* However, the directional words *to* and *from* are preferred even for large territories, except where the territories border one another:

He sailed *from* Europe *to* Canada.

but: He drove $\left\{ \begin{array}{l} from \\ out\ of \end{array} \right\}$ France *into* Belgium.

173

For buildings or groups of buildings either *at* or *in* can be used, but *at* is preferred when the building is thought of as an institution rather than in physical terms. (Many such nouns with *at* take no definite article: *at school, see* 495.)

{He works *at the post office.*
but: I left my purse *at/in the post office.*

{He studies *at Oxford* (=the university).
but: He lives *at/in Oxford* (=the city).

At and *to*
174

At is used instead of *to* when what the following noun refers to is being treated as a target:

He threw the ball *at me* (*ie* 'He tried to hit me').

He threw the ball *to me* (*ie* 'for me to catch').

Note also a similar contrast between:

Peter shouted *at me* (suggests that Peter was angry with me).

Peter shouted *to me* (suggests that Peter was trying to communicate with me at a distance).

Other contrasts of the same general kind are seen in:

He pointed *at/to me.*

He passed/handed a note *to me.*

He {aimed the gun / shot} *at me.*

Overlap between *on*-type and *in*-type prepositions
175

There is a difference between 'surface' and 'volume' in:

We sat *on the grass.*   (SURFACE: *ie* the grass is short)

We sat *in the grass.*   (VOLUME: *ie* the grass is long)

Another difference (between 'surface' and 'area') is seen in:

Robinson Crusoe was marooned *on a desert island* (SURFACE: *ie* the island is small).

He was born *in Cuba* (AREA: *ie* Cuba is a large island, and a political unit with boundaries).

Position
176

Position as a relation between two objects can best be explained by a picture. Imagine that a car is standing on a bridge:

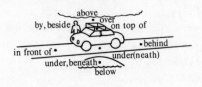

The river is *below the car*.	A bird hovered *over us*.
There are clouds *above the car*.	A man is standing *by/beside the car*.
The road is *under(neath) the car*.	
The roofrack is *on top of the car*.	The road stretches *in front of* and *behind the car*.

177

The main difference between *over/under* and *above/below* is that *over* and *under* tend to indicate a direct vertical relationship, or nearness: 'The man had a bad cut *over his left eye*'; 'He was leaning *over the injured man*'. *Above* and *below* may mean simply that one object is on a higher or lower level than the other. *Underneath* often means that one object is actually touching the other. In this respect it is the opposite of *on top of*.

178

By and *beside* mean 'at the side of', but can also be used more generally to indicate the nearness of one object to another:

She sat in a chair *by* (= 'near') *the door*.

179

The following prepositional adverbs (*see* 746) or fixed phrases correspond to the prepositions of position we have just dealt with:

overhead	(over)	above	(above)
underneath	(under)	below	(below)
in front	(in front of)	behind	(behind)
on top	(on top of)	beneath	(beneath)

Examples:

He tumbled off the bridge into the water *below*. (= below the bridge)

An airliner flew *overhead*. (= 'over us', *etc*)

Would you like to sit *in front*? (= 'in the front seat of the car')

Some other positions

180

Between, among and *amid: Between* normally relates an object to two other objects, and *among* to more than two:

The house stands *between two trees*.

The house stands *among trees*.

But *between* can relate more than two objects, if we have a definite number in mind:

Switzerland lies *between France, Germany, Italy and Austria*.

Amid ⟨formal⟩ means 'in the midst of', and like *among*, can apply to an indefinite number of objects: 'The house stands *amid trees*'. Unlike *among*, it can also be followed by a mass noun:

A child's doll was found *amid the wreckage of the plane*.

Opposite means 'facing':

> His house is *opposite mine* (*ie* 'facing mine, on the other side of the street').

(A)round refers to surrounding position or motion:

> The police were standing on guard *around the building*.

About and *around* in 〈informal〉 English often have a vaguer meaning of 'in the area of' or 'in various positions in':

> The guests were standing *about/around the room*.

> There aren't many shops *about/around here*.

In 〈AmE〉, *about* is rarer and more 〈formal〉 in this sense than *around*.

Motion
181

In 164–7, those meanings illustrated by diagrams 1, 3, 5, and 6 involve MOTION. The prepositions in the other diagrams (2 and 4) indicate STATE.

Different aspects of motion can be pictured as follows:

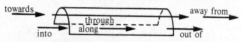

> The train sped *towards/into/etc the tunnel*.

But the prepositions used to indicate position in 176–80 can also signify MOTION TO the position concerned:

1   The bush was a good hiding-place, so I dashed *behind it*.
2   When it started to rain, we all ran *underneath the trees*.

Passage
182

The same prepositions can also be used, like *through* and *across*, to indicate motion towards, then away from a place (*ie* PASSAGE):

1   The photographers ran *behind the goal-posts*.
2   I crawled *underneath the fence*.

Other prepositions can be used similarly:

1   We drove *by/past the town hall*.
2   We passed *over/across the bridge*.
3   We turned *(a)round the corner*.

(A)round can also refer more generally to circular motion:

> The earth moves *(a)round the sun*.

Direction
183

Up, down, along, and *across/over* represent motion with reference to a direction or axis.

HORIZONTAL AXIS   VERTICAL AXIS

He walked *along/across the street.*   [1]

He ran *up/down the hill.*   [2]

He drove *up/down the street.*   [3]

Sentence [3] does not necessarily mean that the street was on a hill: ⟨informally⟩, we use *up* and *down* with practically the same meaning as *along*. (*Downtown* ⟨AmE⟩ means simply the central or business part of a town.)

Repeated motion
184

We can express repeated motion by joining two prepositions with *and*:

> He walked *up and down the room* (in one direction and then in another).
>
> The oars splashed *in and out of the water.*
>
> They danced *round and round the room.*

Orientation (or viewpoint)
185

The preposition *beyond* makes reference not only to two objects, but to a third factor, the 'viewpoint' at which the speaker is standing (or imagines he is standing):

> I could see the town *beyond the lake* (*ie* 'on the other side of the lake [from me']).

We can also express a similar meaning by using *across, over, through, past, etc* in a sense related to their 'passage' or 'direction' sense (*see* 182–3):

the people *over the road* ⟨*esp* BrE⟩	the cafe *round the corner*
	the garage *past the supermarket*
friends *across the sea*	the hotel *down the road*
the house *through the trees*	the man *up a ladder*

We can, if we like, specify the viewpoint by using a *from*-phrase:

> He lives up/down/along/across the road *from me.*

Resulting meaning
186

Prepositions which have the meaning of 'motion' can also have a 'state' meaning, indicating the state of having reached a particular destination:

> The horses are *over the fence* (*ie* 'have jumped the fence').
>
> The divers are *out of the water* already.

Pervasive meaning
187

Over and *through* can have 'pervasive' meaning, especially when preceded by *all*:

> He painted (*all*) *over the walls* (*ie* 'he covered the walls with paint').
>
> The noise could be heard *all over/through* the building.

Through is restricted to areas and volumes (*see* 166–7). *Throughout* can be used instead of *all through*:

> The epidemic has spread *throughout the country.*

Abstract place meaning

188

Many place prepositions are used in more abstract senses, which have a meta-phorical relation to their basic sense. Some examples are:

> *In, out of* (condition or inclusion): *in danger, out of danger; in practice, out of practice; in a race, in plays, in a group.*
>> People never behave *in real life* as they do *in plays.*
> *Above, below, beneath* (level):
>> His grades are *above the average.* Such behaviour is *beneath* (=not worthy of) *him.*
> *Over, under* (power, surveillance): *under suspicion, under orders:*
>> The King had absolute power *over his subjects.*
> *Up, Down* (movement on a scale): *up the scale, down the social ladder.*
> *From, to* (giving and receiving):
>> I got a letter *from Jill.*
>> He lent some money *to his son.*
> *Between, among* (relations between two or more people):
>> There was a fight *between two boys.*
>> They agree *among themselves.*
> *Past, beyond* (excess):
>> He's *beyond* (=too ill for) *recovery.*
>> I'm *past* (=too old for) *falling in love.*

Place adverbs

189

Most place prepositions (except the *at*-type prepositions) correspond in form to prepositional adverbs (*see* 746), and in general their meanings correspond as well. Here are some examples:

> We stopped the bus and got *off* (*ie* 'off the bus').
> Have you put the cat *out* (*ie* 'out of the house')?
> The child ran *across* in front of the car (*ie* 'across the road').
> When they reached the bridge, they crossed *over*, looking *down* at the water *beneath.*

190

But some prepositional adverbs have special uses:

> They travelled *on* (*ie* 'they continued their journey').
> The thieves snatched her handbag and ran *off* (='away').
> A man came *up* (*ie* 'approached') and introduced himself.
> You don't see many trams *about* nowadays ⟨informal BrE⟩ (*ie* 'about the place').

In this last example, *about* is so vague as to be almost meaningless.

In addition to *up* and *down*, the following adverbs of direction can be noted: *upward(s), downward(s); forward(s), backward(s); inward(s), outward(s); homeward(s).*

Distance
191
Distance can be expressed by noun phrases of measure such as *a foot*, *a few yards*, *ten miles*, *a long way*, etc. These phrases can modify a verb of motion:

He ran *several miles*.

They can also precede and modify an adverbial of place:

They live *a long way away*.
The valley lay *two thousand feet below them*.

Here the reference is to static location. Notice the corresponding question forms:

How far did he run?
But: How *far away* do they live?

Manner, means and instrument

Answering the question '*how*'
192
If you want to specify HOW an action is performed or HOW an event takes place, you can use an adverbial of MANNER, MEANS, or INSTRUMENT:

(A)   How did he write the letter?

(B)   He wrote it $\begin{cases} \textit{hurriedly.} & \text{(MANNER)} \\ \textit{by hand.} & \text{(MEANS)} \\ \textit{with a ball-point pen.} & \text{(INSTRUMENT)} \end{cases}$

You can ask a more specific question about the instrument with which an action is performed as follows:

What did he write it *with*? ⟨informal⟩
With what did he write it? ⟨formal⟩

Manner
193
The three chief ways of expressing manner are (A) adverb (usually ending in -*ly*), (B) *in . . . manner* (or *way*), (C) *with* + abstract noun phrase. Most adjectives have matching -*ly* adjectives, and many adjectives have matching abstract nouns. Thus there may be three ways of expressing the same idea:

He spoke $\begin{cases} \text{(A)} & \textit{confidently.} \\ \text{(B)} & \textit{in a confident manner/way.} \\ \text{(C)} & \textit{with confidence.} \end{cases}$

When a manner adverb is available, use the adverb, as it has the advantage of being shorter and ⟨less formal⟩ than the other constructions. Further examples of manner phrases are:

We'll let you know *in the usual manner/way*.
The task was done *in a workmanlike manner/way*.
She greeted us *with great courtesy* (*ie* 'very courteously').
I answered *without hesitation* (*ie* 'unhesitatingly').
He rides *cowboy-style* (or *in the style of a cowboy*).

Like this, like that (or *this way, that way*) are phrases with the meaning 'in this/that manner':

You don't spell 'hysteria' *like that*; you spell it *like this* ⟨informal⟩.

Notice that *in* can be omitted before *way* in certain ⟨informal⟩ constructions:

She cooks turkey
$$\begin{cases} \textit{the way I like.} \\ \textit{the same way as I do / as me.} \\ \textit{a number of different ways.} \end{cases}$$

194

A manner phrase sometimes expresses a comparison:

She sings *like a professional* (*ie* 'in the manner of a professional, as well as a professional').

Manner clauses introduced by *as* can be used in a similar way:

She cooks turkey
$$\begin{cases} \textit{like my mother.} \\ \textit{as my mother did.} \\ \textit{in the way my mother did.} \ \langle\textit{formal}\rangle \\ \textit{the way my mother did.} \ \langle\textit{informal}\rangle \end{cases}$$

They hunted him *as a tiger stalks its prey.* ⟨formal⟩

Comparisons with unreal situations can be expressed by a clause beginning *as if* or *as though*:

She treats me $\begin{Bmatrix} \textit{as if} \\ \textit{as though} \end{Bmatrix}$ *I were a stranger.*

(On the verb form *were* here, *see* 286.)

Means and instrument: *by* and *with*
195

MEANS is expressed by a prepositional phrase introduced by *by*:

I usually go to work *by bus*.

The thief must have entered *by the back door*.

We managed to sell the house *by advertising it in the paper*.

INSTRUMENT is expressed by a prepositional phrase introduced by *with*:

He caught the ball *with his left hand*.

Someone killed him *with an arrow*.

The verb *use* and its object also convey the idea of instrument:

He always opens his letters with a knife.

= He always uses a knife to open his letters.

The non-use of an instrument can be expressed by *without*:

$=\begin{cases} \text{He drew the lines without a ruler.} \\ \text{He didn't use a ruler to draw the lines.} \\ \text{He drew the lines without using a ruler.} \end{cases}$

196

We sometimes prefer to replace a phrase of means by a different type of prepositional phrase, *eg* one of place:

(A) How did he get in?   (B) He came in *through the window*.
                                               (more usual than *by the window*)

(A)   How did you hear the news? (B)   I heard it *on the radio*. (*Compare:* They sent the message *by radio*.)

The article is omitted in *by*-phrases denoting communication: *by car, by train, by letter, by post, by radio* (*see* 495).

Cause, reason and purpose

Direct cause
197
There are many different answers to the question 'What caused such-and-such an event'. The means and instrument, just discussed, may be said to be kinds of direct cause. More important, though, is the *person* who causes an event, *ie* the ACTOR in an action. The actor is usually specified by the subject of a clause, or by the agent in the passive (*see* 676–9):

(A)   How did the fire start?

(B) $\begin{cases} \textit{Some children} \text{ started it (}\textit{ie}\text{ 'caused it to start').} \\ \text{It was started by } \textit{some children.} \end{cases}$

Start in the second sentence here may be called a CAUSATIVE VERB, and *some children* names the actor.

Many adjectives and intransitive verbs in English have a corresponding causative verb. The causative verb may match them in form (*open, grow, blow up, narrow* (adj) and *narrow* (verb)), or may be different in form (*fall, fell; die, kill; come, bring*):

The dam *blew up*.	The terrorists *blew up* the dam.
The road became *narrower*.	They *narrowed* the road.
The tree has *fallen*.	Someone has *felled* the tree.
The supplies *came* yesterday.	They *brought* the supplies yesterday.

198
Sometimes, when the actor is not mentioned, the instrument or means takes the position of subject, *ie* the role of the 'causer' of the action:

They killed him *with a bullet*.	*A bullet* killed him.
They brought the supplies *by train*.	*A train* brought the supplies.

In the passive, the actor can be expressed by an agent *by*-phrase (*see* 676–9):

The dam was blown up *by terrorists*.

The same is true of instrument:

He was killed *by a bullet*.

Cause and result: *Because, etc*
199
More generally, you may indicate cause (whether direct or indirect) by an adverbial *because*-clause, or by a prepositional phrase beginning *because of, on account of* ⟨formal⟩, *from, out of*:

Because: The car crashed *because the driver was careless.*   [1]

Because of: He lost his job *because of his age.*   [2]

On account of ⟨formal⟩: Many fatal accidents occurred *on account of icy road conditions.*   [3]

From, out of (mainly to express motive, *ie* psychological cause):
Some support charities *out of duty,* others *from a sense of guilt.*

200

Other prepositions of cause are *for* (mainly with nouns of feeling) and *through*:
He jumped *for joy.*

The car crashed *through the driver's carelessness.*   [1a]

Cause as subject
201

The above sentences answer the question *Why?* rather than the question *How?* But 'cause' in these sentences is not very different from 'actor', 'instrument' and 'means' (*see* 195–7): we can often make the 'cause' the subject of the sentence. *Compare* [1], [1a] and [2] in 199–200 with [1b] and [2b] below:

The driver's carelessness $\begin{cases} \textit{caused the car to crash.} \\ \textit{made the car crash.} \\ \textit{caused the crash.} \end{cases}$ [1b]

(*Cause* and *make* are general causative verbs.)

His age *lost him* (=caused him to lose) *his job.*   [2b]

Other verbal constructions expressing cause are these:

He argues that higher wages inevitably $\begin{cases} \textit{lead to} \\ \textit{result in} \\ \textit{give rise to} \\ \textit{bring about} \end{cases}$ higher prices.

We can also say:

The effect of higher wages is to raise prices.

Result
202

Result is the opposite of cause (*cf* [3] in 199):

$= \begin{cases} \text{The icy conditions } \textit{caused} \text{ many accidents.} \\ \text{Many accidents } \textit{resulted from} \text{ the icy conditions.} \end{cases}$ [3a]

Result can be expressed by a clause beginning with *so (that)*:   [4]

I took no notice of him, *so (that)* he flew into a rage.

This is equivalent to:

He flew into a rage *because* I took no notice of him.   [4a]

In this context, *so* is more ⟨informal⟩ than *so that.*

Purpose
203

The intended result (*see* 338) or PURPOSE of an action is described by an adverbial of purpose, which is usually a *to*-infinitive clause, but may also be a finite verb clause beginning *so that.* (The *so that*-clause often contains *should, see* 289.)

He left early *to catch the last train.*

To improve the railway service, they are electrifying the main lines.

They advertised the concert *so that everyone should know about it.*

In order ⟨more formal⟩ and *so as* can precede *to* in the infinitive clause: *in order to catch the last train*; *so as to improve the railway service*. Also *in order that* is a ⟨more formal⟩ alternative for *so that*: *in order that everyone should know about it*. In ⟨informal BrE⟩, *in case* can introduce the idea of negative purpose (*compare* 209):

He left early *in case he should miss the last train* (*ie* '. . . so that he should not miss it').

Reason and consequence
204

Because, because of, and *on account of* can express REASON as well as cause. Cause and reason are overlapping notions (both answering the question *Why?*), but we can see a difference between them in that reason concerns not the events themselves, but the way a person interprets the events, and acts upon his interpretation:

I lent him the money $\begin{cases} \textit{because he needed it.} \\ \textit{because of his children.} \end{cases}$

Reason can also be expressed by *as*-clauses and *since*-clauses:

As Jane was the eldest, she looked after the others.

Since we live near the sea, we can often go swimming.

We can say that the main clause indicates the CONSEQUENCE of the reason clause. Another way to express the same idea would be:

The city is situated near the sea and *consequently* enjoys a healthy climate. ⟨rather formal⟩

205

Now that and *seeing that* are conjunctions which have a meaning very close to *as* and *since*, except that *now that* has also an element of time meaning:

Now that the weather has improved, we'll be able to enjoy the game.

Seeing that he could not persuade the other members of the committee, he gave in.

Another ⟨more formal⟩ way to express the same idea is a participle clause (*see* 515):

The weather having improved, the game was enjoyed by players and spectators alike. ⟨formal⟩

Being a man of fixed views, he refused to listen to our arguments. ⟨formal⟩

206

Yet another construction expressing reason is a *for*-phrase, which accompanies certain adjectives and verbs conveying emotion and attitude:

I was angry with him *for being late* (='because he was late').

He was punished/commended/praised *for his outspoken defence of free speech.*

207

The following are linking adverbials of cause or reason (*see* 380) meaning 'because of that' or 'for that reason': *therefore*, *thus* ⟨rather formal⟩, *so* ⟨informal⟩, *accordingly* ⟨formal⟩, *hence* ⟨formal⟩, *consequently*. A linking adverbial corresponding to *seeing that* is *in that case*:

(A)   The weather has improved.   (B)   *In that case*, we can enjoy our
                                                                    game.

Condition and contrast

Open and hypothetical conditions
208

Conditional clauses are related to reason clauses, but they discuss the consequence of something which may or may not be a real event. Notice the difference between:

> I'll lend Peter the money *because he needs it*.   [1]
> I'll lend Peter the money *if he needs it*.   [2]

The speaker of sentence [2] does not know whether Peter needs the money, while the speaker of [1] knows that he does. A sentence like [2] expresses what we call an OPEN condition, because the truth or falsehood of what the sentence describes is 'open', *ie* unknown. The conditional clause often precedes the main clause:

> *If you feel seasick*, take one of these pills.

There is another type of conditional sentence, which expresses an unreal or HYPOTHETICAL condition; *ie* for this type of sentence the speaker assumes the falsehood or unlikelihood of what he is talking about:

> I'd lend Peter the money *if he needed it*.

The speaker's assumption here is 'but he doesn't need the money'. As this example shows, the hypothetical meaning is signalled by the use of the hypothetical past tense (*see* 284).

209

Less common indicators of condition are the conjunctions *in case*, *on condition that*, *provided that*, and the preposition *in case of* ⟨formal⟩:

> Take these pills, *in case you feel ill on the boat*.
> I'll lend you the money *on condition that you return it within six months*.
> *Provided that* ⎱ they had plenty to eat and drink, the men were happy.
> *So long as* ⎰
> *In case of difficulty* call the operator. ⟨formal⟩

In case specifies a future condition that may or may not arise. *On condition that* stipulates or lays down a condition to which a person must agree. *Provided that* and *so long as* resemble *on condition that* in having the restrictive implication of 'if and only if . . .'. *In that case* and *then* ⟨informal⟩ are sentence adverbials of condition:

(A)   He may have missed the train.

(B)   ⎰ *In that case*, he would have taken a taxi.
      ⎱ He would have taken a taxi, *then*.

Negative condition

210

Unless expresses a negative condition. Thus we could change the emphasis of [2] by saying:

> I won't lend Peter the money *unless he needs it*.

Note the equivalence of:

$$= \begin{cases} \textit{Unless} \text{ Peter } \textit{improves} \text{ his work, he'll fail the exam.} \\ \textit{If} \text{ Peter } \textit{doesn't improve} \text{ his work, he'll fail the exam.} \end{cases}$$

Negative hypothetical conditions can be expressed by *but for* + noun phrase:

> *But for John*, we would have lost the match (*ie* 'If it hadn't been for
> John'; 'If John hadn't played well', *etc*).

Otherwise is a sentence adverb expressing negative condition (*see* 382).

Use of *any, ever, etc*

211

Because they indicate uncertainty, conditional clauses usually contain *any*-words like *any, ever, yet, etc* instead of *some*-words like *some, always, already* (*see* 803–7):

> Unless *anyone* has *any* questions, the meeting is adjourned.

> If you *ever* have *any* problems, let me know.

But to express special positive bias (*see* 248), conditional clauses can contain *some*-words:

> Help yourself if you want *something* to eat.

Clauses of contrast: *although, etc*

212

A type of adverbial meaning that overlaps with conditional meaning is that of CONTRAST (often called CONCESSION). If two circumstances are in contrast, it means that the one is SURPRISING or UNEXPECTED in view of the other:

$$\begin{cases} a & \text{The weather is bad.} \\ b & \text{We are enjoying ourselves.} \end{cases} \quad \begin{cases} a & \text{He looked strong and healthy.} \\ b & \text{He hadn't eaten for days.} \end{cases}$$

We can put the two contrasting statements *a* and *b* together by making one of them into a subclause beginning *although* or *though* ⟨informal⟩:

> We are enjoying ourselves, *although/though the weather is bad*.

> (*Even*) *though he hadn't eaten for days*, he looked strong and healthy.

(*Even though* is slightly more emphatic than *though*.) We can link the contrasting ideas *a* and *b* in another way, by using the coordinating conjunction *but*:

> He hadn't eaten for days, *but* he looked strong and healthy.

The conjunctions *while* and *whereas* ⟨more formal⟩ can express contrast between two equivalent ideas:

> Elizabeth was lively and talkative, *whereas her sister was quiet and
> reserved*.

213

The following are special constructions for expressing the meaning of 'even though':

Much as I would like to help, I have other work I must do. ('Even
   though I would like to help very much . . .')
Strange as it may seem, nobody was injured in the fire. ('Even though
   it may seem strange . . .')

In sentences like these, the conjunction *as* occurs in the middle of the subclause,
after a subject complement (*strange*) or an adverbial (*much*). Sometimes *though* is
used instead of *as*: *Strange though it may seem . . .*. These constructions can
sound rather ⟨elevated⟩ and ⟨rhetorical⟩:

Unarmed as/though he was, he bravely went forward to meet his
   enemies.

Phrases and adverbs of contrast: *in spite of, etc*
214

In spite of, despite ⟨formal⟩, *notwithstanding* ⟨very formal⟩, *for* (*all*) are prepositions of contrast:

We are enjoying ourselves *in spite of the weather*.
Despite a shortage of steel, industrial output has increased by five per
   cent. ⟨formal⟩
Notwithstanding the rise in prices, luxury goods are still much in
   demand. ⟨formal⟩
For all his skill, he has accomplished very little. (= 'Despite his great
   skill . . .')

There are also a number of sentence adverbials (*see* 479) expressing the meaning
'in spite of this/that': *yet, however, nevertheless* ⟨formal⟩, *all the same* ⟨informal⟩,
still, even so:

The weather was absolutely dreadful; *however*, the children enjoyed
   themselves.

Yet can be used in the main clause to reinforce the contrast made by the subclause:
Although he hadn't eaten for days, *yet* he looked strong and healthy.

The adverb *even* is used to imply a contrast with what we might usually expect:
My father won't give me the money—he won't *even* lend it to me.

The contrast here is with the usual expectation that fathers are willing to lend
money to their children.

Condition + contrast
215

The ideas of condition (*if*) and implied contrast (*even*) are combined in the conjunction *even if*:

I always enjoy sailing, *even if the weather is rough*. ('You wouldn't
   expect me to enjoy sailing in rough weather, but I do.')

The meaning of *even if* is sometimes conveyed by *if . . .* (*at least*):
If he's poor, at least he's honest.

The same contrastive meaning is expressed in hypothetical conditions by both
even if and *even though* ⟨more formal⟩:

He wouldn't give me the money, *even if I begged him for it*.

Alternative conditions: *whether . . . or, whatever, etc*

216

Condition is combined with the meaning of *either . . . or* in the parallel conjunctions *whether . . . or*, which specify two contrasting conditions:

> *Whether we beat them or they beat us*, the match will be enjoyable
> ('If we beat them, or even if they beat us . . .').
>
> You'll have to pay, *whether you like it or not* ('. . . if you like it, or
> even if you do not').

The meaning of 'contrary to expectation' is also present here, as the examples show.

A similar meaning is present in the conjunctions *whatever, whoever, wherever, etc*:

> She looks pretty, *whatever she wears*.   [3]
>
> *Wherever he goes*, he makes friends.   [4]

The meaning is that the statement in the main clause is true in ANY OF THE CONDITIONS covered by the subclause. Again, contrasting meaning is present, in that [3] implies, for example, 'She looks pretty *even if* she wears ugly clothes.' The same meaning can be expressed by an adverbial clause beginning *no matter wh-*:

> She looks pretty, no matter what she wears.

Two general adverbials with this type of meaning are *anyway* and *in any case* (= 'whatever the circumstances'):

> She looks pretty *anyway*. ⟨informal⟩

Degree

217

We come now to a class of expressions, DEGREE expressions, which usually modify the meaning of a particular word in the clause. Degree is largely expressed by adverbs, which either act (A) as PREMODIFIERS of adjectives, adverbs, *etc* (*see* 480–8), or else act (B) as ADVERBIALS in clause structure.

(A) PREMODIFYING DEGREE ADVERBS (*see* 583)

> *a* *How* hungry are you?   *b* (I'm) *very* hungry.
>
> *a* *How* soon are they leaving?   *b* (They're leaving) *quite* soon.

(B) DEGREE ADVERBS AS ADVERBIALS (*see* 477, 583). Here the degree adverbs usually modify the meaning of the verb:

> *a* *How much* does she love him? *b* (She loves him) *passionately*.

Applied to nouns, degree is expressed by quantifiers (*see* 772–3):

> *a* *How much* of a scholar is he? *b* (He's) *not much* of one. ⟨rather
>   informal⟩

Degree expressions can answer the questions *How?* (for adjectives and adverbs); *How much?* (for verbs); and *How much of?* (for nouns). More ⟨formal⟩ questions of degree are *To what degree?* and *To what extent?* Applied to verbs, degree adverbials sometimes answer the question *How far?* rather than *How much?*

> *a* *How far* do you agree with me? *b* (I agree with you) *absolutely*.

Gradable words and degree
218
Not all verbs, adjectives, *etc* can be modified by a degree adverbial. Degree can only apply to GRADABLE WORDS, *ie* words whose meaning can be thought of in terms of a SCALE. Most pairs of words of opposite meaning, like *old* and *young*, are gradable:

(A)   *How old* is that dog?   (B)   It's *very old* / *quite young*.

If you want to make the degree more exact, you can use a measure phrase (*five years*, *six foot*, *etc*) as a degree adverbial: *He's five years old. He's six foot tall.*

There are two main kinds of gradable words: SCALE words indicate a relative position on a scale (*eg large*, *small*) and LIMIT words indicate the end-point of a scale (*eg black*, *white*):

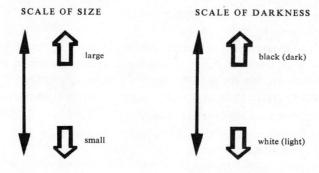

(For the idea of darkness, we also have the scale words *dark* and *light*.)

219
Degree adverbs and degree phrases can sometimes act either as premodifiers or as adverbials:

The performance of Hamlet was
absolutely magnificent.   (PREMODIFIER)
I agree with you *absolutely*.   (ADVERBIAL)

In other cases a different adverb has to be used in the different functions: for example, *very* and *too* are limited to the modifying function. The most important differences concern scale words and are given in this table, which also shows the differences between types of adverbs modifying scale words:

Degree with scale words

WITH ADJECTIVE SCALE WORDS	WITH VERB SCALE WORDS
(A) Indicating extreme position on the scale	
very (see 222): He's very friendly.	(*very*) *much* (see 222) *a lot* ⟨informal⟩, *a great deal*: I like him very much.

(B)   Intensifying the meaning slightly

quite, rather, fairly; pretty ⟨informal⟩:	*considerably, rather; quite a lot* ⟨informal⟩:
It's quite expensive.	Prices have increased considerably.
He was rather annoyed.	I rather like him.

(C)   Toning down or decreasing the effect of the scale word

a bit ⟨informal⟩, *a little, slightly:*	*a bit* ⟨informal⟩, *a little, slightly:*
It's slightly uncomfortable.	Prices have fallen slightly.
	I know him a little.

Degree with limit words.
220

With limit words (*see* 218) the same adverbs can function as modifiers and as adverbials. The two main classes of such adverbs are:

(A)   Those indicating that the limit word's meaning is used to its fullest extent: *absolutely, altogether, completely, entirely, quite, totally, utterly:*

> The story is *totally* false.
>
> I *completely* disagree with you.

(B)   Those indicating a position near the limit of the scale: *almost, nearly, practically* ⟨informal⟩, *virtually:*

> The bottle is *almost* empty.
>
> I've *nearly* finished my work.

Note

Notice that *quite* has two uses: *quite* (= 'considerably') goes with scale words, and *quite* (= 'absolutely') goes with limit words.

221

The same degree words which modify adjectives can also modify adverbs. But comparative adjectives and adverbs are modified by the degree words which function elsewhere as adverbials:

$$I \ am \ feeling \begin{cases} much \\ a \ great \ deal \\ a \ lot \ \langle informal \rangle \end{cases} more \ healthy \ than \ I \ was.$$

(*not* *I am feeling *very* more healthy . . .)

Superlatives can be intensified by degree adverbs which apply to limit words:

> It is *quite*⟨esp BrE⟩/*altogether*/*absolutely* the best show in town.

But *very* can also have an intensifying effect if placed directly before the superlative word (but not before *most*):

> This is my *very* best suit.

Very and *much*
222

We have noted (*see* 219) that *very* acts as a premodifier, whereas *much* acts as an adverbial. However, *much* on its own is limited to mid-position in the clause (*see* 477). In end-position, it has to be preceded by *very*:

> The party was *very* enjoyable.   (PREMODIFIER)
> I (*very*) *much* enjoyed the party.   (MID-POSITION ADVERBIAL)
> I enjoyed the party *very much*.   (END-POSITION ADVERBIAL)

Some verbs cannot go with *much* alone: we can say (for example) *I much prefer . . .*, but *not *I much like . . .*; *I very much like . . .*, however, is acceptable.

Positive and negative attitude
223

Some degree adverbs, although they have the same meaning with respect to 'scale' and 'limit', tend to be distinguished in terms of positive and negative ATTITUDE:

POSITIVE ATTITUDE	NEGATIVE ATTITUDE
It's *quite* warm today.	It's *rather* cold today.
She's *entirely* satisfied.	She's *completely/utterly* dissatisfied.

Fairly (= 'considerably') and *entirely* sometimes suggest a positive or 'good' meaning, whereas *rather*, *completely*, and *utterly* sometimes suggest a negative or 'bad' meaning. Thus *fairly warm* implies that warmth is a good thing; if someone said *It's rather warm today*, on the other hand, he would probably be thinking that the weather was a little TOO warm. The expressions *a bit* and *a little* also tend to go with negative meanings:

> These boxes are *a bit/little* heavy.

Other aspects of degree adverbs
224

Some words, like the adjectives *new*, *full*, and *empty*, can be used both as scale words and as limit words:

> The furniture is { *very* new. / *absolutely* new. }
> The glass is { *very* full. / *absolutely* full. }

In other cases, we can have a scale word and a different limit word dealing with the same area of meaning:

	SCALE			LIMIT
very / *somewhat*	(1) tired / (2) rare / (3) unlikely		*absolutely* / *nearly*	(1) exhausted / (2) unique / (3) impossible

A scale word *very* often corresponds to one or more limit words, which intensify its meaning, and add emotive emphasis; for example, *terrible* intensifies the meaning of *bad*:

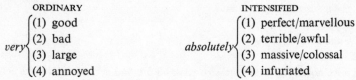

	ORDINARY			INTENSIFIED
very	(1) good / (2) bad / (3) large / (4) annoyed		*absolutely*	(1) perfect/marvellous / (2) terrible/awful / (3) massive/colossal / (4) infuriated

Note

[a] You can also intensify meaning by repeating the word *very*, or by adding *very . . . indeed*: *very very large*; *very quickly indeed*.

[b] Scale words and limit words are sometimes difficult to separate because there is a tendency to 'convert' limit words to scale words in everyday language. Hence combinations like *too perfect* and *rather unique* are sometimes heard. Some speakers regard such expressions as slovenly and 'bad English'.

225

In addition there are negative degree adverbs (*barely*, *hardly*, and *scarcely*), and the *any*-type (*see* 806) degree adverbial *at all*:

I *scarcely* noticed him (= 'I almost didn't notice him').

I didn't notice him *at all* (= 'I totally failed to notice him').

Was it *at all* enjoyable?

226

Apart from the degree adverbs listed so far, there are many degree adverbs which are more restricted in their use, and tend to go with a particular set of gradable words, *eg badly* goes with the verbs *need*, *want*; *thoroughly* goes with the verbs *enjoy*, *disapprove*, *dislike*, *etc*; *hard* goes with the verbs *work*, *try*, *etc*:

We *thoroughly* enjoyed the show (= 'very much enjoyed').

He *badly* needs a haircut (= 'needs . . . very much').

Such adverbs usually intensify the meaning of the gradable word.

Role, standard and viewpoint

227

Degree is not the only type of meaning which specifies more exactly the scope of a gradable word. By *at* or *as* you can also specify the ROLE which the gradable word implies; by *for* you can specify the STANDARD by which the speaker is judging its use:

John is CLEVER.	
John is *very* CLEVER.	(DEGREE)
John is CLEVER *at swimming*.	(ROLE)
As a swimmer, he's OUTSTANDING.	(ROLE)
John is a GOOD swimmer *for a youngster*.	(STANDARD)
For a learner, he swims WELL.	

(Here the gradable words are in SPACED CAPITALS.)

228

Further, you can specify the VIEWPOINT or RESPECT in terms of which a word or phrase is used:

Morally, it was not an easy problem (*ie* 'From a moral point of view . . .').

In a way, I was surprised at his behaviour (*ie* 'In one respect/from one point of view . . .').

He is a good swimmer *in a technical sense* (*ie* 'from a technical point of view').

He is a good writer *in that he has an elegant style*.

You can also name the person(s) whose point of view is in question:

To his parents, his behaviour was astonishing.

Comparison

229

If you want to compare two things with respect to their position on a scale of degree or amount, use comparative words *taller, happier, etc* or comparative phrases *more careful, less careful, etc* (*see* 523–4). A postmodifying phrase or clause introduced by *than* can indicate the 'standard' against which the comparison is made.

To describe the picture, you may say:

Jack is *taller than* Jill (is).	[1]
Jill is *shorter than* Jack (is).	[2]
Jill is *less tall than* Jack (is).	[3]
Jack is *less short than* Jill (is).	[4]

Sentences [1]–[4] have the same meaning, but are listed in order of their commonness. A sentence like [4] is very unusual, and would only be said if both Jack and Jill were short.

Equal comparisons
230

For an equal comparison, *eg* when Jack and Jill are the same height, we use *as . . . as* instead of *more . . . than*:

Jack is *as* tall *as* Jill (is).

Jill is *as* tall *as* Jack (is).

To negate equal comparison, we say *not as . . . as*, or *not so . . . as*:

Jill is *not as* tall *as* Jack (is).	[5]
Jack is *not so* short *as* Jill (is).	[6]

Sentences [5] and [6] have the same meaning as [1]–[4].

Comparative and superlative
231

When comparing only two things, we use the comparative forms:

Jill is *the shorter* of the two children.

Jack is *the taller* of the two children.

When comparing more than two objects we use superlative forms *tallest, most useful, least tall, etc*:

Susan is *the tallest* of the three.

Jill is *the shortest* of the three.

To name the objects, you use *of*, as above, followed by a plural noun phrase:

Luxembourg is the *smallest of the Common Market countries*.

The *of*-phrase is sometimes placed for emphasis at the beginning of the clause:

Of the (*two*) *boys*, John behaves the *more* politely.

Of all the capital cities in the world, Bangkok is the one I would *most* like to visit.

To name the group or sphere within which the comparison is made, use *in* with a singular noun phrase:

Susan is the oldest girl *in the class*.

It was the worst moment *in/of my life*.

Other constructions which can specify the range of comparison with superlatives are possessive pronouns, genitives, adjectives and relative clauses:

my best friend

the world's highest mountain

the greatest *living* composer

the most enjoyable book *I have ever read*

Comparison with a definite norm
232

Sometimes a comparison is made between an object and a definite standard or 'norm' understood in context (often through back-pointing). In such cases, use *than that* or *as that*, or simply omit the comparative phrase or clause altogether:

(A)   Jack must be six foot tall.   (B) $\begin{cases} \text{No, he's taller } (than\ that). & [7] \\ \text{Is he as tall } as\ that? & [8] \end{cases}$

For [8], you can also say: *Is he* THAT *tall?* ⟨informal⟩.

The *than*-phrase is usually omitted when we are comparing not two different things, but the same thing at an earlier and at a later time:

Nowadays food is *more expensive* (*ie* 'more expensive than it was').

Foreign cars are becoming *more popular* (than they were).

233

To indicate continuing change, repeat the comparative word with *and*:

Jill is getting *taller and taller*.

The world is changing *more and more quickly*.

Fewer and fewer people are attending church these days.

In these sentences, we cannot use a *than*-construction.

Enough and *too*
234

Enough and *too* are words indicating 'sufficiency' and 'excess'. The norm to which these words refer can be indicated by a *to*-infinitive clause (*see* 515):

He's rich enough *to own a car*.   [9]

The grass is too long *for me to cut*.   [10]

Notice that [9] and [10] mean the same as:

He's not too poor to own a car.   [9a]

The grass isn't short enough for me to cut.   [10a]

The viewpoint or standard from which the sufficiency or excess is judged may be expressed by a *for*-phrase:

> The room is too noisy *for us*.
>
> It's too cold *for tennis* today.

Often, where the meaning is obvious, reference to norm and viewpoint is omitted:

> Is the coffee *sweet enough*? (*ie* 'sweet enough for you to drink'?)
>
> The butter is *too expensive* (*ie* 'too expensive for me to buy').

So . . . (*that*) and *such* . . . (*that*)
235

Degree or amount constructions with *so* . . . (*that*) and *such* . . . (*that*) (*see* 831) express a meaning similar to *enough* and *too*:

> Donkey Queen is *so* fit *that she may well win the race*. (meaning roughly 'She is fit enough to win the race')
>
> It's *such* a good chance (*that*) *we mustn't miss it*. (meaning roughly 'It's too good a chance to miss')

But the *so* . . . (*that*)/*such* . . . (*that*) construction also adds a meaning of result (*see* 202), expressed by a *that*-clause:

> She polished the floor *so* hard *that* you could see your face in it.
>
> The animal was *such* a nuisance *that* we let it escape.
>
> He earns *so* much money *that* he doesn't know what to do with it.

So and *such* in these sentences add emotive emphasis, and this emphasis can also be expressed without the *that*-clause:

> The animal was 'such a nuisance!
>
> I'm 'so hungry! (*see* 311)

Comparison with nouns: *more of a, etc*
236

The various constructions just illustrated can be applied to gradable nouns (like *success, fool, coward*) by the use of *more of a, as much of a, less of a, etc*:

> He's *more of a* sportsman than his brother.
>
> It was *as much of a* success as I expected (it would be).
>
> You're *less of a* fool than I thought (you were).
>
> He's *enough of a* man to tell the truth.
>
> He's *too much of a* coward to tell the truth.

Proportion
237

To compare circumstances in terms of equivalent tendencies, you can use a clause of PROPORTION introduced by *as*:

> *As time went on*, things got worse and worse.

There is a more ⟨formal⟩ construction in which *so* is added to the main clause:

> *As* you go farther north, *so* the winters become longer and more severe.

Yet another construction expressing proportion consists of two clauses beginning with *the* + a comparative word:

The farther north you go, *the* more severe the winters are.

The more you argue with him, *the* less notice he takes.

Notice that *the* here is a conjunction, and not the definite article. This construction involves placing the comparative element of the clause first, and so often requires a change from normal word order:

He takes less notice *but* . . . the less notice he takes.

The subject and verb of the second clause, or of both clauses, may be omitted if their meaning is obvious:

The more tickets you can sell, the better. (*ie* '. . . the better it will be')

The more the merrier. (proverb)

We'll have to begin our journey early tomorrow; in fact, the earlier,
the better.

Addition, exception and restriction

Addition
238

To express ADDITION we can use the prepositions *in addition to*, *as well as*, and *besides*:

They stole three valuable paintings, *in addition to* the money.   [1]

As well as ⎱ eating a seven-course meal, they drank three
Besides ⎰ bottles of wine.   [2]

In a coordinate construction, the idea of addition can be simply conveyed by *and*, or (with more emphasis) by *not only* . . . *but* (*also*) (*see* 547). Thus [1] is equivalent to:

The money (was stolen) and three valuable paintings were
stolen.   [1a]

Not only the money, but (also) three valuable paintings were
stolen.   [1b]

The adverbials *also*, *too* ⟨informal⟩, *as well* ⟨informal⟩, and *in addition* ⟨rather formal⟩ have the meaning 'in addition to that' (where *that* points back to something mentioned earlier):

They ate a seven-course meal; they *also* drank three bottles of wine.

(*ie* 'in addition to eating a seven-course meal')

. . . They drank three bottles of wine, *too*/*as well*.

. . . *In addition*, they drank three bottles of wine.

The preferred positions of these adverbials are different: *also* prefers mid-position (*see* 470), *too* and *as well* end-position, and *in addition* front-position (but *see* 242).
239

So (when placed first in the sentence and followed by inversion of subject and operator) combines the meaning of *also* or *too* with the function of a substitute form (*see* 433):

John plays tennis, and *so* does his sister (= 'and his sister does, too').

While *so*, *too*, *etc* have a positive meaning, *neither* and *nor* have the corresponding negative meaning. For negative clauses, there is also the corresponding *any*-word (*see* 803) and the adverb *either* ⟨informal⟩, which occurs at the end of a clause. Note that *so*, *neither*, and *nor* cause inversion (*see* 432–3):

(A)   I'm hungry.
$\begin{cases} \text{(B)} & \text{I am, } too. \\ \text{(B)} & So \text{ am I.} \end{cases}$ POSITIVE

(A)   I'm not hungry.
$\begin{cases} \text{(B)} & Neither \text{ am I.} \\ \text{(B)} & Nor \text{ am I.} \\ \text{(B)} & \text{I'm not, } either. \end{cases}$ NEGATIVE

Exception
240

EXCEPTION is the opposite of addition, in that it indicates 'subtraction' from a total. This meaning may be expressed by a number of prepositions: *except*, *except for*, *apart from*, *bar*, *but* (*but* occurs only in postmodification):

> None of us had any money *except* (*for*) *James*.
> We had a pleasant time, *apart from the weather*.
> They stole everything $\begin{cases} but \text{ the typewriter.} \\ bar \text{ the typewriter. (less common)} \end{cases}$

An adverbial clause beginning with the conjunction *except that* can also be used:

> We had a pleasant time, *except that the weather was cold*.

Otherwise and *else* are adverbs of exception:

> The weather was appalling, but *otherwise* (= 'apart from that') we
>   had a pleasant time.
> The typewriter was too large, but we carried everything *else* (= 'apart
>   from that').

In this sense, *otherwise* occurs only as a sentence adverb, and *else* only as a postmodifier.

The adverb *even* expresses the negation of exception, normally with an effect of surprise and emphasis (*see* 214):

> They stole everything—*even* the clothes in the cupboard ('not ex-
>   cepting the clothes in the cupboard').

Even is also closely related to the notion of addition:

> He knows several languages; he even claims to speak Chinese ('that
>   as well as all the others').

Restriction: *only, etc*
241

The word *only* is RESTRICTIVE, in that it combines negative meaning with the idea of exception:

> He was wearing *only* his pyjamas (= 'he was wearing *nothing but* his
>   pyjamas').
> *Only James* had any money (= 'no one except James . . .').

With expressions of amount (*see* 57–68) and degree *etc*, *only* means 'no more than . . .':

> *Only a few people* attended the meeting (= 'no more than a few . . .').

I didn't give him the book; I *only lent* it to him. (= '. . . I did no more
  than lend it to him')

I know her *only slightly* (= '. . . no more than slightly').

Other words with a meaning similar to *only* are *just, merely, simply*. The restrictive meaning of *only* can be applied, in a slightly different way, to time:

I saw him *only last week* (= 'no earlier than', 'as late as').

Notice the contrast between *only* and *even*:

Only my coat was wet ('that and nothing else').

Even my underclothes were soaked ('that as well as everything else').

Ambiguity with *also, only, etc*

242

Adverbs of addition, exception and restriction (like *also, even, only*) often 'focus'
their meaning on a particular part of the sentence, such as a noun phrase or a
verb or the whole of the sentence following the subject. A sentence can be ambiguous, depending on the element that is 'focused': *I only lent him the books*.
But contrastive intonation (*see* 415) can help to clarify the meaning:

(I didn't g̀ive him ány̆thing—) I only *l̲e̲n̲t̲* him the books.   [3]

(I didn't lend him the typ̆ewriter—) I only lent him the *b̀o̲o̲k̲s̲*.   [4]

An example with *also* is:

(He's not only a g̀o̲o̲d̲ áctor—) He's also a *s̀uccessful* actor.

(He's not only a successful b̆u̲s̲i̲n̲e̲s̲s̲m̲a̲n̲—) He's also a successful

  àctor.

(He's not only a w̆r̲i̲t̲e̲r̲—) He's also *a successful àctor*.

(The parts in *italics* are those which are 'focused'.) In writing, it is best to put the
focusing adverb as near to the focused element as possible, *only* and *even* before it,
and *also* and *too* after it. Thus you could pick out the meaning of [4] by writing
I lent him only the books, instead of *I only lent him the books*.

Only and *even* in front-position focus on the next element of the sentence—
usually the subject:

Only *one of us* had a sleeping bag.

Even *the BB̀C̲* makes mistakes sómetimes.

Compare:

His wife àl̲so̲ has a degree.

I t̀o̲o̲ thought he looked ill.

Subject matter: *about* and *on*

243

About and *on* can both indicate the subject of a communication or discussion:

He *told* me *about* his adventures.

She gave *a lecture on* European history.

Have you any *books on/about* stamp-collecting?

Some verbs and nouns go with *about* or *on*, others go with *about* only:

speak about/on	teach (someone) about
lecture about/on	learn about
argue about/on	read about
write about/on	quarrel about
a book about/on	a story about
a discussion about/on	ignorance about

On, unlike *about*, tends to be limited to deliberate, formal acts of ⟨speaking⟩ and ⟨writing⟩, and also suggests a more definite focusing on the subject. *About* can also be used of mental states: *think about, know about, etc.*

Note

Of is sometimes used instead of *about*: *I wouldn't dream of asking him*; *All you think of is money.* But notice the difference between *He thought about the problem* (= 'He considered the problem') and *He thought of the problem* (= 'He brought the problem to his mind').

Section B: Information, reality and belief

Statements, questions and responses

244

Why do we need to use language? Probably the most important reason (but not the only one) is that we wish to give someone some piece of information which we think he doesn't know about. STATEMENTS (*see* 799) are typically sentences which give information. QUESTIONS (*see* 777-81, 800) are typically sentences by which someone asks his hearer to give information. In this section, we shall discuss the ways in which information is given and received and we shall also consider people's attitudes to information, and the reality it deals with. This means considering such notions as truth, hypothesis, belief, probability, *etc.*

Questions and answers
245

In conversation, both statements and questions often provoke a RESPONSE. For questions, the most natural response is an answer to the question, giving the speaker the information he needs:

Yes-No QUESTION (*see* 778)

(A)   Is the dinner nearly réady?

    (B)   Yes, it's already cȯoked.
            (POSITIVE ANSWER)   [1]

    (B)   No, it's not cȯoked yét.
            (NEGATIVE ANSWER)   [2]

You can generally shorten the answer by omitting some or all of the informa-

tion already contained in the statement. Thus a shorter version of [1] is: *Yes, it is*
or simply *Yes*. Shorter versions of [2] are:

No, it isn't.
No, not yet.
Not yet.
No.

Wh-QUESTION (*see* 779-80)

(A)   Where are you going?   (B)   (I'm going) to the office.

Here again, part of the answer (the part in brackets) can be omitted.

Questions about alternatives
246

Yes-no questions are LIMITED: only one of two answers (positive or negative) is
possible. *Wh*-questions are UNLIMITED, because any number of answers can be
given, so long as they give information required by the *wh*-word (*who, what,
when, where, how, etc: see* 578-83).

Another type of limited question is one which expects as an answer one of two
or more alternatives mentioned in the question:

(A)   Shall we go by train or by   (B)   By bus.
        bus?

(A)   Would you like coffee, tea,   (B)   Coffee, please.
        or cocoa?

Notice that the intonation rises on each alternative except the last, on which it
falls.

There is a type of alternative question which is like a *yes-no* question in expecting a positive or negative answer:

yes-no   Are you coming?

ALTERNATIVE   { Are you coming or not?
                        { Are you coming or aren't you (coming)?

Such alternative questions have a rather impatient tone.

247

Another type of alternative question is more like a *wh*-question in form:

How shall we go? By bus or by train?

What would you like to drink? Coffee, tea, or cocoa?

Questions with positive or negative bias
QUESTIONS WITH *some, always, already, etc*
248

Most *yes-no* questions are neutral as between positive and negative replies, and
have *any*-words like *any, ever, yet, etc* (*see* 803-7). You can, however, use forms

like *some*, *always*, *already*, *etc*, and this indicates that you expect a positive answer to your question:

> Did *someone* cáll last night? ('Is it true that someone called last night?')
>
> (*Compare:* Did *anyone* call last night? (neutral))
>
> Has she gone to bed *alréady*? ('Am I right in thinking that she's gone to bed already?')
>
> (*Compare:* Has she gone to bed *yet*? (neutral))

For ⟨politeness⟩, it is customary to use *some*-forms in making an offer:

> Would you like *something* to éat? ('I expect you would!')
>
> Do you need *some* money for the phóne?

Questions in statement form
249

You can strengthen the positive bias of a question by putting it in the form of a statement (using, however, the rising tone of a question):

> You got home sáfely then?
>
> The guests have had something to éat?

These questions are rather casual in tone. It is as if you are assuming in advance that the answer is 'Yes'. With a negative, such questions assume the answer 'No':
The shops weren't ópen? (You might say this on seeing someone come home with an empty shopping basket.)

Tag questions: requests for confirmation
250

Tag questions (*see* 781) added to the end of a statement ask for confirmation of the truth of the statement. The answer expected is 'Yes' if the statement is positive, and 'No' if the statement is negative. (If the statement is positive, the tag-question is negative, and vice versa.)

> He likes his jób, dóesn't he? ('I assume he likes his job. Am I right?')
>
> Nobody was wàtching me, wére they? ('I assume nobody was watching me. Am I right?')

If the tag question has a falling tone, the positive or negative bias is stronger, and the tag question merely asks for routine confirmation of what the speaker already believes. The sentence is more like a statement than a question.

> It's beautiful wèather, ìsn't it?
>
> You have mèt my wífe, hàven't you?
>
> (said by a man introducing his wife to an acquaintance)

(*See* 251 on how negative questions are answered in English.)

Note

There is a less common type of tag question for which both statement and question are positive: *You've had an àccident, háve you?* Here the statement expresses a conclusion which the speaker has arrived at from the situation. The tone is sometimes sarcastic:

So you call that hard w\`ork, d/o you?

Negative questions
251

One might expect *yes-no* questions which contain a negative form to assume a negative answer. In fact, such questions have a mixture of positive and negative bias:

Have*n't* you had br/eakfast yet, Mary? ('Is it really true that
you haven't had breakfast? You ought to have had it by
now!')   [3]

Ca*n't* you dr/ive straight? ('I thought you could, but
apparently you can't!')   [4]

Will *nobody* help us to clear /up?   [5]

As the examples suggest, this construction usually expresses some degree of surprise (or even disappointment or annoyance). The speaker would normally assume the positive meaning, but now expects the negative. Thus a situation in which you would say [3] might be: you visit Mary at 10.30 a.m. and find that she is still cooking bacon and eggs. Your earlier (and normal) assumption is that she has had breakfast; your later assumption (when you see her cooking) is that she hasn't.

Note

Some languages answer negative questions in a different way to English. To the question *Isn't he here yet?*, the English answer *No* means 'He is *not* here', while *Yes* means 'He *is* here': the answer is given to the underlying meaning rather than to the grammatical form of the question.

Questions with more than one *wh*-word
252

It is possible (though unusual) to have more than one *wh*-word in the same *wh*-question. In this case, only one of the *wh*-elements is moved to the front of the sentence (unless the two *wh*-elements are coordinated):

(A)   *Who's* bringing *wh\`at?*
(B)   I'm bringing the drinks, and John's bringing the sandwiches.
(A)   *How* and *when* did you arr\`ive?
(B)   I arrived by train, on Friday.
(A)   *Who* did you send those b\`ooks to, and *wh\`y?* ⟨informal⟩
(B)   I sent them to Frank, because he asked me for them.

Polite questions
253

You can make a question more ⟨polite⟩ (*eg* when addressing a stranger) by adding *please*, or by using an introductory formula like *Could you tell me:*

What's your n\`ame, pl/ease?

Would you mind telling me your na´me?

Please could I have your address and te´lephone number?

May/could I ask you if you are driving to the sta´tion?

(On *can*, *may*, and *could* here, *see* 340.)

Responses to statements
254

Unlike a question, a statement does not demand a response. But in conversation, we often make a response to a statement in order to express interest, surprise, pleasure, regret, *etc*, or simply to show the speaker that we are still attending:

(A) I've just had a phone call from the travel agent ... (B) Ye´s?

(A) ... you know those plane tickets to Sydney that you ordered for next Tuesday ... (B) Mm´? (A) well, he says they are now ready to be collected ... (B) Go˅od. (A) ... but unfortunately, he says there's been a mistake ... (B) Oh de˅ar. (A) Yes, apparently the plane doesn't arrive in Australia until 9.00 a.m. on Wednesday. (B) I se˅e.

(*Mm* /m/, *Mhm* /mhm/, *Uh-huh* /əhə/ and *Yeah* /jeə/ are casual alternatives to *Yes*.) These 'attention signals' are particularly important in telephone conversations. Other signals of this kind are *Oh?* and *Really?*, to express surprise and interest:

(A)   I hear Paula's getting married.   (B)   Re´ally?

Other attention signals of more limited use are: *Well! Fancy that! etc*.

Short questions
255

Questions can be used as responses to statements, when the hearer wants more information than has been given. Like other responses, these questions are often shortened by omitting repeated matter. They can often be shortened to the question word alone:

(A)   The old lady's buying a house.

(B)   Whe˅n? / Whe˅re? / Why˅? / Whi˅ch house? / Wha˅t old lady?

There are also two-word questions with an end-placed preposition:

(A)   I'm going to write an adventure story.

(B)   What fo˅r? / Who fo˅r? / What abo˅ut?

Likewise *Who wi˅th?*, *Where to˅?*, *etc*. (These questions with end-placed prepositions are 〈informal〉 in style: in 〈formal〉 English we would say *With who˅m? etc*, *see* 579.)

All these shortened questions are rather 〈familiar〉 and abrupt. For greater 〈politeness〉, use a fuller question: *When is she going to buy it? etc*.

Such questions can also be used when what the speaker says isn't clear in some respect, *eg* where the meaning of definite words like *this* is not specified:

(A)   Take a look at thi˅s.   (B)   (Take a look at) wha˅t?

Note

For a negative statement, use *Why not?* rather than *Why?*:

(A)   Joan is very upsèt.   (B)   Whỳ?

(A)   She hasn't been invìted.   (B)   Why nòt?

Echo questions: requests for repetition
256

Another type of response question is an ECHO QUESTION, in which we ask the speaker to repeat some information (usually because we failed to hear it, but sometimes also because we can't believe our ears):

(A)   I didn't enjoy that meal.   (B)   Did you say you didn't enjóy it?

Here the request is explicit, but you may leave out *Did you say*, and simply 'echo' part or all of what has been said, using a (sharply rising) question intonation:
You didn't enjóy it? In these examples, brackets show how some repeated elements may be omitted:

(A)   The Browns are emigrating. (B)   (They're) émigrating?

(A)   Switch the light off, please. (B)   (Switch) the líght (off)?

You can also use a *wh*-echo question, indicating by the *wh*-word the part of the sentence that you didn't hear:

(A)   It cost five dollars.   (B)   Hów much did (you say) it
                                          cost?   [6]

(A)   He's a dermatologist.   (B)   Whát is he?   [7]

Note that the nucleus occurs on the *wh*-word in these questions.

257

The *wh*-word can also be placed later in the sentence, in its statement position. Thus instead of [6] and [7], you could say: *It cost hów much? He's (a) whát?*

But such questions, again, are ⟨familiar⟩ and often ⟨impolite⟩, unless preceded by an apology or mark of politeness:

Sorry, whát was his job?

I'm sorry, I didn't quite hear: whát does he do?

Note

Echo questions sometimes refer back to other questions:

(A)   Have you ever been to Valladolid?   (B)   (Sorry), have I ever been whére?

258

General requests for repetition are very commonly used:

(A)   I'll make some coffee.
- (B)   ((I) beg your) párdon?
- (B)   Excúse me? ⟨AmE⟩
- (B)   Sórry? ⟨BrE⟩
- (B)   Whát? ⟨familiar, often impolite⟩

(A) (I said) I'll make some   (B) Oh, $\begin{cases} \text{thanks.} \\ \text{thank you.} \\ \text{thank you very much.} \end{cases}$
coffee.

A more explicit general request for repetition (*eg* where you have heard most, but not all, of what was said) can take one of the following forms:

I'm sorry, I didn't quite hear/follow what you said.

Sorry, I didn't quite get that. ⟨informal⟩

I'm very sorry, would you mind $\begin{cases} \text{repeating that?} \\ \text{saying that again?} \end{cases}$

Omission of information

259

The last section has already amply illustrated the general rule that we omit information which is already obvious from the preceding context. The rule is further illustrated by the following statement and six possible replies:

(A) This country must economise if it's going to increase its prosperity.

(B) I agree.

(B) Absolutely.

(B) Certainly not.

(B) Nonsense!

(B) True enough, but the problem is how to economise.

(B) And the only way to do it is by greater taxation.

All these responses in some way lack the structure of a 'complete sentence' (*see* 797), but are acceptable in communication, because the structure omitted contains information already understood.

260

In other circumstances, it is the situation outside language which makes certain information (and therefore certain linguistic elements) unnecessary. Examples are the brief 'incomplete' or formulaic utterances you may hear in various situations:

COMMANDS	Off with the lid! Out with it! Faster! Not so fast!
QUESTIONS	More coffee? How about joining us?
SLOGANS	Republicans out; Republicans for ever.
EXCLAMATIONS	Goal! Good! Excellent! You lucky boy; (What a) pity! Shame! Poor John; Silly boy! Oh for a drink! Now for some fun! You and your jokes!
ALARM CALLS	Help! Fire!

261

Sometimes, in casual ⟨familiar⟩ speech, you will notice that words are omitted from the beginning of a sentence. These are usually words which carry little information, such as a pronoun subject and/or an auxiliary verb. They are bracketed in the following examples:

'Beg your párdon. (I . . .)   Want a drínk? (Do you . . .)

Serves you rìght. (It . . .)   Sorry I mìssed you. (I am . . .)

No wònder he's late. (It is . . .)   See you làter. (I will . . .)

262

In public notices, headings *etc*, a noun phrase, nominal clause, or adjective phrase often stands on its own:

EXIT	WHERE TO EAT IN LONDON
ENGLISH DEPARTMENT	FRESH TODAY

Prohibition notices are often put in the form of a noun phrase: NO SMOKING, NO ENTRY, NO PARKING, *etc*.

263

Also in some broadcasting situations, such as sports commentaries, a great deal of grammatical structure is omitted. This extract could be from a television football commentary:

Cruyff to Neeslens; a brilliant pass, that. And the score still: Holland 1, West Germany 0. The ball in-field to – oh, but beautifully cut off, and . . .

Reported statements and questions

Reported statements
264

To report what somebody has stated, you can either use quotation marks (DIRECT SPEECH) or a *that*-clause (*see* 638–40) (INDIRECT SPEECH):

He said: 'I need more money'.   (DIRECT SPEECH)

He said that he needed more money.   (INDIRECT SPEECH)

He said (in this example) can be called the REPORTING CLAUSE, and the rest of the sentence can be called the REPORTED CLAUSE. In direct speech, the reporting clause can also be placed after (or in the middle of) the reported clause, and the subject (if it is not a pronoun) can be placed after the verb of saying:

'I need more mòney,' {
John exclaimed.
exclaimed John.
he exclaimed.
but not *exclaimed he.

Indirect speech
265

In narrative, the reporting verb is usually in the past tense. In this case, certain changes are normally made in converting from direct speech to indirect speech:

a Change present tense verbs into the past tense (to match the reporting verb).

b Change 1st and 2nd person pronouns into the 3rd person.

c (Sometimes) change pointer words (*see* 87–90) like *this, now, here,
   tomorrow* into *that, then, there, the next day,* etc.

Examples:

DIRECT SPEECH (*ie* what the speaker actually said)		INDIRECT SPEECH
'I *moved* here two years ago.'	→	He explained that he *had moved* there two years [1] before.
'Our team *has won*.'	→	They claimed that their team *had won*. [2]
'I *will marry* you tomorrow.'	→	She promised that she *would marry* him the next day. [3]
'They *can sleep* in this room.'	→	She suggested that they *could sleep* in that room. [4]

Notice that the change to the past tense applies not only to ordinary present
tense verbs, but to the present perfect (*has won → had won*) (*see* 882), and to
modal auxiliaries (*will → would, can → could,* etc) (*see* 501).

The shifting of a verb to an earlier time reference generally applies also to past
tense verbs, which are shifted to the past perfect (the pluperfect) in indirect
speech. Thus

'I *saw* them yesterday.'	→	He told me that he *had seen* them the day before.

But sometimes the shift does not take place *see* 266(3).

Exceptions

266

There are four exceptions to the shifting of tense in indirect speech.

(1) Past perfect verbs in direct speech are not changed in indirect
    speech:

'I *had left* before they arrived.'	→	He said (that) he *had left* before they (had) arrived.

(2) Modal auxiliaries like *must, ought to,* and *should* do not normally
    change. But *must* can also be reported as *had to:*

'You *must go*.'	→	She said that they $\begin{cases} must\ go. \\ had\ to\ go. \end{cases}$

Should (after *I* or *we*) is changed to *would:*

'I *should* be grateful if . . . '	→	He said he *would* be grateful if . . .

But the *should* of obligation remains unchanged, *eg* You should be
more careful → I told him he should be more careful.

(3) When the idea expressed in the reported statement can also be applied to
    the time of reporting, there is no need to change the tense or other forms:

'The world *is* flat.'   →   Ancient philosophers argued
                                that the world *is/was* flat.

This is because the question of whether the world is flat or round can apply as much to the present time as to the time of the ancients. Similarly, example [1] could be reported: *He said that he moved here two years ago* if the person were reporting this statement near the time and place of the original statement.

(4)   Some verbs of saying used in direct speech narrative cannot be easily used in indirect speech. For example:

'The game is up,' growled Trent.

but hardly:

*Trent growled that the game was up.

These verbs include verbs which emphasise vocal effect (like *cry*, *gasp*, *grunt*, *laugh*, *shout*). Other verbs like *answer*, *declare*, *reply*, *say* can be readily used for both direct and indirect speech, while verbs of assertion like *assert*, *confirm*, *state* occur mainly in indirect speech.

Indirect questions
267

The rules for indirect speech apply to indirect questions as well as to indirect statements. The only difference is that for indirect questions, a *wh*-clause (*see* 641-3) is used instead of a *that*-clause:

DIRECT SPEECH	INDIRECT SPEECH
'*Do* you *live* here?'	→ She asked him if (*or* whether) he *lived there*. [5]
'*Did* our team *win*?'	→ They asked if (*or* whether) their team *had won*. [6]
'Why *won't* you *marry* me?'	→ He asked her why she *wouldn't marry* him. [7]
'Which chair *shall* I *sit* in?'	→ He wondered which chair he *should sit* in. [8]

Indirect *yes-no* questions ([5], [6]) are introduced by *if* or *whether* (*see* 644). Indirect *wh*-questions are introduced by the *wh*-word which begins the question in direct speech.

268

Questions about alternatives (*see* 246-7) behave in the same way. The *yes-no* type of alternative question is generally introduced by *whether* in indirect speech:

'Is it *your* turn or *Susan's*?'   →   She asked him whether it was his
                                           turn or Susan's.

There is also a type of indirect question in which the reported clause is a *to*-infinitive clause beginning with a *wh*-word:

I asked him what to do (= 'I asked him what I ought to do').

He wondered whether to leave (= 'He wondered whether he ought to leave').

(Reported commands: *see* 352.)

Denial and affirmation

Negative sentences
269
When a speaker wishes to deny the truth of something, he uses a NEGATIVE SENTENCE containing one of the negative items *not* (or *n't*), *no*, *nothing*, *nowhere*, *etc* (*see* 632–3). A part of a sentence or clause which follows the negative word is called the SCOPE OF NEGATION, and it is this part of the sentence that is negated. The scope of negation is here signalled by **bold type**:

He definitely has**n't taken the job.** ('It's definite that he hasn't')   [1]

He has**n't definitely taken the job.** ('It's not definite that he has')   [2]

In these examples, the meaning is different because in [1] *definitely* is outside the scope of negation, while in [2] it is within the scope of negation. A final adverbial may or may not be in the scope of negation:

They were**n't at home** | for the whole day. ('For the whole day, they weren't at home'.)

They were**n't at home for the whole day.** ('It's not true that they were at home for the whole day'.)

(On the intonation here, *see* 35–43, 412.) Notice the difference in meaning between the first and second sentence in the following pairs:

Crime necessarily does**n't pay.** (= 'Crime never pays')

Crime does**n't necessarily pay.** (= 'It doesn't always pay')

I really do**n't mind waiting.** (= 'I don't mind at all')

I do**n't really mind waiting.** (= 'I DO mind, but not too much')

270
In the scope of negation, *any*-words like *any*, *yet*, *ever* (*see* 803–7) are used:

I did**n't attend any of the lectures** ('I attended none of the lectures').   [3]

We have**n't had dinner yet.**   [4]

But we can also use *some*-words like *some*, *already*, *sometimes* after the negative word, and these words lie outside the scope of negation. Therefore the meaning of [3] is different from that of [5]:

I did**n't attend** some of the lectures ('There were some lectures that I didn't attend').   [5]

271
Occasionally a negative word applies not to the verb at all, but to a phrase or part of a phrase elsewhere in the sentence:

No food at all is better than unwholesome food (*ie* 'Eating nothing at all is better than eating . . . ').

We *not infrequently* go abroad (*ie* 'We quite often go abroad').

They stayed at a *not very* attractive hotel (*ie* '... at a rather un-attractive hotel').

Affirmation
272
To place emphasis on the positive meaning of a sentence, we put the intonation nucleus on the operator (or first auxiliary in the verb phrase *see* 672–5). This is done especially for contrast, when someone has suggested or assumed the negative:

(A) Why haven't you had a bath?   (B) (But) I have had a bath.

(A) What a pity Mary isn't here!   (B) (But) she is here.

If the response is not a straightforward denial, but contains new information, the new information is stressed by a fall-rise tone (*see* 43):

(A) Surely he can't drive a bus?   (B) No, but he can drive a car.

If there is no other operator, *do* is used as dummy operator (*see* 674–5):

So you did go to the concert this evening. ('I thought you might not')

(A) So you don't enjoy Julie's conversation?   (B) No, but I do think she's a good cook.

Denial
273
To DENY what someone has suggested or supposed, you can again place the nucleus on the operator, but this time on the negative operator (*can't, didn't, etc*):

So you haven't lost your keys. ('I thought you had')

(A) When did he pass his exam?   (B) Well actually he didn't pass it.

When the negative is not contracted, the nucleus falls on *not*:

... he did not pass it.

Short affirmations
274
There is a shortened type of affirmation in which everything is omitted after the operator. This is usual when you are simply affirming a question or statement, and do not need to repeat what has already been said:

(A) This book is interesting.   (B) Yes, it is. (*ie* 'It is interesting')

(A) I assume John will be late.   (B) Yes, he will.

(A) Your mother looks well.   (B) Yes, she does.

(A)   Can you speak German?   (B)   Yes, I c̀an.

(A)   Have I missed the bus?   (B)   Yes, I'm afraid you hàve.

To agree with a negative statement, use a negative operator:

(A)   Your mother doesn't look
        well.   (B)   No, she d̀oesn't.

Short denials
275

Similar shortened statements (in the negative) are used to deny a statement, or to answer a question in the negative:

(A)   You worry too much.   (B)   No, I d́on't.   [6]

(A)   I'll probably fail my dri- (B)   No, you w̌on't.   [7]
        ving test.

(A)   Can you speak German?   (B)   No, I'm afraid I c̀an't.   [8]

Notice that when we deny or contradict a statement, as in [6] and [7], we use a rise or fall-rise tone. More ⟨formal⟩ or emphatic sentences contain operator + *not*.

In these cases the nucleus is on *not: No, he did ǹot.*

To deny a negative statement, use the positive operator with a rising or fall-rise tone:

(A)   I understand most people
        didn't agree with me.   (B)   Yes, they d́id.

(A)   I won't pass the exam.   (B)   I bet you will.

276

A denial can seem blunt and ⟨impolite⟩ unless we tone it down in some way. We can make a denial more ⟨tactful⟩ by only ⟨tentatively⟩ expressing the contrary view:

(A)   He's m̀arried, ìsn't he?

(B)   Actually, I don't think he ̀is.

(B)   ́Is he? I thought he was a b̀achelor.

(B)   Are you śure? I had the impression that he was still s̀ingle.

Denial combined with affirmation
277

The construction *not* (or *n't*) . . . *but* is used to deny one idea and to affirm another, contrasting, idea:

I do*n't* agree with his principles, *but* at least he's sincere.
The land does*n't* belong to me, *but* to the government.

We can also say:

= {The land belongs *not* to me, but to the government.
{The land belongs to the government, *not* to me.

Notice a nucleus can be on the operator in both the positive and negative clause:

I don't like mathematics, but I do enjoy biology.

Agreement and disagreement

278
Agreement and disagreement are types of affirmation and denial in which the expression of JUDGEMENT or OPINION rather than the assertion of FACT is involved. It is all the more necessary not to offend standards of politeness when the other person's judgement is in question.

Agreement
279
In agreeing with an unfavourable opinion, you may wish to qualify your agreement with an expression of regret, *etc:*

(A)   His speech was boring.

   (B)   Yes, I'm afraid it was.

   (B)   I have to agree that it was.

   (B)   I must say I found it so.

In other cases, you can be as enthusiastic as you like in emphasising your agreement:

(A)   It was an interesting exhibition, wasn't it?

(B)   (Yes,) it was superb / absolutely splendid, *etc.*

(A)   A referendum will satisfy everybody.

(B)   (Yes,)

   definitely.

   quite.

   absolutely.

   I quite/absolutely agree.

   I couldn't agree more.

(A)   A referendum won't satisfy everybody.

(B)

   Definitely not.

   It certainly won't.

   You're absolutely right, it won't.

   I agree (that it won't).

Tactful disagreement
280
When you deny or contradict what someone else has stated, the effect is often ⟨impolite⟩, unless the denial is qualified in some way. You can qualify it by an apology or by adjusting to the speaker's point of view:

(A)   English is a difficult language to learn.

(B)   I'm afraid I disagree with you: some languages are even more
        difficult, I think.

(B)   True, but the grammar is quite easy.

(B)   Yes, but it's not so difficult as Russian.

(B)   Do you think so? Actually, I find it quite easy.

(A)   The book is tremendously well written.

(B)   Yes, (well written) as a whole—but there are some rather boring
        patches, don't you think?

Partial or qualified agreement
281

In discussion and argument, there is often a need to agree with one aspect of a
speaker's view, and to disagree with another. Here are some of the methods you
might use to express this sort of qualified agreement (x and y here stand for
statements, and x and y for noun phrases).

> Certainly it's true that x, but on the other hand y.
>
> I can see that x, but surely y.
>
> I'm in total agreement with you/Jones/*etc* about *x*, but we also
>   have to consider *y*.
>
> Agreed, but if we accept *x*, then it must (also) be true that y.

Corroboration
282

We can also agree, and add a further point to corroborate or confirm the argument:

> Yes, and in fact x.
>
> Yes, and what is more, x.
>
> I agree, and in fact one might go so far as to say x.
>
> Absolutely. Actually, I would go further, and say x.

Fact, hypothesis and neutrality

283

We have considered the truth and falsehood of statements in terms of affirmation, denial, negation, etc. But there are many circumstances in which the issue
of truth or falsehood is ASSUMED rather than directly stated. Compare:

> I'm glad that John has agreed.   (FACT)   [1]
>
> I wish that John had agreed.   (HYPOTHESIS)   [2]

In [1], the speaker assumes the truth of the statement *John has agreed*, while in
[2], he assumes its falsehood. We will call something assumed to be false HYPO-
THETICAL.

Hypothetical meaning
284

A FACT (or factual meaning) is usually expressed by a finite verb clause, as in [1],
or by an *-ing* clause (*see* 515):

I'm surprised $\left\{\begin{array}{l}\text{that he made}\\ \text{at his making}\end{array}\right\}$ that mistake.

A HYPOTHESIS (or hypothetical meaning) is usually expressed by the past tense in dependent clauses, as in [2], and by *would* (or *'d*) + infinitive in main clauses. These two constructions can be seen respectively in the conditional subclause and in the main clause of hypothetical conditions (*see* 208):

SUBCLAUSE

If we *had* enough money, I *would buy* a radio today/tomorrow.

Notice that the past tense (*had, would*) here has nothing to do with past time: reference is to PRESENT or FUTURE time.

PAST time when combined with hypothesis is expressed by the perfective construction *have* + *-ed* participle:

If we *had had* enough money, I *would have bought* a tape-recorder last year.

Would in the verb of the main clause can be replaced by another past tense modal auxiliary:

If we *had* enough money, I *could* (= 'would be able to') *buy* a tape-recorder today.

Other constructions containing hypothetical clauses
285

Apart from conditional clauses, hypothetical meaning may occur in a few other special constructions. The main ones are illustrated here:

It's *time* you were in bed.   ('but you're not in bed')

He behaves *as if* he owned the place.   ('but he doesn't own
                                                                          . . .')

It's not *as though* he $\left\{\begin{array}{l}\text{were poor.}\\ \text{was poor.}\\ \langle\text{informal}\rangle\end{array}\right.$ ('he's not poor')

Just *suppose* someone had seen us.   ('but they didn't see us')

If only I hadn't listened to my parents!   ('but I did listen . . . ')

In that case,
Then,   } he would have taken a taxi. (*see* 209–10)
Otherwise,

In your place, I would have taken a taxi.

(On the special hypothetical use of modal auxiliaries for tentative meaning, *see* 295, 337, 340.)

Other ways of expressing hypothetical meaning
286

In addition to the past tense, there are three less common ways of expressing hypothetical meaning in subclauses:

(A)   THE *were*-SUBJUNCTIVE (*see* 825):

I'd play football with you if I *were* younger.

(The ordinary past tense *was* can replace *were* in ⟨informal⟩ style.)

(B)   *Were to* (or *was to* ⟨informal⟩) + INFINITIVE:

> If it *were to rain* tomorrow, the match would be postponed.

(This construction expresses hypothetical future.)

(C)   *Should* + INFINITIVE:

> If a serious crisis *should arise*, the government would take
> immediate action.

Constructions (B) and (C) are also slightly ⟨formal or literary⟩, and suggest ⟨tentative⟩ conditions. The last two constructions are in general limited to conditional clauses (and constructions related to conditions, like *Suppose he were to see us!*).

287

Another type of hypothetical conditional clause has no subordinating conjunction *if*, but instead begins with an operator placed before the subject (inversion). The three operators which occur in this construction are *had*, subjunctive *were*, and putative *should* (see (C) above):

> *Had I known*, I would have written before. ('If I had known . . . ')
> *Were a serious crisis to arise*, the government would have to act
>   swiftly. ('If a serious crisis were . . . ')
> *Should you change your mind*, no one would blame you. ('If you
>   should . . . ')

The constructions with *were* and *should* are rather ⟨literary⟩ in tone, and can always be replaced by an *if*-construction.

Note

In the negative of clauses beginning *had*, *were* and *should*, there is no contracted form: instead of **Hadn't I known, etc*, we must say *Had I not known, etc*.

Neutrality

288

In addition to fact and hypothesis, there is a third type of situation, in which the speaker assumes neither the truth nor the falsehood of a statement. We will call this situation NEUTRALITY. (We have already met a type of neutrality with respect to the EXISTENCE of something that a phrase refers to: this is the neutrality expressed by such forms as *any, ever, yet*.) For example:

a   It's best *for Sarah to be patient*.

b   I want *John to agree*.

In these sentences, we do not know a whether Sarah will be patient or not; b whether John will agree or not. In this sense, the assumptions are NEUTRAL. Infinitive clauses often express neutrality; also *wh*-clauses, which in this respect sometimes contrast with *that*-clauses:

> Did you know *that* John has agreed? ('John has agreed')
> Do you know *whether* John has agreed? ('Please tell me')

There is the same contrast between:

> He told me *that* they had passed the exam.
> He told me *whether* he had passed the exam.

To the second sentence, a listener would be inclined to reply with a question: *Well, and did he pass it?*

Doubt is another verb that can be followed by either a *that*-clause or a *wh*-clause. *Not + doubt* expresses certainty, and so takes a *that*-clause:

I doubt whether ⎫
I don't doubt that⎭James will co-operate with us.

Putative *should*
289
We have already said that *should* expresses a tentative condition in *if*-clauses. This is true not only for hypothetical conditions, but for OPEN conditions (*see* 208):

If you ⎰hear   ⎱ the news, Jane, please let me [3]
   ⎱should hear ⟨tentative⟩⎰ know.

Open conditions are, in fact, another case of a construction which is NEUTRAL with regard to truth and falsehood. We do not know from [3] whether or not Jane will hear the news and let me know.

In other dependent clauses, too, *should* is used neutrally, to represent something as a neutral 'idea' rather than as a 'fact'. We call this use of *should* PUTATIVE. Contrast these two sentences:

FACT   ⎰The fact is⎱ that the railways will be improved.
     ⎱We know ⎰

IDEA   ⎰The idea is   ⎱ that the railways *should* be
     ⎱Someone is suggesting⎰ improved.
     (' . . . but whether they *will* be improved is another
      matter')

290
Putative *should* occurs quite widely in *that*-clauses (*see* 828):

It's a pity that you *should have* to leave. [4]
I'm surprised that your wife *should object*. [5]
It's unthinkable that he *should resign*. [6]
What worries me is that men *should be able* to threaten
 ordinary peaceful citizens with bombs and bullets. [7]

In some of these sentences, there is no neutrality: for example, the speaker of [5] assumes that 'your wife objects'. Even so, there is a difference between [5] and the factual sentence *I'm surprised that your wife objects*, because in [5] it is the 'very idea' of the objection that surprises me, not the objection as a fact.

Note
[a] Putative *should* is also found in some questions and exclamations:
 How should I know? Why should he resign? Who should come in but the mayor himself!

[b] In some sentences, putative *should* is difficult to distinguish from *should* in the sense of 'ought to': *He has urged that private firearms should be banned.*

The subjunctive
291
The subjunctive (*see* 823-5) also has neutral meaning. It can be used:
 a In some *that*-clauses, where the clause expresses an intention:

Congress has voted/decided/decreed/insisted that the present
law *continue* to operate.

Here *should* + infinitive can also be used. This use of the subjunctive is
quite common in ⟨AmE⟩, *eg* in newspaper language.

b In some conditional and contrast clauses (*see* 208–16):

Whatever *be* the reasons for it, we cannot tolerate dis-
loyalty. (= 'Whatever the reasons for it may be . . . ')

c In certain idioms, usually in main clauses:

God *save* the Queen!

So *be* it then;

Heaven *forbid*!

These constructions are all ⟨formal⟩ and rather ⟨elevated or archaic⟩.

Degrees of likelihood

292

Instead of thinking of truth and falsehood in black-and-white terms, we can think
in terms of a SCALE OF LIKELIHOOD. The extremes of the scale are IMPOSSIBILITY
and CERTAINTY (or LOGICAL NECESSITY); other, intermediate concepts to be considered are POSSIBILITY, PROBABILITY, IMPROBABILITY, *etc.* These notions are
expressed in various ways:

a most importantly, by modal auxiliaries (*can, may, must, etc, see* 501):

You *may* be right.

b more ⟨formally⟩, by a sentence with introductory *it* and a *that*-clause:

It is *possible that* you are right (*see* 584–7).

c by an adverbial such as *necessarily, perhaps, probably* (*see* 479):

Perhaps you're right.

These various constructions will now be illustrated in 293–301. We shall give
special attention, where necessary, to the use of auxiliaries in negative sentences,
in questions, in reference to past time, and in hypothetical clauses.

Auxiliaries such as *can, may,* and *must* can refer to the future as well as to the
present: *You may feel better tomorrow* (= 'It's possible that you *will* feel better').

Possibility
Can, may, could, might
293

(A) POSSIBILITY OF THE FACT (*factual*)

$$= \begin{cases} \text{The railways } \textit{may} \text{ be improved.} & [1] \\ \textit{It is possible that} \text{ the railways will be improved.} & [2] \\ \textit{Perhaps/possibly/maybe} \text{ the railways will be improved.} & [3] \end{cases}$$

(B) POSSIBILITY OF THE IDEA (*theoretical*)

$$= \begin{cases} \text{The railways } \textit{can} \text{ be improved.} & [4] \\ \textit{It is possible for} \text{ the railways to be improved.} & [5] \end{cases}$$

Theoretical possibility (*can*) is 'weaker' than factual possibility (*may*). Sentence
[4], for example, says merely that IN THEORY the railways are 'improvable', *ie* that

they are not perfect. Sentence [1], on the other hand, could suggest that there are definite plans for improvement.

Note

Can in general statements of possibility has roughly the same meaning as *sometimes:*

$$= \begin{cases} \text{Lightning } \textit{can} \text{ be dangerous.} \\ \text{Lightning is } \textit{sometimes} \text{ dangerous.} \end{cases}$$

294

NEGATION: For impossibility, use *cannot* or *can't* ⟨informal⟩ (but not *may not*):

> He can't be working at this time! ('It is impossible that he is working . . . ')

He may not be working, on the other hand, means 'It is possible that he is not working'.

QUESTIONS: Use *can* (not *may*): *Can he be working?* (= 'Is it possible that he is working?')

PAST TIME: For something which was possible in the past, use *could:*

> In those days, a man could be sentenced to death for a small crime.

For the (present) possibility of a past happening, use *may* + the perfect:

> *We may have made a mistake.* ('It is possible that we (have) made a mistake')

HYPOTHETICAL: For hypothetical possibility, use *could* or *might:*

> If someone were to make a mistake, the whole plan *could/might* be ruined.

Tentative possibility (could, might)

295

Could and *might* in their hypothetical sense are often used to express ⟨tentative⟩ possibility, *ie* to talk of something which is possible, but unlikely:

> He *could/might* be telling lies. ('It is just possible that he is telling lies'.)
>
> *Could* you have left your purse on the bus? ('Is it just possible . . . ?')

Ability (*can, be able to,* etc)

296

The notion of 'ability', also expressed by *can*, is closely related to that of 'theoretical possibility':

> He *can* speak English fluently.
>
> Will you *be able to* meet us in London tomorrow?
>
> He *is capable of* keeping a secret when he wants to.
>
> She *knows how to* type and take shorthand.

NEGATION: For inability, use *can't* (or *be unable to,* or *be incapable of*):

> He *can't* speak German very well.

QUESTIONS: *Can you drive a car?*

PAST TIME: *Could* usually means 'knew how to'; it refers to a permanent or habitual ability:

> He *could* play the piano when he was five.

Was/were able to often combines the ideas of 'ability' and 'achievement':

> By acting quickly, we *were able to* save him from drowning. (*ie* 'We could, and did save him').

HYPOTHETICAL: *I'm so hungry, I could eat a horse!*

Certainty or logical necessity (*must, have, to,* etc)

297

Must + infinitive and *have* + *to*-infinitive (or, ⟨*esp* in BrE⟩, *have got to*) can express certainty or logical necessity:

> There *must* be some mistake.
>
> You *have to* be joking! ⟨*esp* AmE⟩
>
> The bombing'*s got to* stop sometime. ⟨*esp* BrE⟩
>
> *It is certain that* the bombing will stop soon.
>
> = { Many people will *certainly/necessarily* lose their jobs.
>   { Many people are *certain/sure* to lose their jobs.
>
> *Inevitably*, some changes will take place.

The contrasting relation between possibility and certainty can be seen in:

> = { His father *can't* still be *alive*.
>   { His father *must* be *dead*.
>
> = { It is *impossible* that his father is still *alive*.
>   { It is *certain* that his father is *dead*.

All four sentences have in effect the same meaning.

Negatives and questions

298

> = { *Does* there *have to* be a motive for the crime?
>   { Is there *necessarily* a motive for the crime?
>   { *Need* there be a motive for the crime? ⟨*esp* BrE⟩
>
> = { Strikes *don't have to* be caused by bad pay (they can also be caused by bad conditions, *etc*).
>   { Strikes are *not necessarily* caused by bad pay.
>   { Strikes *need not be* caused by bad pay. ⟨*esp* BrE⟩

The auxiliary *need* is used ⟨*esp* in BrE⟩, in place of *must* in questions and negatives.

299

PAST TIME: We have to distinguish a past certainty (*had to*) from a certainty about the past (usually expressed by *must* + the perfect):

> Someone *had to* lose the game. ('It was necessary, by the rules of the game, for someone to lose')
>
> John *must* have missed his train ('It is (almost) certain that John missed his train').

HYPOTHETICAL: Use *have to:*

> If God did not exist, someone *would have to* invent him. (*ie* 'it would be necessary for someone . . . ')

Prediction and predictability (*will, must*)
300

As illustrated above (*see* 297), *must* often expresses a certainty about an event which we do not observe, but about which we draw a conclusion from evidence. On hearing the phone ring, you might say '*That* MUST *be my wife*' ('I KNOW that she is due to phone at about this time, and I therefore CONCLUDE that she is phoning now'). In a similar way, you can use *will* to express a 'PREDICTION' about the present, just as you can use *will* to make a prediction about the future: *That* WILL *be my wife*. There is little difference here between *must* and *will*:

$=\begin{cases} \text{John } will \text{ have arrived } by\ now. \quad (also: \text{John } will \text{ have arrived by} \\ \qquad\qquad\qquad\qquad\qquad\qquad\qquad\qquad tomorrow) \\ \text{John } must \text{ have arrived } by\ now. \quad (but\ not: \text{ *They } must \text{ have} \\ \qquad\qquad\qquad\qquad\qquad\qquad\qquad\qquad \text{arrived by } tomorrow.) \end{cases}$

This sort of prediction with *will* often occurs with conditional sentences:

If litmus paper is dipped in acid, it *will* turn red.

Will can also be used in a habitual sense, to express the idea of 'predictability' or 'characteristic behaviour':

Accidents *will* happen.

A lion *will* only attack a human being when it is hungry.

We have noted (*see* 120) the equivalent use of *would* to express habitual or characteristic ('predictable') behaviour in the past:

He *would* often go all day without eating.

Probability *ought to, should,* etc
301

The auxiliaries *ought to* and *should* (*see* 501) can express 'probability', and can be regarded as weaker equivalents of *must* (= 'certainty'). *Compare:*

Our guests *must* be home by now. ('I am certain')

Our guests $\begin{Bmatrix} ought\ to \\ should \end{Bmatrix}$ be home by now. ('They probably are, but I'm not certain')

Should is more frequent than *ought to*. Other ways of expressing probability are:

It is quite *probable/likely* that they didn't receive the letter.

He is *probably* the best chess-player in the country.

They have *very likely* lost the way home.

The concert *is likely to* finish late.

NEGATION: Improbability can be expressed by *shouldn't, oughtn't to,* or *it is improbable/unlikely that:*

There $\begin{Bmatrix} shouldn't \\ oughtn't\ to \end{Bmatrix}$ be any difficulties.

It *is unlikely that* there will be any difficulties.

QUESTIONS (rare):

Should there be any difficulty in getting tickets?

Note

People have a natural tendency to overstate their convictions. Therefore *must* and *will* (*see* 300) are sometimes used in a weakened sense that one feels is nearer to 'probability' than to 'certainty': *You'll be feeling hungry after all that work. They must have spent years and years building this cathedral.*

Attitudes to truth

302

We now consider the ways in which people may be committed or uncommitted to the truth or reality of something. The people concerned may be the speaker ('I') or another person, or a group of people. We often use, to express such attitudes, a *that*-clause or a *wh*-clause (the latter to express a 'neutral' attitude, *see* 288), but adverbials and other constructions are also sometimes available, as well as the type of parenthetical clauses we call comment clauses (*see* 522). In ⟨impersonal⟩ style, people prefer to use the methods of expressing certainty, probability, *etc* discussed in 297–301, rather than those which involve a 1st person pronoun. Thus *It is certain* . . . and *It is unlikely* . . . can be impersonal alternatives to *I am certain* . . . or *I doubt* . . . .

Certainty
303

I *know* that his answer will be 'No'.
I *know* what his answer will be.

= { I am *certain/sure* (that) the party will be a success.
The party will be a success, I'm *sure*.

They were *convinced* { (that) they would succeed.
of their success.

= { It is *obvious/clear/plain* (to us all) that he has suffered a great deal.
He has *clearly/obviously/plainly* suffered a great deal.

= { We *do not doubt* that he is honest.
We *have no doubt* of his honesty.

Without doubt, she is one of the best teachers in the school

Other adverbials which can replace *without doubt* in more ⟨formal⟩ contexts: *doubtless, indubitably, undeniably, unquestionably.*

Doubt or uncertainty
304

= { I am *not certain/sure/convinced* that he deserves promotion.
I am *not certain/sure* whether he deserves promotion.

They were *uncertain/unsure* (*of*) who was to blame.

= { I *doubt* if many people will come to the meeting.
I *don't think* many people will come to the meeting. (*see* 636)

{ There were some *doubts*
We have *doubts* } *about* his honesty.

They were *uncertain of/about* the best course to take.

Belief, opinion, *etc*
305

(A) BELIEF, OPINION

= { *I believe* (that) the lecture was well attended.
The lecture was well attended, *I believe*.

He thinks (that) he can dictate to everybody.

It was everybody's *opinion* that the conference was a success.

It's my *belief* that cars will disappear from our roads by 1990.

In my opinion, he was driving the car too fast.

You may *consider* yourselves lucky.

He was *thought/believed/considered* to be the richest man in Europe.

There is a slight difference between 'opinion' and 'belief' in that an opinion is usually something that someone arrives at on the basis of observation and judgement:

It's my belief that he drinks too much.

('I don't know how much he drinks, but . . . ')

It's my opinion that he drinks too much.

('I know how much he drinks, and in my judgement, it's too much'.)

Further, tag questions with a falling tone can sometimes be used to express an opinion:

He was driving too fast, wasn't he?

(B) ASSUMPTION

We assume/suppose that you have received the package.

$= \begin{cases} \text{All the passengers, } I \text{ presume, have been warned about the delay.} \\ \text{All the passengers have } presumably \text{ been warned about the delay.} \end{cases}$

Will in the sense of 'present prediction' (*see* 300) can be used here:

I assume you *will* all have heard the news.

(C) APPEARANCE

$= \begin{cases} \text{It } seems/appears \text{ (to me) that no one noticed his escape.} \\ \text{No one } seems/appears \text{ to have noticed his escape.} \\ Apparently, \text{ no one noticed his escape.} \end{cases}$

It *looks/seems* as if you're right.

He *looks as if* he's ill. ⟨rather informal⟩ (Here *looks* refers to visual appearance only.)

306

In *that*-clauses in categories (A) and (B), transferred negation (*see* 636) is common. Thus instead of *I think he hasn't arrived*, we prefer to say *I don't think he has arrived*.

Notice that in shortened reply statements in these three categories, the clause which is the object of belief, *etc*, can usually be replaced by *so* (*see* 401):

(A) Has the race been postponed?   (B) $\begin{cases} \text{I think } so. \\ \text{I suppose } so. \\ \text{It seems } so. \\ \text{Apparently } so. \\ \text{I don't think } so. \end{cases}$

(Here *so* replaces '(that) the race has been postponed'.)

Section C: Mood, emotion and attitude

307

In section B, we looked at the English language as a means of giving and receiving information. But language is more than this: it is communication *between people*. It often expresses the emotions and attitudes of the speaker and he often uses it to influence the attitudes and behaviour of the hearer. These are the aspects of English we consider in this section.

Emotive emphasis in speech

308

In this part of the section, we shall be dealing mainly with ⟨familiar⟩ forms of English.

Interjections
309

Interjections are words whose only function is to express emotion. Common English interjections are: *Oh* /oʊ/ (surprise); *Ah* /ɑː/ (satisfaction, recognition, *etc*); *Aha* /əˈhɑː/ (jubilant satisfaction, recognition); *Wow* /waʊ/ (great surprise); *Yippee* /ˈjɪpiː/ (excitement, delight); *Ouch* /aʊtʃ/, *Ow* /aʊ/ (pain); *Ugh* /ʌx/ (disgust); *Ooh* /uː/ (pleasure, pain).

> *Oh*, what a beautiful present!
> *Ah*, that's just what I wanted.
> *Aha*, these books are exactly what I was looking for.
> *Wow*, what a fantastic goal!
> *Yippee*, this is fun!
> *Ouch*, my foot!
> *Ugh*, what a mess.
> *Ooh*, this cream cake's delicious.

Other ways of giving emotion emphasis
310

EXCLAMATIONS (*see* 568)

> What a wonderful time we've had!
> How delightful her manners are!

Exclamations are often shortened to a noun phrase or an adjectival phrase: *What a girl!* ('What a girl she is!'); *How funny!* ('How funny it is!').

311

EMPHATIC *so* AND *such* (*see* 482, 562)

> He's súch a nice mán!
>
> I'm 'so afraid they'll get lòst.
>
> Why is he 'such a bàby!
>
> Don't upsèt yourself 'so!

These have an emotive emphasis similar to that of exclamations, but their tone is rather 'gushy'. The words *so* and *such* are stressed, and for extra emphasis, may receive nuclear stress.

312

REPETITION

It's *far, far* too expensive.

I agree with *every* word you've said—*every* single word.

It's *very very* awkward.

You *bad, bad* boy!

313

STRESS ON THE OPERATOR (*see* 672-5)

That will be nice!

What are you doing?

We have enjoyed ourselves!

The operator often has nuclear stress. *Do* can be used as a dummy auxiliary to express emphasis (*see* 675):

You do look pretty.

You 'did give me a fright.

There is a similar use of *do* to give persuasive emphasis to a command:

'Do be quiet!

Do come if you can!

314

NUCLEAR STRESS ON OTHER WORDS

I wish you'd listen!

I'm terribly sorry!

Intensifying adverbs and modifiers

315

As we noted in 219-20, many degree adverbs and other degree expressions intensify the meaning of the word they modify:

We are *very* happy *indeed*.

I was *utterly* dismayed.

He's an *absolute* saint.

In ⟨familiar⟩ speech, some adjectives and adverbs (such as *terrific, tremendous, awfully, terribly*) have little meaning apart from their emotive force. Thus *terrific, great, grand, fantastic* are simply emphatic equivalents of *good* or *nice*: *The weather was terrific*; *It was a great show*; *etc*. Notice that *awfully* and *terribly* can be used in a 'good' sense, as well as in a 'bad' sense:

She's *terribly* kind to us.

In addition to degree adverbs, certain adverbs like *really* and *definitely* have an emphatic effect:

We *really* have enjoyed ourselves.

He *definitely* impressed us.

It was *truly* a memorable occasion.

She *literally* collapsed with laughter. ⟨familiar⟩

Intensification of questions and negatives
316

You can intensify the emotive force of a *wh*-question by adding *ever*, *on earth*, *etc*, to the *wh*-word:

How *ever* did he escape? ('I just can't imagine')

Why *on earth* didn't you tell me? ('How silly of you!')

What *in heaven's name* does he think he's doing? ('The idiot!')

In ⟨writing⟩, sometimes *ever* is spelled as part of the *wh*-word: *whoever*, *wherever*, *etc*, but so spelled, these words have other uses apart from intensifying (*see* 216). *Why ever* is always spelled as two words.

317

You can intensify a negative sentence by adding *at all* either directly after the negative word, or in a later position in the sentence:

I found nothing *at all* the matter with him.

She didn't speak to us *at all*.

Other negative intensifiers are *a bit* ⟨informal⟩ and *by any means* (both adverbials of degree); and *whatever* (postmodifier of a negative noun phrase):

They weren't *a bit* apologetic.

You have no excuse *whatever*.

Further examples of negative intensifiers are:

I didn't sleep *a wink*. ⟨informal⟩

He didn't give me *a thing* (= 'anything at all'). ⟨informal⟩

A negative noun phrase beginning *not a* can be used for emphasis:

We arrived *not a* moment too soon (= We didn't arrive a moment
    too soon).

318

Another rather ⟨rhetorical⟩ form of negative emphasis is often combined with the forms already mentioned. This is to place the negative element at the beginning of the clause:

Not a penny of the money did he spend.

Never have I seen such a crowd of people.

As the examples show, the operator is placed before the subject in this construction (unless the negative element is itself the subject: *Not a single word passed his lips*) (*see* 432).

For *can't* or *couldn't*, *possibly* is used as an intensifier: *It can't possibly succeed*.

Exclamatory and rhetorical questions
319

An EXCLAMATORY QUESTION is a *yes-no* question spoken with an emphatic falling tone, instead of the usual rising tone. The most common type has a negative form:

Hasn't she gr<u>o</u>wn! ('She's grown very very much!')

Wasn't it a marvellous c<u>o</u>ncert!

Here the speaker vigorously invites the hearer's agreement; the effect is similar to:

> It was a marvellous c̲o̲ncert, w̲asn't it? (*see* 250)

Another type of exclamatory question is positive in form, with stress on the operator and subject:

> 'Am 'I h̲ungry! ('I'm very very hungry'.)

> 'Did 'he look ann̲o̲yed!

> 'Has 'she gr̲own!

320

A RHETORICAL QUESTION is more like a forceful statement than an exclamation. A *positive* rhetorical question is like a strong *negative* statement; a *negative* rhetorical question is like a strong *positive* statement.

POSITIVE

> Is that a reason for desp̲a̲ir? ('Surely that is not a reason ...')

NEGATIVE

> Didn't I t̲e̲ll you he would forg̲e̲t? ('You know I told you ...')

There are also rhetorical *wh*-questions:

> What d̲ifference does it make? ('It makes no difference')

> Who doesn't know th̲a̲t? ('Everyone knows that')

As the name suggests, rhetorical questions are often rather ⟨rhetorical⟩ in tone.

Describing emotions

321

We come now to the description or reporting of emotive behaviour. An emotive reaction to something can be expressed by the preposition *at:*

I was alarmed *at* his behaviour.	[1]
An audience will always laugh *at* a good joke.	[2]
She was very surprised *at* your resignation from the club.	[3]

In ⟨BrE⟩, *with* is often used instead of *at* when what causes the reaction is a person or object rather than an event:

> I was furious *with* John.

> Is he pleased *with* his present?

Other prepositions used are *about* and *of: worried about, annoyed about, resentful of,* etc (*see* 243).

The cause of the emotion is often expressed by a *to*-infinitive clause or a *that*-clause (with or without *should, see* 289–90), and in these cases the preposition is omitted:

> They were alarmed *to find the house empty.*

> She is sorry *to have missed the show.*

> I was delighted *that you came.*

> We're anxious *that everything should go smoothly.*

322

The cause of emotion may also be expressed by the subject (or, in the passive, by the agent). *Compare* [3] above with:

= { Your resignation from the club surprised her very much.
    { She was very surprised by your resignation from the club.

Other constructions for describing emotions do not specify the person affected, and are therefore more ⟨impersonal⟩:

The accommodation was *satisfactory/delightful, etc.*	[4]
The news from the front is *very disturbing.*	[5]
It's amazing that so many passengers were unhurt. (*see* 454, 584)	[6]
It's a pity that you should have missed her.	[7]
It's a pity to have missed her.	[8]

In most of these cases, the person affected is likely to be 'me' (the speaker). The person affected can sometimes be made clear by a phrase introduced by *to* or *for*: *satisfactory for most people, disturbing to me, etc.* Thus [6] can be expanded:

To me, it's amazing that so many passengers were unhurt.

Sentence adverbials
323

Some sentence adverbials (including comment clauses, *see* 522) can express an emotional reaction or judgement:

To my regret, he did not accept our offer.

(*ie* 'I regretted that he did not accept the offer')

Surprisingly, no one has objected to the plan.

(*ie* 'It is surprising that . . . ')

He is *wisely* staying at home today.

The children were rather noisy, *I'm afraid.*

Other sentence adverbs similar to *surprisingly* and *wisely* are *amazingly, strangely, annoyingly, regrettably, fortunately, luckily, hopefully, preferably, foolishly, sensibly.*

Liking and disliking
324

Verbs such as *like, love, hate,* and *prefer* can be followed either by a *to*-infinitive clause or by an *-ing* clause (*see* 515), as well as by a noun phrase object:

	parties.	[9]
	to give parties. (*ie* 'She likes the idea	[10]
She likes/loves/hates	of it', *etc*)	
	giving parties. (*ie* 'She likes it when	[11]
	she does it', *etc*)	

Some English speakers discern a slight difference between [10] and [11]: the infinitive clause expresses an 'idea', while the *-ing* clause expresses a 'fact' (*see* 290). Thus in some contexts (but not in [10]), the infinitive clause may have NEUTRAL meaning (*see* 288):

He likes me *to work* late. { '. . . and that's why I do it.' }
                           { '. . . but I never do it.' }

He likes me *working* late. ('. . . and that's why I do it')

Usually only the infinitive clause can be used when the main verb is hypothetical:

(A)   Would you like *to have* dinner now?

(B)   No, I'd prefer *to eat* later.

Note

Enjoy, *dislike*, and *loathe* only take *-ing* clauses:

He enjoys/dislikes/loathes *working*.

Preference
325

Prefer means 'like more' or 'like better'. The rejected alternative is introduced by a *to*-phrase, or by a clause introduced by *rather than*, which may be followed by an infinitive (with or without *to*) or by an *-ing* participle:

Most people prefer trains *to* buses.

He prefers renting a car *to* having one of his own.

He prefers to rent a car *rather than* to have one of his own.

Rather than buy a car of his own, he prefers to rent one.

She has always preferred making her own clothes $\begin{Bmatrix} \textit{rather than} \\ \textit{instead of} \end{Bmatrix}$
buying them in the shops.

Would prefer + to-infinitive (hypothetical preference) can be replaced by *would rather* + bare infinitive, which may be followed by a *than*-construction (*see* 528):

$= \begin{cases} \text{I'd prefer to stay in a house rather than in a hotel.} \\ \text{I'd rather stay in a house than in a hotel.} \end{cases}$

Some other emotions
326

Here are some of the ways of expressing other emotions. Many of the constructions illustrated here have already been discussed and exemplified. Notice that adverbs of degree (*see* 217–26) can be used to indicate the 'strength' of the emotion. Many of the sentences are ⟨informal⟩ and ⟨familiar⟩.

327
HOPE

I (very much) hope (that) he $\begin{Bmatrix} \text{will arrive} \\ \text{arrives} \end{Bmatrix}$ on time.

I am (rather) hoping that . . .	⟨tentative⟩ (*see* 127)
I hoped that . . .	⟨tentative⟩ (*see* 111)
I was hoping that . . .	⟨more tentative⟩ (*see* 127)

I hope to see you soon.

Hopefully, next spring will bring
an improvement in the economic   ⟨*esp* AmE⟩
situation.

328
ANTICIPATION OF PLEASURE

I am looking forward to receiving your reply.

I know I will enjoy meeting you again.

329

DISAPPOINTMENT OR REGRET

I'm (rather/very) disappointed that . . .

It is (a little bit) disappointing that . . .

It's a (great) shame/pity that . . .

I'm sorry to hear that . . .

I $\begin{Bmatrix} \text{would have} \\ \text{had} \end{Bmatrix}$ hoped that . . . (unfulfilled hope) (*see* 284)

I wish (that) someone had let me know. (unfulfilled wish) (*see* 336–7)

If only I had known! (*see* 337)

Unfortunately, . . .

330

APPROVAL

I (very much) approve of $\begin{cases} \text{the plan.} \\ \text{your asking for his opinion.} \end{cases}$

It wasn't a bad mòvie, wàs it? ⟨familiar⟩ (mild)

I (rather) like the new boss.

I $\begin{Bmatrix} \text{love} \\ \text{'do like} \end{Bmatrix}$ your dress. (enthusiastic)

What a(n) great/excellent/marvellous/ . . . play! (enthusiastic)

331

DISAPPROVAL

I don't like the way she dresses (very much).

I don't (much) care for sweets, actually.

I didn't think $\begin{cases} \text{much of the orchestra.} \\ \text{the orchestra was much/very good.} \end{cases}$

I thought the novel was pòor/drèadful/appálling, didn't yóu?

It would have been better, I think, if you hadn't mentioned it.

You shouldn't have bought such an expensive present. (*see* 343)

I don't think you should have told the children.

I had hoped you would have done more than this.

Disapproval can often be expressed more ⟨tactfully⟩ by means of a question:

Did you have/need to work so late?

Why did you do a thing like that?

Was it really necessary to be so rude to the waiter?

Don't you think it would have been better if you had told me in advance?

332

SURPRISE

It's (rather) surprising/amazing/astonishing that so many people come to these meetings.

I am/was (very) surprised that so many turned up.

What a surprise!

How strange/odd/astonishing/amazing that . . . !

Wasn't it extraordinary that . . . ? (*see* 319)

Surprisingly/strangely/incredibly, . . .

333

CONCERN, WORRY

> I am (a bit) concerned/worried that . . .
>
> I am (rather) worried/concerned about . . .
>
> It's (very) disturbing/worrying that . . .
>
> I find his behaviour very disturbing/worrying.
>
> His health gives (some) cause for anxiety. ⟨formal, impersonal⟩

Volition

334

We distinguish four types of volition: WILLINGNESS, WISH, INTENTION, INSIST-
ENCE. These are listed in order of increasing 'strength': volition becomes 'stronger' to the extent that a person asserts his will, or imposes it on others.

Willingness
335

Willingness can be expressed by the auxiliary *will* (or *'ll* ⟨informal⟩):

(A) Who *will* lend me a cigarette?   (B) Ì *will*.

  ('Who is willing to lend me . . . ')

  The porter *will* help if you ask him.

Here the future meaning of *will* is mixed with that of volition (*see* 129). For past
or hypothetical willingness, use *would:*

> PAST TIME   When he was young, he was so poor (that) he
>   *would* do anything for money.
>
> HYPOTHETICAL   John is so greedy, he *would* do anything for
>   money (if you asked him).

Won't and *wouldn't* express the negative of willingness, *ie* REFUSAL:

> He *won't* take any notice.   (='He refuses/declines to take
>   any notice.')
>
> They *wouldn't* listen to me.   (='They refused . . .')

Note

The adverbs *willingly* and *readily* combine the ideas of 'willingness' and 'performance': *He willingly/readily gave me the money* (*ie* 'He was willing to do it,
and did so').

Wish
336

For neutral volition, *wish* is a more ⟨formal⟩ verb than *want:*

> The manager *wishes* (me) to thank you for your co-operation.
>
> I *want* (you) to read this newspaper report.
>
> Do you *want* me to sign this letter?

For a hypothetical circumstance, use only *wish:*

> I *wish* (that) you would listen to me! (' . . . but you won't')

337

The exclamatory construction *If only . . .* can also be used for hypothetical meaning:

$$=\begin{cases}\text{If only I could remember his name!}\\ \text{I 'do wish I could remember his name!}\end{cases}$$

When expressing your own wishes, or inviting the wishes of others, you can make the wish more ⟨tentative⟩ and ⟨tactful⟩ by using *would like, would prefer,* or *would rather* (*see* 324–5):

> *Would* you *like* me to open these letters?
>
> I *would/should like* to stay in an inexpensive hotel.

(*Should* can replace *would* in the 1st person.)

Another way to consult someone's wishes is to use a question with *shall,* or more ⟨tentatively⟩, with *should:*

> *Shall* I make you a cup of coffee? ('Would you like me to . . . ')
>
> What *shall* we do this evening? *Shall* we listen to some music?
>
> *Should* we tell him that he's not wanted?

Note

[a] For other uses of *shall* connected with volition, *see* 340, 343.

[b] 1st and 3rd person commands with *let* (*see* 521) also express a kind of wish: *Let's listen to some music,* (*shall we?*). *Let everyone do what they can.*

Intention

338

The verbs *intend, mean,* and *aim* (+ infinitive clause) express intention:

> He intends/means/aims to catch the last train.   [1]
>
> That remark was meant/intended to hurt her.   [2]

Intention can also be expressed by *be going to* (*see* 130), or, in the 1st person, by *will/shall* (*see* 129):

> *Are* you *going to* catch the last train?
>
> I *will/shall* write as soon as I can.
>
> We *won't* stay longer than two hours.

These forms also have an element of prediction, and so are more definite about the fulfilment of the intention than [1] and [2].

(On clauses and phrases of purpose, or 'intended result', *see* 203.)

Insistence

339

> He *insists* on doing everything himself.
>
> We *are determined* to overcome the problem.

Insistence is occasionally expressed by *will/shall* with strong stress:

> He 'will try to mend it himself. ('He insists on trying . . . ')
>
> I won't / shan't ⟨BrE⟩ give in! ('I am determined not to . . . ')
>
> Why 'will you make things difficult for yourself?

Permission and obligation

Permission: *can, may, etc*

340

$$\begin{cases} \textit{Can} \text{ we smoke in here?} \quad \text{Yes, you} \begin{cases} \text{can.} \\ \text{may.} \end{cases} \\ \textit{May} \text{ we smoke in here?} \langle \text{more formal, polite} \rangle \\ \text{Are we } \textit{allowed to} \text{ smoke in here?} \\ \text{Are we } \textit{permitted to} \text{ smoke in here?} \langle \text{formal} \rangle \\ \text{Is it all right if we smoke in here?} \langle \text{informal} \rangle \end{cases}$$

We have *allowed/permitted* him *to* take the examination late.

They *let* him do what he wants.

Could can express permission in the past, or hypothetical permission:

When I was a student, I *could* travel at half-price.

('. . . was allowed to . . . ')

If you were a student, you *could* travel at half-price.

('. . . would be allowed to . . . ')

You can also use hypothetical *could* (and sometimes *might*) in ⟨tactful⟩ requests for permission:

Could/Might we ask you what your opinion is?

I wonder if I *could/might* borrow your pen?

Another construction for asking and giving permission involves the verb *mind*:

(A)   Would you mind $\begin{cases} \text{if I opened a window?} \\ \text{my opening a window?} \end{cases}$

(B)   No, $\begin{cases} \text{I don't mind at all.} \\ \text{not at all.} \end{cases}$ (= 'certainly you may').

Again, the hypothetical form is more ⟨tactful⟩.

Note

Shall is occasionally used in the 2nd and 3rd person to express permission given by the speaker:

You *shall* do exactly as you wish.

He *shall* get his money.

Perhaps this meaning is rather one of willingness: 'I am willing to see that he gets his money' *etc*.

Obligation or compulsion

must, have, to, etc

341

$\begin{cases} \text{You } \textit{must} \\ \text{You'll } \textit{have to} \end{cases}$ be back by 2 o'clock ('I want you to do some cleaning').   [1]

You *have to* sign your name here (otherwise the document isn't valid).   [2]

I've *got to* finish this essay by tomorrow. ⟨informal⟩   [3]

The university *requires* all students to submit their work by a given date. ⟨formal⟩   [4]

Must and *have (got) to* + infinitive (*see* 297, 501) both express obligation, but some English speakers feel a difference between them. For such speakers, *must* involves the speaker's authority (see [1]), while *have (got) to* involves some other authority than the speaker; *eg* official regulations (see [2], [4]). With a 1st person subject, *must* expresses the speaker's authority over himself (*ie* his sense of duty, social responsibility *etc*):

> I *must* phone my parents tonight. ('They'll be worrying about me')
> We *must* invite the Stewarts to dinner. ('It's months since we saw them')

In the past tense and in hypothetical clauses, *had to* and *would have to* express obligation:

> They *had to* work fifty hours a week in those days ('were obliged to . . . ')
> If you went abroad, you *would have to* earn your own living. (' . . . would be obliged to . . . ')

Need, etc
342

In questions and negatives, the auxiliary *need* ⟨*esp* BrE⟩ is a replacement for *must;* otherwise forms of *have (got) to* or *need to* can be used (*see* 298):

$$=\begin{cases} \text{\textit{Need} you work so hard? } ⟨\textit{esp } BrE⟩ \\ \text{\textit{Have} you \textit{got to} work so hard?} \\ \text{\textit{Do} you \textit{have to} work so hard?} \\ \text{\textit{Do} you \textit{need to} work so hard?} \end{cases}$$

$$=\begin{cases} \text{We \textit{needn't} hurry. } ⟨\textit{esp } BrE⟩ \\ \text{We \textit{don't have to} hurry.} \\ \text{We \textit{don't need to} hurry.} \end{cases}$$

(A) *Has* he *got to* start school tomorrow? ⟨informal⟩
(B) No, he *hasn't got to* be there before Friday. ⟨informal⟩

> There's no *need* to buy the tickets yet.

Note

Must sometimes occurs in questions expecting a negative answer:

> *Must* you leave already? ('Surely you don't have to!')

Other ways of expressing obligation
343

(A) *Ought to* and *should* (*see* 301) express an obligation which may not be fulfilled. *Compare* [3] and [4] above with

> I *ought to* phone my parents tonight ('but I probably won't have time').
> All students *should* submit their work by a given date (' . . . but some of them don't!').

(B) *Need to* + infinitive (where *need* is a main verb, not an auxiliary, *see* 503) indicates 'internal obligation' caused by the state of the person referred to:

> He needs to practise more if he is to improve his playing.

We can also use *need* with a direct object:

> He needs more practice.

(C) *Had better* ⟨informal⟩ + infinitive (without *to*) has the meaning of 'strong recommendation or advisability':

> You'd better be quick, $\begin{cases} \text{or you'll miss the train.} \\ \text{if you want to catch the bus.} \end{cases}$
>
> He'd better not make another mistake.
>
> I suppose I'd better lock the door.

(D) *Shall* in the sense of 'obligation' or 'insistence' is normally limited to official regulations and other formal documents:

> The Society's nominating committee shall nominate one person for the office of President. ⟨very formal⟩

Prohibition

344

Prohibition can be thought of as the negation of permission ('He is not allowed to do something') or, in a different sense, as the negation of obligation ('He is obliged *not* to do something'). *Can* and *may* (= 'permission') and *must* (= 'obligation') can all have the meaning of 'prohibition' with a negative:

(A) *Can* the children play here?   (B)   No, I'm afraid they *can't*.

> You *may not* go swimming.   ('You're not allowed to . . . ')
>
> You *mustn't* keep us all waiting.

A weakened prohibition (more like negative advice) can be indicated by *oughtn't to* ⟨*esp* BrE⟩, *shouldn't, had better not, etc*:

> You *oughtn't to* waste money on smoking.
>
> He *shouldn't* be so impatient.
>
> I'*d better not* wake them up.

Influencing people

Commands

345

With the aim of getting someone to do something, a direct command can be used: *Shut the door*; *Follow me*; *Just look at this mess*; *etc* (*see* 520). A negative command has the effect of forbidding an action: *Don't be a fool; Don't worry about me*.

In addition, with a 2nd person subject, the verb forms expressing obligation and prohibition (*see* 341, 344) can have almost the same effect as a command: *You must be careful; You mustn't smoke*.

The construction *be to* + infinitive can refer to a command given either by the speaker, or (more usually) by some official authority:

> He *is to return* to Germany tomorrow ('He has been given orders to return to Germany').
>
> You *are to stay* here until I return ('I tell you to').

Note

[a] Some abbreviated sentences which do not contain an imperative verb have the effect of brusque commands: *Out with it! This way! Here!*

(=‘Bring/put it here’). Another type is especially used in addressing children and pets: *Off you go! Down you get! Up you come!* ⟨familiar⟩

[*b*]   *Will* in its future sense can sometimes be used (*eg* in military contexts)
with the force of a severe command:

> Officers *will* report for duty at 0600 hours.
> You *will* do exactly as I say.

346

You can specify the people who have to obey the command by putting a 2nd or
3rd person subject in front of the imperative verb (*see* 520), or else by using a
vocative:

> 'You take this tray, and 'you take that one. (pointing to the people
> concerned; note that *you* is stressed)
> Jack and Susan stand over there.
> Somebody open this door.
> Come here, Michael.

Elsewhere, a command with *you* has a tone of impatience:

> You mind your own business!

Another form of impatient command begins with *will:*

> Will you be quiet!

Although this has the grammatical form of a question, its falling intonation
gives it the force of a command.

   In many circumstances, commands are ⟨impolite⟩, and therefore we shall
consider in 347–51 various ways of toning down the effect of a command.

Note

It is not impolite to use a command when you are telling someone to do something for his own good: *Have another chocolate*; *Make yourself at home*; *Just
leave everything to me*; *Do come in*. These are in effect offers or invitations
rather than commands.

⟨*Politer*⟩ commands

347

One way to tone down or weaken the imperative force of a command is to use a
rising or fall-rise tone, instead of the usual falling tone:

> Be careful.
> 'Don’t forget your wallet.

Another way is to add *please*, or the tag question *won’t you*:

> Please hurry up.
> Look after the children, won’t you.
> This way, please.

Note

Two other tags, *why don’t you* and *will you* (after a negative command), can
tone down a command:

> Have a drink, why don’t you.
> Don’t be late, will you.

But after a positive command, *will you* has rising intonation, and usually expresses impatience (*see* 346).

Sit down, will you.

Requests
348
It is often more ⟨tactful⟩ to use a request rather than a command: *ie* to ask your hearer whether he is willing or able to do something. The auxiliaries *will/would* (= willingness) and *can/could* (= ability) can be used:

(A)
{
Will you pass the salt, please?
Would you please pass the salt?
}
(B)   Yes, certainly.

(A)   *Can* you possibly give me a lift?
(B)   No, I'm afraid not, because . . .

(A)   *Could* you lend me your pen?
(B)   O.K. ⟨familiar⟩ Here it is.

(These examples also show typical replies.) *Would* and *could* are more ⟨tactful⟩ than *will* and *can*. You can also use a negative question, which expects a positive answer (*see* 251), and is to that extent less ⟨tentative⟩ and more persuasive:

Won't you come in and sit down?

Couldn't you possibly come another day?

Other ⟨polite⟩ forms of request
349
There are many more indirect ways of making a ⟨polite⟩ request; *eg* you can make a statement about your own wishes. The following are listed roughly in order of least to most ⟨polite⟩:

I wouldn't mind a drink, if you have one.

Would you mind typing this letter?

I wonder if you'd mind giving me his address?

Would you be {so kind as / kind enough} to switch the light on?

I would be extremely grateful if you would write a reference for me.

I wonder if you would kindly send us some information about your English courses?

These sentences are typical of ⟨spoken⟩ English. In ⟨formal⟩ letters, useful formulae are: *I would be very grateful if . . .* ; *I would appreciate it if . . .* ; *Would you kindly . . .*

Advice, suggestions and invitations
350
As ways of influencing other people, advice, suggestions and invitations are

milder than commands. Strictly, these leave the decision about what to do in the hands of the hearer. But in practice, as the examples show, they are often ⟨tactful⟩ ways of giving commands or instructions.

ADVICE

> You ought to read this book (*see* 343).
>
> You should stay in bed.
>
> You'd better take your medicine.
>
> I'd advise you to see a doctor.
>
> If I were you, I'd sell this car.

SUGGESTIONS

> I suggest we take the night train.
>
> You can read these two chapters before tomorrow (if you like).
>
> You could be cleaning the office while I'm away.
>
> You might have a look at this book.
>
> Why don't you call on me tomorrow?

Could and *might* indicate ⟨tentative⟩ suggestions.

SUGGESTIONS INVOLVING THE SPEAKER

> I suggest we go to bed.
>
> Shall we listen to some music?
>
> Let's enjoy ourselves! (*see* 521)
>
> Let's not waste time.
>
> Why don't we have a party?   ⟩ ⟨informal, familiar⟩
>
> How about a game of football?
>
> What about (having) a drink?

351

INVITATIONS

> Come in and sit down. ⟨familiar⟩
>
> Would you like to come with me?
>
> How would you like to come and spend a week with us next year?
>
> May I have the pleasure of this dance? ⟨formal, polite⟩
>
> May I invite you to dinner next Saturday? ⟨formal, polite⟩

Here is a typical sequence:

(A) Are you doing anything tomorrow evening?

(B) No.

(A) Then perhaps you'd be interested in joining us for a meal at a restaurant in town.

(B) Thank you very much. ⎰ That is kind of you.
⎱ I'd love to.

In ⟨politely⟩ refusing the invitation, (B) might say:

> Well, that's very kind of you—but I'm afraid I have already arranged/promised to ... What a pity, I would have loved to come.

Reported commands, etc
352

Commands, like statements and questions (*see* 264–8), can be reported either in direct speech or in indirect speech:

DIRECT SPEECH   'Put on your space-suits,' he said.

INDIRECT SPEECH   He told/ordered/commanded/instructed them
                    to put on their space-suits.

In indirect speech, put the command in the form of a *to*-infinitive clause. The hearer can be indicated by an indirect object (*them* in the above example). Note the passive construction:

> They were told to put on their space-suits.

The same construction can be used for advice, requests, permission, obligation, persuasion, invitations, *etc*:

He *advised* me to read this book.	[1]
He *asked/begged* me to help him with his homework.	[2]
She *allowed* him to kiss her.	[3]
They *compelled* him to answer their questions.	[4]
Mary has *persuaded* me to resign.	[5]
We *were invited* to attend the performance.	[6]
They *recommended* us to stay at this hotel.	[7]

Notice also direct object constructions:

> The doctor advised a rest.
>
> He begged our forgiveness.
>
> I (can) recommend the Lobster Newburg.

353

Not all verbs for 'influencing people' take an infinitive. *Suggest* takes a *that*-clause (often with putative *should*, *see* 289–90):

> He suggested that they should play cards.

This construction may also follow other verbs, such as *recommend*:

> The doctor recommends that you do/should not tire yourself.

Requests, acts of permission, *etc* can also be put in the form of indirect statements and questions. Thus instead of [2] and [3] you could say:

He asked me if I would help him with his homework.	[2a]
(DIRECT: 'Will you help me with my homework?')	
She said he might kiss her.	[3a]
(DIRECT: 'You may kiss me.')	

The rules for change into the past tense, *etc* (*see* 265) for indirect statements and questions apply also to indirect commands, requests, *etc* (except that there is no tense-change in the infinitive clauses). After a past-tense reporting verb, *will*, *shall*, *can*, *may*, and *have to* change to their past tense forms *would*, *should*, *could*, *might*, and *had to* (see [2a], [3a]) but *must*, *ought to*, *should*, and *had better* do not change:

'You must be careful.' → I told them they must be careful.
'You ought to stay in bed.' → I said that he ought to stay in bed.

354

The verbs *forbid* ⟨formal⟩, *prohibit* ⟨formal⟩, *dissuade*, *refuse*, *decline*, *deny* and *prevent* already contain a negative meaning, so the clauses which follow them are normally positive:

They were forbidden to smoke.   ⎫ ('They were ordered not to
They were prohibited from smoking.⎭ smoke')
She dissuaded him from leaving the country. ('She persuaded him not to . . . ')
The minister refused/declined to comment on the press report.
He denied that the allegations were true.
They were prevented from taking part.

Warnings, promises and threats
355
Finally, we turn to three types of utterance involving future time:
WARNINGS

Mind (your head)!
Look out!
Be careful (of your clothes).
I warn you it's going to be foggy.
If you're not careful, that pan will catch fire.

Short warnings are often spoken with a fall-rise intonation: Mi̬nd!
PROMISES

I'll let you know tomorrow.
I promise (you) I'll be quick.
You won't lose money, I promise (you).
You shall have the money tomorrow. (On *shall* here, *see* 340 Note)
Assuming that the order reaches our office by tomorrow, our firm will undertake to let you have the goods by the week-end. ⟨formal⟩

THREATS

I'll report you if you do that.
Don't you da̖re tell lies.
You da̖re touch me!
Do that, and I'll tell your mother (*see* 381).
Stop eating those sweets, or I'll take them away (*see* 382).

Warnings, promises and threats in reported speech
356
REPORTED WARNINGS

He warned us to be careful.

They warned us of/about the strike.

We were warned that the journey might be dangerous.

REPORTED PROMISES

He promised/undertook to let me know.

He promised that he wouldn't lose money.

They promised him that he would not lose his job.

Her boss ⟨familiar⟩ has promised her a rise.

She has been promised a rise.

THREATS

He threatened to report me to the police.

He threatened that they would lose their jobs.

He threatened them with dismissal.

Friendly communications

357

Let us now look at some of the simple acts of communication whereby people establish and maintain friendly relations with one another. Common intonations are given where they are important (*see* 31–43).

Beginning and ending conversation
358

GREETINGS

Good morning/afternoon/evening. ⟨polite⟩

Hello.

Hi. ⟨very familiar⟩

Hello (with a rising tone) is also used in answering the phone.

FAREWELLS (temporary)

'Goodbye; Cheers. ⟨very familiar, BrE⟩   Cheerio. ⟨familiar BrE⟩

('Bye)-bye. ⟨very familiar⟩   So long. ⟨very familiar⟩

See you. ⟨very familiar⟩   See you later. ⟨very familiar⟩

See you at six o'clock. ⟨familiar⟩   See you tomorrow. ⟨familiar⟩

'Good-night (final word before parting for the night or before going
     to bed).

FAREWELLS (more permanent): 'Goodbye.

Other remarks may be added for politeness:

It's been nice knowing you.   (I hope you) have a good
                                                      journey.

INTRODUCTIONS

May I introduce (you to) Miss Brown? ⟨formal⟩

This is John Smith.

Meet my wife. ⟨familiar⟩

I don't think you've met our neighbour, Mr Quirk.

GREETINGS ON INTRODUCTION

How do you do? ⟨formal⟩ How are you?

Glad to meet you.   Hello ⟨informal⟩.

359

After a greeting, a conversation may continue with a polite inquiry about health, *etc*:

How are you?

How are you getting on? ⟨familiar⟩

How's things? ⟨very familiar⟩

Common replies to such questions are:

(I'm) fine. How are you?

Very well, thank you. And you?

If someone is liable to poor health, you might begin: *How are you feeling today/ these days?* or *I hope you're well.*

Especially in Britain, opening remarks about the weather are common:

(A)   (It's a) lovely day, isn't it? (*see* 250)

(B)   Yes, isn't it beautiful. (*see* 319)

(A)   What miserable weather! (*see* 310)

(B)   Dreadful!

Beginning and ending letters
360
Example of a ⟨formal⟩ official letter

Dear Sir,/Dear Madam,

With reference to your letter of...

....

Yours faithfully,

A R Smith

(Manager)

Example of a ⟨less formal⟩ letter

Dear Dr Smith,/Miss Brown,/George,

Thank you for your letter of..

....

(With best wishes)

⎰ Yours sincerely, ⟨BrE⟩
⎱ Sincerely (yours), ⟨AmE⟩

James Robertson

Example of an ⟨informal⟩ letter between acquaintances

Dear George,

....

(Best wishes)

Yours (ever),

Janet

More intimate letters may begin and end with endearments: *My dear George,*
Dearest George, . . . Love from Janet, etc.

Thanks, apologies, regrets
361
THANKS

Thank you;   Thanks very much.

Many thanks.   Ta. ⟨BrE slang⟩

RESPONSES TO THANKS

Not at all.   You're welcome.

That's all right.

Note that in English such responses are not so common as in some other languages. Often the 'giver' makes no reply. In shops *etc* the customer will say
Thank you for the article he has bought, and the shopkeeper will often likewise
say *Thank you* in return, on receiving the money.

APOLOGIES

(I'm) sorry.   (I beg your) pardon.   Excuse me.

Excuse me in ⟨BrE⟩ is limited to mild apologies for routine impolite behaviour;
eg, for interrupting, for sneezing, for pushing in front of somebody. One would
say *I beg your pardon* for mishaps such as treading on someone's toe. More
lengthy apologies are:

I'm extremely sorry ⟨ (about that letter).
                    ⟨ (for forgetting to send that letter).

⟨ Will you forgive/excuse me if I have to leave early?
⟨ I hope you will forgive/excuse me if I have to leave early.

RESPONSES TO APOLOGIES

'That's all right.   'Please don't worry.

REGRETS

I'm sorry I was unable to come to the meeting. ⟨informal⟩
I regret that I was unable . . . ⟨formal, written⟩

Good wishes, congratulations, condolences
362
(These are normally spoken with a falling tone.)
GOOD WISHES

Good luck!
Best wishes for your vacation ⟨AmE⟩/holiday. ⟨BrE⟩

Have a good time at the theatre.

I wish you every success in your new career. ⟨more formal⟩

GOOD WISHES SENT TO A THIRD PERSON

Please give my best wishes to Sally.

Please remember me to your father.

Please give my kindest regards to your wife. ⟨formal⟩

Give my love to the children. ⟨informal⟩

Say hello to Joe. ⟨AmE⟩

SEASONAL GREETINGS

Merry Christmas.	Happy New Year.
Happy birthday (to you).	Many happy returns (of your birthday).

TOASTS

Good health. ⟨formal⟩	Your health. ⟨formal⟩
Cheers! ⟨familiar⟩	Here's to your job. ⟨familiar⟩
Here's to the future. ⟨familiar⟩	

CONGRATULATIONS

Well done! ⟨familiar⟩ (for a success or achievement).

Congratulations on your engagement.

I was delighted to hear about . . . / that . . . .

May we congratulate you on your recent appointment. ⟨formal⟩

CONDOLENCES

Please accept my deepest sympathy on the death of your father.
⟨formal⟩

I was extremely sorry to hear about . . . / that . . . ⟨informal⟩

Offers
363

In making an offer, you can make use of questions about the wishes of the hearer
(*see* 334–7):

Would you like another helping of túrkey?   [1]

Would you like me to mail these lètters?   [2]

Shall I get you a cháir?   [3]

Can I open the dóor for you?   [4]

In accepting an offer in the form of a question, we say

eiiher   Yès, pléase.   (acceptance)

or   Nò, thànk you.   (refusal)

More ⟨polite⟩ acceptances:

Yès, pléase. That's very kìnd of you.

Yès, thànk you, I'd lòve some more.

(Note that *thank you* can be used in accepting, as well as refusing.)

More ⟨polite⟩ refusals include an explanation of the refusal:

That's very kind of you, but I couldn't possibly manage any more.

No, thank you very much. I'm just leaving. [answer to 3]

No, please don't bother. I can manage, thank you. [answer to 4]

In ⟨familiar⟩ English, commands are often used in making offers:

Have some more coffee.

Do sit down.

Let me get a chair for you.

After the offer has been accepted, the other person need not say anything when he/she performs the service. Quite often people just smile, or say *Here you are* (*eg* on bringing some food), or *There you are* (*eg* on opening a window, bringing a chair, *etc*).

Vocatives

364

To get someone's attention, you can use a vocative such as *John, Mrs Johnson, Dr Smith*:

John, I want you.

Have you got a minute, Mr Johnson?

Dr Smith, have you seen this report?

Vocatives can be used more generally to mark the speaker's relation to the hearer. *Sir* and *madam* are vocatives which mark respect to a stranger:

Did you order a taxi, madam? ⟨formal⟩

(After a rising tone, the intonation continues to rise through the vocative.) Other titles of respect, and some professional titles, can be used as vocatives: *Ladies and gentlemen!* (⟨formal⟩ opening of a speech); *My Lord* (to a peer, a bishop, a British judge, *etc*); *Your Honor* (to an American judge); *Your Excellency* (to an ambassador); *Mr President*; *Prime Minister*; *Father* (to a priest); *Doctor* (to a medical doctor); *etc*.

In contrast, the following are some of the many examples of the ⟨familiar⟩ use of vocatives: *dad(dy)*; *old man*; *you guys* ⟨familiar AmE⟩; *my dear*; *darling*.

365

English is restricted in forms of address to strangers. *Sir* and (especially) *madam* are too ⟨formal⟩ to be used in most situations. *Miss* as a vocative is by many considered ⟨impolite⟩. Some people even feel that occupational vocatives like *waiter* or *driver* are ⟨rather impolite⟩, although others, like *nurse* (= 'nursing sister') or *operator* (telephone) are acceptable:

Operator, could you put through a call to Copenhagen, please?

Thus to get the attention of a stranger, you may often have to rely on *Excuse me!* or (in ⟨AmE⟩) *I beg your pardon!*

Section D: Meanings in connected discourse

366

In Sections A, B and C we have been considering aspects of meaning in isolation, but in this final section we shall be thinking about how meanings may be put together and presented in a spoken or written discourse. That is, we shall be discussing style and presentation of ideas. We start with the organisation of connections within and between sentences.

Linking signals

367

Whether in speech or in writing, you help people to understand your message by signalling how one idea leads on from another. The words and phrases which have this connecting function are like 'signposts' on a journey. Most of them in English are sentence adverbials, and they generally come at the beginning of a sentence. Their most important functions are as follows.

Making a new start
368

Well and *now*, placed at the front of a sentence in ⟨speech⟩, signal a new start in the train of thought:

(A)   You remember that puppy we found?

(B)   Yes.

(A)   Well, we adopted it, and now it has some puppies of its own.

Well here means roughly 'I am now going to tell you something new'. It is particularly common when a person is asked for an opinion:

(A)   What do you think of the oil crisis?

(B)   Well, I don't think it's quite as serious as it seems.

Now often signals a return to an earlier train of thought:

> Well, that's settled at last. Now, what was the other thing we
> wanted to discuss?

Changing the subject
369

Incidentally or *by the way* ⟨informal⟩ can be used to change the subject:

> The airlines charge half-price for students. $\left\{\begin{array}{l}\text{By the way,}\\\text{Incidentally,}\end{array}\right\}$ have you
> bought your ticket for New York yet?

Listing and adding
370

In ⟨writing⟩ and ⟨formal speech⟩ you can list a series of points by such adverbs as *firstly* (or *first*), *second(ly)*, *next*, *last(ly)* (or *finally*). Phrases such as *to begin with, in the second place,* and *to conclude* can also be used. Similar to these adverbials are *also, moreover, furthermore, what is more, etc* which indicate that an additional point is being made (*see* 238):

> Several reasons can be given for the change in the attitude of many students. *To begin with,* they fear the outbreak of nuclear war. *Secondly,* they are concerned over the continuing pollution of the environment. Not enough progress, *moreover,* has been made in reducing poverty or racial strife ... And *to conclude,* they feel frustrated in their attempts to influence political decisions.

Reinforcement
371
Besides, in any case ⟨informal⟩ and *anyway* ⟨informal⟩ are other sentence adverbials indicating an additional point in an argument, but with a slightly different meaning. They are used to reinforce an argument in a situation where a preceding argument might not seem sufficient:

> I won't be coming to the football game this afternoon. I have some work to do in the garden. *Besides,* if they play as badly this time as they did last week, it won't be worth watching.

Furthermore ⟨more formal⟩ and *what is more* can be used in a similar way.

Summary and generalisation
372
To lead into a summary of points already made, you can write *in a word, in short,* or *to sum up.* The following passage from a book review illustrates their use:

> The techniques discussed are valuable. Sensible stress is laid on preparatory and follow-up work. Each chapter is supported by a well-selected bibliography. *In short,* this is a clearly-written text-book that should prove extremely valuable to teachers.

Other linking phrases serve to indicate a generalisation from points already made: *in all, altogether, more generally, etc.* These are used in a similar way to the summary signals. Thus *in all* could replace *in short* in the quotation above.

Explanation
373
A point already made can be explained in three ways:
(A) by expanding and clarifying its meaning: *that is, that is to say, ie*
(B) by giving a more precise description: *namely, viz*
(C) by giving an illustration: *for example, for instance, eg*

(The Latin abbreviations *ie, viz* and *eg* are mainly found in ⟨formal written⟩ texts. They are normally read aloud as 'that is', 'namely', and 'for example', respectively.)

> It is important that young children should see things, and not merely read about them. *For example,* it is valuable experience to take them on a trip to a farm.

These forms can also link two structures in apposition (*see* 489–91) in the middle of a sentence:

> At least one person, *namely* the President himself, supports the proposal for disarmament.

Reformulation
374
Sometimes, to make our ideas clearer, we explain or modify them by putting them in other words. Such reformulations can be introduced by adverbials like *in other words, rather, better*;

> They are enjoying themselves, or rather, they appear to be (enjoying themselves).

> He admits that he took the book without permission. In other words, he stole it.

Linking constructions

375
We can think of a clause—the unit which may contain a statement—as the basic unit of meaning in a discourse. Grammar provides three main ways of putting such units together:

(A) COORDINATION: You can coordinate them by the conjunctions *and, or, but, both . . . and, etc* (*see* 542, 547).

(B) SUBORDINATION: You can subordinate one clause to another (*ie* make it into a subclause, *see* 826–34), using such conjunctions as *when, if,* and *because.*

(C) ADVERBIAL LINK: You can connect the two ideas by using a linking sentence adverbial (*see* 479), such as *yet, moreover,* and *meanwhile.*

Contrast
376
The three methods (coordination, subordination, and adverbial link) are illustrated below for the relation of CONTRAST (*see* 212–14):

(A) He was extremely tired, *but* the noise kept him awake.

(B) { *(Al)though* he was very tired, the noise kept him awake until after midnight.
{ The noise kept him awake, *(al)though* he was very tired.

(C) He had travelled many miles, and was extremely tired. *However,* because of the noise he was unable to go to sleep until the early hours of the morning. ⟨more formal⟩

For a stronger and more emphatic connection, you can combine a sentence adverbial with coordination or subordination:

(A)+(C) He was extremely tired, *but* he was *nevertheless* unable to sleep until after midnight.

(B)+(C)   *Although* he was suffering from fatigue as a result of the
            long journey, *yet* because of the noise, he lay awake in his
            bed, thinking over the events of the day until the early
            hours of the morning. ⟨formal, rather rhetorical⟩

Choice between coordination, subordination and linking adverbial
377
(A)   Coordination is often a 'looser' connection than the others, because
      it is more vague (*see* 386) and less emphatic. It is more character-
      istic of ⟨speech⟩ than of ⟨writing⟩.
(B)   Subordination tends to give a clause a less important part in the
      information given by a sentence. Thus an adverbial subordinate
      clause is often used when the information in the clause is already
      wholly or partly known or expected by the hearer (*see* 420):

      John went fishing in the afternoon. *When he returned*, the
      dinner was on the table.
(C)   An adverbial link is often used to connect longer stretches of
      language, perhaps whole sentences which themselves contain co-
      ordinate or subordinate clauses.

Other relations of meaning
378
We now give, for illustration, some other examples of relations of meaning to
show how English offers a choice between coordination, subordination, and
adverbial links. In the case of coordination (and sometimes of subordination),
we place an adverbial in brackets where it can be added to make the relation
more specific. Most of the types of meaning relation illustrated have been dis-
cussed in Section A, and so no further explanation is needed at this point.
379
Time-when (*see* 140–50)
(A)   He loaded the pistol carefully, and (*then*) took aim.
(B)   *After* loading the pistol carefully, he aimed it at the marshal.
(C)   He drew the pistol from his holster, and loaded it carefully. *Then* he
      aimed it at the unsuspecting figure of the marshal.
380
Cause, reason, result (*see* 197–207)
(A)   He ran out of money, and (*therefore*) had to look for a job.
(B)   { *Because* he had run out of money, he had to look for a job.
      { He ran out of money, *so* (*that*) he had to look for a job.
(C)   After six months abroad, he ran out of money. He *therefore* had to
      look for a job.

381
Positive condition (*see* 208–9)
The conjunction *and* can indicate condition, but only in limited contexts such as
commanding, advising, *etc*:
(A)   Take this medicine, and (*then*) you'll feel better. ⟨informal⟩

(B) *If* you take this medicine, you'll feel better.

(C) You ought to take your medicine regularly, as the doctor ordered. You'll feel better, *then*. 〈informal〉

Then here has roughly the meaning 'on that condition', or 'in that event'.

382

Negative condition (*see* 210)

Or can be used to indicate negative condition in limited contexts:

(A) You'd better put your overcoat on, or (*else*) you'll catch a cold. 〈informal〉

(B) *Unless* you put on your overcoat, you'll catch a cold.

(C) I should wear an overcoat if I were you; *otherwise*, you'll catch a cold.

383

Condition + contrast (*see* 215–6)

Coordination alone cannot indicate this meaning:

(B) *However* much advice we give him, he (*still*) does exactly what he wants.

(C) It doesn't matter how much advice we give him: he *still* does exactly what he wants.

384

Addition (*see* 238)

(A) { She's (*both*) a professional artist *and* a first-rate teacher (*see* 547).
       { She's *not only* a professional artist, *but* (*also*) a first-rate teacher.

(B) *As well as* (being) a professional artist, she's (*also*) a first-rate teacher.

(C) She's well known all over the country as a professional artist. Incidentally, she's *also* a first-rate teacher.

385

Alternatives

This meaning cannot be indicated by subordination:

(A) We can (*either*) meet this afternoon, *or* we can discuss the matter at dinner (*see* 547).

(C) Would you like us to have a meeting about the matter this afternoon? *Alternatively* we could discuss it at dinner.

Other adverbs: *otherwise*, (*or*) *else*. 〈informal〉

'General purpose' links

386

As you can see from 379–81, 384, *and* is a 'general purpose' linking word, which can adapt its meaning according to context. Any positive link between two ideas can be expressed by *and*. English has three other methods of vague or 'general purpose' connection of this kind. They are: (A) RELATIVE CLAUSES (*see* 783–96), (B) PARTICIPLE AND VERBLESS CLAUSES (*see* 515–16) and (C) grammatically UN-LINKED CLAUSES.

Relative clauses

387

Notice the equivalence between a coordinate clause with *and*, and a non-restrictive relative clause (*see* 100, 795):

$=\begin{cases}\text{We have arrived at the hotel, and find it very comfortable.}\\ \text{We have arrived at the hotel, } \textit{which we find very comfortable.}\end{cases}$

The same equivalence is seen in sentence relative clauses (*see* 796), in which the relative pronoun points back to a whole clause or sentence:

$=\begin{cases}\text{He's spending too much time on girls, and that's not good for his}\\ \quad\text{school work.}\\ \text{He's spending too much time on girls, } \textit{which is not good for his}\\ \quad \textit{school work.}\end{cases}$

Restrictive clauses also have a flexible connecting function; in the sentences below, the implied links are reason, time-when, and condition:

REASON

> I don't like people *who drive fast cars.*
>
> ('Because they drive fast cars, I don't like them')

TIME-WHEN

> The man *I saw* was wearing a hat.
>
> ('*When* I saw him, he was wearing a hat')

CONDITION

> Anyone *who bets on horses* deserves to lose money.
>
> ('If anyone bets on horses, he deserves to lose money')

Participle and verbless clauses

388

These clauses (*see* 515–16), characteristic of ⟨formal written⟩ English, also have a broad 'general purpose' linking function, as these examples show:

REASON

> *Being a farmer*, he has to get up early.
>
> ('As he is a farmer . . . ')

TIME-WHEN

> *Cleared*, the site will be very valuable.
>
> ('When it is cleared . . . ')

CONDITION

> *Cleared*, the site would be very valuable.
>
> ('If it were cleared . . . ')

MEANS

> *Using a sharp axe*, he broke down the door.
>
> ('By using a sharp axe . . . ')

REASON

> He stared at the floor, *too nervous to reply.*
>
> (' . . . because he was too nervous . . . ')

Unlinked clauses
389

Two neighbouring clauses may be grammatically unlinked; for example, they may be separated in writing by a period (.) or a semi-colon (;) or a colon (:). But this does not mean there is no connection of meaning between them; it means, rather, that the connection is implicit, and has to be inferred by the reader.

In ⟨informal speech⟩, a speaker frequently relies on such implied connections, whereas in ⟨writing⟩, he would make the connection clear by sentence adverbials or coordination. These examples may be compared with the (C) sentences of 379–81 (the 'missing link' is indicated in [square brackets]):

> He loaded the pistol carefully; [then] he took aim . . . a shot rang
> out.   (TIME)
> He had to look for a job—[because] he had run out of money.
>   (REASON)
> Take this medicine: [if you do,] it'll make you feel better.
>   (CONDITION)

Substitution and omission

390

Clauses are often connected not only because of a meaning-link of the kinds we have considered, but because they SHARE some content, *eg* they may be talking about the same person:

> *My brother* was wearing a raincoat. *My brother* didn't get wet.

We can, if we like, link these two sentences into one sentence without changing them: *My brother was wearing a raincoat and my brother didn't get wet.* But generally, we avoid repeating the shared words and content (1) by SUBSTITUTING a pronoun (or other substitute form) such as *he*; (2) by OMITTING the repeated element(s):

> { My brother was wearing a raincoat, and (he) didn't get wet.
> { My brother, who was wearing a raincoat, didn't get wet.

Obviously, substitution and omission are very useful and important, in that (A) they shorten the message, and (B) they can make the connections of meaning more easy to grasp. We may say that they make the structure of the sentence 'tighter'. The general rule is: substitute and omit wherever you can, except where this leads to ambiguity. We shall now consider some of the ways in which the English language allows you to do these things. We shall consider substitution and omission together, and see how the repetition of various grammatical units can be avoided by these methods. Sometimes one method is available, sometimes the other, and sometimes both.

Substitutes for noun phrases
3rd person pronouns
391

The personal pronouns *he, she, it, they, etc* (*see* 683–7) substitute for noun phrases, and agree with them in number and gender (*see* 569, 654–9). In these examples, the noun phrase and its substitute are in *italics*:

Elizabeth has cut *her* finger. ('Elizabeth's finger')

The *electrician* is here. Shall I ask *him* in?

Could you mend *this table*? I broke *it* yesterday.

$\begin{cases} John\ and\ Mary \\ The\ children\ next\ door \end{cases}$ stole a toy from my son. *Their* mother told

them to return the toy, but *they* said it was *theirs*.

Notice that in the last sentence the plural pronouns *they*, *them*, *etc* substitute not only for plural noun phrases, but for coordinated singular noun phrases such as *John and Mary*.

Reflexive pronouns (*himself, themselves, etc*) and relative pronouns (*who, which, etc*) behave in the same way (*see* 691–4, 785–95):

He hurt *himself*. / She hurt *herself*. / They hurt *themselves*.

The man *who* was injured. / The house *that* was destroyed.

1st and 2nd person pronouns

392

Occasionally, 1st and 2nd person pronouns substitute for coordinate noun phrases. If a 1st person pronoun is present in the noun phrase, agreement is with the 1st person:

You and I ought to share *our* ideas.

My wife and I are going to Argentina. *We* hope to stay with some friends.

If a 2nd person pronoun is present without a 1st person pronoun, agreement is with the 2nd person pronoun:

You and John can stop work now. *You* can both eat your lunch in the kitchen.

Special cases

393

(1) QUANTIFIERS (*see* 765–76). Sometimes a plural pronoun substitutes for quantifier pronouns like *everybody, somebody, no one*, and *anyone*:

$= \begin{cases} \text{Everybody looked after } \textit{themselves.} \\ \text{Everybody looked after } \textit{himself.} \end{cases}$ ⟨more formal⟩: (*see* 540)

(2) GROUP NOUNS. For substitution, a singular noun referring to a group of people is treated either as a singular inanimate noun (when we are thinking of the group as a unit), or as a plural human noun (when we are thinking of the members of the group):

a family *who* quarrel among *themselves*

but: a family *which* traces *its* history from the Norman Conquest (*see* 537).

Quantifier pronouns

394

Other pronouns such as *one, some, each, none* (*see* 765–76) can act as substitutes for a noun phrase. As the examples show, we could alternatively treat most of these cases as omissions of some part of the phrase:

SUBSTITUTION FOR SINGULAR COUNT NOUN PHRASES

Have you seen *my cigarettes*? I want to smoke *one*. (*ie* 'smoke a cigarette')

SUBSTITUTION FOR PLURAL COUNT NOUN PHRASES

Can you give me *a few nails?* I need *some.* (*ie* 'some nails')

When *the children* entered, *each* was given a small present. (*ie* 'each of the children', 'each child')

We lost *most of the games,* but not quite *all.* ('all of them')

Proust and James are great novelists, but I like Tolstoy better than *either.*

Proust and James are great novelists, but *neither* is easy to read.

These books are heavy. You carry one *half,* and I'll carry the *other.* (*ie* 'You carry half of them, and I'll carry the other half of them')

John and I went looking for *mushrooms.* He found *a few,* I found *several* more, and we soon had *enough* for breakfast.

SUBSTITUTION FOR MASS NOUN PHRASES

Some of the equipment has been damaged, but *none* has been lost.

I'd like *some paper,* if you have *any.*

Substitutes for nouns and parts of noun phrases
395

The pronoun *one* can substitute for a noun, as well as for a whole noun phrase:

Have you seen any *knives?* I need a sharp *one.* ('a sharp knife')

I like this *coat* better than *the one* (= 'the coat') you showed me before.

The plural of *one* in this sense is *ones:*

I can get you several sharp *ones,* but this is the best *one* I have.

Notice that *one* cannot replace mass nouns; instead, they are omitted: *Which wine would you like? The red or the white?* ('the red wine or the white wine?') Both count and mass nouns can be omitted, but count nouns cannot be omitted after the indefinite article *a(n).* The choice between *one* and omission is shown in these examples:

COUNT SINGULAR   { I'd prefer the large bottle to the small (one).
                  { I'd prefer a large bottle to a small one.

                      (*not* * ... to a small)

COUNT PLURAL   { I'd prefer the large bottles to the small (ones).
                 { I'd prefer large bottles to small (ones).

MASS   I'd prefer (the) red wine to (the) white.

396

Other examples of the choice between *one* and omission:

This house is bigger than my last (one).

I broke the coffee-pot, so we have to buy another (one).

The first runner finished a few yards in front of the next (one).

I know her two older children, but I don't know the youngest (one).

397

With postmodifiers, the pronouns *that* and *those* can act as substitutes with definite meaning (= 'the one', 'the ones'). *That* always has non-personal reference:

Towards the end of his life, Schubert wrote two remarkable trios:

that (= 'the one') in B flat, and *that* in E flat. ⟨rather formal⟩

The paintings of Gauguin's Tahiti period are more famous than
those (= 'the ones') he painted in France.

That can also be used as a substitute with a mass noun:

The plumage of the male pheasant is far more colourful than *that*
(= 'the plumage') of the female.

These uses of *that* and *those* are rather ⟨formal⟩, and are largely restricted to
⟨written⟩ English. The relative pronoun *which* cannot normally be omitted
after *that*:

The problem confronting us today is not dissimilar from *that which*
Britain faced in the 1930s. (*Compare*: '... the one Britain faced
in the 1930s.')

Substitutes for structures containing a verb

THE AUXILIARY VERB *do*

398

The dummy auxiliary verb *do* (or its negative forms) can act as a substitute for the
whole of a clause apart from the subject:

He can *cook* as well as she *does*. ('as she cooks')

(A)   *Who wants to play tennis this afternoon?*   (B) $\begin{cases} \text{I } do. \\ \text{I } don't. \end{cases}$

You can also omit the whole clause following the subject:

He can *cook* as well as $\begin{array}{l}\text{she} \langle\text{formal}\rangle \\ \text{her} \langle\text{informal}\rangle\end{array}$

(A)   Who wants to play tennis?   (B) $\begin{cases} \text{Me.} \\ \text{Not me.} \end{cases}$ $\begin{array}{l}\langle\text{in-} \\ \text{formal}\rangle\end{array}$

Notice that in ⟨informal⟩ English, the pronoun subject is changed to its objective form (*me*, *etc*) when the rest of the sentence is omitted.

   Do can also substitute for the part of a clause excluding subject and adverbials:

(A)   *Have* you *written to your father* yet?

(B)   Yes, I *did* last week. ('I wrote to my father ... ')

Occasionally *do* acts as a substitute for a verb phrase alone:

She plays the piano better than he *does* the guitar. ('plays')

399

In all such cases, you can use other auxiliaries in a parallel position to *do;* that is,
you can omit the whole or part of the sentence following an auxiliary:

I'll *open a bank account* if you *will* (= '... if you will do so').

He *can cook* as well as she *can*.

(A)   He *is working* late this week.   (B)   Yes, he *was* last week, too.

   You *can play* in the garden, but you *mustn't* in the garage.

Do and the other auxiliaries are unstressed, except in cases of affirmation and
denial (*see* 272–3), or where they have some sort of contrastive meaning:

(A)   Are you going to clean the car?

(B)   I *could*, and I *ought* to, but I don't think I *will*.

The omission also occurs after two or three auxiliaries:

He was working harder than he *ought to have been.*

(A)   Is the kettle boiling?   (B)   It may be.

(A)   Did you lock the door?   (B)   No, I should have, but I forgot.

Note

[a]   *Be* as a main verb (*see* 500) cannot be omitted after an auxiliary:

If they're not asleep, they should be.

[b]   In ⟨BrE⟩, *do* or *done* is sometimes added after another auxiliary:

He can't promise to come tonight, but he may *do.*

(A)   Would you please unlock the door?   (B)   I have *done.*

THE MAIN VERB *do*

400

The main verb *do* (*see* 498) acts as a substitute for a main verb, normally a verb denoting some action or activity. Since this *do* is transitive, it requires an object, which may be one of the substitute words *it, that,* or *so:*

He *got her home,* but I don't know how he managed to *do it.*

('. . . managed to get her home')

They have promised *to increase pensions by 20 per cent.* If they *do so,* it will make a big difference to old people.

Do that is generally more emphatic and ⟨informal⟩:

They say he sleeps in his shoes and socks. Why ever does he *do that*?

Do it and *do so* cannot always replace one another. Notice the difference between:

Bob's getting *his house painted,* and moreover, he wants me to *do it.*

('He wants me to paint his house')

Bob's *getting his house painted,* and moreover, he wants me to *do so.*

('He wants me to get *my* house painted')

Note

There is a similar use of *do* in *wh-*questions and in *wh-*subclauses:

(A)   What is he *doing*?   (B)   He's painting.

What he *did* was lose the game.

Substitutes for *that*-clauses

401

So is a substitute for *that*-clauses representing reported statements, beliefs, assumptions, emotions, *etc:*

Oxford will win the next boat race. All my friends say *so.*

('. . . say that Oxford will win the next boat race')

John hasn't found a job yet. He told me *so* yesterday.

('. . . that he hasn't found a job yet')

(A)   Are the Browns coming to dinner?

(B)   I think *so.*/I suppose *so.*/ I hope *so.*/I'm afraid *so.*

Not replaces *so* in negative clauses: *I hope not, I'm afraid not, etc.* But, with verbs taking transferred negation (*see* 636), it is more natural to say: *I don't think so;*

I don't suppose so; *etc.* In sentences expressing certainty and doubt (*see* 303–4) we cannot use *so*, but have to say: *I'm sure they are*; *I'm sure of it*; *I doubt if they are*; *I doubt it*; *etc.*

In comparative clauses, the whole of a *that*-clause can be omitted:

He's older than I thought ('. . . than I thought he was').

Also, after the verbs *know*, *ask*, and *tell*, a whole *that*-clause is frequently omitted in conversation:

(A)   She's having a baby.   (B)   I *know*.

(A)   How do you *know*?   (B)   She *told* me (so). Why do you *ask*?

So cannot be used after *know* and *ask*.

Substitutes for *wh*-clauses
402

The whole of a *wh*-clause following the *wh*-word can be omitted:

Someone has hidden my notebook, but I don't know *who/where/why*.

(='I don't know who has hidden my notebook', *etc*)

This cannot be done with *whether* and *if.*

Substitutes for *to*-infinitive clauses
403

With infinitive clauses, you can omit the whole of the clause following *to:*

(A)   Why don't you come and stay with us?

(B)   I'd love to (do so).

You can *borrow my pen*, if you wȧnt to (do so).

He *borrowed my pen*, although I told him nȯt to (do it).

Somebody ought to *help you*. Shall I ask Pėter to (do so)?

With some verbs, such as *want* and *ask*, the whole of the infinitive clause, including *to*, can be omitted in ⟨informal⟩ English:

You can borrow my pen, if you want.

Shall I ask Peter?

I*t*, that, this
404

The definite pronouns *it*, *that*, and *this*, are widely used as substitutes for clauses as well as for noun phrases (*see* 87–90, 391):

If *you don't take the examination*, you'll regret *it*.

('regret not taking the examination')

(A)   She's having a baby.   (B)   How do you know *thȧt*?

(*ie* '. . . know that she's having a baby'; *it* cannot replace *that* here.)

After many weeks of rain, *the dam burst*. *This* resulted in widespread flooding and much loss of livestock and property. ('The bursting of the dam resulted in . . . ')

In such cases, the pronoun replaces a *that*-clause (with factual meaning, *see* 283–90) or an *-ing* clause.

Other structures with omission
405
Other structures which allow us to shorten a sentence by omitting repeated matter are coordinated structures, non-finite clauses, and verbless clauses. All these structures will be discussed in Part Four, so here we merely give a few examples of the varied types of omission that occur in them, showing how these provide briefer alternatives to substitution and repetition.

Omission through coordination
406
(The elements which are or can be omitted in coordination are in *italics*.)
> Peter ate the food but left the drink.
>> (= 'Peter ate the food, but *he* left the drink.')
> We are flying to Madrid tonight, and to Athens next week.
>> (= 'Tonight we are flying to Madrid; next week *we are flying* to Athens.')
> Peter cut himself a slice of bread and some ham.
>> (= 'Peter cut himself a slice of bread; *he* (also) *cut himself* some ham.')
> Not only classical, but popular art is being seriously studied these days.
>> (= 'Classical art is being seriously studied these days; popular art *is*, (too).')
> Either West Germany or Holland will win the World Cup.
>> (= 'West Germany will win the World Cup; or (else) Holland *will do so*.')
> John washes and irons his own shirts.
>> (= 'John washes his own shirts; he irons *them*, (too).')

In general, the same omissions cannot be made when one of the clauses is subordinate to the others. *Compare*:
> He was exhausted and went to sleep.
> *but not*: *He was so exhausted that went to sleep.

But there are a few cases where subclauses follow the coordinate clause pattern:
> He ate the fruit, *though* not the nuts.

Omission in non-finite clauses
407
Non-finite clauses (*see* 515) have no operator, and most of them have no conjunction or subject. Thus in comparison with finite subclauses they are more economical and avoid repetition; *ing*-clauses and *-ed* clauses, probably for this reason, are particularly favoured in ⟨formal or written⟩ styles of English. We shall illustrate these points with equivalent finite clauses.

> *to*-INFINITIVE CLAUSE: I hope to be present.
>> (= 'I hope *that I shall* be present.')
> *-ing* CLAUSE: Living in the country, we had few social visits.
>> (= '*Since we* lived in the country, . . . ')

-ed CLAUSE: The man injured by the bullet was taken to hospital.
(= 'The man *who was* injured by the bullet . . . ')

408

The same applies to non-finite clauses introduced by a subordinator:

-ing CLAUSE: He wrote his greatest novel while working as an ordinary seaman.

(= ' . . . while *he was* working as an ordinary seaman')

-ed CLAUSE: Though defeated, he remained a popular leader.
(= 'Though *he had been* defeated . . . ')

Omission in verbless clauses
409

Verbless clauses (*see* 516) have no verb and usually no subject:

Whether right or wrong, he usually wins the argument.

(= 'Whether *he is* right or wrong . . . ')

A man of few words, Uncle George declined to express an opinion.

(= '*Being* a man of few words /*As he was* a man of few words . . . ')

Verbless clauses, like participial clauses, often belong to a more ⟨formal⟩ style.

Note

Not all subordinators can introduce participial and verbless clauses. For example, *because*, *as*, and *since* (as conjunctions of reason) cannot. Notice the difference, in this connection, between *since* denoting time and *since* denoting reason:

TIME

Since he left school, ⎫
Since leaving school, ⎭ he's had several different jobs.

REASON

Since you know the answer, ⎫
*Since knowing the answer, ⎭ why didn't you speak up?

Presenting and focusing information

410

We now deal with the various ways in which meanings can be presented and arranged for effective communication. For a message to be properly understood,

a   the message has to be cut up into individual pieces of information (*see* 411–13)

b   the ideas have to be given the right emphasis (*see* 414–24)

c   the ideas have to be put in the right order (*see* 425–49)

Pieces of information
411

In ⟨written⟩ English, a PIECE OF INFORMATION can be defined as a piece of language which is separated from what goes before and from what follows by punctuation marks (. , ; : — ? !), and which does not itself contain any punctuation marks. In ⟨spoken⟩ English, a piece of information can be defined as a tone unit (*see* 36), *ie* a unit of intonation containing a nucleus. Notice the difference, in ⟨written⟩ English, between:

Peter has a charming wife and two children.   [1]

Peter has a charming wife; he also has two children.   [2]

In a sense, as we show in 375–85, [1] and [2] 'mean the same', but [1] presents the message as ONE piece of information, while [2] presents it as TWO pieces of information, separated by a punctuation mark (;). In ⟨speech⟩, the same contrast is seen in:

|Peter has a charming wife and two children|

(ONE TONE UNIT) [1a]

|Peter has a charming wife | he also has two children|

(TWO TONE UNITS) [2a]

Dividing the message into tone units
412
There is no exact match between punctuation in ⟨writing⟩ and tone units in ⟨speech⟩. Speech is more variable in its structuring of information than writing. Cutting up speech into tone units depends on such things as the speed at which you are speaking, what emphasis you want to give to parts of the message, and the length of grammatical units. A single sentence may have just one tone unit, like [1a]; but when the length of a sentence goes beyond a certain point (say roughly ten words), it is difficult not to split it into two or more separate pieces of information:

|The man told us we could park it here.|

|The man told us | we could park it at the railway station.|

|The man told us | we could park it | in the street over there.|

413
For guidance, the following general rules are useful:
(A) Use a single tone unit for each sentence, except in the circumstances (B)–(G) below.
(B) If a sentence begins with a clause or adverbial phrase, give the clause or adverbial element a separate tone unit:

The year before last, | we spent two weeks in Wales.|

(This does not usually apply when the adverbial is a fronted topic, *see* 426–9.)
(C) If a sentence contains a non-restrictive postmodifier (*see* 100), *eg* a non-restrictive relative clause (*see* 795), give the postmodifier a separate tone unit:

|The blue whale | which is the world's largest animal | has

been hunted almost to extinction.|

(D)   Similarly, give any medial phrase or clause a separate tone unit:

|And thàt | in shórt | is why I refúsed.|

(E)   A vocative or linking adverb usually has its own tone unit (or at least ends a tone unit):

|Mǎry | are you cóming?|

|The polìce | howéver | thought he was guìlty.|

(F)   Give a separate tone unit to a clause or long noun phrase acting as subject:

|What we něed | is plenty of tìme.|

(G)   If two or more clauses are coordinated, give them each a separate tone unit:

|He opened the dóor | and walked straight ìn.|

End-focus and contrastive focus
414
The nucleus is the most important part of a tone unit: it marks the FOCUS OF INFORMATION, or the part of the unit to which the speaker especially draws the hearer's attention. Normally, the nucleus is at the end of the tone unit; or, to be more precise, on the last major-class word (noun, main verb, adjective, or adverb, *see* 884) in the tone unit. Which syllable of the word is stressed, if it has more than one syllable, is determined by ordinary conventions of word stress: to¹day, ¹working, ¹photograph, conver¹sation, *etc.* This neutral position of the nucleus, which you see in all the examples in 413, we call END-FOCUS.
Note
Constructions consisting of two or more nouns together often behave, for stress purposes, like a single word (*ie* like a noun compound), with the main stress on the first noun: ¹export records; ¹building plan; ¹traffic problem. (But contrast town ¹hall, country ¹house, lawn ¹tennis etc.)
415
But in other cases you may shift the nucleus to an earlier part of the tone unit. You may do this when you want to draw attention to an earlier part of the tone unit, usually to contrast it with something already mentioned, or understood in the context. For this reason, we call earlier placing of the nucleus CONTRASTIVE FOCUS. Here are some examples:

|Òne of the parcels has arríved.| (but the other one hasn't)   [3]

(Was Dylan Thomas married in Swansea?) |Nò, | but he was
   bòrn in Swánsea.| [4]

(I hear you're painting the kitchen blue.) |Nò, | I'm painting the
   children's bèdroom blue.| [5]

(Have you ever driven a sports car?) | Yès, | I've òften driven
   one.| [6]

In cases like [3] and [4], contrastive meaning is signalled by a fall-rise tone (*see* 37), with a fall on the nucleus and a rise on the last stressed syllable in the tone unit. In other sentences, there may be a double contrast, each contrast indicated by its own nucleus:

|Her f̬ather | is A̬ustrian, | but her m̬other | is French.|

416

Sometimes contrastive focus draws attention to a whole phrase (*eg the children's bedroom* in [5]); at other times, it is a single word that receives the focus (*eg often* in [6]). Even words like personal pronouns, prepositions, and auxiliaries, which are not normally stressed at all, can receive nuclear stress for special contrastive purposes:

(I've never been to Paris) | but I will go there | some dáy.| [7]

(A)   (What did John say to Mary?)

(B) |He was speaking to me| (not to Mary).   [8]

(I know she works with John) | but who does she work for?| [9]

(I don't know if you mean to see Peter,) | but if you see him |
    (please give him my good wishes).   [10]

In some cases, *eg* [8] and [9], contrastive focus comes later rather than earlier than normal end-focus. Thus the normal way to say *Who does he work for?* [9] would be with focus on the verb, not the preposition:

Who does he work for?

In exceptional cases, contrastive stress in a word of more than one syllable may shift to a syllable which does not normally have word stress. For example, if you want to make a contrast between the two words normally pronounced *bu'reau-cracy* and *au'tocracy* you may do so as follows:

|I'm afraid that b̬ureaucracy | can be worse than a̬utocracy.|

Given and new information

417

We can roughly divide the information in a message into GIVEN INFORMATION (something which the speaker assumes the hearer knows about already) and NEW INFORMATION (which the speaker does not assume the hearer knows about already). In [8] above, 'He was speaking' is given information: it is already given by the preceding clause; in [10], 'you see him' is given information for the same reason:

|He was speaking	to me|	|If	you see him ...	
GIVEN	NEW	NEW	GIVEN

As new information is obviously what is most important in a message, it receives the information focus (*ie* nucleus), whereas old information does not. Naturally, personal pronouns and other substitute words, because they refer to something already mentioned or understood, normally count as old information.

Note

Notice that given information and new information are what the speaker *presents* as given and new respectively. What *in fact* the hearer knows or assumes may be a different thing. For example, a speaker might say:

(Margaret likes Picasso,) |but Jane h̬ates modern painting.|

The position of the nucleus here means that the speaker assumes that the hearer knows that Picasso is a modern painter. But of course, the hearer might not have heard of Picasso, or might not regard him as a modern painter.

Information given by situation
418
'Given information' suggests information which has already been mentioned or alluded to. But we may extend this notion to include information which is 'given' by the situation outside language. In this respect 'old' information is like definite meaning and there is indeed a strong connection between old information and definiteness (*see* 69–90).

In the following examples, for which we give the most natural intonation, the definite items *today*, *here*, and *mine* in [11, 12, 13] do not have a nuclear stress because their meaning is given by the situation. In contrast, the items *Saturday*, *factory*, and *father's* in [11a, 12a, 13a] are most likely to be new information, and therefore receive nuclear stress:

|What are you doing today?| [11]

|What are you doing on Saturday?| [11a]

|I work here.| [12]

|I work in a factory.| [12a]

|Mr Smith is a friend of mine.| [13]

|Mr Smith is a friend of my father's.| [13a]

But the definite items *today etc*, could have nuclear stress if some contrast were implied:

(I know what you did yesterday,) |but what are you doing

today?| [11b]

(I used to work in a factory,) |but now I work here.| [12b]

419
In other examples, the information given by the situation outside language is more a matter of what is expected in a given context:

|The kettle's boiling.| |The doctor has called.|

|Is your father at home?| |Dinner's ready.|

In a natural context, the final part of each of these sentences conveys little information, and therefore does not receive the nucleus. In a home, the one thing to announce about kettles is that they are 'boiling'; and the one thing you expect the doctor to do is to 'call' *etc*. Therefore the nucleus occurs, contrary to end-focus, on the earlier and more informative part of the sentence.

Main and subsidiary information
420
Degrees of 'informativeness' are also relevant to the choice of tone (*see* 37–43) on the nucleus. We tend to use a falling tone to give emphasis to the main

information in a sentence, and a rising tone (or, with more emphasis, a fall-rise tone) to give subsidiary or less important information, *ie* information which is more predictable from the context. Subordinate clauses and adverbials often give information which is subsidiary to the idea in the rest of the main clause:

(A) |I saw your bròther | at the game yésterday.|

MAIN		SUBSIDIARY

(B) |Yĕs, | watching fŏotball | is his favourite pàstime.|

	SUBSIDIARY		MAIN	

Subsidiary information may either precede or follow the main information. Speaker (B) could also say here:

|Yès, | his favourite pàstime | is watching fòotball.|

	MAIN		SUBSIDIARY	

But if there had been no allusion to the subject of football, the speaker would normally put the main focus on *football:*

(A) |What does he like to do in his spare tìme?|

(B) |His main pastime is watching fòotball.|

or, on the pattern of the first example;

(B) |Watching fòotball| is his favourite pástime.|

Adverbials as main and subsidiary information
421
Adverbials following the main clause often have a rising tone to indicate subsidiary information added as an afterthought:

|It was snòwing | when we arríved.|

|She'll do ànything | if you ask her nícely.|

But a final adverbial clause can also occasionally contain the main information:

|She had just finished dréssing | when her gùests arrived.|

Shorter final adverbials are often included in the same tone unit as the rest of the clause, and may bear the main focus:

|She plays the piano bèautifully.|

Main and subsidiary information in writing
422
In ⟨writing⟩, you cannot point to important information by using intonation, so you have to rely on ordering and subordination of clauses instead. The general rule is that the most important information is saved up to the end, so that the sentence finishes with a sort of climax (here indicated by *italics*):

> Arguments in favour of a new building plan, said the mayor, included suggestions that if a new shopping centre were not built, the city's traffic problems *would soon become unmanageable.*

In reading this sentence aloud, it is natural to put a rising or fall-rise tone on all points of information except the last, which receives a falling tone.

| ... bŭilding plan | ... mᾴyor | ... suggéstions | ... bᵘilt | ...
traffic problems | ... unmanageable|

End-focus and end-weight
423

When you are deciding in which order to place the ideas in a sentence, there are two principles to remember:

(A) END-FOCUS (*see* 414): the new or most important idea in a piece of information should be placed towards the end, where in speech the nucleus of the tone unit normally falls. As we saw in 422, this principle may be extended to apply not just to a single piece of information, but to a whole sentence containing many pieces of information. This is because a sentence is generally more effective (especially in ⟨writing⟩) if the main point is saved up to the end.

(B) END-WEIGHT: The more 'weighty' part(s) of a sentence should be placed towards the end. Otherwise the sentence may sound awkward and un-balanced. The 'weight' of an element can be defined in terms of length (*eg* number of syllables) or in terms of grammatical complexity (number of modifiers, *etc*).

424

Both end-focus and end-weight are useful guiding principles, not invariable rules. As we have said, although end-focus is normal, you are allowed in speech to shift the nucleus to an earlier position in the tone unit, for CONTRASTIVE focus. Similarly, there are exceptions to end-weight:

My father owns *the largest betting-shop in London.*   [14]
The largest betting shop in London belongs to my father.   [15]

In [14], a long object phrase (*the largest betting-shop in London*) follows a short subject (*my father*) and a short verb (*owns*). This sentence keeps to the principle of end-weight. But in [15], the long noun phrase comes first. This sentence breaks the end-weight principle, and is less natural than [14]; but it could easily be said by someone wanting to place the focus of information on *father*. In such a case the two principles of end-weight and end-focus conflict. Generally, however, the two principles work together: it is usual for a short element in a sentence (*eg* a pronoun) to have less information than a longer element.

Order and emphasis

Topic
425

In the rest of this chapter, we shall show that English grammar has quite a number of sentence processes which help to arrange the message for the right order and the right emphasis. Because of the principles of end-focus and end-weight, the final position in a sentence or clause is, in neutral circumstances, the most important.

But the first position is also important for communication, because it is the starting-point for what the speaker wants to say: it is (so to speak) the part of the sentence which is familiar territory in which the hearer gets his bearings. Therefore we call the first element in a clause (leaving aside conjunctions and many adverbials, *see* 429 Note) the TOPIC. In most statements, the topic is the subject of the sentence. If the statement has only one tone unit, usually the topic does not receive focus, because it often contains old information, and links the statement in meaning to what was said before:

(Have you seen Bill?) | He   owes me   five dollars.|

|TOP- | INFORMATION|
| IC | FOCUS |

But sometimes topic and information focus coincide, and in this case, the topic is doubly prominent:

(Who gave you that magazine?) | Bill   gave it to me.|

|TOPIC |
| AND |
|FOCUS |

Fronted topic
426
Instead of the subject, you may make another element the topic, by moving it to the front of the sentence. This shift gives the element a kind of psychological prominence, and has three different effects:

(A)   EMPHATIC TOPIC
427

In ⟨informal⟩ conversation, it is quite common for a speaker to front an element (particularly a complement) and to give it nuclear stress, thus giving it double emphasis:

|Joe | his name is.| [1]⎫
|An utter fool I felt | too.| [2]⎬ (TOPIC = COMPLEMENT)
|Relaxation you call it.| [3]⎭

|Excellent food they serve here.| [4]   (TOPIC = OBJECT)

It is as if the speaker says the most important thing in his mind first, adding the rest of the sentence as an afterthought. The ordering of the elements here is CSV (in [1] and [2]), CSVO (in [3]), and OSVA (in [4]), instead of the normal order SVC, SVOC, SVO (*see* 506–8).

(B)   CONTRASTIVE TOPIC
428

Here the fronting helps to point dramatically to a contrast between two things mentioned in neighbouring sentences or clauses, which often have parallel structure:

|His face | I'm not fond of | (TOPIC = PREPOSITIONAL COMPLEMENT)

but his character | I despise.| (TOPIC = OBJECT)

|Bloggs | my name is| (TOPIC = COMPLEMENT)

so Bloggs | you might as well call me.|

|Willingly | he'll never do it| (TOPIC = ADVERBIAL)

(he'll have to be forced.)

|Rich | I may be| (TOPIC = COMPLEMENT)

(but that doesn't mean I'm happy.)

This construction is not very common, and is mainly confined to ⟨rhetorical⟩ speech.

(C)   'GIVEN' TOPIC

429

Another type of fronting is found in more ⟨formal⟩, especially ⟨written⟩ English:

> *Most of these problems* a computer   (TOPIC = OBJECT)
>   could solve easily.

> *This subject* we have examined in an   (TOPIC = OBJECT)
>   earlier chapter, and need not reconsider.

> *Everything that can be done* the adminis-   (TOPIC = PREPOSITIONAL
>   tration has attended to already.   OBJECT)

The fronting here is more negative: a less important idea is shifted to the front so that end-focus can fall on another, more important idea. The word *this* or *these* is often present in the fronted topic, showing that it contains given information. Nevertheless, the topic receives a kind of emphasis as the starting-point of the sentence.

Note

We shall not normally consider an initial adverbial to be a 'fronted topic', because most adverbials can occur fairly freely in front of the subject (*see* 470):

> *Yesterday* John was late for school.

But some adverbials which are closely connected with the verb, such as those of manner and direction, do not usually occur in front position. These may be said to be 'fronted' for special prominence in clauses like

> *Willingly* he'll never do it.
> *Into the smoke* we plunged.

Inversion

430

Fronting is often accompanied by INVERSION; that is, not only the topic element, but the verb phrase, or part of it, is moved before the subject. There are two types of inversion:

SUBJECT-VERB INVERSION

SUBJECT	VERB	X	...	→	X	VERB	SUBJECT	...
The rain	came	down	(in torrents).		Down	came	the rain	(in torrents).

SUBJECT-OPERATOR INVERSION

SUB-JECT	OPERATOR	X	...	→	X	OPERATOR	SUB-JECT	...
I	have	never	seen him so angry.		Never	have	I	seen him so angry.
I	—	never	saw him so angry.		Never	did	I	see him so angry.

431

Subject-verb inversion

Subject-verb inversion is normally limited as follows:

- *a* The verb phrase consists of a single verb word.
- *b* The verb is an intransitive verb of position (*be, stand, lie, etc*) or a verb of motion (*come, go, fall, etc*).
- *c* The topic element (x in the diagram above) is an adverbial of place or direction:

> Here's *the milkman.*
> Here *comes the bus.* ⟩ ⟨informal speech⟩
> There *are our friends.*

> There, at the summit, *stood the castle* in its medi-
>   eval splendour.
> Away *went the car* like a whirlwind. ⟩ more ⟨formal, literary⟩
> Slowly out of its hangar *rolled the gigantic air-*
>   *craft.*

The examples from ⟨informal speech⟩ give end-focus to the subject. In ⟨literary⟩ style, the fronted topic is more useful in giving end-weight to a long subject.

Subject-verb inversion does not take place with a fronted topic when the subject is a personal pronoun: *Here it is* (not **Here is it*); *Away they go!* (not **Away go they*).

Note

[a] The adverb *there* is stressed in the examples above; this stress distinguishes it from the introductory subject *there* (see 590–4).
Contrast:

> 'There are our friends.
>
> There are 'too many people here.

[b] The introductory subject *there* can bring about subject-verb inversion with some verbs:

> There rose in his imagination visions of a world
>   empire.
> There may come a time when we are less fortunate. ⟩ rather ⟨literary⟩
> On the following day, there was held a splendid
>   banquet.

But in a sense, *there* itself is the subject here, as we see from its inversion
with the operator in questions: *Will there come a time . . . ?*

[c] Occasionally subject-verb inversion occurs with a complement as topic
when the complement expresses a comparison:

> For a long time, he refused to talk to his wife, and kept her
> in ignorance of his troubles. *Equally strange was his be-
> haviour to his son.* ⟨literary⟩

432

Subject-operator inversion

The inversion of subject and operator is of course obligatory in most questions
(*see* 777–81); more relevant here is the obligatory subject-operator inversion
when a negative element is fronted for emphasis (especially in ⟨rhetorical⟩
style) (*see* 318):

Not a word *did he* say. (='He didn't say a word')

Under no circumstances *must the door* be left unlocked. ⟨formal⟩

Inversion is also obligatory after fronting of words of negative meaning such as
never, hardly, scarcely, few, little, seldom, rarely, (not) only (see 633–4):

Hardly *had I* left before the trouble started.

> (='I had hardly left before . . . ')

Only later *did they* realise what a terrible thing had happened.

> (='They didn't realise until later . . . ')

Little *does he* know how much suffering he has caused.

> (='He little knows . . . ')

Notice that the dummy operator *do* is used for the inversion with *be* where there
is no other operator in the normal-order sentence:

They realised only later . . . → Only later *did* they realise . . .

  In journalistic English, subject-operator inversion sometimes serves the
purpose of end-weight, where the subject is long and complex:

> Throwing the hammer here *is champion William Anderson, who,
> when he's not winning prizes, is a hard-working shepherd in the
> Highlands of Scotland.*

Note

Be as a main verb can count as an operator for subject-operator inversion:
Seldom is he sober. But it also counts as a verb for subject-verb inversion of the
kind discussed in 431: *Here is the milkman.*

Fronting with *so*
433

Notice the following constructions in which *so* is placed first:

(A) *So* as a substitute form with the meaning of 'addition' (*see* 238) has
subject-operator inversion (for end-focus) in sentences like:

(A) (I've seen the play.)   (B) |So have I.| (='and I have, too')

(I enjoyed the play) | and so did my friends.|

(B) But *so* as a pro-form does NOT have inversion when it is fronted to express emphatic affirmation:

(A) (You've spilled coffee   (B) |Oh dear, | so I have.|
    on your dress.)

(A)   (It's raining hard outside.)   (B) |So it is.|

The *so*-construction here expresses the hearer's surprise at discovering that what the speaker says is true. As with affirmation in general (*see* 272), the nucleus comes on the operator, not on the subject.

(C)   *So* introducing a clause of degree or amount (*see* 235) can be fronted for emphasis, with subject-operator inversion: *So absurd did he look that everyone stared at him* (= 'He looked so absurd that . . . ').

Other constructions affecting the topic

CLEFT SENTENCE (*it*-TYPE)

434

The cleft sentence construction with introductory *it* (*see* 518–19) is useful for fronting an element as topic, and also for putting focus (usually for contrast) on the topic element. It does this by splitting the sentence into two halves, 'highlighting' the topic by making it the complement of *it + be*:

(A)   (Would you like to borrow this book?)

(B) |No, | it's the other book | that I want to read.| [1]

(TOPIC = OBJECT; *cf* I want to read the other book.)

(For centuries London had been growing as a commercial port
of world importance.) But it was *in the north of England*
that industrial power brought new prosperity to the country.   [2]
(TOPIC = ADVERBIAL)

The constrastive meaning of the topic can be seen if we make clear the implied negative in [1] and [2]:

It's the other book, *not that book*, that I want to read.

But it was in the north of England, *not in London*, that . . .

The cleft sentence is particularly useful in ⟨written⟩ English, where we cannot mark contrastive emphasis by intonation.

CLEFT SENTENCE (*wh*-TYPE)

435

A nominal-relative clause (*see* 645–6), like an *it*-cleft sentence, can be used to highlight one element for contrast. It can be either subject or complement of the verb *be* (the subject position is more common):

NORMAL PATTERN	CLEFT SENTENCE	
	|It's more time	that we need.|	(*it*-type)
We need more time. →	|What we need is more time.|	(*wh*-type)
	|More time	is what we need.|	(*wh*-type)

The *wh*-type cleft sentence, like the *it*-type, usually implies a contrast; *eg*
We don't need more money—what we need is more time.

Comparison of *it*-type and *wh*-type cleft sentences
436

The *it*-type and the *wh*-type cleft sentences cannot always be used in the same circumstances. For example, the *it*-type is more flexible in certain ways:

a The focus of the *wh*-type sentence normally has to be in the form of a noun phrase or nominal clause. An adverbial clause or prepositional phrase can sometimes be the focus of the *wh*-type sentence, but it sounds less natural in this construction than in the *it*-type sentence:

> It was by train that we reached Istanbul.
> (*but not*: *How we reached Istanbul was by train.)
> It was in 1950 that he first achieved fame as a writer.
> (*better than*: When he first achieved fame as a writer was
>   in 1950.)
> It was on this very spot that I first met my wife.
> (*better than*: Where I first met my wife was on this very
>   spot.)

The *wh*-type sentence sounds somewhat better when the *wh*-clause comes last:

> On this very spot is where I first met my wife.

b But if an adverbial can be put in the form of a noun phrase, it can be the focus of a *wh*-type sentence with a final *when*- or *where*-clause:

> $=\begin{cases} \text{It is in autumn that the countryside is most beautiful.} \\ \text{Autumn is (the time) when the countryside is most beautiful.} \end{cases}$

> $=\begin{cases} \text{It was at Waterloo that Napoleon was finally defeated.} \\ \text{Waterloo was (the place) where Napoleon was finally de-} \\ \text{feated.} \end{cases}$

c A *wh*-type sentence using the *wh*-words *who, whom,* or *whose* is usually awkward or impossible:

> It was the ambassador that met us.
> *but not*: *Who met us was the ambassador.

We can, however, say:

> The one/person who met us was the ambassador.

437

The *wh*-type cleft sentence is more flexible than the *it*-type in these ways:

a The *wh*-type can focus on the complement of a clause, whereas the *it*-type normally cannot:

> He is a genius. → $\begin{cases} \text{What he is is a genius.} \\ \textit{but not}: \text{*It's a genius that he is.} \end{cases}$

b The *wh*-type can focus on the verb, by using the substitute verb *do*:

> He's spoilt the whole thing. → $\begin{cases} \text{What he's done is spoil the} \\ \text{whole thing.} \\ \textit{but not}: \text{*It's spoil the whole} \\ \text{thing that he's done.} \end{cases}$

Notice that the complement of the *wh*-type sentence here takes the form of a non-finite clause (*spoil the whole thing*). The non-finite verb may be *a* a bare infinitive, *b* a *to*-infinitive, *c* an *-ed* participle, *d* an *-ing* participle:

What he'll do is spoil the whole thing.   *a*

What he's done is {spoil the whole thing.   *a*
{to spoil the whole thing.   *b*
{spoilt the whole thing.   *c*

What he's doing is spoiling the whole thing.   *d*

The bare infinitive is the most usual construction, except after *done* (where the
-ed participle is just as acceptable), and after *doing*, where the *-ing* participle has
to be used.

Sentences with *wh*-clauses and demonstratives
438

A common type of sentence in ⟨informal⟩ English is one in which a *wh*-clause is
linked by the verb *be* to a demonstrative pronoun (*this* or *that*). These sentences
are similar to *wh*-cleft sentences both in structure and in their focusing effect:

This is where I first met my wife.

This is how you start the engine.

(A)   (He was psycho-analysed by a pupil of Freud's.)

(B)   So that's why he's always talking about his mother fixation!

(I had difficulty in starting the car today.) That's what always
happens when I leave it out in cold weather.

Postponement
INTRODUCTORY-*it* CONSTRUCTION
439

The introductory-*it* construction (*see* 584–9) (not to be confused with the *it*-type
cleft sentence) is a means of postponing a subject to a later position in the sentence, either for end-weight or for end-focus:

That income tax will be reduced is unlikely.

→ *It* is unlikely *that income tax will be reduced.*

The *it*-construction is, in fact, more usual than the construction without postponement. If you keep the clause in front position, this is exceptional, and
suggests that you want to put special contrastive emphasis (*see* 428) on the rest
of the main clause:

|That income tax will be reduced | is unlikely; | that it will be

abolished | is out of the question.|

In some instances, such as the passive construction (*see* 585, 676–82), it is impossible to keep the clause in subject position:

It is said that she slipped arsenic in his tea.

(*but not*: *That she slipped arsenic in his tea is said.)

For other examples of *it* replacing a postponed clause as subject, *see* 584.
440

Main focus often occurs in the postponed clause:

It is likely that they will hold an election.

But when an -*ing* clause is the postponed subject, the main focus normally falls
on the rest of the main clause, and the -*ing* clause is treated as an afterthought:

| It's fún | being a hóstess. |

441

Occasionally introductory *it* displaces a clause in object position:

You must find *it* enjoyable *working here.*

(='You must find working here enjoyable';

Compare: It is enjoyable working here.)

I owe *it* to you *that the jury acquitted me.*

(*Compare*: I owe my acquittal to you.)

Something put *it* into his head *that she was a spy.*

(*Compare*: It came into his head that she was a spy.)

This displacement MUST occur when the object clause is a *that*-clause or an
infinitive clause. Thus we can have:

I'll leave it to you to lock the door.

BUT NOT: *I'll leave to lock the door to you.

POSTPONING PARTS OF SENTENCE ELEMENTS

442

The *it*-construction postpones a whole sentence element, whether a subject or
object. You may also wish to postpone a part of a sentence element, for example
by splitting an adjective from its postmodifiers:

How *ready* are they *to make peace with their enemies?*

This can avoid the awkwardness of a long or emphatic element coming in non-
final position, as in *How ready to make peace with their enemies are they?* The
most important cases of such postponement are discussed in 443–6.

POSTPONING THE POSTMODIFICATION OF A NOUN PHRASE

443

The time had come *to decorate the house for Christmas.*   [3]

(*Better than*: The time to decorate the house for
    Christmas had come.)

The problem arose *of what to do with the money.*   [4]

(*Better than*: The problem of what to do with the
    money arose.)

What business is it *of yours?*   [5]

(*More idiomatic than*: What business of yours is it?)

We heard *the story* from his own lips *of how he was stranded
    for days without food.*   [6]

This avoids awkwardness particularly when the rest of the sentence is short in
comparison with the subject. In contrast to [4], the following is normal:

The problem of what to do with the money was discussed by all the
    members of the family.

POSTPONING THE EMPHATIC REFLEXIVE PRONOUN

444

When the reflexive pronouns *myself, himself, themselves, etc* are used for emphasis, they normally have nuclear stress. If such a pronoun is in apposition as part
of the subject, it is common to postpone it for end-focus:

John himself told me. → John told me himself.

    (='It was John, and no one else, who told me')

POSTPONING COMPARATIVE CLAUSES, *etc*

445

A comparative clause or phrase is often separated, by postponement, from the word it postmodifies. In some cases, the same sentence without postponement would be extremely awkward:

    More people own houses these days *than used to years ago.*

        (*not*: *More people than used to years ago own houses
           these days.)

    He showed *less pity* to his victims *than any other tyrant in history.*

        (*not*: *He showed less pity than any other tyrant in history
           to his victims.)

446

Other constructions which, like comparative clauses, are often postponed are postmodifying phrases of exception (*see* 239–40), and clauses of amount or degree following *too, enough,* and *so* (*see* 234–5):

    All of them were captured *except the leader of the gang.*

    Too many people were there *for the thief to escape unseen.*

    I was *so excited* by the present *that I forgot to thank you.*

Other choices of position

The passive

447

Another example of a grammatical process which changes the positions of elements in the sentence is the rule for forming passive sentences (*see* 676–82).

(A) (Who makes these chairs?) (B) They're made by Ercol.   [7]

    The President was mistrusted by most of the radical and left-
    wing politicians in the country.   [8]

In [7], the passive gives the sentence end-focus, where the active (*Ercol makes them*) would not. In [8], the passive gives end-weight, where the active sentence (*Most of the radical . . . mistrusted the President*) would be awkward.

    You can readily use the passive for end-weight where the subject of the sentence is a clause:

    I was astounded that he was prepared to give me a job.

        (*Better than*: That he was prepared to give me a job
           astounded me.)

The preposition *by* is omitted here because a *that*-clause cannot be complement of a preposition *see* 639.

Position of direct object

448

In normal order, a direct object precedes an object complement or a final-position adverbial (*see* 508). But if the object is long, it can be postponed to the end for end-weight:

{ NORMAL ORDER He has proved *them* wrong.

{ FINAL OBJECT   He has proved wrong *the forecasts made by the*
                          country's leading economic experts.

NORMAL ORDER   He condemned *them* to death.
FINAL OBJECT   He condemned to death *most of the peasants who had*
                 taken part in the rebellion.

The same choice can be made when a noun phrase object comes before a particle (*eg* the second part of a phrasal verb such as *make up, give away, let down*):

He gave all his books awáy.   She made the story úp.
He gave awáy all his books.   She made up a stóry.

The choice may be made either for end-weight, or, as in these examples, for end-focus. Notice that personal pronoun objects cannot be moved to the end in this way: *He gave them away*, but not **He gave away them.*

Position of indirect object

449

In a similar way, an indirect object can in effect be postponed, by converting it into a prepositional phrase:

> The twins told their mother all their sécrets.   [9]
> The twins told all their secrets to their móther.   [10]

This change, like the others, can be used for a different end-focus. For example, [9] answers the implied question 'What did the twins tell their mother?', but [10] answers the implied question 'Who did they tell their secrets to?'.

Avoiding intransitive verbs

450

Connected with the principle of end-weight in English is the feeling that the predicate of a clause should be longer or grammatically more complex than the subject. This helps to explain why we tend to avoid predicates consisting of just a single intransitive verb. Instead of saying *Mary sang*, we would probably prefer to say *Mary sang a song*, filling the object position with a noun phrase which adds little information but helps to give more weight to the predicate.

451

For such a purpose English often uses a general verb (such as *have, take, give,* and *do*) followed by an abstract noun phrase:

He's having a swim. ⟨BrE⟩   (*Compare*: He's swimming)
      taking a bath.

He took a rest.   (*Compare*: He rested)
The man gave a shout.   (*Compare*: The man shouted)
He does little work.   (*Compare*: He works little)

The sentences on the left are more idiomatic than those on the right.

In a similar way a transitive verb can be replaced by an indirect object construction with the verb *give, etc:*

I gave the door a kick.   (= 'I kicked the door')
I paid her a visit.   (= 'I visited her')

Part Four

Grammatical Compendium

How to use the Compendium

This Grammatical Compendium covers all the important areas of English grammatical form and structure, and is arranged alphabetically under topic headings. The arrangement is alphabetical because the Compendium is primarily meant to be used for reference, especially as an explanation of grammatical terms and categories referred to in Part Three.

Even so, some students may wish to study the structures of English grammar systematically, and many others may find it generally helpful to see how the topics relate to one another in an overall logical plan. For this reason, we present a visual guide to the Compendium (*see* p 190), showing related topics grouped in boxes, and dependences of one topic on another by arrows. You can, if you wish, see the diagram as a suggested plan for reading the Compendium in a logical order. If you do, notice that the diagram offers you a choice of orders, since often two or more topics lead equally naturally to or from another topic. For example, after reading 'Sentences' and 'Clauses', you could go to any of the groups containing 'Subordination' and 'Coordination'; 'Negation', 'Questions', *etc*; 'Verb Phrases', 'Subjects', *etc*. There is no single 'best way' of putting the topics in a natural sequence.

Another thing to bear in mind is that the diagram attempts to show only the more important relations between topics. Some connections have not been indicated; others, it could be argued, might be just as well shown by arrows pointing in the opposite direction. We have simplified the 'map' in order to make it reasonably easy to follow. Each entry in the Compendium has a reference to the most relevant sections of R Quirk *et al*, *A Grammar of Contemporary English* (Longman 1972), so that, if required, a more detailed treatment of the topic can be consulted in that book.

Adjective patterns (*see GCE* 12.31–43)

452
Adjectives can have three types of complement: (A) prepositional phrase, (B) *that*-clause, and (C) *to*-infinitive.

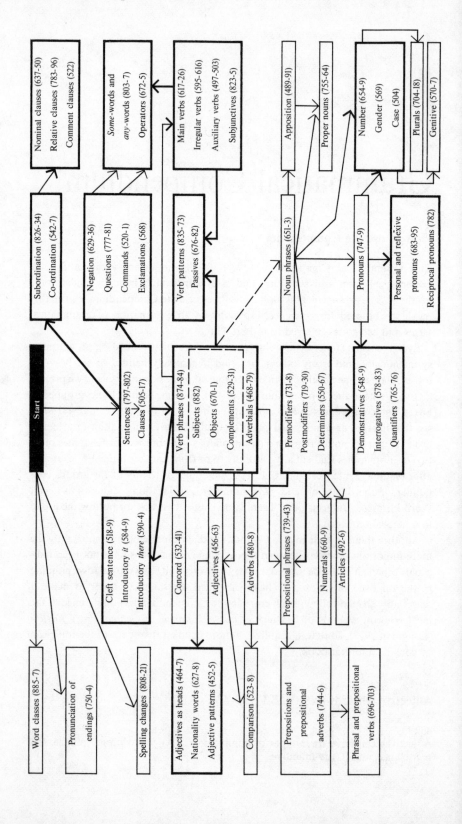

(A) Adjectives with a prepositional phrase
453
Adjectives can have different prepositional complements: *good at, afraid of, ready for, keen on, etc.* Usually, a particular adjective requires a particular preposition. Here are some examples:

They were terribly *worried about* you.
She was awfully *bad at* mathematics.
We were all *annoyed at* his behaviour.
She was *successful in* her last attempt.
You are *interested in* languages, aren't you?
Were they *conscious of* the difficulties?
She was *convinced of* his brilliance.
His plan is *based on* co-operation.
She is *dependent on* your assistance.
Not all income is *subject to* taxation.
This plan is not *compatible with* our principles.
He is *disappointed with* her behaviour.

(B) Adjectives with a *that*-clause
454
a Personal subjects
Some adjectives and adjectival participles have a finite *that*-clause as complement (where *that* can usually be omitted):

I'm *sure (that) he'll be late.*
We're *glad (that) you can come.*

When the *that*-clause expresses a 'putative' idea, it contains *should* (*see* 289–90):

We're *surprised* that he should resign.
I'm *amazed* that he should get the post.

Other adjectives and participles with *that*-clauses: *certain, confident, proud, sad; alarmed, annoyed, astonished, disappointed, pleased, shocked, etc.* Such adjectives elsewhere have a prepositional phrase as complement: *certain of, annoyed at, pleased with, etc.*
b Introductory *it* as subject
Adjectives with *that*-clauses frequently have introductory *it* as subject (*see* 584–9):

It's *true* that she never turned up.
It's *possible* that we'll be a bit late.

Other such adjectives include: *certain, evident, likely, obvious, probable.*
    The *that*-clause often contains putative *should:*

It's *odd* that he should be late.
It's *appropriate* that he should get the post.

Similarly: *curious, extraordinary, fortunate, important, odd, sad; alarming, disconcerting, embarrassing, fitting, frightening, irritating, shocking, surprising, etc.* Notice that many of these adjectives have the form of an *-ing* participle.
    In ⟨formal⟩ style, the verb in the *that*-clause can sometimes be subjunctive (*see* 823):

It's *essential* { that he be here by tomorrow.
{ that he should be here by tomorrow.

(C) Adjectives with a *to*-infinitive
455
There are different types of adjectives with *to*-infinitive constructions, for example:

He was *splendid* to wait.   [1]
He is *hard* to convince.   [2]

He was *furious* to hear about it.   [3]

He was *slow* to react.   [4]

The meanings of the four constructions are different, as can be seen from these paraphrases:

{ It was splendid of him to wait.   [1a]

{ How splendid of him to wait!   [1b]

{ To convince him is hard.   [2a]

{ It is hard to convince him.   [2b]

{ To hear about it made him furious.   [3a]

{ It made him furious to hear about it.   [3b]

He reacted slowly.   [4a]

a Other examples of adjectives like *splendid* in [1] (note the position of *not*, *never* and other 'mid-position' adverbs):

They were *stupid* not to follow your advice.

She was *careful* never to repeat her mistake.

He was *wrong* to go ahead with the plan.

Also: *clever, cruel, good, kind, naughty, nice, rude, silly.*

b Other examples of adjectives like *hard* in [2]:

He is *difficult* to please.

It's *good* to eat.

He's *impossible* to teach.

He's *easy* to deal with.

Also: *convenient, enjoyable, fun* ⟨informal⟩, *pleasant.*

c Other examples of adjectives like *furious* in [3]:

I'll be *glad* to drive you home.

They were *delighted* to hear about your results in the exam.

Also: *amazed, angry, annoyed, disappointed, pleased, sorry, surprised, worried.*

d Other examples of adjectives like *slow* in [4]:

He was *quick* to answer my
letter.   (=‘He answered . . . *quickly.*’)

They were *prompt* to act.   (=‘They acted *promptly.*’)

He is *willing* to give us his
support.   (=‘He'll *willingly* give . . . ’)

e Other adjectives having an infinitive clause as complement do not fit into the other four categories. They are similar to *d* in their range of meaning, but cannot be paraphrased by the use of an adverb:

I am *unable* to answer your question.

They are *bound* to be late.

We're all *anxious* to meet your family.

f There is also a class of adjectives with an infinitive clause after introductory *it:*

It's *important* to have warm clothing.

It will be *necessary* to pay in advance.

Will it be *convenient* to see you this afternoon?

Also: *possible, impossible, nice* ⟨informal⟩, *right, wise, wrong.* With these, and some other adjectives, the infinitive clause can have a subject introduced by *for:*

It's *impossible* for us all to go by car.

They were *anxious* for him to succeed.

Adjectives (*see GCE* 5.2–5, 5.12–41)

456

(A) Most adjectives can be both attributive (acting as premodifiers of nouns, *see* 732) and predicative (acting as complements of verbs, *see* 841):

She's a *pretty* girl.   ATTRIBUTIVE
All the girls here are *pretty*.   PREDICATIVE

(B) Most adjectives can be modified by intensifiers like *very, quite, rather, etc* (*see* 217–19):

She looks *quite young* for her age.

(C) Most adjectives can take comparative and superlative forms (*see* 524). Regular comparison may be expressed *a* by adding the endings *-er* and *-est* to the adjective:

The Browns seem a lot *happier* now than they used to.

They are the *kindest* people I know, too.

or *b* by placing *more* and *most* before the adjective:

I think she's *more intelligent* than her husband.

These are the *most beautiful* paintings I've ever seen.

Attributive adjectives
457
Although most adjectives can be either attributive or predicative, some can only be used in attributive position. One group of them can be related to adverbials (*see* 468):

ADJECTIVES	ADVERBIALS
my *former* friend	He was *formerly* my friend.
an *occasional* visitor	She was *occasionally* a visitor.
the *late* president	He was till *lately* the president (now dead).
a *hard* worker	a worker who works *hard*
a *big* eater	someone who eats *a lot*

Other attributive adjectives are derived from nouns, for example:

criminal law = 'law concerning crime'
an *atomic* scientist = 'a scientist specialising in atomic science'
a *medical* school = 'a school for students of medicine'

Predicative adjectives
458
Adjectives can be used predicatively as subject complement after linking verbs like *be, seem, look, feel* (*see* 510, 838):

I feel *awful* this morning.

or as object complement after verbs like *consider, believe, find* (*see* 865, 867):

We found the place absolutely *delightful*. (= 'We found that the place was absolutely *delightful*.')

Adjectives can be complement to a subject which is a finite clause (*see* 514):

Whether the minister will resign is still *uncertain*.

or a non-finite clause (*see* 515):

Driving a bus isn't so *easy* as you may think.

Similarly, adjectives can be object complement to clauses:

They considered $\begin{Bmatrix} \text{what he did} \\ \text{working so hard} \end{Bmatrix}$ *foolish*.

Whereas the adjectives like *awful, delightful, uncertain, easy* and *foolish* can be used both attributively (*see* 457) and predicatively, some groups of adjectives are usually restricted to predicative position. One such group is 'health adjectives':

She felt *faint*.
You look *well*.
He's seriously *ill* (*sick* ⟨*esp* AmE⟩).

In attributive use, however, *sick* is common in both ⟨BrE⟩ and ⟨AmE⟩:

He's a very *sick* man.

Another group of predicative adjectives includes the following, many of which are regularly followed by phrases or clauses:

We are very *fond* of her. (= 'We like her very much.')

He is *ready* to do it. (= 'He is prepared to do it.')

I'm *afraid* that you're mistaken. (= 'I fear that you're mistaken.')

Most of the committee members were *present* at the meeting.

Notice that many of these adjectives CAN precede a noun, but in a different sense: *a ready answer* (= 'an answer which was given readily'), *the present situation* (= 'the situation at the present time').

Postmodifying adjectives
459

Adjectives (especially predicative adjectives) are sometimes postmodifiers, *ie* they follow the item they modify (*see* 719). Such an adjective can usually be regarded as a reduced relative clause (*see* 783):

The people (who were) *involved* were reported to the police.

The men (who were) *present* were his supporters.

Is there anything (which is) *interesting* in the papers?

Quantifiers ending in *-body, -one, -thing, -where* can only have postmodification: *something nice* (*see* 730). In other cases, the postmodifying adjective is one that cannot be attributive: we cannot say **the involved people* or *the present men in the above sentences.

A few adjectives have special meanings when they occur after the noun:

the president *elect* (soon to take office)

the City of London *proper* (as strictly defined)

The adjective is a postmodifier in several compounds (*see* 705):

attorney *general*   court *martial*

notary *public*   postmaster *general*

An adjective combined with its complement cannot come before the noun:

*The *easiest to teach* boys were in my class.

Such adjective phrases can usually be postmodifiers:

The boys *easiest to teach* were in my class.

Our neighbours have a house *much larger than ours*.

It is however more usual to separate the adjective and its complement:

The *easiest* boys *to teach* were in my class.

Our neighbours have a *much larger* house *than ours*.

But if the adjective is itself modified by the adverb *so* or *too*, it cannot normally be separated from its complement:

These boxes are *too heavy to carry*.

but not: *These are *too heavy* boxes *to carry*.

The box is *so heavy that I can't carry it*.

but not: *This is a *so heavy* box *that I can't carry it*.

An exception is where the indefinite article is placed between the adjective and the noun head:

This is *too heavy* a box *for me to carry*.

He was *so eloquent* a speaker *that even his enemies listened with respect*. ⟨formal⟩

In ⟨informal⟩ use, it is more natural to use *such* rather than *so:*

This is *such a heavy* box *that I can't carry it*.

Adjectives and participles
460

There are many adjectives that have the same form as *-ing* or *-ed* participles (*see* 621–2):

His views on politics were rather *surprising*.

He seems quite *satisfied* with his new job.

These adjectives can also be attributive: *his surprising views*. The *-ed* participle of intransitive verbs can also be used attributively: *the escaped prisoner* (= 'the prisoner who has (had) escaped').

Sometimes a verb corresponding to the adjective has a different meaning. We can therefore have ambiguous sentences like *They were relieved,* where we cannot tell whether *relieved* is a participle or an adjective. The ambiguity disappears with more context:

ADJECTIVE   They were very *relieved* to find her at home.

PARTICIPLE   They were soon *relieved* by the next group of sentries.

The difference between the adjective and the participle is not always obvious. It is clear that an *-ing* form is a present participle and not an adjective when a direct object is present:

He was *entertaining* the guests with his stories.

Similarly, the verbal force is explicit for the *-ed* form when a personal *by*-agent is present (*see* 677):

The man was *offended* by the policeman.

For both *-ed* and *-ing* participles, modification by the adverb *very* clearly indicates that the forms are adjectives:

His views were very *alarming*.

The man was very *offended*.

But sometimes we find a construction with both *very* and a *by*-agent:

I was very *irritated* by the man in the blue suit.

She was very *shaken* by the news.

In these 'mixed' constructions, we cannot say whether the *-ed* form is a participle or an adjective.

Adjective or adverb? (*see GCE* 5.7–9, 5.17, 5.65–7)

461

Many adverbs in English are derived from adjectives by the addition of *-ly: quick—quickly, careful—carefully, etc.* Some adverbs, however, do not end in *-ly*, but have exactly the same form as adjectives:

ADJECTIVE	ADVERB
an *early* train	The train arrived *early*.
a *late* dinner	I've been working *late*.
a *straight* line	He went *straight* to the door.
a *hard* task	We tried *hard* to convince them.
a *direct* hit	We flew *direct* to Stuttgart.
a *wrong* answer	You've got it all *wrong*. ⟨informal⟩
a *short* distance	The arrow fell *short* of the target.
a *long* rest	You mustn't stay too *long*.
a *high* wall	Don't aim too *high*.

These adverbs are mostly connected with time, position and direction. In some cases, there is also an adverb in *-ly* (*lately, hardly, directly, shortly, etc*), but with a different meaning:

He drove home *directly* after arriving (= 'immediately').

I haven't seen him *lately* (= 'recently').

A few ⟨informal⟩ adverbs with adjective form have a premodifying function:

He's *pretty* (= 'quite') tall.

He was *dead* (= 'absolutely') drunk.

462

There are also cases in which an adjective is used after the verb or object where we might expect an adverb. Notice that here we consider the adjective to be a complement (subject complement or object complement, *see* 529), not an adverbial at all:

> The food tasted *good*. (= 'The food was good to taste.')
> The flowers smell *sweet*.
> We live quite *close* to you.
> Keep *still*!
> The moon shone *clear* and *bright*.

Both *good* and *well* are adjectives (but with different meanings) in:

> Those cakes look *good* (= '. . . look as if they taste good').
> Your mother looks *well* (= '. . . in good health').

There is a contrast between *strong* (adjective) and *strongly* (adverb) in:

> He felt *strong* enough to win the contest.
> He felt *strongly* enough about it to object.

463

The difference between an adverb form and an adjective form does not always involve a difference of meaning. In these examples, the two are more or less equivalent, although the adjective form tends to be more ⟨informal⟩:

> He spoke $\begin{cases} loud \text{ and } clear. \\ loudly \text{ and } clearly. \end{cases}$
> She buys her clothes *cheap/cheaply*.
> We had to drive *slow/slowly* all the way.
> We had to lie *quiet/quietly* until the danger was over.
> I saw him as *clear* ⟨informal⟩/*clearly* as if he was standing here.
> It all happened so *quick* ⟨informal⟩/*quickly* that I could do nothing.

The form without *-ly* is especially common in comparative and superlative constructions:

> Let's see who can run *quickest*.
> Would you mind walking *slower*?
> We must look *closer* at the problems.
> That is *easier* said than done.

In these examples, the normal adverb form would have *-ly:*

> We must look *closely* at the problems (*not* . . . close . . .).

Adjectives as heads (*see GCE* 5.20–3)

464

Adjectives can function as heads of noun phrases. Such adjectives normally take a definite determiner, usually the definite article, and they have no plural inflection. There are two kinds of such adjectives, both with generic reference (*see* 74), those denoting a class of people, and those denoting an abstract quality.

465

(A) A CLASS OF PEOPLE (PLURAL): *the rich* = 'those who are rich'.

> There is often a lack of communication between *the young* and *the old*.
> *The unemployed* cannot be expected to live on their savings.
> *The English* have been called 'a nation of shopkeepers'.

For the difference between *the English* and *Englishmen*, *see* 627–8.

466

(B) AN ABSTRACT QUALITY (SINGULAR): *the absurd* = 'that which is absurd'.

Some people enjoy *the mystical* and *the supernatural* in literature.

He went from *the sublime* to *the ridiculous*.

467

But the article is sometimes omitted before adjective heads in parallel phrases (*see* 495) where the adjectives are linked by a conjunction or a preposition:

Education should be for both *young* and *old*.

Things went from *bad* to *worse*.

Adverbials (*see GCE* Chapter 8)

468

Adverbials can have a number of different structures. They can be

(A) ADVERBS (*see* 480):

Peter was playing *well*.

(B) PREPOSITIONAL PHRASES (*see* 743):

Peter was playing *with great skill*.

(C) FINITE CLAUSES (*see* 514):

Peter was playing well, *although he was very tired*.

(D) NON-FINITE CLAUSES (*see* 515), in which the verb is

a an infinitive:

Peter was playing *to win*.

b an *-ing* participle:

Being captain of the team, Peter played to win.

c an *-ed* participle:

When urged by his friends, he agreed to play again.

(E) VERBLESS CLAUSES (*see* 516):

Peter was playing, *unaware of the danger*.

(F) NOUN PHRASES (less common) (*see* 651–3):

Peter was playing *last week*.

(G) NOUN PHRASES FOLLOWED BY *ago, long, etc*:

Three years ago, Peter was playing football regularly.

469

Adverbials usually tell something extra about the action, happening, or state described by the rest of the sentence. For example, the time when it happened, the place where it happened, or the manner in which it happened:

TIME   My father is working *today*.

PLACE   My father is working *in the kitchen*.

MANNER   My father is working *hard*.

A sentence can have more than one adverbial:

My father is working *hard   in the kitchen   today*.

The meanings of adverbials are dealt with in Part Three (*see* 140–243). Here we are concerned with the POSITIONS of adverbials in relation to other sentence elements, including other adverbials.

Adverbial positions
470

Although some adverbials can only occur in fixed positions, most adverbials are mobile, *ie* they can come at different places in the sentence. We need to distinguish three main positions:

FRONT-POSITION   *Now* Susan is very happy.

MID-POSITION   Susan is *now* very happy.

END-POSITION   Susan is very happy *now*.

FRONT-POSITION is before the subject:
>   *Every Sunday* he went to church.

MID-POSITION is

>   *a* immediately before the main verb if no auxiliaries are present:
>   >   Bill *never* GOES abroad.
>
>   *b* after the operator, *ie* the first auxiliary (*see* 672–5), if there is more than
>   one verb present:
>   >   Bill HAS *never* GONE abroad.
>   >
>   >   Bill MIGHT *never* HAVE GONE abroad if you hadn't invited him.
>
>   *c* after forms of *be* when *be* is a main verb (*see* 500):
>   >   Bill IS *never* at home these days.

Occasionally a mid-position adverbial comes before the operator (*see* 269, 477).

END-POSITION is

>   *a* after an object or complement if there is one present:
>   >   Bill took his car *to the garage*.
>
>   *b* otherwise after the verb:
>   >   Bill drove *very carefully*.

The placing of an adverbial depends partly on its structure (adverb, prepositional phrase, clause, *etc*), partly on its meaning (time, place, manner, *etc*).
Order and emphasis also play a part (*see* 425–51). Long adverbials (clauses,
prepositional and noun phrases) normally occur in end-position, though front-
position is not uncommon, particularly for emphasis or contrast.

>   { We went *to Chicago on Monday*.
>   { *On Monday* we went *to Chicago*.
>   { He was a complete failure *as far as mathematics is concerned*.
>   { *As far as mathematics is concerned*, he was a complete failure.

Long adverbials rarely occur in mid-position, which is usually restricted to
certain short adverbs such as *almost, hardly, just, never*:

>   The chairman *almost* resigned.
>
>   We've *just* returned from Italy.

The main problem, then, in placing adverbials is with *adverbs*. We shall
therefore concentrate on these in the following discussion.

Adverbials denoting manner, means, and instrument (*see* 192–6)
471

Manner, means, and instrument adverbials usually have end-position:

>   They live *frugally*.
>
>   The children go to school *by bus*.
>
>   They examined the specimen *microscopically*.

In the passive, however, mid-position is common:

>   Discussions were *formally* opened here today on the question of
>   international disarmament.

Contrast the position of *well* in the following active and passive sentences:

>   He put the point *well*.   The point was put *well*.
>   *He *well* put the point.   The point was *well* put.

Place adverbials (*see* 161–91)
472

Place adverbials, both those denoting location and those denoting direction,
usually have end-position:

>   The meeting will be *upstairs*.
>
>   He managed to kick the ball *into the goal*.

Some location adverbials, particularly prepositional phrases and clauses, can
easily appear in front-position:

⎰ *Outside*, the boys were jumping and skipping.
⎱ The boys were jumping and skipping *outside*.
⎰ *In the nursery* the children were playing happily but noisily.
⎱ The children were playing happily but noisily *in the nursery*.

Two place adverbials can occur together in end-position, usually with the smaller unit before the larger unit:

Many people eat *in Chinese restaurants in London*.

Only the larger unit can be moved to front-position:

In London many people eat *in Chinese restaurants*.

*In Chinese restaurants many people eat *in London*.

If one of the adverbials is an adverb, it normally comes before a prepositional phrase:

They drove *downhill to the college*.

Time adverbials
473

Time adverbials can be divided into three classes according to their meaning: adverbials denoting time-when, duration and frequency (*see* 140–60).

Time-when adverbials
474

We may distinguish two groups of time-when adverbials.

Group A adverbials denote a point or period of time:

Do come and see us *again*.

We lived in Baltimore *last year*.

The meeting starts *tomorrow at 8 o'clock*.

As these examples show, Group A adverbials normally have end-position. But there are exceptions. For example, *just* always has mid-position:

I'm *just* finishing my homework.

Now and *then* can occur in front-, mid-, or end-position:

⎧ *Now* he's living in New York.
⎨ He's *now* living in New York.
⎩ He's living in New York *now*.

Group B adverbials denote a point of time but also imply the point from which that time is measured. Most of these adverbials occur either in front-, mid-, or end-position:

⎧ |*Recently* | they had an accident.|
⎨ |They *recently* had an accident.|
⎩ |They had an accident | *recently*.|

⎧ |*Once* we owned an Alsatian dog.|
⎨ |We *once* owned an Alsatian dog.|
⎩ |We owned an Alsatian dog | *once*.|

As indicated, in end-position these adverbs usually have a rising-tone nucleus (*see* 421).

Time duration adverbials (*see* 151–6)
475

Time duration adverbials denote (A) length of time or (B) duration from some preceding point of time. Both groups normally have end-position:

(A)   I'll be in California *for the summer*.

They were on duty *all night long*.

(B)   Britain has had decimal currency *since 1971*.
        I've been staying hear *since last Saturday*.
(Note that the second group requires the perfective aspect, *see* 119, 881.) Single-word duration adverbs, however, usually take mid-position:
        They have *always* tried to be friendly.
        He is *temporarily* out of work.

Time frequency adverbials (*see* 157–60)
476
There are two groups: (A) those denoting definite frequency and (B) those denoting indefinite frequency.
(A)   Definite frequency adverbials usually have end-position:
                Committee meetings take place *weekly*.
                This week I'll be in the office *every day*.
                I go to Japan *twice a year* on business.
(B)   Indefinite frequency adverbs normally have mid-position:
                He *generally* leaves home at seven in the morning.
                We don't *normally* go to bed before midnight.
                Does she *always* dress well?
                They *regularly* take their dog for a walk in the evening.
                I *sometimes* think she doesn't know what she's talking about.
                I'm *rarely* in my office after five.

Other examples of adverbs denoting indefinite frequency: *ever*, *frequently*, *never*, *occasionally*, *often*, *seldom*, *usually*.

However, prepositional phrases of indefinite frequency have front- or end-position:
                As a rule it's very quiet here during the day.
                We've been to see our in-laws *on several occasions*.

Degree adverbs (*see* 217–26)
477
Degree adverbs have a heightening or lowering effect on some part of the sentence. Many of them occur in mid-position:
        He's *definitely* going to emigrate.
        So they *really* want him to be elected?
        We *thoroughly* disapprove of their methods.
        I *entirely* agree with her.
        I *much* prefer the old methods.
        They can *scarcely/hardly* ignore our views.
        We *nearly* missed the plane.
        She *all but* kissed me.
        I *rather* like him.
End-position is also possible for many of these adverbs:
        He *completely* ignored my request.
        He ignored my request *completely*.
Note that degree adverbs in mid-position can come, for positive or negative emphasis, before the operator:
        I *simply* don't believe what she said.
        You *really* will have to be more careful.

Two or more adverbials
478
Time adverbials in end-position tend to occur in the order DURATION + FREQUENCY + TIME-WHEN:
        I used to swim *for an hour or so every day during my childhood*.

I'm paying my rent *monthly this year*.

Our electricity was cut off *briefly today*.

When more than one of the main classes of adverbials occur in end-position, the normal order is MANNER/MEANS/INSTRUMENT + PLACE + TIME:

He was working *with his lawn-mower in the garden the whole morning*.

They go *by bus to the opera every month*.

A clause normally comes after other adverbial structures (adverbs, prepositional phrases, *etc*):

We plan to stop *for a few days wherever we can find accommodation*.

Adverbials which normally occur in end-position are often put in front-position to avoid having too many adverbials in end-position:

The whole morning he was working *with his lawn-mower in the garden*.

It is not usual for more than one adverbial to be in front-position or mid-position.

Sentence adverbials
479
The adverbials we have discussed so far are *integrated* to some extent in the structure of the sentence. For example, they can modify the verb, and be affected by negation.

I *always* drive *carefully*.

I don't *always* drive *carefully*.

(Here both *always* and *carefully* are in the scope of the negative, *see* 269.)

There is also another class called SENTENCE ADVERBIALS, which are *peripheral* to the sentence structure. The difference between the two classes appears clearly with adverbs that can have both functions:

Naturally, the children are behaving well while you are here.   [1]

The children behave *naturally*.   [2]

In [1] *naturally* is a sentence adverbial (= 'of course'), in [2] it is a manner adverbial (= 'in a natural manner'). Similarly, *yet* is a sentence adverbial in [3]:

I've been waiting outside his door the whole day, *yet* (= 'nevertheless') I haven't seen him.   [3]

and a time adverbial in [4]:

I've been waiting outside his door the whole day, but I haven't seen him *yet* (= 'so far').   [4]

Sentence adverbials have a wide range of possible structures. For example, instead of *frankly* in this sentence

Frankly, he hasn't got a chance.

we could put

A PREPOSITIONAL PHRASE	*in all frankness*
AN INFINITIVE CLAUSE	*to be frank, to speak frankly, to put it frankly*
AN *-ing* PARTICIPLE CLAUSE	*frankly speaking, putting it frankly*
AN *-ed* PARTICIPLE CLAUSE	*put frankly* (less common)
A FINITE VERB CLAUSE	*if I may be frank, if I can speak frankly, if I can put it frankly*

Sentence adverbials often convey the speaker's comment on the content of what he is saying:

Of course, nobody imagines that he will repay the loan.

To be sure, we have heard many such promises before.

Other examples of such adverbials are: *admittedly, certainly, definitely, indeed, surely; perhaps, possibly; in fact, actually, really; officially, superficially, tech-*

nically, theoretically; fortunately, hopefully, luckily, naturally, preferably, strangely, surprisingly. Many other sentence adverbials (*eg however, therefore, moreover*) have a connective role (*see* 367–85).

The normal position for most sentence adverbials is front-position. They are usually separated from what follows by a tone unit boundary in speech or a comma in writing:

⟨Written⟩ Obviously, they expected us to be on time.

⟨Spoken⟩ |Ŏbviously | they expected us to be on tìme|

Adverbs (*see GCE 5.42–64*)

480

Most adverbs are formed from adjectives (*see* 461) with the suffix *-ly*: *frank/ frankly, happy/happily,* etc. (For the change in spelling from *y* to *i* in *happy/ happily,* etc, *see* 809.)

Adverbs have two typical functions:

(A)   as adverbial (*see* 468): He *always* drives *carefully*.

(B)   as modifier of *a* adjectives, *b* adverbs, or *c* a number of other constructions (*see* 484–7):

   a He is an *extremely* careful driver.

   b He drives *extremely* carefully.

   c He lives in a house *just* outside the town.

A less common function is

(C)   as a complement of a preposition: *I haven't been here before* NOW.

The adverb used as a modifier
481
Most modifying adverbs fall into the semantic category of degree adverbs (*see* 217–26, 477).

482
a The adverb modifies an adjective
The adverb in general precedes the adjective:

   He's *rather* tall for a ten-year old.

   I thought it was an *absolutely* awful show myself. ⟨familiar⟩

   It's *extremely* good of you to do this for me.

One adverb, *enough*, is placed after its adjective:

   This just isn't good *enough*!

The adverbs *too, so,* and *how* (ie, *how* in interrogative and exclamatory sentences) are exceptional. When they modify an adjective in a noun phrase, the indefinite article is placed after the adjective (*see* 459):

   He's *too* good *an* actor to forget his lines.

   How tall *a* man is he?

   How strange *a* feeling it was! ⟨formal⟩

But with mass and plural nouns, where no indefinite article is present, these adverbs cannot premodify the adjective. Instead, *how* (in exclamations) is replaced by *what*:

   What strange ideas you have!

      (*not* *How strange ideas . . .)

483
b The adverb modifies an adverb
An adverb may premodify another adverb:

   You seem to be smoking *rather* heavily these days.

As with adjectives, the only postmodifying adverb is *enough*:
> Oddly *enough*, nothing valuable was stolen.

484

c The adverb modifies a prepositional phrase
> The nail went *right* through the wall.
> His parents are *dead* against his hitch-hiking. ⟨familiar⟩

485

d The adverb modifies a determiner, pronoun or numeral (see 550, 747, 660–1)
> He has *hardly* any friends.
> *Nearly* everybody came to the housewarming party.
> *Over* two hundred deaths were reported after the disaster.

The indefinite article can be premodified when *a = one*:
> My parents will stay for *about* a week.

The quantifiers *much* and *little* and those ending in *-body*, *-one*, *-thing* and *-where*, and the interrogatives *who*, *what* and *where* are postmodified by *else*: *somebody else, all else, who else, what else, somewhere else, nowhere else*, etc. With determiners, the equivalent word is the postdeterminer *other*:

> Someone else ⎫
> Some other person ⎬ will have to take my place.

Again, *enough* is a postmodifier:
> He gave us little *enough* encouragement.

486

e The adverb modifies a noun phrase
A few degree words can modify noun phrases. They include *quite, rather, such,* and *what* (in exclamations). The noun phrase is normally indefinite, and the adverb precedes any determiners (*see* 562):
> The place was in *rather* a mess. ⟨informal⟩

> He told *such* ⎰ a funny story.
> ⎱ funny stories.

> *What* a fool he is!

487

f The adverb modifies a noun
Some adverbs denoting place or time postmodify nouns (*see* 729):

his journey *home*	the meeting *yesterday*
the sentence *below*	the day *before*
	the years *ahead*

In some phrases the adverb can also be used as a premodifier:

the *above* statement	our *upstairs* neighbour
the statement *above*	our neighbour *upstairs*

The adverb is a complement of a preposition
488
Some place and time adverbs act as complements of prepositions. Of the place adverbs, *here* and *there* occur for example with: *along, around, down, from, in, near, out (of), over, round, through, up. Home* can occur after *at, from, near, toward(s)*. Others are restricted to follow *from: above, abroad, below, downstairs, indoors, inside, outside, within, without.*
> I don't know anybody *around here*. ⟨informal⟩
> Is anybody *at home*?
> He shouted at me *from downstairs*.

Time adverbs which most commonly function as complement of prepositions are, for example:
> I haven't eaten *since yesterday*.

They didn't mention their engagement *till* (a long time) *afterwards*.
After today, there will be no more concerts until October.
I'm saving the chocolates you gave me *for later*.

Apposition (*see GCE* 9.130–180)

489

Two or more noun phrases which occur next to each other and refer to the same person or thing are said to be in APPOSITION:

A neighbour of yours, Fred Long, will be visiting us this evening   [1a]

The elements in apposition can also occur in a different order:

Fred Long, a neighbour of yours, will . . .   [1b]

The relationship expressed by apposition is the same as that expressed by a subject and its complement:

Fred Long is *a neighbour of yours*.

We can regard the second appositional element in cases like [1b] as a reduced non-restrictive relative clause (*see* 795):

Fred Long, (who is) *a neighbour of yours*, will . . .

Restrictive and non-restrictive apposition
490

A distinction similar to that between restrictive and non-restrictive relative clauses can be applied to apposition:

(Which Mr Smith do you mean?) |Mr Smith the árchitect|

   or |Mr Smith the electrician?| (RESTRICTIVE)

|I want to speak to Mr Smith, | the electrician.| (NON-RESTRICTIVE)

The elements in non-restrictive apposition are here separated by a comma ⟨writing⟩ or by separate tone units ⟨speech⟩, as in the case of non-restrictive relative clauses (*see* 411–13).

Restrictive apposition is common especially when the first element defines the meaning of the second element:

the famous critic Paul Jones	my good friend Bob
the number three	this man Smith
the novel *Les Misérables*	the letter 'A'

Sometimes the determiner is omitted ⟨*esp* written AmE⟩:

| Art critic Paul Jones | Democratic Leader Robinson |

In this case, the first element is almost like a title (as in *Professor Brown, see* 756).

Explicit apposition
491

Sometimes the appositional relation is made explicit by an adverbial (*see* 479):

   the passenger plane of the 1980s, *namely* the supersonic jet

We may also include under apposition cases where the second element exemplifies the first, or is in inclusive relation to it. In such cases a connecting adverbial, such as *for example, for instance, especially, particularly, in particular, notably, chiefly, mainly*, is normally present:

   Many famous men, *for example* De Gaulle, Churchill and Roosevelt, have visited this university.

   The children enjoyed watching the animals, *particularly* the monkeys.

For appositive clauses, *see* 725–7.

Articles (see GCE 4.13–16, 4.28–47)

492
The articles are a subclass of the determiners (see 550). There are two articles in English, the definite and the indefinite. Sometimes nouns require no article at all.

The forms of the articles
493
The spelling of the indefinite article and the pronunciation of both the definite and indefinite articles depend on the initial sound of the following word. Articles are normally unstressed, but may be stressed for special emphasis.

The unstressed definite article is always written *the* but is pronounced /ðə/ before consonants and /ðɪ/ before vowels. The indefinite article is *a* /ə/ before consonants and *an* /ən/ before vowels:

the /ðə/ ⎫
a /ə/ ⎭ boy, car, pilot, . . .

the /ðɪ/ ⎫
an /ən/ ⎭ aunt, egg, octopus, . . .

Note that it is the pronunciation, not the spelling, of the following word that determines their form:

a European /ə juərə'pɪən/ car
a UN /ə 'juː en/ spokesman
an X-ray /ən 'eksreɪ/
an FBI /ən ‚ef biː 'aɪ/ agent

Note words beginning with silent *h*: *an hour, an heir*. In one or two words that are written with initial *h*, usage varies: *a(n) hotel, a(n) historical novel*.

The stressed forms of articles are often printed in *italics*. Here the distinction in the pronunciation of the definite article disappears:

the /ðiː/ ⎫
a /eɪ/ ⎭ boy, car, pilot, . . .

the /ðiː/ ⎫
an /æn/ ⎭ aunt, egg, octopus, . . .

The stressed definite article is often used to indicate excellence or superiority in some respect, as in

(A) |Is he *the* /ðiː/ Mr Johnson?|

(B)   No. |He's *a* /eɪ/ Mr Johnson, | but not the famous one.|

The demonstration will be *the* event this week.

Article usage
494
The general grammatical rules are as follows:

The definite article can be used with all kinds of noun except most proper nouns:

SINGULAR COUNT NOUNS	*the ball/child/exam*
PLURAL COUNT NOUNS	*the balls/children/exams*
(SINGULAR) MASS NOUNS	*the gold/milk/knowledge*

The indefinite article, on the other hand, can normally only be used with singular count nouns; for other nouns the ZERO ARTICLE (or unstressed *some* /səm/) is used for indefinite meaning:

SINGULAR COUNT NOUNS	*a ball/child, an exam*
PLURAL COUNT NOUNS	*(some) balls/children/exams*
(SINGULAR) MASS NOUNS	*(some) gold/milk/knowledge*

Summary:

	DEFINITE MEANING	INDEFINITE MEANING
SINGULAR COUNT	*the ball*	*a ball*
PLURAL COUNT	*the balls*	(*some*) *balls*
MASS	*the gold*	(*some*) *gold*

The general rules of meaning for the use of articles with common nouns are discussed in Part Three (*see* 69–78). Here we shall add to that information by discussing some groups of common nouns, and the use of count nouns as complements. (For proper nouns, *see* 755–64.)

Common nouns without article
495
Below are some groups of common nouns without article, chiefly occurring in idiomatic expressions. They appear in the left-hand column. For contrast, parallel examples with regular uses of the article are given in the right-hand column.

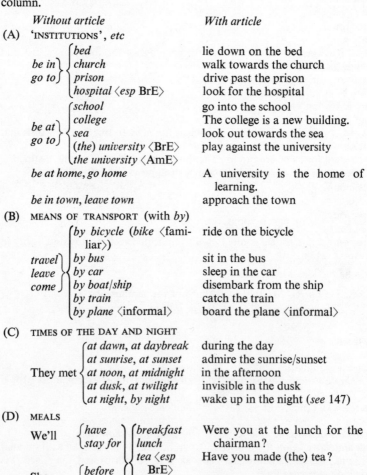

Without article   *With article*

(A) 'INSTITUTIONS', *etc*

be in ⎫ ⎧ bed   lie down on the bed
go to ⎭ ⎨ church   walk towards the church
         ⎩ prison   drive past the prison
           hospital ⟨*esp* BrE⟩   look for the hospital

be at ⎫ ⎧ school   go into the school
go to ⎭ ⎨ college   The college is a new building.
         ⎨ sea   look out towards the sea
         ⎨ (the) university ⟨BrE⟩ play against the university
         ⎩ the university ⟨AmE⟩

be at home, go home   A university is the home of
                                    learning.
be in town, leave town   approach the town

(B) MEANS OF TRANSPORT (with *by*)

travel ⎫ ⎧ by bicycle (*bike* ⟨fami- ride on the bicycle
leave ⎬ ⎨   liar⟩)
come   ⎭ ⎨ by bus   sit in the bus
         ⎨ by car   sleep in the car
         ⎨ by boat/ship   disembark from the ship
         ⎨ by train   catch the train
         ⎩ by plane ⟨informal⟩   board the plane ⟨informal⟩

(C) TIMES OF THE DAY AND NIGHT

         ⎧ at dawn, at daybreak   during the day
         ⎨ at sunrise, at sunset admire the sunrise/sunset
They met ⎨ at noon, at midnight   in the afternoon
         ⎨ at dusk, at twilight   invisible in the dusk
         ⎩ at night, by night   wake up in the night (*see* 147)

(D) MEALS

We'll ⎧ have   ⎫ ⎧ breakfast   Were you at the lunch for the
      ⎩ stay for⎭ ⎨ lunch   chairman?
                  ⎨ tea ⟨*esp*   Have you made (the) tea?
She   ⎧ before ⎫ ⎨   BrE⟩
      ⎨ at   ⎬ ⎨ dinner   She was preparing (the) dinner.
arrived ⎩ after ⎭ ⎩ supper   The supper was cold.

Dinner will be served at 6 o'clock.   The dinner was well cooked.

(E)   PARALLEL PHRASES

They walked $\begin{cases} \textit{arm in arm.} \\ \textit{hand in hand.} \end{cases}$ He took her by the arm.

What have you got in your hand?

They are *husband and wife*.   She's the wife of a famous artist.

We met *face to face*.   He punched me right in the face.

Count nouns as complements
496

Unlike many other languages, English requires an article with singular count nouns as complements (*see* 529, 839). With indefinite reference, the indefinite article is used:

Bill became *a successful businessman*.

Mary always wanted to be *a scientist*.

Mr Heyman was considered (to be) *an excellent music teacher*.

But no article is required after *turn*:

He has turned *traitor*.

With definite reference, the definite article is normally used:

Mr Fillmore was regarded as *the best mason* in the village.

However, the definite article can be omitted when the noun designates a unique role, office or task:

Who's (*the*) *captain of the team*?

We've elected Mr Crook (*the*) *chairman of the committee*.

The definite article can be similarly omitted with a noun phrase in apposition (*see* 489):

Mrs Twentyman, *wife of a leading local businessman*, was fined £50 for reckless driving last Thursday.

Auxiliary verbs (*see GCE* 3.5–8, 3.17–22, 3.43–53)

497

Auxiliary verbs are, as their name suggests, 'helping verbs'. They do not make up a verb phrase on their own, but must usually be accompanied by a following main verb. Auxiliary verbs are a small class of words, made up of primary auxiliaries like *be* and modal auxiliaries like *can* (*see* 874).

Auxiliary verbs are structurally necessary for certain constructions (especially negative and question clauses), and these constructions enable us to distinguish them from main verbs:

(A)   Auxiliary verbs can be placed before the negative word *not*:

I *am* not working today.

(B)   Auxiliary verbs can be placed before the subject in questions:

Can I help?

An auxiliary verb can occur without a main verb, but only where the main verb is omitted because it is supplied by earlier context (*see* 399):

I can speak French as well as she *can*.

Some auxiliary verbs have contracted positive forms which can be used after a pronoun (*He's leaving tomorrow, What'll you have?* etc), a short noun (*The dog's barking, The soup'll be cold*), or the words *here, there* and *now* (*There's going to be trouble, Now's the time*). In addition, most auxiliary verbs have contracted negative forms, is*n't*, can*'t*, *etc* (*see* 630). Contracted forms frequently occur in ⟨spoken⟩ and ⟨informal⟩ English.

The primary auxiliary verbs (*do, have, be*)
Do
498
The auxiliary *do* has the following forms:

		Non-negative	Uncontracted Negative	Contracted Negative
present ⎰	3rd person	⎰ *does*	⎰ *does not*	⎰ *doesn't*
⎱	other	⎱ *do*	⎱ *do not*	⎱ *don't*
past		*did*	*did not*	*didn't*

Note *Do* is also *a* a main verb (='perform', *etc*) and *b* a substitute verb (*see* 398–9) with the full range of forms like other main verbs, including the present participle *doing* and the past participle *done*:

a   What have you been *doing* today?
b   (A)   You said you would finish it.
     (B)   I have *done* (so).

Have
499
Like *do*, *have* is both a main verb and an auxiliary. It has the following forms (*see* 619):

	Uncontracted Non-negative	Contracted Non-negative	Uncontracted Negative	Contracted Negative
base	*have*	*'ve*	*have not, 've not*	*haven't*
-*s* form	*has*	*'s*	*has not, 's not*	*hasn't*
past	*had*	*'d*	*had not, 'd not*	*hadn't*
-*ing* form	*having*		*not having*	
-*ed* participle	*had*			

As a main verb (='possess'), *have* is sometimes constructed as an auxiliary ⟨*esp* BrE⟩. ⟨AmE⟩ prefers the *do*-construction:

    I *haven't* any books. ⟨*esp* BrE⟩
    I *don't have* any books. ⟨AmE⟩ and ⟨BrE⟩

When used as an event verb (*see* 104–5) in the sense of 'receive, take, experience', *etc*, the main verb *have* normally has the *do*-construction in both ⟨AmE⟩ and ⟨BrE⟩:

    Does he *have* coffee with his breakfast?
    Did you *have* any difficulty getting here?

The *do*-construction is also required in such expressions as

    Did you *have* a good time?

There is also the ⟨informal⟩ *have got* 'possess', where *have* is constructed as an auxiliary. It is particularly common in negative and interrogative sentences:

    I *haven't got* any books.
    Have you *got* the tickets?

The normal negative of *You'd better stay* is *You'd better not stay*.

Be
500
Be is constructed as an auxiliary even when it functions as a main verb. For example, it normally has no *do*-construction (*but see* Note *b*). It has eight different forms:

		Non-negative	Uncontracted Negative	Contracted Negative
base		*be*		
present	1st person singular	*am, 'm*	*am not, 'm not*	*(aren't, ain't)*[a]
	3rd person singular	*is, 's*	*is not, 's not*	*isn't*
	2nd person, 1st and 3rd person plural	*are, 're*	*are not, 're not*	*aren't*
past	1st and 3rd person singular	*was*	*was not*	*wasn't*
	2nd person, 1st and 3rd person plural	*were*	*were not*	*weren't*
-ing form		*being*	*not being*	
-ed participle		*been*		

Note

[a] *Aren't I* is widely used in questions in ⟨BrE⟩, but there is no generally acceptable contracted form for *am not* in declarative sentences. *Ain't* is ⟨substandard BrE⟩ and is so considered by many in ⟨AmE⟩. As well as serving as a contracted *am not*, it is used also for *isn't*, *aren't*, *hasn't* and *haven't*.

[b] The main verb *be* may have the *do*-construction in persuasive imperative sentences and regularly has it with negative imperatives (*see* 520):

> Do be quiet!
> Don't be awkward!

[c] In the construction *be + to*-infinitive only the finite (present and past) forms of *be* can be used:

> The Prime Minister *is* to make a statement tomorrow.

*But not** The Prime Minister $\begin{Bmatrix} will\ be \\ is\ being \end{Bmatrix}$ to . . .

The modal auxiliaries

501

The modal auxiliaries do not have *-s* forms, *-ing* forms, or *-ed* participles. *Can, may, shall, will* have special past forms (*could, etc*), but the remainder (such as *must*) do not.

Non-negative	Uncontracted Negative	Contracted Negative[a]
can	*cannot, can not*	*can't*
could	*could not*	*couldn't*
may	*may not*	*(mayn't)*[b]
might	*might not*	*mightn't*
shall	*shall not*	*shan't*[c]
should	*should not*	*shouldn't*
will, 'll	*will not, 'll not*	*won't*
would, 'd	*would not, 'd not*	*wouldn't*
must	*must not*	*mustn't*
ought to	*ought not to*	*oughtn't to*[d]

Non-negative	Uncontracted Negative	Contracted Negative
used to	*used not to*	$\begin{cases} \textit{didn't use(d) to} \\ \textit{usedn't to} \end{cases}$
need	*need not*	*needn't*
dare	*dare not*	*daren't*

Note

[a]   Sometimes there is a choice between two contracted forms, *eg won't* and *'ll not*.

[b]   *Mayn't* is restricted to ⟨BrE⟩, where it is rare.

[c]   *Shan't* is rare in ⟨AmE⟩.

[d]   *Ought* regularly has the *to*-infinitive, but occasionally the bare infinitive is used in negative sentences and in questions (although *should* is commoner in both cases):

> You *oughtn't smoke* so much.
>
> *Ought* you *smoke* so much?

Used to
502

Used always takes the *to*-infinitive and occurs only in the past tense. It may take the *do*-construction, in which case the spellings *use* and *used* |juːst| both occur:

> He *didn't use* to *smoke.*

The interrogative construction *Used he to smoke?* is ⟨*esp* BrE⟩. *Did he use(d) to smoke?* is preferred in both ⟨AmE⟩ and ⟨BrE⟩. However, a different construction is often a more natural choice, for example:

> *Did he smoke when you first knew him?*

Dare and need
503

Dare and *need* can be constructed (A) as modal auxiliaries (with bare infinitive and without the inflected forms *dares/needs*, *dared/needed*) or (B) as main verbs (with *to*-infinitive, *-s* inflection and past forms). The modal auxiliary construction is mainly restricted to negative and interrogative sentences, whereas the main verb construction can always be used and is in fact the more common. *Dare* and *need* as auxiliaries are probably rarer in ⟨AmE⟩ than in ⟨BrE⟩.

	Modal Auxiliary Construction	Main Verb Construction
positive	—	He *needs to* go now.
negative	He *needn't* go now.	He *doesn't need to* go now.
interrogative	*Need* he go now?	*Does* he *need to* go now?
negative-interrogative	*Needn't* he go yet?	*Doesn't* he *need to* go yet?

Note

[a]   The modal auxiliary construction is not confined to negative and/or interrogative sentences but can also occur in other contexts with similar meanings, for example,

> He need do it only under these circumstances.
>
> He need do it but once.
>
> He need have no fear.
>
> No soldier dare disobey.
>
> Nobody would dare predict . . .
>
> All you need do is . . . ('You need do no more than . . . ')

[*b*]   A mixture of the two constructions is sometimes found in the case of
dare, which may have the *do*-construction with a bare infinitive:
>We did not dare speak.

Case (*see GCE* 4.93)

504

In English, the personal pronouns *I, he, she, we, they* have three case forms,
subjective, objective, and genitive (*see* 684, 687). But nouns and other pronouns
(except *who, see* 579, 788) have only two cases: the common case (*the boy*) and
the genitive case (*the boy's*). The common case, which has no special ending, is
the case which is found in all circumstances except where the genitive is required
(*see* 570–2).

Clauses (*see GCE* 7.1–12, 11.4–7)

505

Clauses are the principal structures of which sentences are composed. A sentence
may consist of one, or more than one clause (*see* 797). There are three important
ways in which clauses may be described and classified:
(A)   In terms of the CLAUSE ELEMENTS (subject, verb, *etc*) from which they are
constructed, and the VERB PATTERNS which are formed from these elements (*see* 835–72).
(B)   In terms of the amount of use which a clause makes of verb phrase
structure (*see* 873–79). On this ground, we distinguish between FINITE
CLAUSES, NON-FINITE CLAUSES, and VERBLESS CLAUSES (*see* 513–16).
(C)   In terms of CLAUSE FUNCTION, *ie* the function a clause performs in a
sentence; *eg* whether it is a NOMINAL CLAUSE (acting as a noun phrase),
an ADVERBIAL CLAUSE (acting as an adverbial element), *etc* (*see* 517).
We shall deal with each of these in turn.

Clause elements
506

A clause can be analysed into five different types of clause elements: SUBJECT
(S, *see* 822), VERB (or rather VERB PHRASE, V, *see* 873), COMPLEMENT (C, *see* 529),
OBJECT (O, *see* 670–1), and ADVERBIAL (A, *see* 468–79), for example

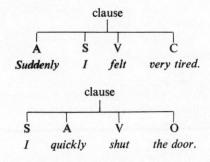

507

We may broadly distinguish the 'MAIN' ELEMENTS of clause structure (subject,
verb, complement, object) and the 'MODIFYING' ELEMENTS (adverbials). Adverbials differ from the other types of clause elements in at least three respects:
(1)   Adverbials are usually OPTIONAL, *ie* they may be omitted without making
the clause unacceptable (optional elements are placed in brackets):
>(Suddenly) I felt tired.
>I (quickly) shut the door.

But not   *I felt.
               *I shut.

(2) Adverbials are NOT RESTRICTED IN NUMBER. Whereas a clause can only have one subject, one finite verb, one complement, and one or two objects, there may be, in theory at least, any number of adverbials (but there are rarely more than three or four adverbials in one clause). (Compare, however, coordinated clause elements, *see* 544.)

SV: The children played.
SV(A):   The children played (*by the lake*).
SV(A)(A):   The children played (*all day*) (*by the lake*).
(A)SV(A)(A):   (*Sometimes*) the children played (*all day*) (*by the lake*).

(3) Adverbials are often MOBILE, *ie* they can occur at different places in the clause:

S(A)V(A):   The children (*sometimes*) played (*by the lake*).
SV(A)(A):   The children played (*by the lake*) (*sometimes*).

(On the position of adverbials, *see* 470–8.)

The basic verb patterns (for more details *see* 835–72)
508
If we concentrate on the main elements in the clause, we can distinguish six basic verb patterns. (We call them 'verb patterns' rather than 'clause patterns', since it is the verb that determines the type of clause structure.)

Verb pattern [L]: LINKING VERBS
    Mary is *a nurse/pretty.*
    Mary is *here.*
Verb pattern [T]: VERBS WITH ONE OBJECT (transitive verbs)
    Everybody admired *her new car.*
Verb pattern [V]: VERBS WITH OBJECT + VERB (+ ...)
    They told *me to stay.*
Verb pattern [D]: VERBS WITH TWO OBJECTS (ditransitive verbs)
    She gave *all the children presents.*
Verb pattern [X]: VERBS WITH OBJECT AND OBJECT COMPLEMENT
    They considered *the car too expensive.*
Verb pattern [I]: VERBS WITHOUT OBJECT OR COMPLEMENT (intransitive verbs)
    The children laughed.

The active-passive relation (*see* 676–82)
509
There are certain relations between clause elements: one is the relation which makes it possible to change an active clause into a passive clause. Of the active verb patterns in 508, the following can normally occur in the passive:

PATTERN	ACTIVE	PASSIVE
[T] (SVO)	Everybody admired her new car.	Her new car was admired by everybody.
[V] (SVOV)	They told me to stay.	I was told to stay.
[D] (SVOO)	She gave all the children presents.	All the children were given presents. / Presents were given (to) all the children.
[X] (SVOC)	They considered the car (to be) too expensive.	The car was considered (to be) too expensive.

Since the object of the active clause is converted into the subject of the passive clause, we find here that only four of the six basic verb patterns can occur in the passive, namely, those patterns which contain an object. Pattern [D] usually has two passive forms, because it has two objects, either of which can usually become subject in the passive.

The complements of subjects and objects (Patterns [L] and [X])
510
The commonest verb in verb pattern [L] is *be*. Here *be* is not an auxiliary, as in *He is coming* (*see* 872), but a main verb (*see* 500). Since *be* links together the subject and the complement, we call it a LINKING VERB. There are also other linking verbs (*see* 838):

a   You *look* a lot better today, Ann.   verbs of 'appearance'
    We *felt* terribly annoyed at their behaviour.   and 'sensation'
b   They *became* very good friends.   verbs of 'becoming'
    She soon *got* tired of waiting.

511
An adjective complement can usually become a premodifier of a noun (*see* 732):

    The nurse was *pretty*.

    (She was) a *pretty* nurse.

If the complement is a noun, as in

    My daughter is *a nurse*.

the subject and its complement refer to the same person or thing.

512
Verb pattern [X] SVOC can often be expanded by a *to be* infinitive or paraphrased by a *that*-clause (*see* 848, 867):

    They considered *the car to be too expensive*.

    They thought *that the car was too expensive*.

This shows that the object and the complement of the SVOC verb pattern have the same relation of meaning as the subject and complement of an SVC pattern [L]: *The car was too expensive*.

Finite, non-finite, and verbless clauses
513
A second way of classifying a clause is on the basis of what kind of verb phrase (if any) acts as its V element. The three types of clause that have to be distinguished are: (A) finite clauses, (B) non-finite clauses, and (C) verbless clauses.
514
(A)   FINITE CLAUSES are clauses whose verb element is a finite verb phrase (*see* 875–6), *ie* where the first word of the verb phrase is finite, and (in general) alters its form for past tense:

    Bill *has/had gone* to the office.

    He *won't be* back until ten, because he*'s working* late.

    He *loves* hard work.

All the clauses which have illustrated the verb patterns above (*see* 508) have been finite clauses. The finite clause is the most important of the three types because a complete sentence has at least one independent finite clause.

515
(B)   NON-FINITE CLAUSES are clauses whose verb element is a non-finite verb phrase, *ie a* an *-ing* participle (*see* 621), *b* an *-ed* participle (*see* 622), or *c* an infinitive (*see* 624). Non-finite clauses can be constructed without a subject, and they usually are. Apart from the frequent omission of the subject, the verb patterns described earlier apply to non-finite as well as to finite clauses.

a *-ing* PARTICIPLE CLAUSES (or *-ing* CLAUSES)

without a subject: *Entering the house*, he tripped over the welcome mat. (VO)

with a subject: *The matter having been settled so amicably*, I felt quite satisfied with the results. (SVA)

b *-ed* PARTICIPLE CLAUSES (or *-ed* CLAUSES)

without a subject: *Covered with confusion*, she hurriedly left the room. (VA)

with a subject: *The job finished*, we went home straight away. (SV)

c *to*-INFINITIVE CLAUSES

without a subject: The best thing would be *to tell everybody*. (VO)

with a subject: The best thing would be *for you to tell everybody*. (SVO)

The subject of an infinitive clause is often introduced by the preposition *for*.

d BARE INFINITIVE CLAUSES (*ie* containing an infinitive without *to*)

These are much less common than *to*-infinitive clauses.

without a subject: All I did was *hit him on the head*.

with a subject: Rather than *John do it*, I'd prefer to do the job myself.

516

(C) VERBLESS CLAUSES are clauses which contain no verb element, and often also no subject. They are regarded as clauses because they function in ways which make them equivalent to finite and non-finite clauses, and because they can be analysed in terms of one or more clause elements. We can usually assume that a form of the verb *be* has been omitted:

Dozens of tourists were stranded, *many of them children* (*ie* 'many of the tourists *were* children').   [1]

A sleeping bag under each arm, Mr Johnson tramped off on his vacation (*ie* 'there *was* a sleeping bag under each of his arms').   [2]

The verbless clause in [1] has the structure SC (subject + complement); the verbless clause in [2] has the structure SA (subject + adverbial).

The subject, when omitted, can usually be understood as equivalent to the subject of the main clause:

The oranges, *when ripe*, are picked and sorted (= 'when they are ripe').

Whether right or wrong, Michael always comes off worst in an argument (= 'whether he is right or wrong').

An adjective (alone or as head of the adjective phrase) can function as a verbless clause. The clause is mobile, though it usually precedes or follows the subject of the main clause:

{ *By then nervous*, the man opened the letter.
{ The man, *by then nervous*, opened the letter.

Long and untidy, his hair waved in the breeze.

Anxious for a quick decision, the chairman called for a vote.

An adverb may sometimes replace, with little difference in meaning, an adjective functioning as a verbless clause:

Nervously, }
Nervous, } the man opened the letter.

Clause functions
517
In terms of function, *ie* what role they have in a sentence, clauses can be divided into MAIN CLAUSES and SUBCLAUSES (subordinate clauses) (*see* 826–7). Subclauses are those which are part of another clause: we can further divide them into categories such as nominal clauses, adverbial clauses, *etc.* The various functions of clauses are treated elsewhere under the following entries:

(A) NOMINAL CLAUSES (*see* 637–50), *ie that*-clauses, interrogative clauses, *-ing* clauses, and infinitive clauses as subject, object, complement, prepositional complement, *etc.* For example, in

> *That he gave a false name* shows *that he was doing something dishonest.*

both the subject and the object are *that*-clauses.

(B) RELATIVE CLAUSES (*see* 783–96), *ie* clauses introduced by *wh*-pronouns or *that*, for example

> The family *who live opposite our house* are French.

Relative clauses are usually postmodifiers in noun phrases.

(C) COMMENT CLAUSES (*see* 522), for example

> *To be honest*, I'm not sure what to do.

Comment clauses function as sentence adverbials.

(D) COMPARATIVE CLAUSES (*see* 527), for example

> This road is less crowded *than the other one was.*

(E) ADVERBIAL CLAUSES (*see* 468), which have a large number of different meanings, are discussed in Part Three: clauses denoting time (*see* 140–60), place (*see* 161), contrast (*see* 212–15), cause or reason (*see* 199, 204), purpose (*see* 203), result (*see* 202), and conditional clauses (*see* 208–10).

Cleft sentences (*see GCE* 14.18–23)

(A) The *it*-type cleft sentence
518
A single clause, for example,

> John bought an old car last week.   [1]

can be divided into two separate parts, each with its own verb:

> It was John who bought an old car last week.   [1a]

A construction like [1a] is called a CLEFT SENTENCE (*see* 434). Sentence [1] can be changed into different cleft sentences depending on what element is considered the most important in the sentence (focus, *see* 414–15):

> |It was an old car that John bought last week.|
>
>   (OBJECT IS FOCUS)   [1b]

> |It was last week that John bought an old car.|
>
>   (ADVERBIAL IS FOCUS)   [1c]

The second part of a cleft sentence is very similar to a restrictive relative clause (*see* 794): the relative pronouns are also used in cleft sentences.

(B) The *wh*-type cleft sentence
519
Besides the *it*-type, there is also a *wh*-type of cleft sentence [2b] (*see* 435). Compare [1b] with

> |What John bought last week | was an old car.| [2b]

Cleft sentences are to be contrasted with sentences with introductory *there* (*see* 590–4) and introductory *it* (*see* 584–9). In introductory *it*-sentences, *it* introduces a clause, and there is no emphasised clause element to act as focus:

> It's no use *trying to wake him up.*

Commands (*see GCE* 7.72–77)

2nd person commands
520

A command is usually a sentence with an imperative verb, *ie* the base form of the verb, without endings for number or tense.

> *Come* here.

Commands are apt to sound abrupt unless they are toned down by signals of politeness such as *please* (*see* 347):

> Please *eat* up your dinner.
>
> *Shut* the door, please.

There are no auxiliary verbs in commands except *do* (*see* 675), which must occur in negative commands, and may also occur in positive commands:

> *Don't stay* too late, John.   (NEGATIVE COMMAND)
>
> *Do sit* down.   (EMPHATIC OR PERSUASIVE COMMAND)

Notice that in commands, but not elsewhere, *do* can be followed by *be:*

> *Don't be* noisy.   *but*: They *weren't* noisy.
>
> *Do be* careful.   *but*: They *are* careful.

Although commands usually have no subject, we can say that, when the subject is missing, there is an IMPLIED subject *you*. This is evident when a reflexive pronoun (*see* 691–5) or a tag (*see* 781) is used:

> Be quiet, will *you*!
>
> Behave *yourself*.

However, a subject *you* does sometimes occur in commands:

> *You* just listen to me.
>
> *You* go ahead.

Here *you* is always stressed, whereas in statements it is not stressed:

> 'You 'put it do̱wn.   (COMMAND)
>
> You 'put it do̱wn.   (STATEMENT)

1st and 3rd person commands
521

1st person and 3rd person commands also occur, but less frequently than 2nd person commands.

A 1st person command begins with *let* followed by *me* in the singular, or *us* (normally abbreviated to *'s*) in the plural:

> *Let me* have a look at your essay.
>
> *Let's* have dinner. ⟨informal⟩

A 3rd person command has a 3rd person subject, which is preceded by *let* in ⟨formal⟩, often ⟨elevated⟩ style:

> *Somebody let* me out. ⟨informal⟩
>
> *Let somebody* else attempt this task. ⟨formal⟩

Comment clauses (*see GCE* 11.65–66)

522

Comment clauses are so called because they do not so much add to the information in a sentence as comment on its truth, the manner of saying it, or the attitude of the speaker. They are only loosely related to the rest of the main clause they belong to, and function as sentence adverbials (*see* 479). They are usually marked off from the other clause, in ⟨written⟩ English by commas, and in ⟨speech⟩ by having a separate tone unit. Comment clauses can freely occur in front-, mid- and end-positions in the clause, but the end-position is mainly restricted to ⟨informal speech⟩.

At that time, *I believe*, Bill worked as a mechanic.

What's more, we lost all our belongings.

Stated bluntly, he has no chance of recovery.

|The Smiths | *as you probably know* | are going to America|

|He's a pacifist | *you see*|

|I'm not sure what to do | *to be honest*|

Other everyday examples of comment clauses are:

you know	you bet ⟨familiar⟩
I know	I see
I think	I suppose
I'm afraid	as you see
as I said	to be frank
so to say	so to speak
put frankly	what's more likely

Comment clauses are of varied types, as these examples show. The most frequent type is probably that of finite clauses without any introductory word: *you see, you know, I think, etc.* These are closely parallel to main clauses introducing a *that*-clause (*see* 848). Compare:

I see that the Joneses have a new pet.

The Joneses have a new pet, *I see*.

Comparison (*see* 229–37, *see GCE* 5.68–77, 11.53–64)

523

Gradable adjectives and adverbs (*see* 218, 456) have degrees of comparison. Comparison is expressed either by the endings *-er* and *-est* or by the words *more* and *most*:

		COMPARATIVE	SUPERLATIVE
ADJECTIVES	{ tall	{ taller	{ tallest
	{ beautiful	{ *more* beautiful	{ *most* beautiful
ADVERBS	{ soon	{ sooner	{ soonest
	{ easily	{ *more* easily	{ *most* easily

Comparison of adjectives

524

The endings are generally used with

a Adjectives consisting of one syllable:

great   greater   greatest

b Adjectives consisting of two syllables and ending in *-y, -ow, -le, -er,* and *-ure*:

funny (funnier, funniest), friendly, lively, *etc*

hollow (hollower, hollowest), narrow, shallow, *etc*

feeble (feebler, feeblest), gentle, noble, *etc*

clever (cleverer, cleverest), mature, obscure, *etc*

c Some common two-syllable adjectives, for example *common, handsome, polite, quiet*, which can have either type of comparison:

common	{ commoner	{ commonest
	{ more common	{ most common

The endings sometimes involve changes in spelling or pronunciation (*see* 809, 817, 820), for example:

pretty	prettier	prettiest
big	bigger	biggest

Other adjectives than those mentioned in *a*, *b*, or *c* can form comparison only with *more* and *most*, for example:

interesting	more interesting	most interesting

A small group of highly frequent adjectives have irregular comparison:

bad	worse	worst
good	better	best
far	further/farther	furthest/farthest

Old is regularly inflected *older*, *oldest*, but in a specialised use, restricted to family relations, the irregular forms *elder*, *eldest* are normally substituted in attributive and head position:

My *elder brother* is an artist.

John is *the elder* of the two brothers.

Note that before a *than*-construction, we always use *older*:

My brother is *older than* I am.

Comparison of adverbs
525
Adverbs have the same general rules of comparison as adjectives. (This is of course true also for adverbs that are identical in form with adjectives, *early*, *etc*):

early	earlier	earliest

Note that adverbs of two syllables ending in *-ly* do not follow the rule of adjectives ending in *-y* (*eg funny, see* 524):

quickly	more quickly	most quickly

As with adjectives, there is a small group of adverbs with irregular comparison:

well	better	best
badly	worse	worst
little	less	least
much	more	most
far	further/farther	furthest/farthest

Comparison of quantifiers
526
The quantifiers *much*, *many*, *little* and *few* (*see* 766, 773) also have special comparative and superlative forms, as follows:

much	more	most
many	more	most
little	less	least
few	fewer/less	fewest/least

Comparative clauses
527
The comparative form of adjectives and adverbs is used when we want to compare one thing with another in order to point out some difference (*see* 229, 231). For this purpose, a subclause beginning with *than* can be added after the comparative word:

His most recent book is *more interesting* than his previous ones
were.   [1]

She can knit *better* than she can sew.   [2]

Bill speaks French $\begin{Bmatrix} worse \\ less\ well \end{Bmatrix}$ than he writes it.   [3]

The part of the sentences in *italics* may be called the 'hinge' element of the comparison. The hinge element is the phrase which contains the comparative word, and which the *than*-clause postmodifies. This element may be a noun phrase, an adjective phrase, or an adverbial phrase. It is called a 'hinge' because it belongs, in terms of meaning, both to the main clause and to the comparative subclause. Thus in terms of meaning, the hinge element *more interesting* in [1] acts as the complement of *is* in the main clause and of *were* in the subclause. In terms of structure, however, the subclause in [1] does not contain a complement. In general, a comparative clause lacks at least one element of clause structure: namely, the element corresponding to the 'hinge' element.

Comparative phrases
528
In addition, other elements of a subclause can be omitted if they repeat the information in the main clause. If these elements are omitted, however, we are left with a COMPARATIVE PHRASE rather than a comparative clause. That is, *than* is more like a preposition than a conjunction:

There are more pubs *than shops* in this village.

Jack is five years older *than his sister* (= than his sister is).

Bill can speak French more fluently *than* $\begin{cases} I. & \text{⟨formal⟩} \\ me. & \text{⟨informal⟩} \end{cases}$

We scored three more goals *than* $\begin{cases} they. & \text{⟨formal⟩} \\ them. & \text{⟨informal⟩} \end{cases}$

(= '. . . than they scored')

Notice that in ⟨informal⟩ English, the *than*-phrase behaves like a prepositional phrase, in that the following pronoun is in the objective case (*see* 504). In ⟨formal⟩ English, on the other hand, the subjective pronoun is used if the pronoun is notionally the subject of the omitted verb.

In ⟨informal⟩ English such clauses can be ambiguous:

Mr Pettigrew is more fond of his secretary than his wife.

The most likely meaning is:

Mr Pettigrew is more fond of his secretary than he is (fond) of his wife.

But another possible meaning is:

Mr Pettigrew is more fond of his secretary than his wife is.

Adverbials (such as *ever, usual, in the water*) can follow *than* in comparative phrases:

There were more people on the beach than $\begin{cases} ever. \\ usual. \\ in\ the\ water. \end{cases}$

Some other types of comparative phrase cannot be related to comparative clauses. One type is illustrated in:

There were fewer than twenty people at the meeting.

I have better things to do than watching television.

The plane flies faster than 1,000 miles per hour.

Another type of construction is not so much concerned with comparison of degree and amount as with comparison of descriptions:

They pulled him out of the water *more dead than alive*.

The meaning here is roughly: 'he might have been better described as dead rather than alive'. Comparison with *-er* cannot be used in this construction (**deader than alive*). Instead, *more* and *less* are used even where in ordinary comparison they would not be acceptable. For example:

The performance was more good than bad.

(*not*: . . . better than bad)

The constructions we have discussed here are found not only with unequal comparisons (*more, less*), but with 'equal' comparisons (*as much as, etc*) (*see* 230).

Complements (*see GCE* 6.1–3, 7.2–3, 7.11, 12.29–70)

529

The term COMPLEMENT, in a general sense, means something that is necessary to complete a grammatical construction. We distinguish three types of complement: (A) CLAUSE COMPLEMENTS, (B) ADJECTIVE COMPLEMENTS, and (C) PREPOSITIONAL COMPLEMENTS.

(A) Clause complements (*see* 510–12)
The complement of a clause can be

    a a noun phrase (*see* 838–9):   Mary is *a capable girl.*
    b an adjective (*see* 841):   Mary is *capable.*
    c a nominal clause (*see* 637):
          The trouble with Mary is *that she never does any homework.*

The complement can be distinguished from the subject of a clause in that it normally comes after the verb. If there is both an object and a complement in the sentence, the complement normally comes after the object:

    Bad jokes make John *angry.*

Unlike the object, the complement does not become subject if an active sentence is turned into a passive sentence (*see* 677).

A complement often expresses a quality or attribute of the subject or object (*John was absolutely furious*). In other cases (*My best friend is John*), it tells us the identity of the subject or object.

The complement cannot, normally, be omitted. If we take away the complement, the remaining part does not make a good English sentence:

    Bad jokes make John *angry.*
    *Bad jokes make John.

(B) Adjective complements
530
Adjectives and adjectival participles may take different complements (*see* 452–5):

             glad.
She'll be   glad (*that*) *you are coming.* (*that*-CLAUSE)
             glad *to hear the good news.* (*to*-INFINITIVE)
             glad *of your success.*   (PREPOSITIONAL PHRASE)

(C) Prepositional complements
531
A prepositional phrase consists of a preposition and its complement, which is usually a noun phrase, a *wh*-clause, or an *-ing* clause (*see* 739–43):

             the change.
They argued *about*   *what was to be changed.*
             changing the agreement.

Concord (*see GCE* 7.23–36)

532
CONCORD (also called AGREEMENT) means that certain grammatical items agree with each other in (A) number (*see* 654–9) or (B) person (*see* 683).

(A) Concord of number
a Subject-verb concord
533
In English, the question of number concord arises only with present tense verbs, and with the past tense of *be*: *He* KNOWS | *They* KNOW; | *He* WAS | *They* WERE. A clause acting as subject counts as singular:

    To treat them as hostages IS criminal.

Plural words and phrases count as singular if they are used as names, titles, quotations, *etc*:

> *The Brothers Karamazov* IS undoubtedly Dostoyevsky's master-piece.

b Pronoun concord
534
A pronoun which refers to a singular noun phrase is in the singular, and a pronoun which refers to a plural noun phrase is in the plural:

> *The boy* likes HIS toys.
> *The boys* like THEIR toys.

Notional concord
535
There are two factors which interfere with the number concord rule as stated in 532: notional concord and proximity. We find, for example, that the singular form of a group noun like *government* (*see* 47) can be treated as plural in

$$\text{The government } \begin{Bmatrix} \text{HAVE} \\ has \end{Bmatrix} \text{ broken all } \begin{Bmatrix} \text{THEIR} \\ its \end{Bmatrix} \text{ promises.}$$

This is called NOTIONAL CONCORD, since the verb agrees with the *idea* of plural in the group noun rather than the actual singular *form* of the noun.

Concord with group nouns
536
Group nouns occur with either grammatical or notional concord in examples such as:

> The *public* IS/ARE tired of demonstrations.
> The *audience* WAS/WERE enjoying every minute of the show.
> Our Planning *Committee* HAS/HAVE considered your request.
> The vast *majority* of the students NEEDS/NEED increased financial support.

When the group is being considered as a single undivided body, the singular is used:

> The *public* CONSISTS of you and me.
> The *audience* WAS enormous.
> My *company* IS opening a new factory.

The plural verb after a group noun is more characteristic of ⟨BrE⟩ than of ⟨AmE⟩.

Proximity
537
Another factor which sometimes upsets the concord rule in ⟨informal⟩ English is the principle of PROXIMITY. This means that the verb tends to agree with whatever noun or pronoun closely precedes it, instead of the headword of the subject:

> A large number of *people* HAVE applied for the job.

Here the head of the noun phrase is *number* (singular), and one would expect the verb form *has*. Instead the plural noun *people* in the postmodifying *of*-phrase influences the form of the nearby verb. (This can also be considered a case of notional concord.)

Concord with coordinated subjects
538
When a subject consists of two or more noun phrases coordinated by *and*, the verb is usually in the plural if the coordination is taken to be a reduction of two clauses (*see* 542–3):

> *Tom and Mary* ARE ready.
> (= 'Tom is ready and Mary is ready.')

But a singular verb is used
> *a* with coordinated elements which represent a single entity:
>> *The hammer and sickle* WAS flying from a tall flagpole.
> *b* when the noun phrases refer to the same thing:
>> *His lawyer and former college friend, Max Fairford,* WAS with
>> him at his death.

It is also possible to have a plural verb following a singular noun phrase where that noun phrase has a mass noun as head, and refers to two or more coordinated ideas:
> *Dutch and American beer* ARE lighter than British (= 'Dutch beer
> and American beer . . . ').

539

When two noun phrases are joined by *or* or *either . . . or*, the general rule is that the number of the verb is determined by the number of the *last* noun phrase (PROXIMITY):
> Either *your brakes* or *your eyesight* IS at fault.   [1]
> Either *your eyesight* or *your brakes* ARE at fault.   [2]

In [1] the proximity rule applies, but is felt to be awkward by some people. To avoid the awkwardness, it is usually possible to use an auxiliary verb which has the same form in the singular and the plural, for example:
> Either *your brakes* or *your eyesight* MUST be at fault.

Concord with indefinite expressions of amount
540

Indefinite expressions of amount, especially *no, none* and *any*, often cause concord problems:
> So far *no money* HAS been spent on repairs.   (MASS)
> *No person* of that name LIVES here.   (SINGULAR COUNT)
> *No people* of that name LIVE here.   (PLURAL COUNT)
> I've ordered the cement, but *none* (*of it*) HAS yet arrived.   (MASS)
> I've ordered the shrubs, but *none* (*of them*)
> HAVE/HAS yet arrived.   (SINGULAR OR PLURAL COUNT)

In the last example, grammatical concord insists that *none* is singular, but notional concord invites a plural verb. *Has* is typical of ⟨written, formal⟩ style, whereas *have* is more idiomatic in ⟨informal⟩ English.

The same rule also applies to *neither* and *either*:
> I sent cards to Mavis and Margery but *neither* (of them) HAS/
> HAVE replied. In fact, I doubt if *either* (of them) IS/ARE coming.

The plural pronoun *they* is often used in ⟨informal⟩ style as a replacement of *everyone, everybody, someone, somebody, anyone, anybody, no one, nobody*:
> *Everyone* thinks *they* have the answer.
> Has *anybody* brought *their* camera?

In ⟨formal⟩ English, the tendency is to use *he* when the sex is not stated:
> *Everyone* thinks *he* has the answer.

(B) Concord of person
541

As well as concord of number, there is concord of person. *Be* has three forms in the present tense (*see* 500); main verbs have only two (*see* 624–5); modal auxiliaries have only one (*see* 501):

Be (the present tense): *I* AM, *he* IS, *they* ARE
MAIN VERBS: *He* (*our friend, etc*) COMPLAINS
MODAL AUXILIARIES: *I* (*you,* | *we* | *they,* | *our friends, etc*) COMPLAIN
                        I (*we, you, he, our friend, our friends, etc*) CAN come.

Coordination (*see GCE* 9.24–129)

Coordination of clauses
542

Clauses or phrases may be linked together (coordinated) by the conjunctions *and*, *or*, *but*. In these examples, the conjunctions are used to link clauses:

John plays the piano *and* his sister plays the guitar.   [1]

You can boil yourself an egg *or* (you can) make some cheese
    sandwiches.   [2]

They may complain *but* (they) haven't said anything yet.   [3]

When the subjects of the two clauses refer to the same person or thing, the second subject is normally omitted, as in [2] and [3]. Further, if the clauses have matching auxiliary verbs, they are also generally omitted, as in [2].

Here are some further examples of coordinated clauses, with the parts that are usually omitted in brackets:

He found his key *and* (he) opened the door.

I'm selling the car *and* (I'm) buying a new one.

He may have received the letter *but* (he may have) forgotten to reply.

Coordination can be used to link parts of clauses (*eg* subjects, verb phrases, objects) rather than whole clauses. Often we can say, as above, that these are cases of clause coordination in which repeated elements are omitted. For example, the meaning of [4] can be expanded as in [5]:

I bought some bacon and a loaf of bread.   [4]

I bought some bacon and I bought a loaf of bread.   [5]

But in other cases we cannot reconstruct two complete clauses:

My closest friends are Fred and his wife.

This does not mean:

*My closest friend is Fred and my closest friend is his wife.

In addition, there are cases of coordination which may indicate a 'reciprocal' relationship:

Roderick and Mabel are in love. (= 'Roderick is in love with Mabel,
    and Mabel is in love with Roderick.')

Our poodle and the dog down the road were having a fight. (= 'Our
    poodle and the dog . . . were having a fight with *each other*.')

Because of these different functions of coordination in phrases we shall treat coordination of phrases in terms of what elements are *linked*, rather than what elements are *omitted*. We deal with the omission of repeated elements elsewhere (*see* 406).

Coordination of clause elements
543
Some examples are:

SUBJECTS

Fred and *his wife* are my closest friends.

VERB PHRASES

He *speaks*, or *used to speak*, with a very strong accent.

COMPLEMENTS

The hotel was *very expensive* but *rather dirty*.

ADVERBIALS

You can wash this sweater *by hand* or *in the washing machine*.

PREPOSITIONAL COMPLEMENTS

Our team plays in *red shirts* and *white shorts*.

Coordination of words
544
Coordination can also link two words of the same word class. For example:
NOUNS
>Many *boys* and *girls* prefer to dress in the same way nowadays.

ADJECTIVES
>The house was so *old* and *dirty* that no one wanted to buy it.

CONJUNCTIONS
>*If* and *when* the agreement is signed, we can look forward to a period of peace and cooperation.

Coordination of combinations and parts of phrases
545
In addition, coordination can link combinations of phrases (*eg* combinations of sentence elements), even where these do not occur next to one another in the sentence:
SUBJECT AND VERB PHRASE
>*The papers say*, and *most people believe*, that the Democrats will win the next election.

SUBJECT AND COMPLEMENT
>*Martha* is *secretary* and *John chairman*.

Also combinations of words which do not make a complete phrase can be linked:
>The fund gives help to many *orphan children* and *unmarried mothers*.

In this example, we have a single noun phrase (*many . . . mothers*) within which the adjective+noun sequences are coordinated. Another example, in which parts of an adjective phrase are linked, is:
>He is very *friendly* and *willing to help*.

Here *very* modifies (we assume) both *friendly* and *willing to help*.

But notice that sentences can be ambiguous, depending on what parts are understood to be coordinated:
>She's wearing *a white scarf* and *gloves*.

can mean either ' . . . a white scarf and white gloves' or ' . . . gloves and a white scarf'.

But is in general limited to coordination of clauses (with or without the omission of subject and auxiliary verb(s)), or to coordination of adjective phrases, as in
>The weather was warm but rather cloudy.

However, when it comes after a negative construction (*not* [*only*] *. . . but*), *but* can be used more freely (*see* 547).

Omission of conjunctions
546
When more than two items are coordinated, the conjunction is normally omitted before each item except the last:
>| I would like a ham sándwich, | an íce-cream | and a cup of teà. |

In ⟨writing⟩, a comma is used to separate all the items except (normally) the last two; in ⟨speech⟩, a rising tone is normally used on all items in the list except the last.

>We often omit the conjunction before the linking adverbs *then*, *so* and *yet*:
>>The car swerved, (and) *then* crashed into a wall.
>>He wants her to learn to drive, (and) *yet* he won't pay for the lessons.

Elsewhere the conjunction can be omitted especially in a rather ⟨literary⟩ style (*but see* 389), or where the list of items is understood to be incomplete:

> The woods were alive with the call of *blackbirds, thrushes, finches, wood-pigeons.*

Correlative coordination
547
Sometimes the coordination of two structures is made more emphatic by the addition of a word at the beginning of the first structure: *both* x *and* y, *either* x *or* y, etc. This is called CORRELATIVE coordination. The most important correlatives in English are illustrated in these examples:

> *Both* America *and* Russia realise the need for an arms agreement.
> *Either* the pump's broken *or* there's a blockage in one of the pipes.
> His doctor allows him *neither* to drink *nor* to smoke.
> She's *not only* an excellent housewife, *but* (also) a first class mathematician.

Demonstratives (*see GCE* 4.121, 10.65–70)

548
The words *this, that, these* and *those* are called DEMONSTRATIVES. They have number contrast (singular and plural) and can function both as determiners (*see* 550) and as pronouns (*see* 747). The general meanings of the two sets can be stated as 'near' and 'distant' (*cf* the pairs *here/there, now/then, see* 89):

	Singular	Plural
'near'	*this*	*these*
'distant'	*that*	*those*

Examples of determiner function:

> I like $\left\{\begin{array}{l} \textit{this book/these books.} \\ \textit{that book/those books.} \end{array}\right.$

Unless they are subjects; as in

> *This* is my $\left\{\begin{array}{l} \text{girl friend.} \\ \text{favourite picture.} \end{array}\right.$

the demonstratives can have pronoun function only with non-personal reference:

> Is he really going to marry $\left\{\begin{array}{l} \textit{that girl}? \\ \textit{*that}? \end{array}\right.$

> I bought *this* (*picture*) in Copenhagen.

549
In ⟨formal⟩ use, *that/those* can appear as relative antecedents (*see* 397, 784) but here *that/those* do not contrast with *this/these*. The combination *that who* does not occur, because *that* cannot refer to people in this construction:

> The butter we import is less expensive than *that* (*which*) we produce ourselves (= 'the butter which').
> These flowers are better than *those* (*which*) we planted last year (= 'the flowers which').
> He admires *those who* succeed (= 'people who succeed').

Determiners (*see GCE* 4.13–27)

550
Determiners are words which specify the range of reference of a noun in various ways, *eg* by making it definite (*the boy*), indefinite (*a boy*), or by indicating quantity (*many boys*).

To understand the grammatical role of determiners, we have to consider what determiners and nouns can occur together. There are three classes of common nouns relevant to the choice of determiners: they are singular count nouns (such as *bottle*), plural count nouns (such as *bottles*), and mass nouns (such as *pork* and *music*) (*see* 45, 49, 53). Proper nouns normally take no determiners (*see* 755).

Determiners always precede the noun they determine, but they have different positions relative to one another. The most important category is that of CENTRAL DETERMINERS, including articles (*see* 492). These may be preceded by PREDETERMINERS and/or followed by POSTDETERMINERS (*see Table 1*).

Table 1

DETERMINERS

PREDETERMINERS	CENTRAL DETERMINERS	POSTDETERMINERS
a all, both, half (see 559)	a Articles: the, a(n) (see 492–6)	a Cardinal numerals: one, two, etc (see 564)
b double, twice, etc (see 560)	b Demonstratives: this, these, that, those (see 548–9)	b Ordinal numerals: first, second, etc (see 565)
c one-third, etc (see 561)	c Possessives: my, your, etc (see 688–9) and genitives (see 570–2)	c General ordinals: next, last, other, etc (see 565)
d what, such, etc (see 562)	d Quantifiers: some, any, no, every, each, either, neither, enough, much (see 765–76)	d Quantifiers: many, few, little, several, more, less, etc (see 567)
	e Wh- determiners: what(ever), which(ever), whoever, whose (see 578, 645–6)	

Central determiners
551
The central determiners form six groups (A–F) as follows:
552
(A) DETERMINERS WITH ALL THREE CLASSES OF NOUN (singular or plural count nouns and mass nouns):

    a the (*see* 492–6):

        I've lost *the pen/the gloves/the money*.

    b Possessives (*see* 688–9):

        Have you seen *my pen/my gloves/my money*?

    c whose, which(ever), what(ever) (*see* 578, 645–6):

        Whose pen/whose gloves/whose money did you borrow?

    d stressed *some* and *any* (*see* 768):

        Any pen/any pens/any information will do.

    e no (*see* 632):

        He's got *no friend/no friends/no news* at all.

The genitive (*see* 570–2) functions like a possessive determiner. *Compare*:

$$\text{I liked} \left\{ \begin{array}{l} \textit{the girl's} \\ \textit{her} \end{array} \right\} \text{new dress.}$$

553
(B) DETERMINERS WITH PLURAL COUNT NOUNS OR MASS NOUNS ONLY:

    a zero article (*see* 494, 654):

        They need *tractors/help* from us.

b Unstressed *some* /səm/ (*see* 494, 768):

I want *some apples*/*some advice*, please.

c Unstressed *any* (*see* 768, 803):

Have you *any clothes* or *any furniture* to sell?

d *enough* (*see* 769):

We haven't got *enough oranges*/*enough rice*.

554
(C) DETERMINERS WITH SINGULAR COUNT NOUNS OR MASS NOUNS ONLY:

a *this* (*see* 548):

This lecture/*this* (*type of*) *research* is very interesting.

b *that* (*see* 548):

I find *that poem*/*that* (*type of*) *poetry* difficult to understand.

555
(D) DETERMINERS WITH SINGULAR COUNT NOUNS ONLY:

a *a(n)* (*see* 492–3):

Wait *a minute*!

b *every* (*see* 62, 766–7):

He comes here almost *every day*.

c *each* (*see* 63, 766–7):

She had a child on *each side* of her.

d *either* (*see* 65, 766):

Either solution is a bad one.

e *neither* (*see* 633, 766):

Neither method is right.

556
(E) DETERMINERS WITH PLURAL COUNT NOUNS ONLY:

a *these* (*see* 548):

I dislike all *these meetings*.

b *those* (*see* 548):

In *those days* life was enjoyable.

557
(F) DETERMINERS WITH MASS NOUNS ONLY:

much (*see* 769):

We don't have *much news* of him.

Predeterminers
558
As the name implies, predeterminers when combined with central determiners, occur before them. There are four classes of predeterminers.
559
(A) ALL, BOTH, HALF (*see* 767)

All goes with plural count nouns or mass nouns:

Are you going to buy *all these cans*/*all this rice*?

Both goes with plural count nouns only:

Both (*the*) *books* were out of the library.

Half goes with singular or plural count nouns or mass nouns:

I want *half a pint*/*half the plums*/*half the butter*.

Note *All the* . . . occasionally occurs with a singular count noun, but *the whole* . . . or *all of the* . . . is preferable:

All (*of*) *the town*⎫
The whole town⎭ was destroyed by fire.

The predeterminers *all, both, half* occur before articles, possessives, or demonstratives. Since they are themselves quantifiers they cannot occur with other determiners denoting quantity: *every, either, neither, each, some, any, no, enough*.

(B) DOUBLE, TWICE, THREE TIMES, ETC.
560
The second type of predeterminer includes *double, twice, three times, etc*, which occur with singular and plural count nouns or mass nouns denoting amount, degree, *etc*:

> The alternative plan would cost *three times this amount* (= 'three times as much as this').
>
> They want at least *double their salaries* (= 'twice as much as they now earn').
>
> I wish I had *twice his strength* (= 'I wish I was twice as strong as he').

Once, twice, three times, etc can occur with *a, every, each* and *per* ⟨formal⟩ to form frequency adverbials (*see* 476):

$$\text{We go there} \begin{Bmatrix} once \\ twice \\ three\ times \\ four\ times \end{Bmatrix} \begin{Bmatrix} a \\ every \\ each \\ (per) \end{Bmatrix} \begin{Bmatrix} day. \\ week. \\ month. \\ year. \end{Bmatrix}$$

(C) ONE-THIRD, TWO-FIFTHS, *etc*
561
The fractions *one-third, two-fifths, three-quarters, etc* can also be followed by central determiners, and have the alternative *of*-construction:

> He did it in *one-third (of) the time* it took me.

(D) WHAT, SUCH, ETC.
562
What and *such* as predeterminers occur *before* the indefinite article with singular count nouns, and without an article with plural count nouns and mass nouns. They may be classified as predeterminers, or alternatively, as modifiers of noun phrases (*see* 486).

$$\text{What} \begin{Bmatrix} a\ nuisance! \\ beautiful\ clothes! \\ awful\ weather! \end{Bmatrix}$$

> It was *such a nuisance.*
> She wore *such beautiful clothes.*
> We had *such awful weather.*

What here expresses an exclamatory degree (*see* 568), whereas, as a central determiner (*see* 552), it is primarily interrogative.

Other degree words can also behave like predeterminers: *rather a strong wind, quite a good crowd, etc.* (*see* 486).

Postdeterminers
563
Postdeterminers follow any central determiners (*see* 551–7) but come before premodifiers (*see* 731). They include cardinal and ordinal numerals, and various quantifiers.

(A) CARDINAL NUMERALS (*see* 660–1)
564
Apart from *one*, which can of course occur only with singular count nouns, all cardinal numerals (*two, three, etc*) occur only with plural count nouns:

> He has *one* sister and *three* brothers.

(B) ORDINAL NUMERALS (*see* 660–1)
565
Ordinal numerals occur only with count nouns and usually precede any cardinal numbers in the noun phrase:

The *first three* planes were American.

but: He won *three* first prizes.

There is also a class of 'general ordinals' (*next, last, other, further, etc*), which can either precede or follow the ordinal numerals. *Compare*:

{His *last/next* two books were novels.
{His two *last/next* books were novels. (less common)

{The *other three* passengers were men.
{There were three *other* (= 'more') passengers on the bus.

Another can be thought of as a combination of two determiners *an + other*:

He's written another novel.

{He's written another two novels. (= 'two more novels')
{He's written two other novels.

(C) QUANTIFIERS (*see* 766)

566

a   *many, (a) few, fewer*, and *several* occur only with plural count nouns:

His *many friends* never deserted him.

There were very *few people* left when we got there.

The *few words* he spoke were well chosen.

Several cars were involved in the accident.

b   *much* and *(a) little* occur only with mass nouns:

There hasn't been *much good weather* recently.

There is *little evidence* that he committed the crime.

Several is rarely (and *much* virtually never) preceded by a determiner. Notice the different meanings of *little* and *few* with or without the indefinite article:

Hurry up. We've *little time* to waste.

Don't hurry. We've *a little time* before the train comes in.

Jack rarely spoke: he was a man of *few words*.

I have something to say. May I have *a few words* with you?

c   The comparative determiner *more* occurs with plural and mass nouns and *less* usually only with mass nouns:

Some *more tea*, please.

There are *more cars* on the road this morning than yesterday.

Please try to make *less noise*!

These can follow other postdeterminers:

We need two/sev̄ral *more chairs*.

d   There are also phrases denoting quantity. Some can occur with both plural count nouns and mass nouns:

$$\text{The room contained} \begin{cases} \textit{plenty of} \\ \textit{a lot of} \\ \textit{lots of} \end{cases} \textit{students/furniture.}$$

A lot of is chiefly ⟨informal⟩, and *lots of* is even ⟨very informal⟩.

567

Quantifying phrases with *number* are used only with count nouns in the plural:

$$\text{The room contained} \begin{cases} \textit{a (great)} \\ \textit{a (large)} \\ \textit{a (good)} \end{cases} \textit{number of students.}$$

Phrases with *deal* and *amount* can only be used with mass nouns:

$$\text{The safe contained} \begin{cases} \textit{a great} \\ \textit{a good} \end{cases} \textit{deal of} \\ \begin{cases} \textit{a large} \\ \textit{a small} \end{cases} \textit{amount of} \end{cases} \textit{money.}$$

Notice that the head of the noun phrase is the noun following *of*, not *plenty*, *lot* and *number*:

> *Plenty of students*
> *A lot of people* } WERE (*was) there.
> *A great number of guests*

> There $\left\{\begin{array}{l}\text{WAS}\\ \text{**were}\end{array}\right\}$ *lots of food* on the table.

However, *number* and *amount* can occur in the plural:

> There WERE large *numbers* of cars on the road.

Exclamations (see GCE 7.78–79)

568

An exclamation is a type of sentence which is used to express the speaker's feeling or attitude. Notice, however, that the exclamation type of sentence is only one way of showing enthusiasm, *etc*. The exclamation as a sentence type begins with *what* as determiner in noun phrases (*see* 562) or *how* as a degree word with adjectives or adverbs (*see* 482–3). To form an exclamation, put the element of the sentence containing *what* or *how* at the front of the sentence, as with *wh*-questions (*see* 779), but do NOT alter the order of subject and operator:

> { She cooked *such a good dinner*.
> {   *What a good dinner* she cooked!
> { Your son is *clever*.
> {   *How clever* your son is!
> { He tells *such awful lies*.
> {   *What awful lies* he tells!
> { She dances *beautifully*.
> {   *How beautifully* she dances!

On other types of exclamatory construction, *see* 260, 309–20.

Gender (see GCE 4.85–92)

569

Gender in English applies strictly only to certain pronouns, where the categories masculine/feminine and personal/non-personal can apply, for example:

personal	{ masculine	*he*		
			who	*somebody*
	{ feminine	*she*		
non-personal		*it*	*which*	*something*
		(*see* 683)	(*see* 579)	(*see* 774–5)

Nouns, adjectives, and articles have no gender distinctions, although in a small number of words the feminine ending -*ess* marks a noun having female reference: *actor/actress*, *manager/manageress*.

Since nouns have no grammatical gender, the choice of *he*, *she*, and *it* is based on natural distinctions of meaning. The choice between *he* and *she*, for example, is almost entirely based on sex (*see* 82–3).

Genitive (see GCE 4.93–105, 13.27–30, 13.55–56, 13.64)

570

In ⟨spoken⟩ English, the genitive case of regular nouns is pronounced only in the singular, where it takes one of the forms /ɪz/, /z/, /s/ following the rules for *s* inflection generally (*see* 751).

In ⟨written⟩ English, the inflection of regular nouns is written in the singular '*s*, and in the plural *s*' by putting an apostrophe after the plural *s*. In the plural, the genitive is not pronounced.

Regular -s plural

| | ⟨Spoken⟩ | | ⟨Written⟩ | |
	singular	plural	singular	plural
common	/bɔɪ/	/bɔɪz/	boy	boys
genitive		/bɔɪz/	boy's	boys'

571

The '*s* is always added to a noun which does not already end in *s* /s/. This means that it is added to irregular plurals which do not end in -*s* (*see* 707–18):

An irregular plural

| | ⟨Spoken⟩ | | ⟨Written⟩ | |
	singular	plural	singular	plural
common	/tʃaɪld/	/ˈtʃɪldrən/	child	children
genitive	/tʃaɪldz/	/ˈtʃɪldrənz/	child's	children's

Similarly: *people's, men's, women's, etc*

572

In addition to its use with regular plurals, the 'zero' form occurs with some singular nouns ending in -*s*:

a   with Greek names of more than one syllable, as in *Euripides' /*–diːz/ *plays*.

b   with many other names ending in -*s* (*Burns, Jones, etc*). The genitive is written either *Burns'* or *Burns's*. In speech it is pronounced either /ˈbɜːnzɪz ‖ ˈbɜrnzɪz/ or (less commonly) /bɜːnz ‖ bɜrnz/.

c   with certain fixed expressions such as *for goodness' sake, for conscience' sake*.

The *of*-construction

573

In many instances a noun in the genitive case is similar in function to the same noun as head of a noun phrase following *of*:

What's *the ship's name*?

What's *the name of the ship*?

Usually, either the *s*-genitive or the *of*-phrase is preferred in a given case: with people and things, respectively. In numerous contexts only one construction is grammatically acceptable; *eg* we can say *the leg of a table* but not **a table's leg*. We can say *John's car* but not **the car of John*. (On the choice of construction, *see* 95–6.)

The genitive as a feature of noun phrases

574

Although the genitive is generally discussed as a case of nouns, in some respects it is better to regard it as an ending belonging to noun phrases (*see* 651–3) rather than of nouns. In the following examples, preceding determiners and premodi-fiers belong to the genitive noun phrase rather than to the noun which is head of the whole phrase:

MAIN NOUN PHRASE

GENITIVE NOUN PHRASE

a horse's	hind leg
some people's	opinions
older boys'	books
every teacher's	guide to child psychology
the British government's	recent decision

The genitive noun phrase occupies determiner position (*see* 550) in the main noun phrase. This is seen more clearly when we compare equivalent *of*-phrases:

the hind leg of	*a horse*
the opinions of	*some people*
the recent decision of	*the British government*

The group genitive (*see* 575) shows that genitive noun phrases can also contain postmodifiers.

In other cases, however, the genitive behaves more like a single-word noun modifier, and the preceding determiners and premodifiers belong to the head noun of the whole phrase:

best calves' liver (= 'calves' liver of the best quality')
new boys' books (= 'new books for boys')

The group genitive
575
In postmodified noun phrases it is necessary to add an *-s* genitive to the end of the postmodification (rather than to the head noun itself):

UNMODIFIED NOUN: the *Chairman's* business
POSTMODIFIED NOUN: the *Chairman of the Finance Committee's* business
Also: *someone else's* house
          the heir apparent's name
          an hour and a half's discussion
          a week or so's sunshine

The genitive with ellipsis
576
The noun modified by the *-s* genitive may be omitted if the context makes its identity clear (compare 395–6):

My car is faster than *John's* (*ie* 'than John's car').
But *John's* is a good car, too.

With the *of*-phrase, a pronoun is normally required:

The population of New York is greater than *that* of Chicago.

Omission of the head noun is typical of expressions relating to houses, shops, *etc*:

Tonight we're going to *Bill's/the Johnsons'*, *etc.* (= 'the place where Bill lives/the Johnsons live')
I've already been to *the dentist's/the butcher's*, *etc.*

The double genitive
577
An *of*-phrase can be combined with an *-s* genitive into a DOUBLE GENITIVE. The noun with the *-s* genitive must be both definite and personal:

This is an opera *of Verdi's* (= 'one of Verdi's operas').
She's a friend *of my wife's.*

Unlike the simple genitive, the double genitive usually implies non-unique meaning, *ie* that 'Verdi wrote several operas', and that 'my wife has several friends'. *Compare:*

He is $\begin{cases} \textit{my brother} \text{ (suggests I have one, or more than one brother).} \\ \textit{a brother of mine} \text{ (suggests I have more than one brother).} \end{cases}$

Interrogatives (*see GCE* 4.120, 5.48, 7.63–67)

578
Interrogatives are words which introduce *wh*-questions (*see* 779–80) and interrogative subclauses (*see* 641–3). The interrogative words of English are *who, whom, whose, which, what, where, when, how, why, whether, if* (= '*whether*'). They belong, with relative pronouns, to the class of words we call for convenience *wh*-WORDS (since most of them begin with *wh*-). *Whether* and *if* are restricted to interrogative subclauses (*see* 828).

Interrogatives in the noun phrase
579
In the noun phrase, the interrogatives *which* and *what* can act as both determiner and pronoun and can have both personal and non-personal reference. The different interrogative determiners and pronouns are set out in *Table 2*.

Table 2
Interrogative determiners and pronouns

	DETERMINERS	PRONOUNS	
	Personal and non-personal	Personal	Non-personal
Subjective case Objective case	*what, which*	*who, what, which* *who, whom* ⟨formal⟩, *which*	*what, which*
Genitive case	*whose*		
Interrogative . . . + preposition (*see* 642)	*what, which* . . . + preposition	*who, whom* ⟨formal⟩ . . . + preposition	*what, which* . . . + preposition
Preposition + interrogative (*see* 642)	preposition + *what, which* ⟨formal⟩	preposition + *whom* ⟨formal⟩	preposition + *what, which* ⟨formal⟩

580
Who, whom, whose, which, and *what* are also used as relative pronouns (*see* 788). Note, however, that the INTERROGATIVE *which* is used not only with non-personal but also with PERSONAL reference:

The author *who* is my favourite is . . .   (RELATIVE)
Which is your favourite author?   (INTERROGATIVE)

Who can also be used about persons:

Who is your favourite author?

However, they are not identical in meaning. There are two groups of interrogatives, those with INDEFINITE REFERENCE and those with DEFINITE REFERENCE:

Determiner with personal nouns:

(INDEFINITE)	*What conductors* do you like best?
(DEFINITE)	*Which conductor* do you prefer: von Karajan or Stokowsky?

Determiner with non-personal nouns:

(INDEFINITE)	*What newspapers* do you read?
(DEFINITE)	*Which records* do you like best: classical or popular?

Pronouns referring to persons:

(INDEFINITE)	*Who* is your favourite conductor?
(DEFINITE)	*Which* is your favourite conductor: von Karajan or Stokowsky?

Pronouns not referring to persons:

(INDEFINITE)	*What*'s the name of this tune?
(DEFINITE)	*Which* do you prefer: classical or popular music?

The definite interrogative *which* indicates that the speaker is thinking of a definite set of people, objects, *etc* from which the choice can be made.

581

Here are some more examples of interrogatives:

INTERROGATIVE DETERMINERS

Personal and non-personal

What ⎫ ⎰*candidate* will you vote for?
Which⎰ ⎱*party* are you in favour of?
Whose children are they?
Whose racket is this?

INTERROGATIVE PRONOUNS

Personal only:

Who told you where I was?
Who(*m*) is he marrying?

In the objective case, *whom* is ⟨formal⟩ and *who* ⟨informal⟩.

Personal and non-personal:

Which are your children in this photo?

Which can also be followed by an *of*-phrase:

Which of the girls do you like best?	[1]

Sentence [1] can have the same meaning as either [2] or [3]:

Which girl do you like best?	[2]
Which girls do you like best?	[3]

That is, it invites us to choose from a group either one (singular) or more than one (plural).

582

What has a wide range of use, having either personal or non-personal reference both as a determiner and as a pronoun:

(A)	*What*'s your address?	(B) (It's) 18 Reynolds Close.
(A)	⎰*What* nationality is he? ⎱*What*'s his nationality?	(B) He's Finnish.
(A)	*What* date is it?	(B) (It's) the 15th of March.
(A)	*What*'s the time?	(B) (It's) five o'clock.
(A)	*What* is he doing?	(B) (He's) mending the phone.
(A)	*What* was the concert like?	(B) (It was) excellent.

When it refers to a person, however, *what* as a pronoun is limited to questions about profession, role, status, *etc.*

Contrast:

(A)	*What*'s her husband?	(B) He's a film director.

(A) *Which* is her husband?   (B) He's the man on the right
                                              smoking a pipe.
(A) *Who* is her husband?   (B) He's Paul Jones, the famous
                                              art critic.

Interrogative adverbs and conjunctions
583
Besides interrogative determiners and pronouns, there are interrogative adverbs
and conjunctions (*see* 641–3).

Where (place at or place to, *see* 161–91):
> *Where* (= 'At what place') is he staying?
> *Where* (= 'To what place') are you going on your vacation this year?

When (time, *see* 140–50):
> *When* (= 'At what time') are you leaving?

Why (cause, reason, and purpose, *see* 197–207):
> *Why* (= 'For what reason') are you going there?

How (manner, means, and instrument, *see* 192–6):
> *How* (= 'By what means') are you travelling?

How is also an interrogative adverb of degree (*see* 217), in which function it can
premodify adverbs, adjectives and determiners:

How soon will you leave?   *How often* does he see her?
How tall are you?   *How much* money do you have?

Whether and *if* are interrogative conjunctions introducing indirect *yes-no*
questions (*see* 267, 644).

Introductory *it* (*see GCE* 14.23, 14.35–38)

584
The regular word order in English is subject + verb:
> *Her appearance* doesn't matter.

When the subject is a clause (*see* 637), however, the order is normally changed:

> *What she looks like* doesn't matter. (unusual order)
> *It* doesn't matter *what she looks like*. (usual order)

The subject clause is placed at the end of the sentence, and the subject position is
filled by the introductory *it*.

The new sentence contains two subjects: the introductory subject (the pronoun
it) and the postponed subject (the clause *what she looks like*).

Here are some more examples of sentences with introductory *it*:

> *It*'s said *that she slipped arsenic into his tea.*
> *It*'s actually been suggested *that income tax should be abolished.*
> *It*'s a pity *to make a fool of yourself.*
> *It* surprised me *to hear him say that.*
> *It* makes her happy *to see others enjoying themselves.*
> *It* was considered impossible *for anyone to escape.*
> *It* was easy *getting the equipment loaded.*
> *It*'s no use *telling him that.*
> *It* would be no good *trying to catch the bus now.*

585

The introductory-*it* construction is used in the passive in the following cases:
  a introducing a *that*-clause:

> Biologically *it may be found* that there are few differences
> between a black African and a white Scandinavian.

  b introducing direct or indirect speech:

> *It might be asked* at this point: 'Why does not the Govern-
> ment alter the law?'

  c introducing a *to*-infinitive:

> *It may be decided* not to rely exclusively on fixed-site missiles.

586

Any kind of nominal clause may have an introductory *it* except a nominal relative clause (*see* 645–6):

> *Whoever said that* was wrong.

For certain constructions which look just like introductory-*it* sentences there is no corresponding 'regular' construction: *it seems/appears/happens, etc.* For example, there is no such sentence corresponding to *It seems that everything is fine* (**That everything is fine seems*).

587

Sentences with introductory *it* must be distinguished from sentences where *it* is a personal pronoun (*see* 683) which acts as a replacement for a noun phrase in the context, for example:

> I don't like the look of *this fish*, but *it*'s good to eat.

where *it* refers to *fish*. Similarly:

> *It*'s too wet to play tennis.

where the infinitive clause is the complement of the adjective phrase *too wet*.

She's a pleasure to teach
588

There is another type of construction that gives the emphasis in the main clause to *a* the object or *b* the prepositional object of a nominal clause. The object item is 'lifted out' from the clause and placed as subject in the main clause (the objective case form *her* becomes of course the subjective case form *she*):

  a
> *To teach her* is a pleasure.
> It's a pleasure *to teach her*.
> *She's* a pleasure *to teach*.

  b
> *For us to be with Margaret* is great fun.
> It's great fun *for us to be with Margaret*.
> *Margaret* is great fun *for us to be with*.

589

There is a similar construction for *be sure, be certain, appear, seem, be said, be known, etc* + *to*-infinitive:

> *You seem to have* made a mistake.
> *He's known to be* an excellent pianist.

In these cases, however, the corresponding *it*-construction requires a *that*-clause, and it is the subject of the nominal clause that has front-position:

> *It seems that you've* made a mistake.
> *It's known that he's* an excellent pianist.

Introductory *there* (*see GCE* 14.24–30)

590

An English sentence like *A book is on the desk* is possible but uncommon. The natural way of putting it is to begin the sentence with an unstressed *there* and thus postpone the indefinite subject (*a book*):

> There's a book on the desk.

This is called a sentence with introductory *there*. All main verb patterns (*see* 835–72) can be turned into such sentences with *there*, so long as the subject is indefinite and the verb phrase contains *be*:

Pattern [I]:	A BUS is coming.
	There's A BUS coming.
Pattern [L]:	SOMETHING must be wrong.
	There must be SOMETHING wrong.
Pattern [L]:	Was ANYONE around?
	Was there ANYONE around?
Pattern [T]:	PLENTY OF PEOPLE are getting promotion.
	There are PLENTY OF PEOPLE getting promotion.
Pattern [X]:	TWO BULLDOZERS have been knocking the place flat.
	There have been TWO BULLDOZERS knocking the place flat.
Pattern [D]:	SOMETHING is causing her distress.
	There's SOMETHING causing her distress.
Pattern [V]:	TOO MANY PEOPLE are trying to buy houses.
	There are TOO MANY PEOPLE trying to buy houses.

Passive sentences also occur:

> A WHOLE BOX has been stolen.
> There's been A WHOLE BOX stolen.

591

Introductory *there* differs from *there* as a front-placed adverb (*There you are!* see 431) both in lacking stress, and in behaving in most ways like the subject of the sentence:

a   In ⟨informal⟩ English, *there* often determines concord (*see* 533) so that the verb is singular even when the postponed subject is plural:

> *There's* TWO PATIENTS in the waiting room. ⟨informal⟩

occurs alongside the regular ⟨formal⟩ plural:

> *There are* TWO PATIENTS in the waiting room.

b   *There* can act as subject in *yes-no* questions (*see* 778) and tag questions (*see* 781):

> Is *there* ANY MORE SOUP?
> *There's* NOTHING WRONG, is *there*?

c   *There* can act as subject in infinitive and *-ing* clauses (*see* 515):

> I don't want *there* to be any misunderstanding.
> He was disappointed at *there* being so little to do.

592

There is another type of introductory-*there* sentence which consists of *there* + *be* + a noun phrase + a clause which is like a relative clause (*see* 783). Here the verb need not be a form of *be* (and, although there must be an indefinite clause element, it need not be the subject):

> { SOMETHING keeps upsetting him.
> { *There's* SOMETHING (that) keeps upsetting him.
>   *Is there* ANYONE (that) you want to speak to?

Note Here *that* can be omitted even when it is subject, which is not possible in normal relative clauses.

593

Another common sentence pattern with introductory *there* is *there + be +* noun phrase + *to*-infinitive clause:

> *There* was NO ONE for us to talk to.

594

There is also another type which is most likely to occur in ⟨literary⟩ contexts where *there* is followed by a verb other than *be* (such as *lie, stand, exist*):

> *There* may come A TIME (= 'A time may come') when Europe will be less fortunate.

With a place adverbial in front-position, *there* may be omitted in ⟨literary⟩ style:

> In front of the carriage (*there*) rode TWO MEN in magnificent uni-forms. (*see* 431)

Irregular verbs (*see GCE* 3.63–72)

595

The irregular main verbs of English form a rather small, but important group of verbs. They are like regular verbs in having regular *-s* and *-ing* forms, for example, *walks, walking* and *spends, spending* (*see* 620–1). But they differ from regular verbs in that we cannot predict their past form and/or their past participle form from the base (compare the *-ed* form of regular verbs, *see* 622). We distinguish three types of irregular verbs:

- (I)   Verbs in which all these three parts (the base, the past, the past participle) are identical, for example, *cut—cut—cut*.
- (II) Verbs in which two of the three parts are identical, for example, *spend—spent—spent* and *come—came—come*.
- (III) Verbs in which all three parts are different, for example, *speak—spoke—spoken*.

Within each type, the verbs are here arranged according to similarity, for example, 'the *spend*-group', 'the *speak*-group', *etc*. The following list is not exhaustive (*see* further *GCE* 3.63–72). 'R' denotes that the verb also has regular forms. For auxiliary verbs, *see* 497–503.

Irregular main verbs

(I) *All three parts are identical*

596

THE *put*-GROUP

BASE	PAST	PAST PARTICIPLE	
bet	bet	bet	*Also* R: *betted*
bid	bid	bid	
burst	burst	burst	
cast	cast	cast	
cost	cost	cost	
cut	cut	cut	
hit	hit	hit	
hurt	hurt	hurt	
knit	knit	knit	Usually R: *knitted*
let	let	let	
put	put	put	
quit	quit	quit	⟨Informal⟩ verb *Also* R: *quitted*
set	set	set	
shut	shut	shut	
split	split	split	

BASE	PAST	PAST PARTICIPLE	
spread	spread	spread	
wed	wed	wed	*Also* R: *wedded*

(II) *Two parts are identical*

597

(A) THE *learn*-GROUP

These verbs can be either regular (*learned*) or irregular (*learnt*). The regular /d/-form is especially ⟨GA⟩ and the /t/-form especially ⟨RP⟩ (*see* pp 17–18).

burn	burned/burnt	burned/burnt
learn	learned/learnt	learned/learnt
smell	smelled/smelt	smelled/smelt
spell	spelled/spelt	spelled/spelt
spill	spilled/spilt	spilled/spilt
spoil	spoiled/spoilt	spoiled/spoilt

598

(B) THE *spend*-GROUP

bend	bent	bent
build	built	built
lend	lent	lent
send	sent	sent
spend	spent	spent

599

(C) THE *read*-GROUP

bleed	bled	bled
breed	bred	bred
feed	fed	fed
flee	fled	fled
hold	held	held
lead	led	led
read /riːd/	read /red/	read /red/

600

(D) THE *sleep*-GROUP

Where there are regular variants, these are usually preferred in ⟨AmE⟩.

creep	crept	crept	
deal /iː/	dealt /e/	dealt /e/	
dream /iː/	dreamt /e/	dreamt /e/	*Also* R: *dreamed* /iː/
feel	felt	felt	
keep	kept	kept	
lean /iː/	leant /e/	leant /e/	*Also* R: *leaned* /iː/
leap /iː/	leapt /e/	leapt /e/	*Also* R: *leaped* /iː/
leave	left	left	
mean /iː/	meant /e/	meant /e/	
meet	met	met	
sleep	slept	slept	
sweep	swept	swept	
weep	wept	wept	

601

(E) THE *strike*-GROUP

cling	clung	clung
dig	dug	dug

BASE	PAST	PAST PARTICIPLE	
fling	flung	flung	
hang	hung	hung	*hang* = 'execute' is usually R: *He was hanged.*
sling	slung	slung	
spin	spun	spun	
stick	stuck	stuck	
sting	stung	stung	
strike	struck	struck	
string	strung	strung	
swing	swung	swung	
win	won	won	
wring	wrung	wrung	

602

(F) THE *bring*-GROUP

All past and past participle forms have the vowel /ɔː/. Notice that *caught* and *taught* have *-au-* spellings; the rest *-ou-*.

bring	brought	brought
buy	bought	bought
fight	fought	fought
seek	sought	sought
think	thought	thought
catch	caught	caught
teach	taught	taught

603

(G) THE *find*-GROUP

All past and past participle forms have the diphthong /aʊ/:

bind /aɪ/	bound /aʊ/	bound /aʊ/
find /aɪ/	found	found
grind /aɪ/	ground	ground
wind /aɪ/	wound	wound

604

(H) THE *get*-GROUP

get	got	{ got ⟨BrE⟩ { got/gotten ⟨AmE⟩	*gotten* = 'acquired', 'caused', or 'come' (*see* 4)
lose /luːz/	lost /lɒst ‖ lɔːst/	lost	
shine	shone /ʃɒn ‖ ʃoʊn/	shone	*shine* = 'polish' can be R, *esp* ⟨AmE⟩
shoot	shot	shot	

605

(I) THE *sell*-GROUP

sell	sold /soʊld/	sold
tell	told /toʊld/	told

606

(J) THE *come*-GROUP

become /–ʌm/	became	become
come /–ʌm/	came	come
run	ran	run

607

(K) OTHER VERBS WITH TWO FORMS IDENTICAL

BASE	PAST	PAST PARTICIPLE	
beat	beat	beaten	
hear /hɪəʳ/	heard /hɜːd ‖ hɜrd/	heard	
light	lit	lit	*Also* R: *lighted*
make	made	made	
say	said /sed/	said	
sit	sat	sat	
spit	{ spat / spit	{ spat / spit	*spat is esp* ⟨BrE⟩
stand	stood /stʊd/	stood	
lay	laid	laid ⎫	Pronunciation
pay	paid	paid ⎭	regular, spelling only irregular

(III) *All three forms are different*

608

(A) THE *mow*-GROUP: the past participle can be regular or irregular.

hew	hewed	hewn/hewed
mow	mowed	mown/mowed
saw	sawed	sawn/sawed
sew /soʊ/	sewed	sewn/sewed
show	showed	shown/showed
sow	sowed	sown/sowed
swell	swelled	swollen/swelled

609

(B) THE *speak*-GROUP

break /eɪ/	broke	broken	
choose /uː/	chose /oʊ/	chosen /oʊ/	
freeze	froze	frozen	
speak	spoke	spoken	
steal	stole	stolen	
(a)wake	(a)woke	(a)woken	*Also* R: *(a)waked*
weave	wove	woven	

610

(C) THE *wear*-GROUP

bear	bore	born/borne	Note spelling: 'She has *borne* six children and the youngest was *born* a month ago.'
swear	swore	sworn	
tear	tore	torn	
wear	wore	worn	

611

(D) THE *know*-GROUP

blow /oʊ/	blew /uː/	blown /oʊ/
grow	grew	grown
know	knew	known
throw	threw	thrown

612

(E) THE *bite*-GROUP

BASE	PAST	PAST PARTICIPLE
bite	bit	bitten
hide	hid	hidden/hid

613

(F) THE *take*-GROUP

shake	shook /ʊ/	shaken
take	took /ʊ/	taken

614

(G) THE *write*-GROUP

drive /aɪ/	drove /oʊ/	driven /ɪ/
ride	rode	ridden
rise	rose	risen
write	wrote	written

615

(H) THE *drink*-GROUP

begin	began	begun
drink	drank	drunk
ring	rang	rung
shrink	shrank/shrunk	shrunk
sing	sang	sung
sink	sank	sunk
spring	sprang	sprung
stink	stank	stunk
swim	swam	swum

616

(IV) *Other verbs with all three parts different*

eat	ate $\left\{ \begin{array}{l} \text{/et/}\langle RP\rangle \\ \text{/eɪt/}\langle GA\rangle \end{array} \right\}$	eaten
fall	fell	fallen
dive	$\left\{ \begin{array}{l} \text{dived }\langle BrE, AmE\rangle \\ \text{dove }\langle AmE\rangle \text{ } only \end{array} \right\}$ dived	
do /duː/	did	done /dʌn/
draw	drew	drawn
fly	flew	flown
forget	forgot	forgotten
give	gave	given
go	went	gone
lie	lay	lain
see	saw	seen

Compare lay
in 607.

Main verbs (*see GCE* 3.9, 3.55–7)

Regular and irregular verbs
617

There are two types of verbs: MAIN VERBS and AUXILIARY VERBS (*see* 497–503). Main verbs are either REGULAR (such as *call*, *like*, *try*) or IRREGULAR (such as *buy*, *drink*, *set*).

618

'Regular' means that we can state *all* the verb forms of an English verb once we know its BASE form. (The base is the uninflected form which is given in dictionaries.) Even irregular verbs are not, however, entirely irregular (*see* 595). The irregular verbs are listed in 595–616.

619

A regular English verb has the following four forms:

THE BASE	*call*	THE -*ing* FORM	*calling*
THE -*s* FORM	*calls*	THE -*ed* FORM	*called*

The vast majority of English verbs are regular. Furthermore, all new verbs that are coined or borrowed from other languages adopt this pattern, for example *xerox, xeroxes, xeroxing, xeroxed.*

THE -*s* FORM

620

The -*s* FORM, also called the 3RD PERSON SINGULAR PRESENT, of both regular and irregular verbs is formed in ⟨written⟩ English by adding *s* or *es* to the base. In ⟨spoken⟩ English, the *s*-form is pronounced /ɪz/, /z/, or /s/.

BASE	-*s* FORM
press /pres/	*presses* /'presɪz/
play /pleɪ/	*plays* /pleɪz/
help /help/	*helps* /helps/

The rules for the choice of these alternatives are stated in 751; on changes in spelling, for example *try/tries, see* 809.

Exceptions:

do /duː/	*does* /dʌz/ (also /dəz/ as unstressed auxiliary)
say /seɪ/	*says* /sez/
go /goʊ/	*goes* /goʊz/

THE -*ing* FORM

621

The -*ing* FORM, or the PRESENT PARTICIPLE, of both regular and irregular verbs is formed by adding -*ing* /ɪŋ/ to the base:

press /pres/	*pressing* /'presɪŋ/
play	*playing*
help	*helping*

On changes in spelling, for example *beg/begging, see* 817–19.

THE -*ed* FORM

622

The -*ed* FORM of regular verbs is formed by adding -*ed* to the base. It corresponds to *two* forms of many irregular verbs: the PAST FORM and the PAST PARTICIPLE (or -*ed* PARTICIPLE). *Compare*:

REGULAR VERBS			IRREGULAR VERBS		
BASE	-*ed* FORM		BASE	PAST FORM	PAST PARTICIPLE
	PAST FORM	PAST PARTICIPLE			
press	*pressed*	*pressed*	*drink*	*drank*	*drunk*
play	*played*	*played*	*know*	*knew*	*known*
help	*helped*	*helped*	*hit*	*hit*	*hit*

The -*ed* form is pronounced /ɪd/, /d/, or /t/:

pat	*patted* /'pætɪd/
praise	*praised* /preɪzd/
push	*pushed* /puʃt/

On the choice of these alternatives, *see* 752; on changes in spelling, for example *pat/patted, see* 817–19.

The uses of the verb forms
623
After stating what the *forms* of English verbs are, we shall now describe how they are *used*. The uses are further discussed in the sections referred to below.
624
THE BASE FORM is used
   a in all persons of the present tense (*see* 520) except the 3rd person singular:
        I/you/we/they (the boys, *etc*) *like* milk.
   b in the imperative (*see* 520):
        Phone him at once.
   c in the present subjunctive (*see* 823–4):
        It is necessary that every member *inform* himself of these
          rules.
   d in the infinitive (*see* 515):
        We saw them *leave* an hour ago. (the bare infinitive)
        I want you *to type* this letter. (the *to*-infinitive)
625
THE -*s* FORM is used in the 3rd person singular of the present tense (*see* 880), *ie*
the only person where the base form is not used:
   He/she/it (the boy, the cat, *etc*) *likes* milk.
626
THE -*ed* FORM corresponds to both the past tense and the past participle of many
irregular verbs. Unlike the present tense, the past tense has only one form in all
persons:

   I/you/he (the boy, the boys, *etc*) $\left\{ \begin{array}{l} liked \\ drank \end{array} \right\}$ milk.

The past participle is used
   a with a form of *have* to form the perfective aspect (*see* 881–2):

        He has never $\left\{ \begin{array}{l} liked \\ drunk \end{array} \right\}$ milk.

   b with a form of *be* to form the passive (*see* 676):
        She was *injured* in an accident.
        She was *hidden* by the kidnappers.
   c to form -*ed* participle clauses (*see* 515):
        Many of those *injured* in the accident were taken to a
          hospital.
        They found her *hidden* in a cellar.

Nationality words (*see GCE* 4.33, 5.21–22)

627
When speaking about English people *in general* we can say either *the English*
(adjective as head, *see* 465) or *Englishmen* (plural noun without the article):
   $\left. \begin{array}{l} \textit{The English} \\ \textit{Englishmen} \end{array} \right\}$ drink beer in pubs.   [1]
When referring to some *particular* English persons we say:
   The Englishmen who live here drink tea in the garden every day.   [2]
We call these two types of reference [1] GENERIC and [2] SPECIFIC, respectively. In
some cases, such as with *English/Englishman* (*Englishmen*) there are different
forms for different types of reference. Where nationality words have no double
form, *the*+plural can be both generic and specific (*see* 74–8):
   The Germans (in general) are musical.
   The Germans that I know are musical.

628

The following table shows the names of some countries and continents and the corresponding adjectives and nouns (with specific and generic reference).

NATIONALITY WORDS

name of country or continent	adjective	specific singular	specific plural (two, . . .)	generic plural
China	Chinese	a Chinese	Chinese	the Chinese
Japan	Japanese	a Japanese	Japanese	the Japanese
Portugal	Portuguese	a Portuguese	Portuguese	the Portuguese
Switzerland	Swiss	a Swiss	Swiss	the Swiss
Vietnam	Vietnamese	a Vietnamese	Vietnamese	the Vietnamese
Israel	Israeli	an Israeli	Israelis	the Israelis
Pakistan	Pakistani	a Pakistani	Pakistanis	the Pakistanis
Germany	German	a German	Germans	the Germans
Greece	Greek	a Greek	Greeks	the Greeks
Africa	African	an African	Africans	the Africans
America	American	an American	Americans	the Americans
Europe	European	a European	Europeans	the Europeans
Asia	Asian	an Asian	Asians	the Asians
Australia	Australian	an Australian	Australians	the Australians
Italy	Italian	an Italian	Italians	the Italians
Russia	Russian	a Russian	Russians	the Russians
Belgium	Belgian	a Belgian	Belgians	the Belgians
Brazil	Brazilian	a Brazilian	Brazilians	the Brazilians
India	Indian	an Indian	Indians	the Indians
Hungary	Hungarian	a Hungarian	Hungarians	the Hungarians
Norway	Norwegian	a Norwegian	Norwegians	the Norwegians
	Arab[1] / Arabian / Arabic	an Arab	Arabs	the Arabs
Denmark	Danish	a Dane	Danes	the Danes
Finland	Finnish	a Finn	Finns	the Finns
Poland	Polish	a Pole	Poles	the Poles
Spain	Spanish	a Spaniard	Spaniards	the Spanish / the Spaniards
Sweden	Swedish	a Swede	Swedes	the Swedes
England	English	an Englishman	Englishmen	Englishmen / the English
France	French	a Frenchman	Frenchmen	Frenchmen / the French
Holland, the Netherlands	Dutch	a Dutchman	Dutchmen	Dutchmen / the Dutch
Ireland	Irish	an Irishman	Irishmen	Irishmen / the Irish
Wales	Welsh	a Welshman	Welshmen	Welshmen / the Welsh
Britain	British	a Briton[2]	Britons[2]	the British / Britons[2]
Scotland	Scots / Scottish	a Scotsman / a Scot	Scotsmen / Scots	Scotsmen / the Scots

[1] The term *Arab* is used for example in *the Arab nations*, while *Arabian* is used for example in *the Saudi Arabian government*. *Arabic* refers to the language and literature: *He's learning Arabic*.
[2] The noun *Briton* is not often used.

Negation (*see GCE* 7.41–52)

Not-negation
629

To negate a finite clause (*see* 514), you place *not* (or, in ⟨informal⟩ use, its contracted form *-n't*) immediately after the operator (*see* 673):

POSITIVE	NEGATIVE
He is coming.	He is *not* / is*n't* coming.
We may win the match.	We may *not* win the match.
We have been defeated.	We have *not* / hav*en't* been defeated.

In these instances, there is an auxiliary (*be, may, have*) in the positive sentence that can serve as operator. When there is no such operator present, the auxiliary *do* has to be introduced. This is called the *do*-construction (*see* 674). Like modal auxiliaries, *do* is followed by the bare infinitive:

She enjoys reading.	She *does not* / *doesn't* enjoy reading.
They understood the problem.	They *did not* / *didn't* understand the problem.

(On the constructions with *be* and *have* as main verbs in negative sentences and on the forms of the modal auxiliaries, *see* 499–501.)

Contracted negation
630

As well as the contracted negative, English has contracted verb forms (*see* 497), which can be tagged on to the subject (usually only if it is a pronoun). There are two forms of ⟨informal⟩ negation possible, one with a contracted verb, and one with a contracted negative:

CONTRACTED VERB	CONTRACTED NEGATIVE
He'*s not* coming.	He *isn't* coming.
We'*re not* ready.	We *aren't* ready.
They'*ve not* caught him.	They *haven't* caught him.
She'*ll not* miss us.	She *won't* miss us.

Both sets of contracted forms are used in ⟨informal⟩ English. In ⟨formal⟩ English, the full forms are used: *He is not coming*, etc.

As there is no widely acceptable contraction for *am not* (*see* 500, Note *a*), only the verb contraction is possible in a sentence like *I'm not ready*.

631

In questions with inversion, *not* can be placed either after the auxiliary in its contracted form *-n't*, or after the subject in its full form *not*:

$$=\begin{cases} \text{Haven't you heard the news? ⟨informal⟩} \\ \text{Have you } not \text{ heard the news?} \end{cases}$$

Negative pronouns and determiners
632

Instead of the following sentence with *not*-negation:

There is*n't any* butter left.

we may equally well say:

There is *no* butter left.

No is a negative determiner (*see* 550), and is one of a number of negative items in English with different functions, as appears from *Table 3*:

Table 3

NUMBER	FUNCTION	COUNT		MASS
		PERSONAL	NON-PERSONAL	
singular	pronoun	*no one* *nobody*	*nothing*	*none* (of)
		none (of)		
	pronoun and determiner	*neither* (of)		
plural	pronoun	*none* (of)		
singular and plural	determiner	*no*		

As the table shows, *none* can be treated as either singular or plural as far as concord is concerned (*see* 540): *None of them has/have arrived.*

Other negative items
633
Other negative items beginning with *n-* are:

> *nowhere* (adverb of place)
> *never* (adverb of time when or frequency)
> *neither* (adverb of addition, *see* 238)
> (*neither*) . . . *nor* (coordinating conjunction, *see* 547)

Also, there are certain words which are negative in meaning and behaviour, although they do not appear negative in form:

> *hardly, scarcely, barely* (= 'almost . . . not')
> *few, little* (= 'not many', 'not much')
> *rarely, seldom* (= 'not often')

The grammatical behaviour of negative items
634
The usual effect of all these negative items is to make the whole clause in which they occur negative (but *see* 269–71). This means that certain characteristics of negative clauses are found not only with *not*, but also with other negative items:

(A) After a negative item, normally *any*-words occur instead of *some*-words (*see* 803–7):

> *No one* has *any* doubts about his ability.
> I *seldom* get *any* sleep after the baby wakes up.
> I've spoken to *hardly anyone* who disagrees with me on this point.

(B) A negative item at the beginning of a clause brings about the inversion of subject and operator, *ie* the order is operator + subject (unless the negative item belongs to the subject). This construction can sound rather ⟨elevated⟩ and ⟨rhetorical⟩ (*see* 432):

> *Only* after a long argument *did he* agree to our plan.

(C) Negative words are followed by positive rather than negative tag-questions (*see* 781):

> |She *never/scarcely* seems to c͟a͟re| d͟oes she?|

> |You won'*t* forget the sh͟opping| w͟ill you?|

Compare:

> |You'll remember the sh͟opping| |w͟on't you?|

Negation in phrases and non-finite clauses
635

Sometimes the word *not* is attached not to the verb phrase of a clause, but to another element of the clause, such as a noun phrase. *Not* then comes before the word or phrase which it negates. There is no inversion when the negated noun phrase is itself subject:

> *Not all* of the passengers escaped unhurt.
> *Not a single word* did he utter.
> No nation can afford to offend its allies—*not even* the United
>   States of America.

To negate non-finite clauses (*see* 515), we place the negative before the verb phrase:

> *Not* having read the book, I can't tell you whether it is worth buying.
> I asked him *not* to interfere.
> He told her *never* to do it again.

Transferred negation
636

After some verbs like *believe*, *suppose*, and *think*, a *not* which belongs, in terms of meaning, to a *that*-clause is usually transferred to the main clause:

> I *don't believe* (that) you two have met, have you?
>   (= 'I believe you two haven't met')
> I *don't suppose* (that) anyone will object to my absence.
>   (= 'I suppose no one will object . . . ')
> I *don't think* (that) you need worry.
>   (= 'I think you needn't worry.')

Nominal clauses (*see GCE* 11.16–25)

637

Nominal clauses function like noun phrases (*see* 651). Just as noun phrases may occur as subject, object, complement, appositive, and prepositional complement, so every nominal clause may occur in some or all of these roles:

SUBJECT	*Whether we need it* is a different matter.
OBJECT	I don't know *whether we need it*.
COMPLEMENT	The problem is *whether we need it*.
APPOSITIVE	That question, *whether we need it*, has not yet been considered.
PREPOSITIONAL COMPLEMENT	The decision must depend on *whether we need it*.

638

There are five main types of nominal clause:

> *That*-clauses (*see* 639–40)
> Interrogative subclauses (*see* 641–4)
> Nominal relative clauses (*see* 645–6)
> Nominal *to*-infinitive clauses (*see* 647–8)
> Nominal *-ing* clauses (*see* 649–50)

That-clauses
639

That-clauses can occur as:

SUBJECT	*That she's still alive* is sheer luck.
DIRECT OBJECT	I told him *that he was wrong*.

SUBJECT
  COMPLEMENT   The assumption is *that things will improve*.
  APPOSITIVE   Your assumption, *that things will improve*, is
                            not well-founded.

COMPLEMENT OF AN
  ADJECTIVE   I'm sure *that things will improve*.

640

When the *that*-clause is object or complement or postponed subject (*see* 584), *that* is frequently omitted in ⟨informal⟩ use:

I told him⎫
I'm sure ⎬ *he was wrong.*

I know   ⎫
It's a pity⎬ *you're leaving*

Wh-interrogative subclauses
641

Interrogative subclauses are introduced by *wh*- interrogative words (*see* 578–583) and occur in the whole range of functions available to *that*-clauses. In addition, they can act as prepositional complement:

SUBJECT   *How the book will sell* largely depends on its
                           author.
DIRECT OBJECT   I can't imagine *what made him do a thing like
                           that*.

SUBJECT
  COMPLEMENT   The point is not *who will go*, but *who will stay*.
  APPOSITIVE   My original question, *why he did it at all*, has
                          not yet been answered.

COMPLEMENT OF AN
  ADJECTIVE   I wasn't certain *whose house we were in*.
COMPLEMENT OF A   None of us were consulted on *who should have
  PREPOSITION   the job*.

642

Wh-interrogative clauses are like *wh*-questions (*see* 779) in that the *wh*-word is placed first. We have, in the *wh*-interrogative subclause, the same choice between initial and final position where the prepositional complement is the *wh*-element:

He couldn't remember ⎧*on which* shelf he kept it. ⟨formal⟩
                     ⎩*which* shelf he kept it *on*. ⟨informal⟩

643

An infinitive *wh*-clause can be formed with all *wh*-words except *why*:

He explained to me *how to start the motor*.
  (= 'how one should start . . . ')
On British trains, I never know *where to put my overcoat*.
  (= 'where I'm supposed to put . . . ')

Yes-no interrogative subclauses
644

Yes-no interrogative subclauses are formed with *if* or *whether*:

Do you know *if/whether the shops are open now*?

The alternative question (*see* 246) has *if/whether . . . or*:

I don't care *if/whether your car breaks down or not*.

Only *whether* can be directly followed by *or not*:

I don't care *whether or not your car breaks down*.

Nominal relative clauses
645

Nominal relative clauses, also introduced by a *wh*-word, can act as

SUBJECT	*What John really needs* is a wife.
	Whoever wrote this book is a genius (='the person who wrote . . . ').
DIRECT OBJECT	I want to see *whoever deals with complaints*.
	You'll find *what you need* in this cupboard (='the things that . . . ').
INDIRECT OBJECT	She gave *whoever came to the door* a winning smile.
SUBJECT COMPLEMENT	Home is *where your friends and family are*.
OBJECT COMPLEMENT	You can call me *what(ever) names you like*.
APPOSITIVE	Let us know your college address, that is, *where you live during the term*.
COMPLEMENT OF A PREPOSITION	You should vote for *which(ever) candidate you like best*.

646
These clauses are introduced by a *wh*-pronoun or *wh*-determiner (*see* 578–82), which combines the functions of the relative pronoun with that of the determiner and/or head of the whole noun phrase. For example, the proverb
Whoever laughs last, laughs longest.
can be put in the form:
Those who laugh last, laugh longest.
in which *whoever* is replaced by a demonstrative pronoun and a relative pronoun.
Who hardly occurs in contemporary English in this nominal relative function:
**Who told you that was lying*. Other expressions are used:

Whoever
The person who } told you that was lying.
Anyone who

As these examples show, a nominal relative clause can be introduced by a *wh*-word ending in *-ever* (*whatever*, *etc*). These words have general or inclusive meaning. Thus the pronoun *whatever* means roughly 'anything which'.

Nominal *to*-infinitive clauses
647
Nominal *to*-infinitive clauses can occur as:

SUBJECT	*For a bridge to collapse like that* is unlikely.
DIRECT OBJECT	He likes *everyone to be happy*.
SUBJECT COMPLEMENT	His ambition is *to be a pilot*.
APPOSITIVE	His ambition, *to be a pilot*, was never fulfilled.
COMPLEMENT OF AN ADJECTIVE	I'm glad *to be of help*.

648
The subject of a *to*-infinitive is normally introduced by *for*. A pronoun subject is here in the objective case (*see* 684). *Compare*:

The idea is { *that we should meet* on Thursday.
{ *for us to meet* on Thursday.

When the clause is a direct object, the *for* is omitted:
He wants *us to meet on Thursday*.

Nominal *-ing* clauses
649
The nominal *-ing* participle clause can act as:

SUBJECT	*Telling lies* is wrong.

DIRECT OBJECT	No one enjoys *being disturbed in the middle of the night.*
SUBJECT COMPLEMENT	What he likes best is *playing practical jokes.*
APPOSITIVE	He was absorbed in his hobby, *collecting stamps.*
COMPLEMENT OF A PREPOSITION	I'm tired of *being treated like a child.*
COMPLEMENT OF AN ADJECTIVE	The children were busy *building sandcastles.*

650

When the *-ing* clause has a subject there is sometimes a choice between genitive case in ⟨formal⟩ style:

I'm surprised at *his/John's* making that mistake.

and, in ⟨informal⟩ style, objective case (for personal pronouns) or common case (for nouns):

I'm surprised at *him/John* making that mistake.

Noun phrases (*see GCE Chapters* 4 and 13)

651

A noun phrase is a phrase which can act as subject, object, or complement of a clause (*see* 529), or as prepositional complement (*see* 739). It is called a noun phrase because the word which is its HEAD (*ie* main part) is typically a noun. In the following sentence:

John found *the new secretary in his office a very attractive woman.*

John, secretary, office and *woman* are NOUNS. The subject *John*, the object *the new secretary in his office*, the object complement *a very attractive woman* are NOUN PHRASES. Also part of the object, *his office*, is a prepositional complement, constituting yet another noun phrase.

652

The head noun can be accompanied by DETERMINERS (*the, his, a, etc*) and one or more MODIFIERS. Modifiers which precede the head are called PREMODIFIERS (*eg new, very attractive*), and those which follow the head are called POSTMODIFIERS (*eg in his office*).

653

Thus the structure of the English noun phrase can be written:

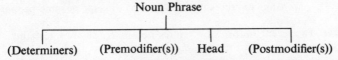

Noun Phrase

(Determiners)   (Premodifier(s))   Head   (Postmodifier(s))

Here the brackets are a reminder that the determiners and modifiers can be left out. However, determiners are more essential to noun phrase structure than modifiers. The only situation in which a noun phrase has no expressed determiner is where it has a 'zero article' (*see* 494). Some examples of noun phrases are:

DETERMINER(S)	PREMODIFIER(S)	HEAD	POSTMODIFIER(S)
the		*boys*	
a	*tall*	*boy*	
		boys	*in general*
all those	*tall*	*boys*	*with long hair*

Any one of these noun phrases could be the object which completes the sentence *Mary likes . . .*

The different parts of noun phrase structure are treated separately as follows: Determiners (*see* 550–67), Premodifiers (*see* 731–8), Postmodifiers (*see* 719–30). Apart from nouns, pronouns (*see* 747) and adjectives (*see* 464) may act as head of a noun phrase.

Number (*see GCE* 4.48–84)

Singular and plural number
654

In English, number is a feature of nouns, demonstratives, personal pronouns and verbs. Nouns have singular or plural number and verbs in the 3rd person vary for singular and plural agreement with the subject noun (*see* 532). The nouns which, according to the main rule, are SINGULAR are

a   singular nouns, *ie* nouns denoting 'one' (*see* 45): *a boy, the table, this idea, etc.*

b   mass nouns (*see* 49): *advertising, our music, the butter, this evidence, etc.*

c   proper nouns (*see* 755–64): *John, Cairo, Mars, the Thames, etc.*

The only nouns which normally occur in the PLURAL are plural count nouns, *ie* nouns denoting 'more than one': *two boys, the tables, these ideas, etc.*

655

The regular plural is formed by adding *-s* or *-es* to the singular (*see* 704). But special mention must be made of

(A)   some nouns which end in *-s* but are singular, and

(B)   some nouns which occur only in the plural.

(On the number of adjectives as head, as in *the supernatural* and *the rich, see* 464–7.)

(A)   SINGULAR NOUNS ENDING IN *-s*

656

a   *News*:

> This is the eight o'clock *news*.

b   Some diseases: *measles, German measles, mumps, rickets, shingles*. (Some speakers also accept a plural verb here.):

> (*The*) *measles is* an infectious disease.

c   Subject names in *-ics* (usually with a singular verb): *classics, linguistics, mathematics, phonetics, etc.*

> *Statistics* (= 'the subject') *is* not as difficult as some people think.

> *but*: The recent *statistics* (= 'figures') on marriage *are* interesting.

d   Some games: *billiards, darts, dominoes, fives, ninepins:*

> *Billiards is* my favourite game.

e   Some proper nouns: *Algiers, Athens, Brussels, Flanders, Marseilles, Naples, Wales*; *the United Nations* (*the UN*) and *the United States of America* (*the USA*) have a singular verb when considered as units:

> *The United States of America is* one of the most powerful nations in the world.

(B)   NOUNS WHICH OCCUR ONLY IN THE PLURAL

657

a   *Cattle*:

> *Many cattle have* died in the drought.

> *People* as the plural of *person*:

> There *were a great many people* waiting at the airport.

> (*People* is however regular in the sense of 'nation': *the peoples of Africa*.)

Police:

>*The police were* checking all the cars entering the city.

but: A *policeman was*
Two *policemen were* } searching the building.

658

b   Some nouns denoting a tool, instrument or article of dress consisting of two equal parts which are joined together. These are always plural, but can be turned into ordinary count nouns by means of *pair of*:

>(A)   'Where *are my trousers*?'   (B)   '*They are* here.'
>'I'd like *a pair of scissors*, please.'
>'There are *two pairs of glasses* on the table. *Which pair* do you want?'

Here is a list of other nouns which are used in the same way as *trousers*, *scissors* and *glasses*:

binoculars	jeans
spectacles	pants
pincers	{ pyjamas ⟨BrE⟩
pliers	{ pajamas ⟨AmE⟩
tongs	shorts
scales	tights

659

c   There are also many other nouns which, in a given sense, only occur in the plural, for example *contents*:

>Have you studied the *contents* of the book?

In many cases they have a singular form (without *-s*), with a different meaning (which a dictionary will explain), for example:

>What is the silver *content* of this coin?

Here are further examples of plural nouns:

>*the Middle Ages*
>*archives*
>*arms* ('weapons', as in *an arms depot*)
>*ashes* (*but* also mass: *tobacco ash*)
>*funds* ('money'; *but a fund*, 'a source of money')
>*means* (as in *He's a man of means.*)
>*oats* (but *corn, barley, etc*; *oats* can also be a singular noun)
>*odds* (in betting)
>*outskirts* (as in *on the outskirts of a city*)
>*premises* ('building')
>*quarters, headquarters* (but *the Latin quarter*)
>*spirits* ('mood': *He's in good spirits*; but *He has a kindly spirit.*)
>*stairs* (*a flight of stairs*) and *steps*
>*surroundings* (as in *the surroundings of a town*)
>*thanks* ('*Many thanks!*')

Numerals (*see GCE* 4.129)

Cardinals and ordinals (*see* 564–5)
660

The cardinal numerals (*one, two, etc*) and the ordinal numerals (*first, second, etc*) are shown in the following list. Both types can function as pronouns or as determiners. The ordinals are normally preceded by another determiner, usually the definite article:

There are *ten* on the list, so you are *the eleventh*.

They have *five children* already, so this is *their sixth child*.

661

CARDINALS		ORDINALS	
0	nought, *etc* (*see* 662)		
1	one	1st	first
2	two	2nd	second
3	three	3rd	third
4	four	4th	fourth
5	five	5th	fifth
6	six	6th	sixth
7	seven	7th	seventh
8	eight	8th	eighth
9	nine	9th	ninth
10	ten	10th	tenth
11	eleven	11th	eleventh
12	twelve	12th	twelfth
13	thirteen	13th	thirteenth
14	fourteen	14th	fourteenth
15	fifteen	15th	fifteenth
16	sixteen	16th	sixteenth
17	seventeen	17th	seventeenth
18	eighteen	18th	eighteenth
19	nineteen	19th	nineteenth
20	twenty	20th	twentieth
21	twenty-one, *etc*	21st	twenty-first, *etc*
30	thirty	30th	thirtieth
40	forty	40th	fortieth
50	fifty	50th	fiftieth
60	sixty	60th	sixtieth
70	seventy	70th	seventieth
80	eighty	80th	eightieth
90	ninety	90th	ninetieth
100	one hundred	100th	(one) hundredth
101	one hundred and one, *etc*	101st	(one) hundred and first, *etc*
200	two hundred	200th	two hundredth
1,000	one thousand	1,000th	(one) thousandth
100,000	one hundred thousand	100,000th	(one) hundred thousandth
1,000,000	one million	1,000,000th	(one) millionth

662

Nought (⟨AmE⟩ *naught*) /nɔːt/ occurs chiefly as the name of the numeral *0*, and is replaced, in general use, by the negative determiner *no* or the pronoun *none*:

There were no survivors from the air disaster.

None of the passengers or crew survived.

Zero /'zɪərov/ is used for *0* especially in mathematics and for temperature:

It's five degrees below zero.

0 /ou/ is used for example in telephone numbers:

Dial 7050 /sevn ov faiv ov/ and ask for extension 90 /nain ov/.

Nil /nɪl/ or *nothing* is used for example in football:

Brazil won 4–0 (four nil/(to) nothing).

Love /lʌv/ is used in tennis, squash, *etc*:

Borg leads by 30–0 (thirty love).

663

One or *a* must be used with 100, 1,000 and 1,000,000 when they are written with letters or spoken:

one/a hundred (passengers)

one/a thousand (pounds)

one/a million (French francs)

Similarly:

one/a hundred and one (= *101*) etc

664

Hundred, thousand and *million* have the singular form following both singular and plural numbers or quantifiers:

two *hundred* (times)

three *thousand* (casualties)

several *million* (dollars)

Note As a head, *million* sometimes has a plural form:

The population of New Zealand is now three *million(s)*.

(*but*: three *million* five thousand)

But all three have the *-s* plural when they denote an indefinite number:

I've told him so *hundreds of* times.

There were *thousands of* spectators at the demonstration.

Millions of people die every year from starvation.

665

The plural *forties* denotes an age or a period between 40 and 49; similarly with *sixties, etc*:

She was a good-looking woman *in her forties*.

The book was published *in the seventies/in the 70s/in the 1970s*.

Fractions and decimals

666

Fractions are read out in full as follows:

$\frac{1}{2}$	(a) *half*	They stayed (for) $\begin{cases} half\ an\ hour. \\ a\ half\ hour. \end{cases}$
$\frac{1}{4}$	*a quarter*	They stayed (for) *a quarter of an hour.*
$\frac{1}{10}$	*a/one tenth*	*a tenth of the population*
$\frac{3}{4}$	*three quarters*	*three quarters of an hour*
$1\frac{1}{2}$	*one and a half*	$\begin{cases} one\ and\ a\ half\ hours \\ an\ hour\ and\ a\ half \end{cases}$
$3\frac{1}{5}$	*three and one fifth*	*three and one fifth inches*

667

Decimals are read out in full as follows:

2·5   *two point five*

3·14   *three point one four*

Times and dates

668

Times of the clock are read out in full as follows:

at 5	*at 5 (o'clock)*
at 5.15	*at five fifteen, at a quarter past five, at a quarter after five* ⟨AmE⟩
at 5.30	*at five thirty, at half past five*
at 5.45	*at five forty-five, at a quarter to six, at a quarter of six* ⟨AmE⟩
at 5.50	*at five fifty, at ten (minutes) to six*
at 6.10	*at ten (minutes) past six, at ten minutes after six* ⟨AmE⟩; *at six ten* can be used when one is referring *eg* to a timetable.

669

Dates are written and read out as follows:

$\langle$written$\rangle$ He died *on* $\begin{cases} \text{5 May 1974. } \langle\text{BrE}\rangle \\ \text{May 5th 1974. } \langle\text{AmE}\rangle \end{cases}$

$\langle$spoken$\rangle$ He died $\begin{cases} \textit{on the fifth of May, nineteen seventy-four.} \\ \textit{on May the fifth, nineteen seventy-four. } \langle\text{BrE}\rangle \\ \textit{on May fifth, nineteen seventy-four. } \langle\text{AmE}\rangle \end{cases}$

Objects (*see GCE* 7.10, 7.14, 7.19–21, 12.44–70)

670

 a Like the subject, the object of a clause is a noun phrase (*see* 651–3):

Yesterday I met *a strange man.*

or a nominal clause (*see* 637–50):

She told me *that we had met before.*

 b The object usually refers to the person, thing, *etc*, affected by the action of the verb:

John is patting *the dog.*

 c The object normally follows the verb phrase. English typically has SVO order in both main clauses and subclauses (but *see* 426, 568, 780, 787):

After they had seen *the play*, Bill and Mary had *a snack.*

 d The object of an active sentence can usually be turned into the subject of a passive sentence (*see* 676–82):

$\begin{cases} \text{Some friends of ours found } \textit{my cat} \text{ in the woods.} \\ \textit{My cat} \text{ was found in the woods.} \end{cases}$

671

When a clause has two objects, the first is an INDIRECT OBJECT (which is often personal) and the second a DIRECT OBJECT:

I gave *her the flowers.*

I bought *Mabel a new dress.*

The indirect object is often equivalent to a prepositional phrase with *to* or *for* (*see* 856–7):

I gave *the flowers to her.*

I bought *a new dress for Mabel.*

Operators (*see GCE* 2.2, 2.17–23, 3.6, 10.53–60)

672

Auxiliary verbs can vary in their number and in their functions in the verb phrase (*see* 874–83). However, there is one important syntactic function that they have in common when they occur first in the finite verb phrase. Compare the following interrogative sentences:

Will they ask many questions?

Were they asking many questions?

Was he asked many questions?

Have they asked many questions?

Have they been asking many questions?

Would he have been asked many questions?

In each case, the first auxiliary of the finite verb phrase is isolated from the rest of the verb phrase, no matter how complex the phrase is. Because of this syntactic function, we call the first auxiliary of a verb phrase the OPERATOR. *Be* and, sometimes in ⟨BrE⟩, *have* act like operators even when they are main verbs, and so the term operator will be used for the following cases, too:

Is she a good student?

Have you any money? ⟨BrE⟩

673

The operator stands before the subject in *yes-no* questions (as above). In negative statements the operator stands before *not*:

He *will not/won't* ask many questions.

He *is not/isn't* asking many questions.

He *has not/hasn't* asked many questions.

He *has not/hasn't* been asking many questions.

The same position is normally that taken by adverbs with mid-position (*see* 470):

He *will never/rarely/then/always* ask the same questions.

The *do*-construction
674

When a verb phrase contains no auxiliary verbs, it contains no word that can act as operator for the purpose of forming *yes-no* questions and negative sentences with *not*:

He *knows* what I want.

You *need* some advice.

John *came* yesterday.

In such cases, we have to introduce the special 'dummy' operator *do* for forming questions (*see* 778) and *not*-negation (*see* 629):

a $\left\{\begin{array}{l}\textit{Does} \text{ he } \textit{know} \text{ what I want?} \\ \textit{Do} \text{ you } \textit{need} \text{ some advice?} \\ \textit{Did} \text{ John } \textit{come} \text{ yesterday?}\end{array}\right.$ b $\left\{\begin{array}{l}\text{He } \textit{doesn't know} \text{ what I want.} \\ \text{You } \textit{don't need} \text{ any advice.} \\ \text{John } \textit{didn't come} \text{ yesterday.}\end{array}\right.$

675

Apart from *yes-no* questions and *not*-negatives, there are a number of other constructions which require the use of an operator (and hence, sometimes, the use of the 'dummy' operator *do*). They include

c   emphatic sentences (*see* 313):

Do be quiet!   I *did enjoy* that meal!

d   tag questions (*see* 781):

John came yesterday, *didn't* he?

e   *wh*-questions where the *wh*-element is NOT the subject:

When *did* John *come*?

Who *did* he *meet* at the station?

but: Who met him at the station?

f   statements with inversion (*see* 432):

Only after a long delay *did* news of Livingstone's fate *reach* the coast.

Passives (*see GCE* 12.2–18)

676

The term PASSIVE is used to describe

(A)   the type of verb phrase which contains the construction *be* + past participle: *was killed, was seen, etc* (*see* 878–9).

(B)   the type of clause in which a passive verb phrase occurs.

The opposite of passive is ACTIVE. Examples of the contrast between active and passive clauses:

ACTIVE	PASSIVE	
The butler *murdered* the detective.	The detective *was murdered* (by the butler).	[1]
The policeman *persuaded* him to leave.	He *was persuaded* to leave (by the policeman).	[2]
My father *gave* me this watch.	I *was given* this watch (by my father).	[3]
His wife *considered* him a genius.	He *was considered* a genius (by his wife).	[4]

How to construct passive sentences
677

To change an active clause into a passive clause,

a replace the active verb phrase by the matching passive one
b make the object of the active clause the subject of the passive clause
c make the subject of the active clause the agent of the passive clause. The agent is the noun phrase which occurs after the preposition *by* in the passive clause.

These three changes can be pictured as follows:

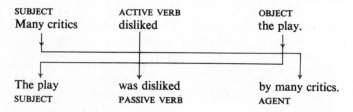

SUBJECT	ACTIVE VERB	OBJECT
Many critics	disliked	the play.

The play	was disliked	by many critics.
SUBJECT	PASSIVE VERB	AGENT

The effect of the change into the passive, as you see, is to reverse the positions of the noun phrases acting as subject and object in the active sentence.

678

Except for a few cases (*see* Note), all active sentences with a noun phrase or pronoun object can be made passive. Sentences [1] to [4] above illustrate this process with four different basic verb patterns (*see* 508–9):

	ACTIVE	PASSIVE	
[T]	SVO	SV (passive) *by*-AGENT	[1]
[V]	SVOV	SV (passive) V *by*-AGENT	[2]
[D]	SVOO	SV (passive) O *by*-AGENT	[3]
[X]	SVOC	SV (passive) C *by*-AGENT	[4]

In the third of these patterns (SVOO), it is usually the first object (the indirect object) that becomes subject of the passive clause. There is, however, another passive construction in which it is the direct object that is made subject. Thus both the following are possible passive forms of the active sentence in [3]:

    { I was given this watch by my father.
    { This watch was given (to) me by my father.

Note

A number of verbs belonging to the [T] pattern do not have a passive. They include *have* (as in *I have a Fiat*), and *hold* (as in *This jug holds two pints*). Also, the passive is sometimes not possible when the object is a clause (*see* 837, 845–52).

679

The *by*-phrase containing the agent of a passive clause is only required in specific cases (in fact, about four out of five English passive clauses have no agent). The passive is especially associated with ⟨impersonal⟩ style (*eg* in scientific and official writing), where the question of who is the agent (*ie* who performs the action described by the verb) is unimportant and often irrelevant:

A police officer *was killed* last night in a road accident.

The question *will be discussed* at a meeting tomorrow.

680

The passive auxiliary is normally *be*, but can sometimes be *get*. The passive with *get* is normally found only in ⟨informal⟩ style, and in constructions without an agent:

The boy *got hurt* on his way home from work.

It is upsetting when a person *gets punished* for a crime that he didn't commit.

681

Another variation of the passive occurs with prepositional verbs (*see* 699). It is possible, in many cases, for the prepositional object (the noun phrase following the preposition of the active sentence) to become the subject of the passive sentence:

ACTIVE   Someone *will have to deal with* this matter right away.

PASSIVE   This matter *will have to be dealt with* right away.

Other examples:

Other possibilities *were talked about* at the meeting.

An improvement in relations between East and West *is to be hoped for* as a result of the conference.

I don't like *being stared at*.

Likewise *ask for, believe in, cater for, look at, talk to, wonder at, etc*.

682

Notice that there are also passive non-finite verb phrases:

	ACTIVE	PASSIVE
to-INFINITIVE CLAUSE	*to understand*	*to be understood*
-ing CLAUSE	*seeing*	*being seen*

I want this *to be* clearly *understood* by everybody.

Without *being seen* by any of the servants, the assassin entered the house.

Personal and reflexive pronouns (*see GCE* 4.112–116)

683

Personal and reflexive pronouns are related in the following way. (The examples include only subjective personal pronouns. See *Table 4* on p. 260.)

(A)   They distinguish between personal and non-personal GENDER, and within personal gender between masculine and feminine (*see* 569):

PERSONAL {masculine   *he*   *himself*
                   {feminine   *she*   *herself*

NON-PERSONAL   *it*   *itself*

(B)   They distinguish between 1st, 2nd, and 3rd PERSON:

1st	*I; we*	*myself; ourselves*
2nd	*you*	*yourself; yourselves*
3rd	*he, she, it; they*	*himself; themselves, etc*

(C)   They distinguish between singular and plural NUMBER (*see* 654):

singular	*I; he, she, it*	*myself; himself, etc*
plural	*we; they*	*ourselves; themselves, etc*

For the 2nd person the same form is used in the singular and plural of personal and possessive pronouns (*you; your, yours*), but there is a separate plural of reflexive pronouns: *yourself* (singular) and *yourselves* (plural).

We, the 1st person plural pronoun, denotes 'I plus one or more others' (*see* 85).

684

In addition, five personal pronouns (together with *who*, *see* 788, 579) are unique in having both subjective and objective case forms (*see* 504) as well as two genitive case forms. The genitives of the personal pronouns are usually called 'POSSESSIVE' (*see* 688–90).

Table 4

PERSONAL AND REFLEXIVE PRONOUNS

			PERSONAL PRONOUNS		POSSESSIVES		REFLEXIVE PRONOUNS
			subjective case	objective case	acting as determiners	acting as pronouns	
1st person	singular		*I*	*me*	*my*	*mine*	*myself*
	plural		*we*	*us*	*our*	*ours*	*ourselves*
2nd person	singular		*you*		*your*	*yours*	*yourself*
	plural						*yourselves*
3rd person	singular	masculine	*he*	*him*	*his*		*himself*
		feminine	*she*	*her*	*her*	*hers*	*herself*
		non-personal	*it*		*its*		*itself*
	plural		*they*	*them*	*their*	*theirs*	*themselves*

Personal pronouns

685

Personal pronouns, as we see from *Table 4*, are classified according to person (1st, 2nd, 3rd person), number (singular, plural), case (subjective, objective, genitive) and gender (masculine, feminine, non-personal).

686

The choice of person, number and gender is determined by meaning (*see* 82–5), which is supplied either by context outside language, or by the sort of noun phrase for which the pronoun acts as a substitute (*see* 391–3). Pronouns generally substitute for a noun phrase which precedes them:

My brother is out, but *he* will be returning soon.

But especially in ⟨formal written⟩ English, a personal pronoun in a subclause can be used as a substitute for a noun phrase which follows it in the main clause. *Compare*:

> As soon as *it* had refuelled, *the plane* took off.
> *The plane* took off as soon as *it* had refuelled.
> As soon as *the plane* had refuelled, *it* took off.

687

The choice of subjective and objective case is made on the basis of grammatical position. The simplest rule to use is that the subjective form is the one used IN SUBJECT POSITION with finite verbs, while the objective form is the one used IN ALL OTHER POSITIONS:

SUBJECTIVE CASE	*He* was late as usual.	(SUBJECT)
	I saw *him* yesterday.	(DIRECT OBJECT)
	Will you give *him* my regards?	(INDIRECT OBJECT)
	I've written to *him* already.	(PREPOSITIONAL COMPLEMENT)
OBJECTIVE CASE	She's several years older than *him*. ⟨informal⟩	(AFTER *than*, *as* IN COMPARISONS)
	(A) Who's there?	(SUBJECT COMPLEMENT)
	(B) It's *me*. ⟨informal⟩	
	(A) Who's going to drive?	(REPLY FORM)
	(B) *Me*. ⟨informal⟩	

(Compare with verb: (B) *I* am.)

But this rule is restricted to ⟨informal⟩ English in the last three cases illustrated. In these cases, traditional grammar tells us that the subjective form is the correct form to use. But in practice, the subjective form sounds rather stilted, and is avoided. Thus you will scarcely ever hear: *It's I*, or *I* in answer to questions like *Who's there*? The comparative form (*older*) *than I* is slightly more common.

Possessives
688

There are two kinds of possessives, each with its separate function. *My, your, her, etc* act as determiners before noun heads, and *mine, yours, hers, etc* as pronouns, *ie* as independent noun phrases:

DETERMINER FUNCTION   This is *her* book.

PRONOUN FUNCTION   The book is *hers*.

In pronoun function, the possessive is always stressed. (Compare the genitive constructions of *This is John's book* and *This book is John's*, see 576.)

Possessive as determiner
689

Unlike many other languages, English uses determiner possessives with reference to, for example, parts of the body and personal belongings:

Mary broke *her* leg when she was skiing in Austria.
Don't tell me they've changed *their* minds again!
There stood a man at the door with *his* hat in *his* hand.
Don't lose *your* balance and fall into the water!

The definite article is, however, usual in prepositional phrases related to the object (or, in passive constructions, the subject):

The little girl took me by *the* hand.
Something must have hit me on *the* head.
He was shot in *the* leg during the war.

Possessive as pronoun
690

The forms *mine, hers, theirs, etc*, can act in all the main positions where a noun phrase is possible:

SUBJECT   Can I borrow your pen? *Yours* (='your pen') works better than mine.

SUBJECT COMPLEMENT	These books are *ours* (= 'belong to us').
OBJECT	Philip wanted a screwdriver, so I let him borrow *yours* (= 'your screwdriver').
PREPOSITIONAL COMPLEMENT	I parked our car directly behind *theirs* (= 'their car').
IN COMPARISONS AFTER *than, as*	My parents are

$$\text{My parents are} \left\{ \begin{array}{l} \text{older than} \\ \text{not so old as} \end{array} \right\} hers$$
(= 'her parents').

Reflexive pronouns
691
Reflexive pronouns are used as objects, complements, and (often) prepositional complements where these elements have the same reference as the subject of the clause or sentence:

> The soldiers tried to defend *themselves*.

> I'm not worried about *myself*. (But I am about you.)

> We have to find *ourselves* a new home.

> Most authors start by writing novels about *themselves*.

> He's not (feeling) *himself* today. (*ie* 'He's feeling ill, out of condition')

Notice that in some cases the reflexive pronoun receives nuclear stress, and in other cases not.

The indefinite pronoun *one* (*see* 776) has its own reflexive as in

> *One* mustn't fool *oneself*.

but other indefinites use *himself* or *themselves* (*see* 540):

> *No one* must fool *himself*.

692
Also reflexives are used in imperative and infinitive constructions, where they point back to the element which is UNDERSTOOD to be the subject of the verb:

> Make *yourself* at home.

> I've asked everyone to help *themselves*.

However, in many prepositional phrases denoting place the ordinary personal pronouns are used:

> He turned around and looked *about him*.

> Have you any money *on you*?

> She had her fiancé *beside her* in the back of the car.

> They placed their papers *in front of them*.

693
The reflexive pronouns *myself, ourselves, etc* are sometimes used as alternatives to *me, us, etc* after *as* (*for*), *like, but* (*for*), *except* (*for*) and in coordinated noun phrases:

> As for *me/myself*, I don't mind what you decide to do.

> For someone like *me/myself*, one good meal a day is quite enough.

> Did you want to speak to my wife or *me/myself*?

694
The reflexive pronouns also have an emphatic use, where they follow a noun phrase or another pronoun, and reinforce its meaning:

> I spoke to the manager *himself*.

> She's getting a divorce: she *herself* told me.

We can also postpone the reflexive pronoun to the end of the sentence (*see* 444).

695

After a determiner possessive, the word *own* can be used for emphatic or reflexive meaning: *my own, your own, his own, etc*:

> He cooks *his own* dinner (= 'He cooks dinner *for himself*').
> The government is encouraging people to buy *their own* homes.

The intensifying adverb *very* can be added before *own*:

> Do you like the soup? The recipe is *my very own*.

The combination possessive + *own* can also occur in an *of*-phrase (*see* 577):

> I'd love to have a house *of my own*.

Phrasal and prepositional verbs (*see GCE* 12.19–28)

Phrasal verbs
696

Verbs may form combinations with ADVERBIAL PARTICLES which, in their form and behaviour are like prepositional adverbs (*see* 746):

The children were *sitting down*.	*Get up* at once.
Drink up quickly.	Did he *catch on*?
The plane has just *taken off*.	He *turned up* unexpectedly.
When will they *give in*?	

Such verb–adverb combinations are called PHRASAL VERBS. Most of the adverbs are place adverbs (*see* 189). Verbs can also combine with prepositional adverbs which function like prepositional phrases. Here we do not speak of 'phrasal verbs':

> They *walked past* (the place).
> She *ran across* (the street).

697

Some phrasal verbs retain the individual meanings of the verb and the adverb (for example *sit down*), whereas for other phrasal verbs the meaning of the combination cannot be built up from the meanings of the individual verb and adverb, for example: *catch on* (= 'understand'), *give in* (= 'surrender'), *turn up* (= 'appear, arrive') *etc*.

698

Many phrasal verbs can take an object:

> *Find out* whether they are coming.
> *Drink up* your milk quickly.
> They *turned on* the light.
> She is *bringing up* her brother's children.
> They *called off* the strike.

With most of these phrasal verbs, the adverb can either come before or follow a noun object:

> = { They *turned on* the light.
> { They *turned* the light *on*.

Personal pronoun objects, however, always have to come before the adverb:

> They *turned* it *on*.

not: *They *turned on* it.

Other examples of phrasal verbs with objects are:

> *blow up* (a bridge)
> *break off* (our relations)
> *bring about* (a change)

> *burn up* (the leaves in the garden)
> *fill out* (a form)
> *get out* (a book)
> *get over* (an idea)
> *make up* (a story)

Most phrasal verbs are ⟨informal⟩.

In some cases phrasal verbs with objects look identical to verbs followed by a prepositional phrase:

a   They *ran over* the bridge (= 'crossed the bridge by running'). (VERB + PREPOSITION)

b   They *ran over* the cat (= 'knocked down and passed over'). (PHRASAL VERB)

Prepositional verbs
699

A verb may also form a combination with a preposition (*see* 744), for example

> He's *applied for* a new job.
> Has anyone *commented on* the results?
> The article also *hinted at* other possibilities.
> Her parents strongly *objected to* her travelling alone.
> Who will be *running for* president at the next election?

The noun phrase following the preposition is termed the PREPOSITIONAL OBJECT. Other examples of prepositional verbs are:

> *add to* (the bill)
> *allow for* (delays)
> *amount to* (50 dollars)
> *approve of* (an action)
> *attend to* (the matter)
> *care for* (somebody)
> *compete with* (somebody)
> *conform to* (a standard)
> *consent to* (a proposal)
> *enlarge on* (a topic)
> *hope for* (improvements)
> *live on* (a small salary)
> *part with* (a car)
> *refer to* (a dictionary)
> *resort to* (violence)
> *shout for* (help)

Differences between phrasal and prepositional verbs
700

Phrasal and prepositional verbs may seem very similar, for example the pair:

a   They *called up* all young men (= 'conscripted').

b   They *called on* their friends (= 'visited').

They are, however, different in at least four respects:

(A)   The adverb in *a* (a phrasal verb) is normally stressed and has nuclear stress in end-position. The preposition in *b* (a prepositional verb), however, is normally unstressed:

a   They called ˈup all young men.

All young men were called up.

b   They called on their friends.

Their friends were called on.

(B)   The preposition in a prepositional verb must come before the prepositional object:

  a { They *called up* all young men.
      { They *called* all young men *up*.
      They *called* them *up*.
  b   They *called on* their friends.
      They *called on* them.

(C)   On the other hand, the prepositional verb allows an adverb to be placed between the verb and the preposition:

  a   *They *called* early *up* all young men.
  b   They *called* early *on* their friends.

(D)   A prepositional verb also accepts a relative pronoun after the preposition:

  a   *All young men *up* whom ⎫
  b   The friends *on* whom   ⎬ they *called* were not at home.

But both types of verb can have the preposition or adverb end-placed:

  The men (whom) they *called ¹up*   ⎫
                                        ⎬ were not at home.
  The friends (whom) they *¹called on* ⎭

Note that, unlike some languages, English often allows the prepositional object to become the subject of a passive sentence (*see* 681):

  They *looked upon* him as   He was *looked upon* as a
  a hero.   hero.

Phrasal-prepositional verbs
701
In ⟨informal⟩ English, some verbs can combine as an idiom with both an adverb and a preposition, for example

  He *puts up with* almost anything (= 'tolerates').
  You shouldn't *break in on* a conversation like that (= 'interrupt').
  We must all *cut down on* spending (= 'reduce').
  Don't imagine you can *get away with* that sort of thing.
  He *walked out on* the project (= 'abandoned').

702
We call these phrasal-prepositional verbs. We can make a clause containing such a verb passive, by changing the prepositional object into the subject (*see* 681):

  { They have *done away with* (= 'abolished') the old laws.
  {   The old laws have been *done away with*.

We cannot insert an adverb between the preposition and the object:

  *He *puts up with* willingly that secretary of his.

though it is possible to do so between the adverb and the preposition:

  He *puts up* willingly *with* that secretary of his.

In relative clauses and questions, where the object is front-placed, the adverb and preposition come after the verb:

  What are the police *checking up on* (= 'investigate')?   ⎫
  You don't realise what I've had to *put up with* (= 'tolerate'). ⎬⟨informal⟩

703
Other examples of phrasal-prepositional verbs in ⟨informal⟩ English are:

  back out of (an agreement)
  catch up on (my reading)
  catch up with (somebody)
  drop in on (a neighbour)
  face up to (the problems)
  get down to (serious talk)
  look down on (somebody)
  make away with (a large sum)
  stand up for (one's ideals)

Plurals (*see GCE* 4.60–84)

Regular plurals
704
Most nouns are count nouns (*see* 45), *ie* they can occur in both the singular (denoting 'one') or in the plural (denoting 'more than one'). Most count nouns have the regular *-s* plural which is formed by adding an *s* to the singular: *one*
> *dog* → *two dogs*
In some cases further spelling changes occur when *-s* is added (*see* 809–14).
For the pronunciation of the *-s* ending, *see* 751.

The plural of compounds
705
    a In most compounds the ending is added to the last part:
> *assistant director* → *assistant directors*

        So also:
> *boy friends, breakdowns, check-ups, grown-ups, sit-ins, stand-bys, take-offs,* etc.

    b But a few compounds take the ending after the first part:
> *notaries public, passers-by,* etc.

    c A few compounds have both the first and the last part in the plural:
> *menservants, women doctors,* etc.

Irregular plurals
(A) VOICING+ *-s* PLURAL
706
Some nouns which in the singular end in the voiceless /θ/ or /f/ sound (spelled *-th* and *-f*) change to the corresponding voiced sound /ð/ or /v/ in the plural, before the regular /z/ ending.

a NOUNS IN *-th*
With a consonant before the *-th*, the plural is regular: *months* (/mʌnθ/ → /mʌnθs/). With a vowel before the *-th*, the plural is also often regular, as with *cloths, deaths, faiths*; but in one or two cases the plural has voicing: *mouths* (/mavθ/ → /mavðz/), *paths*. In several cases we find both regular and voiced plurals: *oaths* (/ovθ/ → /ovθs/, /ovðz/), *truths, wreaths*.

b NOUNS IN *-f(e)*
The voiced plurals /–vz/ are spelled *-ves*:

calf	calves	loaf	loaves
half	halves	shelf	shelves
knife	knives	thief	thieves
leaf	leaves	wife	wives
life	lives	wolf	wolves

Other nouns in *–f* have only the regular plural /–fs/: *beliefs, chiefs, cliffs, proofs, roofs, safes,* etc.

c ONE NOUN IN *-s* has the irregular plural pronunciation /–zɪz/:
> *house* /havs/   *houses* /'havzɪz/

(B) CHANGE OF VOWEL IN THE PLURAL
707
The following nouns form the plural by a vowel change instead of an ending:

foot /fvt/	*feet* /fiːt/
tooth /tuːθ/	*teeth* /tiːθ/
goose /guːs/	*geese* /giːs/

man /mæn/	*men* /men/
mouse /mavs/	*mice* /mais/
woman /'wvmən/	*women* /'wimin/

(C) PLURAL IN *-en* (*with or without vowel change*)

708

child /tʃaild/	*children* /'tʃildrən/
ox /ɒks‖aks/	*oxen* /'ɒksən‖'aksən/
brother /'brʌðəʳ/	*brethren* /'breðrin/ in the special sense 'fellow members of a religious society'; otherwise regular: *brothers*.

(D) NO PLURAL ENDING

709

Some nouns can be used both with a singular and a plural meaning without change: *a sheep/many sheep, etc.*

Some ANIMAL NAMES are, like *sheep*, unchanged, but there is great variation.

Most such nouns are regular: *bird, cow, eagle, hen, rabbit, etc.*

Always unchanged: *deer, sheep, plaice, salmon, grouse.*

Usually unchanged: *pike, trout, carp, moose.*

Both the regular and the unchanged plurals: *antelope, reindeer, fish, flounder, herring.*

710

Dozen, stone ⟨BrE⟩, and *foot*:

I want two *dozen* eggs, please.

(but: *Dozens of eggs* were broken.)

He weighs $\begin{cases} \text{fourteen } stone \text{ two pounds [14st 2 lb]. } ⟨\text{BrE}⟩ \\ \text{198 pounds [198 lb]. } ⟨\text{AmE}⟩ \end{cases}$

(A)   How tall are you?

(B)   I'm $\begin{cases} \text{six } foot \text{ (6 ft). } But: \text{ I'm six } feet \text{ tall)} \\ \text{six } foot/feet \text{ two (inches) [6 ft 2 in].} \end{cases}$

Plural expressions like *five pounds* do not have *-s* when they act as premodifiers (*see* 735): *a five-pound note* ⟨BrE⟩, *a six-lane motorway, a four-piston engine.*

711

Series and *species* can be used as either singular or plural:

He gave *one series/two series* of lectures.

(E) FOREIGN PLURALS

712

In some words borrowed from foreign languages, foreign plurals occur instead of regular plurals. With other foreign words, both a regular plural and a foreign plural can occur. Foreign plurals tend to be commoner in technical usage, whereas the *-s* plural is more natural in everyday language; thus *formulas* (general) but *formulae* (in mathematics); *antennas* (general and in electronics) but *antennae* (in biology). Here is a list of some nouns which have foreign plurals:

713

a NOUNS IN *-us* (Latin)

The foreign plural is *-i* /ai/, as in *stimulus*, → *stimuli* /'stimjulai/.

Only regular plural (*-uses*): *bonus* (→ *bonuses*), *campus, chorus, circus, virus, etc.*

Both plurals: *cactus* (→ *cactuses/cacti*), *focus, nucleus, radius, terminus, syllabus.*

Only foreign plural: *alumnus* (→ *alumni*), *bacillus.*

714

b NOUNS IN in *-a* (Latin)

The foreign plural is *-ae* (pronounced /iː/), as in *alumna* → *alumnae.*

Only regular plural (*-as*): *area* (→ *areas*), *arena, dilemma, diploma, drama, etc.*
Both plurals: *formula* (→ *formulas/formulae*), *antenna.*
Only foreign plural: *alga* (→ *algae*), *larva.*
715
c NOUNS IN *-um* (Latin)
The foreign plural is *-a* /ə/, as in *curriculum, curricula.*
Only regular plural: *album* (→ *albums*), *museum, etc.*
Usually regular: *forum* (→ *forums*), *stadium, ultimatum.*
Both plurals: *aquarium* (→ *aquariums/aquaria*), *medium* (but always *media* in the mass media), *memorandum, symposium.*
716
d NOUNS IN *-ex, -ix* (Latin)
The foreign plural is *-ices* (pronounced /–ɪsiːz/), as in *index* → *indices.*
Both regular and foreign plurals: *apex* (→ *apexes/apices*), *appendix, matrix.*
Only foreign plural: *codex* (→ *codices*).
717
e NOUNS IN *-is* (Greek)
The foreign plural is *-es* (/–iːz/), as in *basis,* → *bases.*
Regular plural: *metropolis* (→ *metropolises*).
Foreign plural: *analysis* (→ *analyses*), *axis, crisis, diagnosis, ellipsis, hypothesis, oasis, parenthesis, synopsis, thesis.*
718
f NOUNS IN *-on* (Greek)
The foreign plural is *-a* /–ə/, as in *criterion* → *criteria.*
Only regular plurals: *demon* (→ *demons*), *electron, neutron, proton.*
Both plurals: *automaton* (→ *automatons/automata*).

Postmodifiers (*see GCE* 13.5–43)

719
Postmodifiers occur after the head in a noun phrase (*see* 651–3). We have the following range of postmodifiers:
(A)   RELATIVE CLAUSES (*see* separate entry 783–95)
        Did you see the girl *who was sitting in the corner*?
(B)   PREPOSITIONAL PHRASES (*see* 783–95)
        Did you see the girl *in the corner*?
(C)   NON-FINITE CLAUSES EQUIVALENT TO RELATIVE CLAUSES (*see* 720)
        Did you see the girl *sitting in the corner*?
(D)   APPOSITIVE CLAUSES (*see* 725–7)
        The fact *that she's good-looking* is not the only reason *why
        I'd like to meet her.*
(E)   CLAUSES OF TIME, PLACE, MANNER AND REASON (*see* 728)
        We visited the house *where Mozart stayed in 1789.*
(F)   ADVERBS (*see* 729)
        The way *out* is over there.
(G)   ADJECTIVES (*see* 730)
        There's something *odd* about her.

Prepositional phrases as postmodifiers
720
The prepositional phrase (*see* 739–43) is by far the most common type of post-modifier in English. Prepositional phrases can often be related to relative clauses:
        Is this the road *to Paris*?
        (= 'Is this the road *that leads to Paris*?')

The house *beyond the church* was for sale.

His life *after the war* was rather dull.

All passengers *on board the ship* had to pass a medical examination.

There is no cause *for alarm*.

(On *of*-phrases, *see* 44–59, 95–6, 573–4.)

Non-finite clauses equivalent to relative clauses as postmodifiers

721

All three types of non-finite clause (*-ing* participle clauses, *-ed* participle clauses, and *to*-infinitive clauses) can function as postmodifiers similar to relative clauses.

-ing PARTICIPLE CLAUSES

The people *working in the factory* asked for a pay increase last
month. (= 'who are/were working in the factory')

When you enter, please hand your tickets to the man *standing at the*

door. (= 'who $\begin{Bmatrix} \text{will be} \\ \text{is} \end{Bmatrix}$ standing at the door')

As the participle clause does not have tense (*see* 407–8, 103), it can be interpreted, according to context, as past or present tense. However, the *-ing* participle clause need not carry the meaning of the progressive aspect (*see* 882, 122):

All articles *belonging to the college* must be returned. (= 'all articles
that belong . . . ')

722

-ed PARTICIPLE CLAUSES

The question *debated in Parliament yesterday* was about abortion
laws. (= 'that was debated in Parliament')

The only car *yet repaired by that mechanic* is mine. (= 'that has yet
been repaired')

The participle clause corresponds in meaning to a passive relative clause, but the participle clause contains none of the distinctions that can be made by tense and aspect.

723

to-INFINITIVE CLAUSES

The question *to be debated tomorrow* is whether income tax should

be increased. (= 'the question which $\begin{Bmatrix} \text{is to} \\ \text{will} \end{Bmatrix}$ be debated')

The next train *to arrive* was from Chicago. (= 'the train which
arrived next')

John is the last person *to cause trouble*. (= 'the person who would
be the last to cause trouble')

Amundsen was the first man *to reach the South Pole*. (= 'who
reached the South Pole first')

As we see, the *to*-infinitive resembles the other non-finite clauses in not making distinctions of tense and aspect, so that its time reference alters according to context. The *to*-infinitive clause is often preceded by *next*, *last*, ordinal numerals or superlatives.

724

In many infinitive clauses, the head of the noun phrase stands in the relation of object or prepositional object to the infinitive verb:

The (best) man *to consult* is Wilson. (= 'the man you/one/*etc*
should consult')

There are plenty of toys *to play with*. (= 'with which to play')

In these cases, a subject preceded by *for* may be added:

The (best) man *for you to consult* is Wilson.

There are plenty of toys *for the children to play with*.

(On other infinitive clauses, such as *the time to arrive*, *see* 728.)

Appositive clauses as postmodifiers
725
Appositive clauses are nominal clauses which have a relation to the head similar to that between two noun phrases in apposition (*see* 489–91). They can be *that*-clauses (*see* 639–40) or *to*-infinitive clauses (*see* 647–8):

> The news *that he was resigning his job* proved to be incorrect. [1]
> The police have been investigating a plot *to kidnap a promi-*
> *nent diplomat.*   [2]

The relation of apposition can be seen if we relate the noun phrase to a subject +*be*+complement construction: [1a]

> The news was that he was resigning his job.   [2a]
> The plot is to kidnap a prominent diplomat.

Notice that the *that*-clause is a nominal clause and not a relative clause. We can show this by contrasting [1] with [3]:

> The news *that was spreading* proved to be incorrect.   [3]

That in [3] is a relative pronoun, and could be replaced by *which*. It acts as the subject of the clause. But in [1] *that* is a conjunction.

726
The head of an appositive clause must be an abstract noun such as *fact, idea, reply, answer, appeal, promise*:

> His wife tried to conceal the fact *that he was seriously ill.*
> We were delighted at the news *that our team had won.*
> Stories *that the house was haunted* had been current for centuries.
> The mayor launched an appeal to the public *to give blood* to the
> victims of the disaster.
> We gratefully accepted his promise *to help us.*

Other types of nominal clause (interrogative and *-ing* clauses, *see* 641–4, 649–50) strictly do not occur as appositive clauses, but they can be put in an appositional relation with the head of the noun phrase by means of the preposition *of*:

> He made the mistake of *attacking a neutral country.* (*Compare*: His
> mistake was attacking . . .)
> We shall soon have to face the annual problem of *what to give Aunt*
> *Matilda for her birthday.* (*Compare*: Our annual problem is what
> to give . . .)

727
Appositive clauses so far illustrated have been restrictive (*cf* 99–102). Examples of non-restrictive appositive clauses are:

> His main argument, *that scientific laws have no exceptions*, was
> considered absurd.
> His last appeal, *for his son to visit him*, was never delivered.
> She suffered from a common misfortune of women at that time:
> *having too much time and too little money.*
> We'll soon have to face that annual problem—*what to give Aunt*
> *Matilda for her birthday.*

All types of nominal clause can act as non-restrictive appositive clauses.

Clauses of time, place, manner, and reason
728
These postmodifying clauses are similar in that they are linked to the head by an adverbial relation (*see* 140–53, 161, 204). They are:

> *a*   Finite clauses introduced by a *wh*-word:

TIME	He is always talking about the years *when he was a student.*
PLACE	We visited the house *where Beethoven was born.*
REASON	Is that the reason *why you came*? ⟨informal⟩

b Finite clauses introduced by *that* or zero:

TIME	It's about time (*that*) *you had a holiday.*
PLACE	I'll show you the place (*that*) *we stayed* (*at*) *last year.* ⟨informal⟩
MANNER	I like the way (*that*) *she does her hair.* ⟨informal⟩
REASON	The reason (*that*) *I came* was to ask your forgiveness.

c *To*-infinitive clauses:

TIME	It will soon be time *to leave.*
PLACE	A good place *to stay* (*at*) is the White Hart.
MANNER	That's not the way *to make an omelette*!

Adverbs as postmodifiers
729
The use of adverbs as postmodifiers is more restricted than the use of other postmodifiers (*see* also 487).

The road *back* was dense with traffic.

(= 'The road *which led back* . . . ')

The people *outside* started to shout.

The weather *tomorrow* will be cloudy.

Adjectives and adjectival constructions as postmodifiers
730
Adjectives normally premodify the noun (*see* 732), but in some constructions (discussed elsewhere, *see* 459), they follow the noun:

There was something *odd* about his behaviour.

Anyone *keen on modern jazz* should not miss this opportunity.

Premodifiers (*see GCE* 13.44–68)

731
Premodifiers in a noun phrase (*see* 651–3) are placed after determiners (*see* 550–67) but before the noun which is head of the phrase. There are the following types of premodifiers, all of which can be related to complements in sentences with a linking verb (*see* 529):

732
(A) ADJECTIVES (*see* 456–7)

He's rented a *delightful* cottage.

(*Compare*: The cottage is *delightful.*)

A premodifying adjective can itself be premodified by degree adverbs (*see* 482):

his *really quite unbelievably delightful* cottage

just as if it were in complement position:

His cottage is *really quite unbelievably* delightful.

733
(B) PARTICIPLES (*see* 621–2)

He's rented a *crumbling* cottage.

(The cottage is *crumbling.*)

He's rented a *converted* cottage.

(The cottage is/has been *converted.*)

734
(C) NOUNS

He's rented a *country* cottage.

(The cottage is *in the country.*)

Genitive nouns can occasionally act as premodifiers, although in general genitives function as determiners (*see* 552). The premodifying function is shown by the position of the genitive in:

He's rented a quaint *fisherman's* cottage.

(= 'a quaint cottage of the kind which belong to fishermen'.)

Compound premodifiers
735
Compound premodifiers are quite common. These are combinations of words which function as a single adjective or noun. They have various patterns:

icy-cold water	*brand-new* dinner plates
a *record-breaking* jump	a *hard-hearted* man
a *hard-working* mother	a *good-looking* girl
a *first-class* performance	a *wrought-iron* gate

(On *a five-pound note, see* 710.)

Premodifiers consisting of more than one word
736
In addition, there are modifiers which consist of more than one word but which make up a syntactic construction rather than a compound word. These are not hyphenated when they occur as complements (*ie* after the verb in a clause), but are often hyphenated when they premodify, and are therefore not easy to distinguish from compounds. They take the form of prepositional phrases, adjective phrases, noun phrases, participial constructions, *etc*:

an *out-of-the-way* cottage	(The cottage is out of the way.)
the *town-hall* clock	(The clock is on the town hall.)
a *ready-to-wear* suit	(The suit is ready to wear.)
a *recently converted* cottage	(The cottage has recently been converted.)
a *red and white* scarf	(The scarf is red and white.)

737
Sequences of three, four, or even five nouns occur quite commonly in a noun phrase; *eg Lancaster City football club supporters*. These are formed either through noun premodification or through noun compounds, or through a combination of both. We can show the way in which the above example is built up as follows:

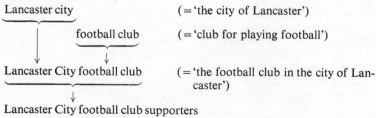

Lancaster city	(= 'the city of Lancaster')
football club	(= 'club for playing football')
Lancaster City football club	(= 'the football club in the city of Lancaster')
Lancaster City football club supporters	
	(= 'the supporters of the Lancaster City football club')

More than one premodifier
738
When a noun head has more than one premodifier, these tend to occur in a certain order. We deal with them in a right-to-left order, *ie* starting from the head (here in CAPITAL LETTERS).

The item that comes next before the head is the type of adjective which means 'consisting of', 'involving', or 'relating to':

This is not a *political* PROBLEM, it's a *social* PROBLEM

Next closest to the head is the noun modifier:

a *world* political PROBLEM

Next before the noun modifier comes the adjective derived from a proper noun:

the *American* spring medical CONFERENCE

Normally, of course, noun phrases do not have *all* these types of premodifiers. We are more likely to find a simpler structure, for example:

a *Russian* trade DELEGATION

Scandinavian furniture DESIGNS

Before this type of adjective we find a variety of other modifiers: participles, colour-adjectives, adjectives denoting age, *etc*:

printed Scandinavian DESIGNS

red oriental CARPETS

a *young* physics STUDENT

These premodifiers may of course themselves have modifiers:

badly copied Scandinavian furniture DESIGNS

really attractive deep-red oriental SILK

a *very, very young* physics STUDENT

a *large enough* lecture HALL

Notice the middle position of unstressed *little*, *old* and *young*:

a '*nice little* 'COTTAGE ⟨informal⟩

a '*fine old* 'GENTLEMAN

a '*pretty young* 'LADY

Prepositional phrases (*see GCE* Chapter 6)

739

A prepositional phrase consists of a preposition (*see* 744–5) followed by a prepositional complement, which is usually

(A)   A NOUN PHRASE (*see* 651–3):

There will be 1400 delegates *at the conference*.

(B)   A *wh*-CLAUSE (*see* 641–6):

No conclusions can be drawn *from what the press reported yesterday*.

(C)   AN *-ing* CLAUSE (*see* 649–50):

By signing the treaty both nations have made an effort towards peace.

Compare:

He was surprised $\begin{cases} \textit{at her remark.} & \text{(A)} \\ \textit{at what she said.} & \text{(B)} \\ \textit{at her saying this.} & \text{(C)} \end{cases}$

740

There are two categories of nominal clause which cannot directly follow a preposition. These are *that*-clauses (*see* 639–40) and *to*-infinitive clauses (*see* 647–8). With such clauses, the preposition is omitted:

He was surprised $\begin{cases} \textit{that she said this.} \\ \textit{to hear her say this.} \end{cases}$

Compare these with preposition + a *wh*-clause:

He was surprised *at what she said*.

Sometimes, the addition of *the fact* (*that*) can serve to convert the *that*-clause construction into a form suitable for a prepositional complement:

She was aware {
of the many problems which still existed.
of the fact that there were still many problems.
that there were still many problems.
}

741

Normally a preposition must come before its complement. However, there are some cases where this does not happen, because the complement is at the front of the clause.

(A) In relative clauses, *wh*-questions, and exclamations the preposition can occur either at the beginning or the end. The first position is ⟨formal⟩.

RELATIVE CLAUSES (*see* 783–96)

{
The party (*which*) most people vote *for* does not necessarily win the election.
The party *for which* most people vote does not necessarily win the election. ⟨formal⟩
}

Wh-QUESTIONS (*see* 779–80)

{
Which house is he staying *at*?
At which house is he staying? ⟨formal⟩
}

EXCLAMATIONS (*see* 568)

What a difficult situation he's *in*!

With what amazing skill this artist handles the brush! ⟨formal⟩

742

(B) In *wh*-clauses, passives, and infinitive clauses the preposition must occur at the end:

Wh-CLAUSES (*see* 641–2, 645)

What I'm convinced *of* is that the world's population will grow too fast.

PASSIVES (*see* 681)

The old woman was cared *for* by a nurse from the hospital.

INFINITIVE CLAUSES (*see* 647–8)

That man is impossible to work *with*. ⟨informal⟩

The functions of prepositional phrases
743

Prepositional phrases may function as:

(A)   ADVERBIALS (*see* 468)

My brother works *in an insurance company*.

To my surprise, the doctor phoned the next morning.

(B)   POSTMODIFIERS IN A NOUN PHRASE (*see* 651–3, 720)

The people *on the bus* were singing.

(C)   VERB COMPLEMENTS (*see* 842, 868)

I want to congratulate you *on your exam*.

(D)   COMPLEMENTS OF ADJECTIVES (*see* 530)

I'm terribly bad *at mathematics*.

(E)   SUBJECT, COMPLEMENT, *etc*

Also prepositional phrases may occasionally take the role of a noun phrase as subject, complement, prepositional complement, *etc*:

Before breakfast is when I do my best work.

The view from *above the shore* is magnificent.

Prepositions and prepositional adverbs (*see GCE* 6.9–10)

Prepositions
744

Prepositions are words which, as their name implies, are PLACED BEFORE a noun phrase (*see* 651–3). The most common English prepositions are SIMPLE, *ie* consist of one word:

We had to wait *at* THE AIRPORT *for* FIVE HOURS *before* TAKE-OFF.

Common simple prepositions are:

about	by	past
above	down	since
after	for	till
along	from	through
around	in	to
at	into	under
before	of	until
below	off	up
beside	on	with
between	over	without

745

Other prepositions, consisting of more than one word, are called COMPLEX, for example:

according to	due to	by means of
along with	except for	in comparison with
as for	out of	in front of
away from	owing to	in relation to
because of	up to	on top of

The following sentences illustrate the use of some complex prepositions:

Two men were interviewed at the police station *in connection with* a theft from a department store.

This development is *in line with* latest trends in fashion.

Prepositional adverbs

746

A prepositional adverb is an adverb which behaves like a preposition with the complement omitted (*see* 189–90):

A car drove past the ga̖te. (*past*=a preposition)

A car drove pa̖st. (*past*=a prepositional adverb)

Prepositions consisting of one syllable are normally unstressed, but prepositional adverbs are stressed:

He 'stayed in the ho̖use.

He stayed i̖n.

All the words listed in 744 (except *at*, *beside*, *for*, *from*, *into*, *of*, *till*, *to*, *until*, *with*) can act as prepositional adverbs (*cf* 179).

Pronouns (*see GCE* 4.106–111)

747

Pronouns are words which can function as a whole noun phrase (*eg* in being subject or object of a clause) or as the head of a noun phrase. Many of them act as substitutes (*see* 391–7) or 'replacements' for noun phrases in the context.

In the majority of cases, a pronoun functions as a whole noun phrase, and therefore does not have any determiners or modifiers. Here are a few examples where determiners and modifiers do accompany the noun phrase:

So you're going to Spain for your holidays. *Lucky you!* ⟨familiar⟩

You have the large room, and I'll have *the small one.*

Those who live in glass houses shouldn't throw stones. (proverb)

748

Many items can function *a* both as determiners (which require a head) and as pronouns (which do not require a head). Others can be *b* determiner only, or *c* pronoun only:

a	DETERMINER	*Which* car ⎫
	PRONOUN	*Which* ⎬ is yours?
	DETERMINER	*This* bike is mine.
	PRONOUN	*This* is my bike.
b	DETERMINER ONLY	*The* bike is mine.
c	PRONOUN ONLY	John has hurt *himself*.
		We don't actually dislike *one another*.

749

Partly because pronouns differ among themselves, partly because many pronouns are related to other categories, pronouns are treated under the following headings:

DEMONSTRATIVES *this, that, these, those* (*see* 548–9)

INTERROGATIVES *who, which, what, where, etc* (*see* 578–83)

NEGATION *no, nobody, no one, nothing, etc* (*see* 632)

PERSONAL AND REFLEXIVE PRONOUNS *I, my, mine, myself, etc* (*see* 683–95)

RECIPROCAL PRONOUNS *each other* and *one another* (*see* 782)

RELATIVE CLAUSES *who, whom, whose, which, that* (*see* 783–96)

QUANTIFIERS *some, any*, and *every* and their combinations with *-body, -one, -thing, each, all, both, either*; *much, many, more, most, enough, several, (a) little, (a) few, less, least, etc* (*see* 765–76)

Pronunciation of endings (*see GCE* 3.54–62, 4.61, 4.96, 5.73)

750

Here we deal with rules for the pronunciation of grammatical endings, whether they are added to nouns, verbs, or adjectives.

The -*s* ending

751

The -*s* ending has three different functions: plural (*see* 704), genitive (*see* 570), and 3rd person singular present (*see* 620). However, the rules for pronouncing the ending are the same in all functions:

FUNCTION	PRONUNCIATION		
	(A) /ɪz/	(B) /z/	(C) /s/
plural	horse → *horses*	dog → *dogs*	cat → *cats*
genitive	George → *George's*	John → *John's*	Ruth → *Ruth's*
3rd person	catch → *catches*	call → *calls*	hit → *hits*

(A) The pronunciation is /ɪz/ after bases ending in voiced or voiceless sibilants, *ie* /z/, /s/, /dʒ/, /tʃ/, /ʒ/, /ʃ/:

church /tʃɜːtʃ‖tʃɜrtʃ/   churches /ˈtʃɜːtʃɪz‖ˈtʃɜrtʃɪz/

Reg /redʒ/   Reg's /ˈredʒɪz/

praise /preɪz/   praises /ˈpreɪzɪz/

(B) The pronunciation is /z/ after bases ending in voiced sounds other than /z/, /dʒ/, /ʒ/ (including vowels):

boy /bɔɪ/   boys /bɔɪz/
pig /pɪg/   pig's /pɪgz/
read /riːd/   reads /riːdz/

(C)   The pronunciation is /s/ after bases ending in voiceless sounds other than /s/, /tʃ/, /ʃ/:

month /mʌnθ/   months /mʌnθs/
week /wiːk/   week's /wiːks/
pick /pɪk/   picks /pɪks/

Note these irregular pronunciations:

do /duː/   does /dʌz/ (or /dəz/ when unstressed)
say /seɪ/   says /sez/

The -ed ending (see 622)
752
The -ed ending of regular verbs has three spoken forms:

(A)   /ɪd/ after bases ending in /d/ and /t/:

pad /pæd/   padded /'pædɪd/
pat /pæt/   patted /'pætɪd/

(B)   /d/ after bases ending in voiced sounds other than /d/ (including vowels):

mow /moʊ/   mowed /moʊd/
praise /preɪz/   praised /preɪzd/

(C)   /t/ after bases ending in voiceless sounds other than /t/:

press /pres/   pressed /prest/
pack /pæk/   packed /pækt/

The -er and -est endings (see 523)
753
(A)   Syllabic l /l̩/ is no longer syllabic before -er and -est:

simple   simpler   simplest
/'sɪmpl̩/   /'sɪmplə˞/   /'sɪmplɪst/

(B)   Adjectives ending in /ŋ/ change /ŋ/ to /ŋg/ before -er and -est:

long /–ŋ/   longer /–ŋgə˞/   longest /–ŋgɪst/
strong   stronger   strongest
young   younger   youngest

Contrast verbs: sing /sɪŋ/ → singing /'sɪŋɪŋ/, etc.

The -ing and -er/-est endings (see 621, 523)
754
Whether or not speakers pronounce final r in words like pour and poor, the r is of course always pronounced before -ing and -er/-est:

The rain is pouring /'pɔːrɪŋ/ down.
It would be fairer /'feərə˞/ to take a vote.

Proper nouns (see GCE 4.2, 4.40–47)

755
Proper nouns have 'unique' reference and, in the singular, usually take no article in English (see 492). The following list gives examples of article usage with some classes of proper nouns:

Proper nouns without an article
756
(A) PERSONAL NAMES (with or without titles)

Mary   Peter Jones

Mr and Mrs Johnson	Lady Churchill
President Roosevelt	Cardinal Spellman
Dr Watson	Judge Darling ⟨mainly AmE⟩
Professor Brown	Uncle Tom

Contrast: *the President of the United States of America, the Lord (God), the Duke of Wellington*

Family terms with unique reference often behave like proper nouns. No article is used in the vocative (*see* 364):

Hello Mother/Mummy ⟨familiar⟩/Mum ⟨familiar⟩.

Elsewhere the article is also omitted in ⟨familiar⟩ use:

Father/Daddy ⟨familiar⟩/Dad ⟨familiar⟩ will soon be home.
Have you thanked Auntie ⟨familiar⟩/Uncle for the present?

Compare: *Your father will soon be home.*

757

(B) CALENDAR ITEMS

  a Names of festivals

      Christmas (Day)   Independence Day
      Easter (Sunday)

  b Names of the months and the days of the week

      January, February, ...   Monday, Tuesday, ...

  c Names of seasons may have the article omitted ⟨*esp* BrE⟩:

      I last saw her in (the) spring.

  but: *in the spring of 1975 (see* 71)

758

(C) GEOGRAPHICAL NAMES

There is normally no article whether or not the name is premodified (*see* 731):

  a Names of continents

      (North) America   (medieval) Europe
      (Central) Australia   (East) Africa

  b Names of countries, counties, states, *etc*

      (modern) Brazil   (industrial) Lancashire
      (Elizabethan) England   (northern) Florida

    Exceptions: *the Argentine* (but *Argentina*), *the Ruhr, the Saar, the Sahara, the Ukraine, the Crimea, (the) Lebanon, the Midwest.*

  c Cities and towns

      (downtown) Boston   (suburban) London
      (ancient) Rome   (central) Tokyo

    But note: *the Hague; the Bronx; the City, the West End, the East End (of London).*

  d Lakes and mountains

      Lake Michigan   (Lake) Windermere
      Mount Everest   Vesuvius

759

(D) NAME + COMMON NOUN

In combinations of name and common noun denoting buildings, streets, bridges, *etc*, the second noun usually has the main stress: *Hampstead He̍ath*, except that names ending in *Street* have the main stress on the first noun: *O̍xford Street.*

Madison A̍venue	Westminster Bri̍dge
Park La̍ne	Leicester Squa̍re
Russell Dri̍ve	Greenwich Vi̍llage

Reynolds Close   Kennedy Airport

Portland Place   Harvard University

But note *the Albert Hall*; also *the Haymarket, the Strand, the Mall* (street names in London); *the Merrit Parkway, the Pennsylvania Turnpike*. Names of universities where the first part is a place-name can usually have two forms: *the University of London* and *London University*. Universities named after a person have only the latter form: *Yale University*.

Proper nouns with the definite article
760
The following classes of proper nouns take the definite article:
761
(A) PLURAL NAMES
    the Netherlands (*but*: Holland)
    the Midlands
    the Hebrides, the Shetlands, the Bahamas, the Canaries
    the Himalayas, the Alps, the Rockies, the Pyrenees
    the Wilsons (= 'the Wilson family')
762
(B) SOME GEOGRAPHICAL NAMES
    Rivers: the Avon, the Danube, the Mississippi, the Thames, *etc*
    Seas: the Atlantic, the Pacific (Ocean), the Baltic, the Mediter-
            ranean, *etc*
    Canals: the Panama (Canal), the Erie Canal, *etc*
763
(C) PUBLIC INSTITUTIONS, FACILITIES, *etc*
    Hotels and restaurants: the Grand (Hotel), the Hilton, *etc*
    Theatres, cinemas, clubs, *etc*: the Globe, the Athenaeum, *etc*
    Museums, libraries, *etc*: the Tate, the British Museum, the Hunt-
    ingdon (Library), *etc*
But note: *Drury Lane, Covent Garden*.
764
(D) NEWSPAPERS
    the Daily Express, the New York Times, the Observer
Magazines and periodicals normally have no article: *Language, Newsweek, Time, Punch, New Scientist, Practical Boat Owner*. However, magazine names modelled on human nouns take the article: *the Spectator, the New Statesman*. After genitives and possessives the article is dropped: *today's Times, this week's New Statesman*.

Quantifiers (*see GCE* 4.18–26, 4.122–128)

765
Quantifiers are determiners and pronouns denoting quantity or amount (*see* 57–68). Of the quantifiers which are determiners, some (like *all*) function as predeterminers in the noun phrase (*see* 558–62), others (like *some*) function as central determiners (*see* 551–7), and yet others (like *many*) as postdeterminers (*see* 563–5). There are five main groups of quantifiers, and within each group we may distinguish:
(1)   Determiners (as in *some friends*)
(2)   Pronouns which may be followed by an *of*-construction (as in *some of the men*)
(3)   Other pronouns (as in *Somebody is knocking*)

766

Determiners

The five groups of quantifiers (A–E) are illustrated in *Table 5*, which shows quantifiers that are determiners.

Table 5

QUANTIFIERS WHICH ARE DETERMINERS

	COUNT		MASS
	Singular	Plural	Singular
GROUP (A): determiners of inclusive meaning (*see* 61–3)	*all* *every* *each* — *half*	*all* — — *both* *half*	*all* — — — *half*
GROUP (B): *some* and *any* words (*see* 803–7)	*some* *any* *either*	*some* *any* —	*some* *any* —
GROUP (C): degrees of quantity/ amount (*see* 58)	— — — — — — —	⎰*many* ⎱*more* *most* *enough* ⎰(*a*) *few* ⎱*fewer*/*less* *fewest* *several*	⎰*much* ⎱*more* *most* *enough* ⎰(*a*) *little* ⎱*less* *least* —
GROUP (D): unitary	*one*	—	—
GROUP (E): negative (*see* 632)	*no* *neither*	*no* —	*no* —

767

Examples:

Group (A)

> *All the world* mourned his death. (Less usual than: *The whole world . . .*)
> I've lost *all my books/money.*
> *Every/each student* will have to take the test.
> *Both carpets* have been cleaned.
> He gave *half the apple/apples/food* to his sister.

All and *both* (but not *half*) can also occur after their heads. If the head is subject, *all* and *both* have the mid-position of adverbs (*see* 470):

> The students/they ⎰*all* like their new professor.
>   ⎱were *all* working hard.

If the head is a pronoun but not a subject, their position is immediately after the pronoun:

> She made us *both/all* welcome (= '. . . *both/all of us . . .* ').

768

Group (B)

Some and *any* can be used as determiners with singular count nouns when they are stressed (on unstressed *some*, see 553):

There was *'some 'book* or other on this topic published last year.
'Any 'pen will do.

In ⟨familiar⟩ style, stressed *some* means '(an) extraordinary' *etc*:

That's *'some 'car* you have there.

More usually, these words are used with plural or mass nouns:

I've found *some glasses/wine* in the cupboard.
Did *any chairs/furniture* get broken?

769

Group (C)

Did you see $\left\{ \begin{array}{l} \textit{many cars} \\ \textit{much traffic} \end{array} \right\}$ on the road?

We've had *more fine days/weather* this summer than last.

Most food is
Most things are $\left. \right\}$ expensive these days.

Have we got *enough glasses/wine*?

There's only $\left\{ \begin{array}{l} \textit{a few minutes} \\ \textit{a little time} \end{array} \right\}$ before the train leaves.

The president has $\left\{ \begin{array}{l} \textit{few supporters} \\ \textit{little support} \end{array} \right\}$ in the army.

There were *fewer/less accidents* on the road this year than last year,
but this doesn't mean there is *less need* for careful driving.

The countries with the *least population* often seem to be those with
the *fewest problems*.

He hasn't been to work for *several days*.

770

Group (D)

Apart from being a numeral (*see* 661) and a pronoun (*see* 776), *one* is used as an
indefinite determiner in such contexts as:

One day I'll come and visit you (= 'at an indefinite time').
One politician is just as bad as another.

771

Group (E)

No problem is $\left. \right\}$ insoluble.
No problems are

He has almost *no money*.

Pronouns which may take an *of*-construction

772

These quantifiers are frequently followed by an *of*-phrase, in which *of* is normally
followed by a pronoun or a definite noun phrase. However, the *of*-phrase may be
omitted if the quantifier acts as a substitute for an earlier noun phrase (*see* 394):

$\left\{ \begin{array}{l} \end{array} \right.$ *Both of them/the men* were wanted by the police.
The two men looked suspicious, and in fact we later discovered that
both were wanted by the police.

Compare *Table 6* (next page) with the table for determiners (*Table 5*).

773

Since the pronouns with the *of*-construction correspond closely to the determiners, we need give only a few examples:

The children had eaten *all of the pie/pears/fruit*.
Both of his parents are German.

Table 6

QUANTIFIER PRONOUNS WHICH MAY TAKE AN *of*-CONSTRUCTION

	COUNT		MASS
	Singular	Plural	Singular
GROUP (A)	*all (of)* *each (of)* — *half (of)*	*all (of)* — *both (of)* *half (of)*	*all (of)* — — *half (of)*
GROUP (B)	*some (of)* *any (of)* *either (of)*	*some (of)* *any (of)* —	*some (of)* *any (of)* —
GROUP (C)	— — — — — — — —	⎧ *many (of)* ⎨ *more (of)* ⎩ *most (of)* *enough (of)* ⎧ *(a) few (of)* ⎨ *fewer/less (of)* ⎩ *fewest (of)* *several (of)*	⎧ *much (of)* ⎨ *more (of)* ⎩ *most (of)* *enough (of)* ⎧ *(a) little (of)* ⎨ *less (of)* ⎩ *least (of)* —
GROUP (D)	*one (of)*	—	—
GROUP (E)	*none (of)* *neither (of)*	*none (of)* —	*none (of)* —

Note that *every* and *no* do not act as pronouns: instead, we use *everyone* and *none*.

(A)   Would *any of you* like some more soup/peas?

(B)   Yes, I'd love *some*.

I haven't read { *many of his poems.*
 much of his poetry.

We've sold *most of the tickets/land*, but we've kept *enough* for our own needs.

I've been to *a few of his lectures*, but understood *little of* what he said.

Several of the passengers were hurt and *one* (*of them*) was taken to hospital. Luckily, *none* was/were killed.

Other pronouns
774
Except for *one*, which merits separate discussion (*see* 776), the other quantifier pronouns are singular pronouns which have either personal or non-personal reference. They are:

	Personal reference	Non-personal reference
GROUP (A)	*everybody, everyone*	*everything*
GROUP (B)	*somebody, someone* *anybody, anyone*	*something* *anything*
GROUP (E)	*nobody, no one*	*nothing*

The pronouns of personal reference have a genitive form (*everybody's*, etc). There is no difference of meaning between the words ending in *-body* and *-one*.

775
Examples:
> *Everybody/everyone* over eighteen now has a vote.
> I've tried *everything*, but *nothing* works.
> *Somebody/someone* told me you've been to America.
> I've got *something* to tell you.
> Has *anybody/anyone* got *anything* to say?
> There was *nobody/no one* at the office.

One
776
One is a numeral, and also a singular count pronoun. As a pronoun, it has three uses:
(A) as a pronoun which may be followed by *of* (*see* 772). *One* so used can follow certain other quantifiers, notably *every*, *each*, and *any*:
> *Every one of* the cups was broken.

With *each* and *any*, *one* is optional:
> *Each/any* (*one*) *of* us could have made that mistake.

(B) as a pronoun which may substitute for an indefinite noun (*see* 395). In this use, *one* has the plural form *ones*:
> I have several maps of the area. Which *one/ones* do you need?

(C) as an indefinite personal pronoun (= 'people in general', *see* 86). This use of *one* has a genitive form *one's* and a reflexive form *oneself.*

Questions (*see GCE* 7.55–71)

777
Questions are either direct:
> *'Where were you last night?'* she asked.

or indirect:
> She asked me *where I was last night.*

Indirect questions are always signalled by an interrogative word. Direct questions, on the other hand, need not contain an interrogative word, for example:
> *'Are you going out again tonight?'* she asked.

On interrogative words, *see* 578–83. On indirect questions, *see* 267. The two most important kinds of questions are *yes-no* questions and *wh*-questions (*see* 245–68).

(A) *Yes-No* questions
778
They are called *yes-no* questions because the answer (which may be expressed or just implied) is *yes* or *no*. To make a statement into a *yes-no* question, simply put the operator (*will*, *is*, etc) before the subject. *Yes-no* questions usually have rising intonation (*see* 41).

STATEMENT	QUESTION	
They'll/will be coming.	Will they be coming?	[1]
Susan is reading a book.	Is Susan reading a book?	[2]
She's a nice girl.	Is she a nice girl?	[3]
She's been working hard.	Has she been working hard?	[4]
His brothers like football.	Do his brothers like football?	[5]

Notice that in the questions [1], [2] and [4] the verb phrase is divided: the subject comes between the operator and the rest of the verb phrase. In [3], the whole verb phrase comes before the subject. Sentence [5] shows the 'dummy operator' *do* in a question. *Do* (*see* 674) has to be used here because there is no operator in the corresponding statement.

(B) *Wh*-questions

779

Wh-questions (unlike *yes-no* questions) normally have falling intonation.

(A)   Where do you live?   (B)   (I live in) London.

(A)   What's your name?   (B)   (My name is) Catherine.

780

Wh-questions begin with an interrogative like *who, what, when, etc* (*see* 578–83). This is how to form *wh*-questions:

   a   Put the sentence element which contains the *wh*-word at the beginning of the sentence.
   b   If the element containing the *wh*-word is object, complement, or adverbial, place the operator in front of the subject.

   Wh-ELEMENT IS OBJECT:

   John asked a question.   What question DID John ask?   [6]

   Wh-ELEMENT IS COMPLEMENT:

   These animals are very clever.   How clever ARE these animals?   [7]

   Wh-ELEMENT IS ADVERBIAL:

   They'll leave tomorrow.   When WILL they leave?   [8]

The operator normally comes just after the *wh*-element. In [6], the *do*-construction has to be used, because the corresponding statement has no operator.

   c   If the element containing the *wh*-word is the subject, the verb phrase remains the same as in the corresponding statement, and no *do*-construction is necessary (*see* 674–5):

   Susan has been reading this book.   *Who's* been reading this book?

   That man is your brother.   Which man is your brother?

(On cases where the *wh*-element is a prepositional complement, see 741.)

(C) Tag questions

781

Tag questions are shortened *yes-no* questions added to a statement. They consist of operator plus pronoun, with or without a negative particle. The choice and tense of the operator depend on the preceding verb phrase, and the pronoun repeats or refers back to the subject of the statement:

   The boat has left, hasn't it?

   The boat left yesterday, didn't it?

   The boat hasn't left, has it?

On tag questions, see further 250.

Reciprocal pronouns

782
We can bring together two sentences such as
John likes Mary.
and
Mary likes John.
into a reciprocal structure:

John and Mary like $\begin{cases} each\ other. \\ one\ another. \end{cases}$

Each other and *one another* are reciprocal pronouns.
Where more than two are involved, *one another* is often preferred:
The four children were very fond of *one another*.
He put all the books on top of *one another*.
The reciprocal pronouns can be freely used in the genitive:
The students borrowed *each other's* notes.

Relative clauses (*see GCE* 4.117–119, 13.5–15)

783
The term RELATIVE CLAUSE is used for various types of subclause which are
linked to part or all of the main clause by a back-pointing element (*see* 70–82),
usually a RELATIVE PRONOUN (but *see* 645–6 on nominal relative clauses). The
principal function of a relative clause is that of postmodifier in a noun phrase
(*see* 719), where the relative pronoun points back to the head of the noun phrase
(THE ANTECEDENT).
784
The relative pronouns of English are *who, whom, whose, which, that*, and zero
(*ie* pronoun omitted). That is, we include in our list a pronoun which is not pronounced, but which 'exists' in that it fills the position of subject, object, *etc* in the
clause. *Compare*:
The records *which he owns* are mostly classical.
(relative pronoun = *which*)
The records *he owns* are mostly classical.
(relative pronoun = zero)

Relative pronouns
785
The choice of relative pronoun depends on
(A)   Whether the clause is *a* RESTRICTIVE or *b* NON-RESTRICTIVE (*see* 99–100):
      a People *who/that live in towns* are deprived of life's greatest bless-
          ing—a healthy environment.
      b Many people, *who live in towns*, are deprived of life's greatest
          blessing—a healthy environment.
(B)   Whether the head of the noun phrase is *a* PERSONAL or *b* NON-PERSONAL:
      a The man *who was following us* seems to have disappeared.
      b The car *which was following us* seems to have disappeared.
(C)   What the role of the pronoun is within the relative clause: *eg* whether it is
      subject, object, *etc*. This determines the choice of *a* SUBJECTIVE or *b* OB-
      JECTIVE case:
      a The girl *who* is going to marry Peter is an extremely attractive
          brunette.
      b The girl (*whom*) Peter is going to marry is an extremely attractive
          brunette.

786

In addition, we have a choice of two constructions when the relative pronoun acts as prepositional complement (*see* 739–43):

The girl (*who/whom*) Peter is engaged *to* . . . ⎫
The girl *to whom* Peter is engaged . . .   ⎬ (*see* 794)

The construction in which the preposition comes at the end of the clause is less ⟨formal⟩ than that in which it precedes the pronoun. Apart from this construction, relative pronouns are always placed first in the clause.

787

Because of the front placing of the relative pronoun, the order of elements in a relative clause is often different from that of normal statements:

(The girl) *who(m) Peter married* . . .	(OSV)
but: Peter married the girl.	(SVO)
(The student) *with whom I share a room* . . .	(ASVO)
but: I share a room with a student.	(SVOA)
(He's not the fool) *that he looks*	(CSV)
but: He looks a fool.	(SVC)

But when the relative pronoun is subject, the normal order is retained:

(The girl) *who marries Peter* . . .   (SVO)

788

The uses of relative pronouns are classified in *Table 7*.

Table 7

RELATIVE PRONOUNS

	RESTRICTIVE AND NON-RESTRICTIVE		RESTRICTIVE ONLY
	personal	non-personal	personal and non-personal
subjective case	*who*	*which*	*that*
objective case	*who(m)*		*that*, zero
genitive case	*whose*	*of which* / *whose*	

We deal now with three classes of relative pronouns: (A) the *wh*-pronouns, (B) *that*, and (C) zero.

(A) *Wh*-PRONOUNS

789

The *wh*-series reflects the personal/non-personal gender of the antecedent:

PERSONAL   *who, whom, whose*
NON-PERSONAL   *which*, [*whose, see* 790]

There's a man outside *who* wants to see you.
I want a watch *which* is waterproof.

790

If a pronoun is in a genitive relation to a noun head, the pronoun can have the form *whose*:

The woman *whose* daughter you met is Mrs Brown.
  (The woman is Mrs Brown; you met *her* daughter.)   [1]

The house *whose* roof was damaged has now been repaired.

(The house has now been repaired; *its* roof was damaged.)   [2]

In examples like [2] where the antecedent is non-personal, there is some tendency to avoid the use of *whose* by using the *of*-phrase:

The house the roof *of which* was damaged has now been repaired.

⟨awkwardly formal⟩

791

With a personal antecedent, the relative pronoun can show the distinction between *who* and *whom*, depending on its role as subject of the relative clause [3], or as object [4] and [5], or as prepositional complement [6], [7] and [8]:

I know the girl
- *who* married him.   [3]
- *who* he met.   ⟨informal⟩   [4]
- *whom* he met.   ⟨formal⟩   [5]
- *who* he spoke *to*.   ⟨informal⟩   [6]
- *whom* he spoke *to*.   ⟨more formal⟩   [7]
- *to whom* he spoke.   ⟨most formal⟩   [8]

When the relative pronoun is object, as in [4] and [5], or when it is the complement of an end-placed preposition, as in [6] and [7], there is some choice between *who* and *whom*. *Whom* is preferred in ⟨formal⟩ English. Among the *wh*-pronouns there is no choice when the pronoun is the subject (*who*), as in [3], or when it is the complement of a preceding preposition (*whom*), as in [8].

(B) *That*

792

That is used with both personal and non-personal reference. However, it cannot follow a preposition (*see* 794c), and is not usually used in non-restrictive relative clauses (*see* 795).

(C) *Zero*

793

The zero relative pronoun is used like *that* except that it cannot be the subject of a clause:

OBJECT   The man { the policeman caught / *that* the policeman caught } received ten years in jail.

SUBJECT   The policeman { *caught him / *that* caught him } received a reward.

Restrictive relative clauses

794

All the relative pronouns can be used in restrictive relative clauses: *who* (*whom, whose*), *which* and, particularly, *that* and the zero relative. We can now complete the picture given so far of the possible choices among all the relative pronouns by four sets of examples.

a   The relative pronoun is the subject:

Have you met anybody { *who* / *that* } has been to China?

There's still one thing { *which* / *that* } is not explained.

b   The relative pronoun is the object:

Do you know the boy
- we met?
- *that* we met?
- *who* we met? ⟨informal⟩
- *whom* we met? ⟨formal⟩

That's the house
- I've bought.
- *that* I've bought.
- *which* I've bought.

c The relative pronoun is the complement of a preposition.

Do you know the boy
{
your daughter writes *to*?
that your daughter writes *to*?
who your daughter writes *to*?
whom your daughter writes *to*? ⟨more formal⟩
to whom your daughter writes? ⟨formal⟩
}

This is the house
{
we wrote to you *about*.
that we wrote to you *about*.
which we wrote to you *about*.
about which we wrote to you. ⟨formal⟩
}

Non-restrictive relative clauses
795
The meaning of a non-restrictive relative clause is often very similar to that of a coordinated clause (with or without conjunction), as we indicate by paraphrases of the examples below. Only *wh*-pronouns are usually used in non-restrictive clauses:

Then he met Mary,
{
who invited him to a party.
and she invited him to a party.
}

Here is John Smith
{
, who(m) I mentioned the other day.
; I mentioned him the other day.
}

(On intonation and punctuation here, *see* 411–13.)

Sentence relative clauses
796
This type of non-restrictive clause points back not to a noun, but to a whole clause or sentence (or even a sequence of sentences):

He admires Mrs Brown,
{
which surprises me.
which I find strange.
}

{
(='and it surprises me that he does')
(='and I find it strange that he does')
}

These clauses have the function of sentence adverbials (*see* 479).

Sentences (*see GCE* 7.1, 7.53, 11.1–2, 11.80–85)

Clauses and sentences
797
Sentences are made up of one or more clauses (*see* 505). Sentences containing just one clause are called SIMPLE, and sentences containing more than one clause are called COMPLEX. There are two main ways of linking clauses together, *ie* of forming complex sentences: COORDINATION and SUBORDINATION.

Two simple sentences, for example

He heard an explosion.
He phoned the police.

may be joined into one sentence, either by coordinating the two clauses by *and* or by making one clause into a main clause and the other into a subclause:

COORDINATION   He heard an explosion *and* (he) phoned the police.

SUBORDINATION   When he heard an explosion, he phoned the police.

(For coordination, *see* 542–7; for subordination, *see* 826–34.)

Four kinds of sentence
798
A simple English sentence, *ie* a sentence consisting of only one clause, may be
—grammatically—a statement, a question, a command, or an exclamation.
799
(A) STATEMENTS are sentences in which the subject is present and generally comes
before the verb (*but see* 426):

> I'll speak to the boss today.

800
(B) QUESTIONS are sentences which are marked in one or more of these ways:
  a The operator is placed immediately before the subject (*see* 778):

> Will you speak to the boss today?

  b The sentence begins with an interrogative word (*see* 780):

> Who will you speak to?

  c The sentence has rising intonation in ⟨spoken⟩ English (*see* 41, 249):

> You'll speak to the boss today?

In ⟨written⟩ English, questions end with a question mark (?).
801
(C) COMMANDS are sentences with the verb in the imperative (*ie* the base form,
see 624). Although they usually have no expressed subject, they sometimes
take *you* (*see* 520):

> (You) speak to the boss today.

Note that in ⟨written⟩ English, command sentences do not normally end with
an exclamation mark, but with a full stop:

> Come here.

802
(D) EXCLAMATIONS are sentences which begin with *what* or *how*, without inversion of subject and operator (*see* 672–5):

> What a noise they are making!

In ⟨written⟩ English exclamations usually end with an exclamation mark (!).

Some-words and *any*-words (see *GCE* 4.127, 7.44–48)

803
Some and *any* as determiners (*see* 552–3) and pronouns (*see* 772) tend to occur in
different grammatical contexts: *some* is the normal word to occur in positive
statements, and *any* is the normal word to occur in *yes-no* questions and after
negatives.
  There are a number of pairs of terms which behave like *some* and *any* in this
respect. Therefore we need to distinguish two classes of words, which we call
some-WORDS and *any*-WORDS:

Some-words are:	*some, someone, somebody, something, somewhere, sometime, sometimes, already, somewhat, somehow, too* (adverb of addition).
Any-words are:	*any, anyone, anybody, anything, anywhere, ever, yet, at all, either.*

804
The contrast between *some*-words and *any*-words is illustrated in these examples
of *some* and *any*:

> Ann has bought *some* new material.   (POSITIVE STATEMENT)   [1]

Ann hasn't bought *any* new material.   (AFTER NEGATIVES)   [2]
Has Ann bought *any* new material?   (QUESTIONS)   [3]

Some can occur in [2] and [3], but these sentences would then require a special context (*see* 248).

Note

Any can be used with stress and with distributive meaning in positive statements *eg Anyone can do that!* (*see* 64), but we are not concerned with this use of *any* here.

805

In negative clauses, *any*-words follow not only *not* or *n't*, but also other negative words such as *nobody, no, scarcely, etc* (*see* 629–34):

Nobody has *ever* given her *any* encouragement.

806

The following illustrate the contrasts between matching *some*- and *any*-words:

some-WORDS	*any*-WORDS	
POSITIVE STATEMENTS	AFTER NEGATIVES	QUESTIONS
DETERMINER They've had *some* lunch.	They haven't had *any* lunch.	Have they had *any* lunch?
PRONOUN He was rude to *some-body*.	He wasn't rude to *any-body*.	Was he rude to *anybody*?
PLACE ADVERB They've seen him *some-where*.	They haven't seen him *anywhere*.	Have they seen him *any-where*?
TIME-WHEN ADVERB I'll see you again *some-time*.	I won't *ever* see you again.	Will I *ever* see you again?
FREQUENCY ADVERB He *sometimes* visits her.	He doesn't *ever* visit her.	Does he *ever* visit her?
DEGREE ADVERB She was *somewhat* annoyed.	She wasn't *at all* annoyed.	Was she *at all* annoyed?

There are similar contrasts between *somehow* and *in any way*, *already* and *yet*, *still* and *any more*.

807

These are a few other contexts in which *any*-words typically occur:

(A)   IN *Yes-No* INTERROGATIVE SUBCLAUSES

I sometimes wonder *whether examinations are any use to anyone*.

(B)   IN CONDITIONAL CLAUSES (*see* 211)

If there were anything wrong, he would certainly let us know.

(C)   AFTER CERTAIN WORDS WITH NEGATIVE IMPLICATIONS

a Verbs: *deny, fail, forget, prevent, etc*

He *denies* I *ever* told him.

b Adjectives: *difficult, hard, reluctant, etc*

It's *difficult* for *anyone* to understand him.

c Prepositions: *against, without, etc*

He arrived *without any* of his belongings.

(D)   IN COMPARISONS (*see* 523–8) after *-er, more, less, as, too*:

The climate here is wet*ter* than *anywhere* else in the country.

It's *too* late to blame *anyone* for the accident.

Spelling changes (*see GCE* 3.55–62, 4.62, 4.96, 5.73)

808
There are a number of changes in the spelling of nouns, verbs, adjectives, and adverbs, which occur when certain endings are added to them. It will be convenient to deal with all such spelling changes here in one place. They involve three types of change: replacing, adding, and dropping letters.

Replacing letters
CHANGING *y* TO *i(e)*
809
In bases ending in a consonant + *y*

(A) *y* becomes *ie* in verbs before 3rd person singular present *-s* (*see* 620):

| they carry | he carries |
| they try | he tries |

(B) *y* becomes *ie* in nouns before plural *-s* (*see* 704):

| a spy | two spies |
| a lady | several ladies |

(C) *y* becomes *i* in adjectives before comparative *-er* or *-est* (*see* 523–5):

| early | earlier | earliest |

(D) *y* becomes *i* in verbs before *-ed* (*see* 622):

| they carry | they carried |
| they try | they tried |

(E) *y* becomes *i* in adverbs before the *-ly* used to form adverbs from adjectives (*see* 480):

| easy | easily |
| happy | happily |

810
But *y* is kept in the following cases:

a in proper nouns: *the Kennedys, the two Germanys*
b in a few words such as *standbys, etc*
c and, of course, after a vowel: *journeys, stays, gayer* (except the *u* of *-quy*: *soliloquy→soliloquies*). In three verbs there is however a change from *y* to *i* also after a vowel:

lay	laid
pay	paid
say	said (Note here also a change of vowel sound: /seɪ/ → /sed/)

y changes to *i* also in certain words in *-ly*:

| gay | gaily |
| day | daily |

CHANGING *-ie* TO *-y*
811
Before the *-ing* ending (*see* 621), *-ie* is changed to *-y*:

| they die | they are dying |
| they lie | they are lying |

Adding letters
ADDING *e* TO NOUNS ENDING IN SIBILANTS
812
Unless already spelled with a final mute *e*, bases ending in sibilants (*ie* /z/, /s/, /dʒ/, /tʃ/, /ʒ/, /ʃ/) receive an additional *e* before the *-s* ending

(A) in the plural of nouns:

box	box*es*
church	church*es*
dish	dish*es*

(B) in the 3rd person singular present of verbs:

they pass	he pass*es*
they polish	he polish*es*

813

Note: An additional *-e* is also added in two irregular verbs ending in *-o*:

they do /du:/	he do*es* /dʌz/ (Note also the change of vowel sound)
they go /gov/	he go*es* /govz/

ADDING *e* TO NOUNS ENDING IN *-o*

814

Nouns ending in *-o* normally have the plural spelled *-oes*:

echoes	potatoes
embargoes	tomatoes
heroes	torpedoes
negroes	vetoes, *etc*

815

Plurals in either *-oes* or *-os* occur, for example, in

archipelagoes	archipelagos
banjoes	banjos
cargoes	cargos

816

The plural is spelled only *-os* after a vowel (*radios, studios, etc*) and in abbreviations (*hippos, kilos, photos, pianos, etc*).

Doubling consonants
817

Final consonants are doubled when the preceding vowel is STRESSED and spelled with A SINGLE LETTER

(A) in adjectives and adverbs before *-er* and *-est*:

big	bigger	biggest
hot	hotter	hottest

(B) in verbs before *-ing* and *-ed*:

drop	dropping	dropped
stop	stopping	stopped
occur	occurring	occurred
permit	permitting	permitted
prefer	preferring	preferred

818

Note: There is no doubling when the vowel is unstressed or written with two letters:

quiet	quieter	quietest
great	greater	greatest
enter /'entəʳ/	entering	entered
visit /'vɪzɪt/	visiting	visited
dread	dreading	dreaded

Compare *hoping/hoped* (from *hope*) with *hopping/hopped* (from *hop*) and *staring/stared* (from *stare*) with *starring/starred* (from *star*).

819

In ⟨BrE⟩ *m* and *l*, are doubled also when they are unstressed:

'cruel	{ crueller	cruellest	⟨BrE⟩
	{ crueler	cruelest	⟨AmE⟩
'travel	{ travelling	travelled	⟨BrE⟩
	{ traveling	traveled	⟨AmE⟩
{ 'program(me)	programming	programmed	⟨BrE⟩
{ 'program	programing	programed	⟨AmE⟩

Dropping letters
DROPPING *e*

820

If the base ends in silent *e*, the *e* is dropped
(A) in adjectives and adverbs before -*er* and -*est*:

| brave | braver | bravest |
| free | freer /ˈfriːəʳ/ | freest /ˈfriːɪst/ |

(B) in verbs before -*ing* and -*ed*:

create	creating	created
hope	hoping	hoped
shave	shaving	shaved

821

Note: Verbs ending in -*ee*, -*ye*, -*oe* and often -*ge* do not drop the -*e* before -*ing* (but they do drop it before -*ed*):

agree	agreeing	(agreed)
dye	dyeing	(dyed)
singe	singeing	(singed)

Compare *dyeing* with *dying* (from *die*) and *singeing* /ˈsɪndʒɪŋ/ with *singing* /ˈsɪŋɪŋ/ (from *sing*).

Subjects (*see GCE* 7.9, 7.13–18)

822

a The subject of a clause is
a noun phrase (*see* 651–3) or pronoun:
> *Bill/He* will be late for the meeting.

a non-finite verb form, or a nominal clause (*see* 637-50), usually with introductory *it* (*see* 584–9):
> *Smoking cigarettes* is a nasty habit.
> { *That he'll be on time* is not very likely.
> { *It*'s not very likely *that he'll be on time*.

b The subject normally occurs before the verb in statements. In questions (*see* 777–81), the subject occurs immediately after the operator (*see* 672–5):
> *They*'ve had some lunch.
> Have *they* had any lunch?

c The subject has number and person concord (where this applies) with the finite verb (*see* 876):
> I*'m* coming, too.   *Mary is* coming, too.

d The most typical function of a subject is to denote the actor: that is, the person, *etc* causing the happening denoted by the verb:
> *John* opened his eyes.

e When an active sentence is turned into a passive sentence (*see* 677), the subject of the active sentence becomes the agent of the passive. The agent occurs in a *by*-phrase, which is however usually omitted (*see* 679):

> *Everybody* rejected the proposal.
> The proposal was rejected (by *everybody*).

Subjunctives (*see GCE* 3.16, 12.35, 12.37)

823

On the whole, subjunctive verb forms are little used in modern English. We may distinguish three categories of the subjunctive:

(A) The MANDATIVE SUBJUNCTIVE in *that*-clauses after expressions like *demand, require, insist, suggest, be necessary, obligatory, etc* has only one verb form, the base (*see* 624). This means there is lack of the usual concord between subject and finite verb in the 3rd person singular present (. . . *he come* . . .), and that the present and past tenses (*see* 880) are indistinguishable. The use of this subjunctive occurs chiefly in ⟨formal⟩ style, and especially in ⟨AmE⟩ (*see* 7). In other contexts, *that*-clauses with *should*+infinitive (*see* 289–90) or *to*-infinitive are more common:

=
> It is necessary *that every member inform himself* of these rules.
>   ⟨formal⟩
> It is necessary *that every member should inform himself* of these rules.
> It is necessary *for every member to inform himself* of these rules.

824

(B) The FORMULAIC SUBJUNCTIVE also consists of the base, but is only used in certain set expressions:

> *Come* what may, . . .
> *Suffice* it to say that . . .
> *Be* that as it may . . .

825

(C) The *were*-SUBJUNCTIVE, when *were* is used instead of the expected *was*, occurs in clauses expressing condition or contrast and in subclauses after verbs like *wish* (*see* 285–6). *Was* can also be used and is more common in ⟨informal⟩ style:

> If she $\begin{Bmatrix} were \\ was \end{Bmatrix}$ to do something like that, . . .

> He spoke to me as if I $\begin{Bmatrix} were \\ was \end{Bmatrix}$ deaf.

> I wish I $\begin{Bmatrix} were \\ was \end{Bmatrix}$ dead.

but: $\begin{Bmatrix} Were \\ *Was \end{Bmatrix}$ I to yield to your demand . . . (*see* 286–7)

Subordination (*see GCE* Chapter 11)

826

Two clauses in the same sentence may be related either by coordination (*see* 542–7) or by subordination. In the case of coordination, the two clauses are 'equal partners' in the same structure. But in subordination one clause, which we call a SUBCLAUSE, is included in the other, which we call the MAIN CLAUSE. A subclause can also have another subclause inside it, which means that it behaves as a 'main clause' with respect to the other subclause. For example, the sentence *I know that you can do it if you try* is made up of three clauses, each within the other:

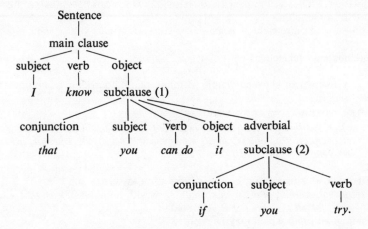

Subclauses can have various functions in their main clause. They may be subjects, objects, adverbials, prepositional complements, postmodifiers, *etc* (*see* 517).

827

A main clause is almost always a finite clause (*see* 514). A subclause, on the other hand, can be a finite, non-finite, or verbless clause:

FINITE SUBCLAUSE   *After its owner had been forced to leave,* the castle was allowed to fall into ruin.

NON-FINITE SUBCLAUSE   The castle, *abandoned by its owner,* was allowed to fall into ruin.

VERBLESS SUBCLAUSE   The castle, *now empty,* was allowed to fall into ruin.

All three types of clause (finite, non-finite, and verbless) may of course themselves have subclauses inside them. Here is a non-finite clause containing a finite subclause:

Having left BEFORE THE LETTER ARRIVED, he was surprised to find his wife at the station.

Here is a verbless clause containing a non-finite subclause:

Never slow TO TAKE ADVANTAGE OF AN OPPONENT'S WEAKNESS, Borg moved ahead confidently to win the fourth set 6–3.

Signals of subordination

828

A subclause is not usually capable of standing alone as the main clause of a sentence. This is because subclauses are usually marked as subclauses by some signal of subordination. The signal may be

a *that*, which may usually be omitted (*see* 639–40):
   I hope (*that*) *you'll like this place.*

b a subordinating conjunction, for example *if* (*see* 208):
   I'll be surprised *if he can do it.*

c a *wh*-word (*see* 578–83):
   We asked him *where he'd been all night.*

d inversion ⟨rather formal⟩ (*see* 287):
   Had I known, I wouldn't have come.

e lack of a finite verb (*see* 876):
   I hope *to see you tonight.*

Apart from *that*-clauses with *that* omitted (including relative clauses, *see* 793) there is only one type of subclause that contains no expressed signal of subordination. This is a comment clause (*see* 522) which can be related to the MAIN clause of a *that*-clause:

You're right, *I suppose*. (='I suppose (that) you're right.')

Subordinating conjunctions
829
We can distinguish between simple, compound, and correlative conjunctions.
830
SIMPLE SUBORDINATING CONJUNCTIONS:

after, (al)though, as, because, before, if, how(ever), like ⟨familiar⟩, *once, since, that, till, unless, until, when(ever), where(ver), whereas, whereby, whereupon, while, whilst* ⟨esp BrE⟩.

831
COMPOUND SUBORDINATING CONJUNCTIONS ENDING WITH *that*:

in that, so that, in order that (*in order to* with infinitives), *such that, except that, for all that, save that* ⟨elevated⟩.

ending with *that* which may be omitted:

but (that), now (that), providing (that), provided (that), supposing (that), considering (that), given (that), granting (that), granted (that), admitting, (that) assuming (that), presuming (that), seeing (that), immediately (that)

ending with *as*:

as far as, as long as, as soon as, so long as, in-so-far as, so far as, inasmuch as ⟨very formal⟩, *according as, so as* (+ *to*-infinitive)

ending with *than:*

sooner than (+ non-finite clause), *rather than* (+ non-finite clause)

other compound subordinating conjunctions:

as if, as though, in case

832
CORRELATIVE SUBORDINATING CONJUNCTIONS:

(A)   *if . . . then, (al)though . . . yet/nevertheless, as . . . so*

(B)   *more/less/-er . . . than, as . . . as, so . . . as, so . . . (that)* (with *that* omitted, *so is* ⟨informal⟩), *such . . . as* ⟨formal⟩, *such . . . (that), no sooner . . . than*

(C)   *whether . . . or*

(D)   *the . . . the*

The various uses of subordinating conjunctions are discussed in Part Three (see the index).
Note
Some subordinating conjunctions (*as, like, since, until, till, after, before, but*) also function as prepositions (*see* 744–5): *since the war* (*ended*).

The functions of subclauses
833
Subclauses may function grammatically as subject, object, complement, or adverbial in a main clause:

SUBJECT	*That we badly need new equipment* is obvious.
DIRECT OBJECT	I know *that she's bright.*
INDIRECT OBJECT	I gave *whoever it was* a drink.
SUBJECT COMPLEMENT	The point is *that they're leaving right away.*
OBJECT COMPLEMENT	I can't imagine John *overcome with grief.*
ADVERBIAL	*When we meet,* I'll explain everything.

In addition, they may function as:

POSTMODIFIER IN A NOUN PHRASE	I like a friend *who remains a friend*.
COMPLEMENT OF A PREPO-SITION	That depends on *what is decided at the meeting*.
COMPLEMENT OF AN AD-JECTIVE	The workers are ready *to go on strike*.

834

NOMINAL CLAUSES (*see* 637–50) are those which can function as subject, object, complement, or complement of a preposition (*ie* which have the same kinds of position in the sentence as noun phrases). ADVERBIAL CLAUSES take the position of adverbial in a main clause. On these and other types of subclause, *see* 517.

Verb patterns (*see GCE* 12.29–70)

835

The part of a clause following the verb phrase depends on the verb for its basic structure. For example, we can use the verb *want* with the following objects:

He wants
$\begin{cases} \textit{a bicycle.} & \text{(A NOUN PHRASE)} \\ \textit{to see you.} & \text{(A \textit{to}-INFINITIVE)} \\ \textit{the man to come.} & \text{(A NOUN PHRASE} + \text{A \textit{to}-INFINITIVE)} \end{cases}$

However, *want* cannot, for instance, have a *that*-clause (like the corresponding verb in many other languages):

*He wants *that she comes*.

836

We have distinguished six basic verb patterns in English (*see* 508):

[L] Linking verbs
[T] Verbs with one object
[V] Verbs with object + verb . . .
[D] Verbs with two objects
[X] Verbs with object and object complement
[I] Verbs without object or complement

Within each basic verb pattern, we can distinguish a varying number of sub-patterns, which are numbered [T1], [T2], *etc*.

In various senses, the same verb can sometimes occur in different basic verb patterns. For example *find* may be [T], [D], and [X]:

[T1]   I found her (in the library).
[D1 (*for*)]   I found her a new job.
[X (*to be*) 1] I found her (to be) an entertaining partner.

837

Although we can state the different verb patterns, it is not possible to list here all the verbs which can occur in each pattern. For this you will need to consult a dictionary, such as *A Dictionary of Contemporary English* (ed. by P. Procter, Longman, forthcoming). We use the same system here as in that dictionary.[1] Only those patterns which give learners the greatest difficulty will be exemplified more fully here. In the examples, optional adverbials are placed in brackets. The patterns are given in the active, but, where passives (*see* 676–82) are common, this is indicated by one passive example in each pattern. Notice, however, that where a passive example is given, this does not necessarily mean

[1] We thank the publishers and the editor of DOC for permission to use and adapt this system of verb patterns. For a chart explaining *see Table 8* on page 308.

that all verbs in that pattern can have a passive. For example, in Pattern [V3]:

They $\left\{\begin{array}{l}\text{allowed}\\\text{wanted}\end{array}\right\}$ us to stay another week.

Only the first of these sentences can be changed into the passive:

> We were allowed to stay another week.

but not: *We were wanted to stay another week.

Linking verbs: [L]
838

In this pattern, the verb is a linking verb (also called a copula, *see* 510). There are two groups of linking verbs: CURRENT LINKING VERBS and RESULTING LINKING VERBS.

Current linking verbs, such as *look* and *feel*, indicate a state. Other current linking verbs are:

> *appear* (happy)
> *lie* (scattered)
> *remain* (uncertain, a bachelor)
> *seem* (restless, an efficient secretary)
> *stay* (young)
> *smell* (sweet)
> *sound* (surprised)
> *taste* (bitter)

Resulting linking verbs, such as *become* and *get*, indicate that the role of the verb complement is a result of the event or process described in the verb:

> *grow* (tired)
> *fall* (sick)
> *run* (wild)
> *turn* (sour, teetotaller)

We can distinguish the following patterns with linking verbs.

839

[L1] The complement is a noun phrase (*see* 651–3) or nominal clause (*see* 637–50):

> This *is* a really good book.
> The answer *is* that we don't want to stay in.
> He *became* a beggar.

840

[L (*to be*) 1] *To be* can occur between the linking verb and the complement, but this *to be* is not necessary:

> She *seems* (to be) a sweet girl.
> He *proved* (to be) a fool.

841

[L7] The complement is an adjective (which may have the form of a participle):

> He *became* very sick (on board their yacht).
> Your garden *looks* awfully nice.
> She *sounded* rather surprised (on the phone).
> Just *stay* calm.

842

[L (*to be*) 7] *To be* can occur between the linking and the complement, but this *to be* is not necessary:

> The task *proved* (to be) impossible.
> He *seems* (to be) tired.

843

[L9] The verb is followed by an adverbial:

> John *is* at school (between 9 and 4).

Their wedding will *be* in late June.

The road *leads* there, through the forest, *etc.*

He *leaned* out of the window, down, *etc.*

The verb may have an adverbial particle to complete or intensify its meaning (*down, up, etc*):

She *cut* the cake (with a knife).

He *landed* (*up*) in jail. ⟨informal⟩

She *lay* (*down*) on the bed.

In the case of *lie* the word *down* may occur as the only adverbial, whereas with *land, up* must be accompanied by another adverbial.

Verbs with one object (monotransitive verbs): [T]

844

[T1] The object is a noun phrase:

She *cut* the cake (with a knife).

He *boiled* the water (in the pan).

The verb may be a phrasal verb (*see* 696), *ie* verb + adverbial particle + object. When the object of these verbs is a noun, it may be placed either before or after the adverbial particle. If it is a pronoun, it may only be placed before the particle:

They *blew* $\begin{cases} up \text{ the bridge.} \\ \text{the bridge } up. \end{cases}$

He *blew* it *up.*

PASSIVE

The bridge (It) was blown up.

The verb may have an adverbial particle to complete or intensify its meaning (*out, up, etc*):

$= \begin{cases} \text{He } cleaned \text{ the room } (out). \\ \text{He } cleaned \text{ (out) the room.} \end{cases}$

$= \begin{cases} Eat \text{ (up) your dinner.} \\ Eat \text{ your dinner (up).} \end{cases}$

PASSIVE

The room was cleaned (out).

The verb may be a prepositional verb (*see* 699), *ie* verb + preposition + object:

I *bumped into* George the other day (= 'met'). ⟨informal⟩

He *came across* an interesting letter to his grandfather (= 'discovered').

They *came by* these facts only yesterday (= 'acquired').

PASSIVE

These facts were come by only yesterday.

The verb may be a phrasal-prepositional verb (*see* 701), *ie* verb + adverbial particle + preposition + object:

They should *do away with* these prejudices (= 'abolish, get rid of').

PASSIVE

These prejudices should be done away with.

845

[T2] These verbs are used with a bare infinitive (without *to*):

Can I *help* clean the windows?

Don't you *dare* speak to me like that!

This behaviour is rare for main verbs, although it is the usual case with the modal auxiliaries (*see* 501). *Help* and *dare* also belong to [T3].

846

[T3] The object is a *to*-infinitive:

We *agreed* to stay over night.
They *decided* to go home at once.
You *deserve* to win this time.
I *expect* to be back by noon.
She has *promised* to write every week.

847

[T4] The verb is followed by an *-ing* form:

We all *enjoyed* seeing them again.
Why have you *stopped* doing your exercises?

Other [T4] verbs include:

acknowledge	dislike	resent
avoid	fancy	resist
consider	finish	risk
deny	miss	cannot stand
detest	postpone	suggest

The verb may have an adverbial particle before the *-ing* form to complete or intensify its meaning:

She *kept* (*on*) working.

848

[T5a] The verb has a *that*-clause (where *that* may be omitted):

They *agree* (that) she is efficient.
We *discovered* (that) we had lost our keys.

Passive with introductory *it* (*see* 584–9):

It was agreed that she is efficient.

Other [T5a] verbs include:

accept	doubt	indicate
admit	feel	remark
claim	forget	understand

849

[T5b] The *that*-clause can be replaced by *so* (in a positive clause) or *not* (in a negative clause):

I *believe* (*suppose*) so.
I *hope* (*think*) not.

850

[T5c] The verb has a *that*-clause with putative *should* (*see* 289–90) or a subjunctive verb (*see* 823–4). *That* is rarely omitted with *should*, never with the subjunctive:

I *request* that she (should) go alone.
He *suggested* that John (should) leave at once.

Other [T5c] verbs include:

ask	insist	recommend
command	order	require
demand	propose	urge

851

[T6a] The verb has a finite clause introduced by a *wh*-word (*see* 578–83): *how, why, where, who, whether* (or sometimes *if*) etc:

He *asked* $\begin{Bmatrix} \text{if} \\ \text{whether} \end{Bmatrix}$ they were coming.

Other [T6a] verbs include:

decide	doubt	guess
discuss	forget	wonder

and, with the verb typically in the negative,

> *know*   *notice*   *say*

852

[T6b] The verb has a non-finite clause introduced by a *wh*-word:

> I don't *know* how to address this letter.
> She *forgot* where to look.

Verb + object + verb: [V]

These transitive verbs have an object which is followed by another verb.

853

[V2] Verb + object + infinitive without *to*:

> Will you *help* me write the invitations?
> Please *let* her stay!
> You *made* me change my mind.

Note that the *to*-infinitive is used in the passive:

> I was made to change my mind.

In this pattern, *let* is not used in the passive.

854

[V3] Verb + object + *to*-infinitive:

> He *allowed* the neighbours to use his car.
> They *asked* us not to be late for the train.
> What *caused* them to revise their decision? ⟨formal⟩
> What *got* them to change their minds? ⟨informal⟩
> They *advised* us to stay another week.

PASSIVE

> We were asked not to be late for the train.

Other [V3] verbs include:

force	*order*	*teach*
help	*permit*	*tell*
intend	*require*	*urge*

Note: *Want, like, etc* as in *He wants us to help* are better classed under [T3] (*see* 647–8, 845).

855

[V4] Verb + object + *-ing* form:

> And please don't *keep* us waiting!
> I don't *like* him being rude to you.
> We *saw* her crossing the lawn.

856

[V8] Verb + object + *ed*-form:

> I must *get* my shoes mended.
> He *had* the house rebuilt.

Verbs with two objects (ditransitive verbs): [D]

857

[D1 (*to*)] The verb has an indirect object + a direct object. This construction can be replaced by a direct object + *to* + noun phrase:

> = { He *gave* George the money.
>   { He *gave* the money to George.

PASSIVE

> = { George was given the money.
>   { The money was given (to) George.

Other [D1 (*to*)] verbs include:

bring	*hand*	*owe*
grant	*offer*	*promise*

read	*show*	*teach*
send	*take*	*write*

858

[D1 (*for*)] The verb has an indirect object + a direct object. This construction can be replaced by a direct object + *for* + noun phrase:

$$= \begin{cases} \text{He } \textit{bought} \text{ his wife a gold watch.} \\ \text{He } \textit{bought} \text{ a gold watch for his wife.} \end{cases}$$

Other [D1 (*for*)] verbs include:

cook	*leave*	*peel*
find	*make*	*save*
get	*order*	*spare*

859

[D1] The verb has two objects which cannot be replaced by prepositional constructions with *to* or *for*. Each object can appear alone in [T1]:

He *asked* me some awkward questions.

He *struck* him a heavy blow.

860

[D1] With these verbs, only the second object can appear alone. There is no corresponding passive:

The coat *cost* (George) 30 pounds.

861

[D5a] The verb has an object + a *that*-clause (*see* 639–40), where *that* is often omitted:

He *told* her (that) he would be back early.

PASSIVE

She was told that he would be back early.

Other [D5a] verbs include:

assure	*inform*	*remind*
convince	*persuade*	*warn*

862

[D5b] *So* can be put in the place of the *that*-clause as substitute:

I *told* you *so* (that he would come).

863

[D6a] The verb has an object + a finite *wh*-clause (*see* 641–3).

He *asked* us who she was.

They didn't *tell* us where he had gone.

PASSIVE

We were asked who she was.

864

[D6b] The *wh*-word is followed by a *to*-infinitive:

I *told* her how to do it.

I *showed* him where to park.

Verbs with object and object complement (complex-transitive verbs): [X]

865

[X1] The complement is a noun phrase:

The parents *named* the baby Susan.

They *voted* him Sportsman of the Year.

PASSIVE

He was voted Sportsman of the Year.

After verbs such as *name* and *vote*, the complement has no article when the office is unique (*see* 496). Other [X1] verbs are:

appoint	*christen*	*make*
call	*elect*	

866

[X (*to be*) 1] *To be* may be inserted before a noun phrase complement:

They *considered* him (to be) the best player on the team.

He *found* her (to be) a very efficient secretary.

PASSIVE

He was considered (to be) the best player on the team.

Other [X (*to be*) 1] verbs include:

appoint	*pronounce*	*think*
imagine	*suppose*	*vote*

867

[X7] The complement is an adjective:

He *painted* the door blue.

She *served* the coffee black.

PASSIVE

The door was painted blue.

Other [X7] verbs include:

keep	*make*
leave	*wash*

868

[X (*to be*) 7] *To be* may be inserted before an adjective complement:

They believed him (to be) innocent.

Many students *thought* the exam (to be) rather unfair.

PASSIVE

He was believed (to be) innocent.

Other [X (*to be*) 7] verbs include:

feel	*know*
imagine	*suppose*

869

[X9] The verb has an adverbial following the object:

Put your coat in the cupboard.

(*Put your coat)

She *showed* me to the door, out, *etc.*

Verbs without object or complement (intransitive verbs): [I]

870

[Iφ]   He *paused*.

The water *boiled* (in the saucepan).

The verb may be a phrasal verb without an object:

The bridge *blew up* (= 'exploded').

Don't ever *give up* (= 'surrender').

There is no object but an object is understood:

John smokes. (understood object = cigars, cigarettes, *etc*)

871

[I] The verb is used with a *to* + infinitive:

He *lived* to be ninety.

872

[I] The verb is followed by an *-ing* form:

He *went* shopping.

She *came* running.

Verb phrases (*see GCE* 3.10–15, 3.23–42)

873

Verb phrases consist either of a MAIN VERB (*see* 617):

She *writes* several letters every day.   [1]

or of one or more AUXILIARY VERBS together with a main verb. As the name implies, auxiliary verbs 'HELP' the main verb to make up verb phrases:

> She *is writing* a long letter home. [2]
>
> She *has been writing* letters all morning. [3]
>
> Those letters *might* never *have been written*, if you hadn't re-
> minded her. [4]

874

There are two types of auxiliaries: PRIMARY AUXILIARY VERBS and MODAL AUXILIARY VERBS. The primary auxiliary verbs are *do, have,* and *be.*
Do helps to form the *do*-construction (*see* 674–5):

> She *didn't write* many letters.

Have helps to form the perfective aspect (*see* 878):

> She *has written* only one letter.

Be helps to form the progressive aspect, as in [2], and the passive, as in

> The letters *were written* in two hours.

The modal auxiliaries help to express a variety of meanings (*see* 129, 292–301, 335–44), for example future time and ability, as in

> The letter *will reach* you tomorrow.
>
> She *cannot spell* very well.

Here is a table showing the different types of verbs:

MAIN VERBS (*see* 617–26)		*write, walk, frighten, etc*
AUXILIARY VERBS	Primary (*see* 498–500)	*do, have, be*
	Modal (*see* 501–3)	*can, may, shall, will, could, might, should, would, used to, must, ought to, need, dare*

Finite and non-finite verb phrases

875

There are two kinds of verb phrase: FINITE and NON-FINITE. Finite verb phrases are distinguished by containing a finite verb as their first (or only) word. The finite verb is the element of the verb phrase which has present or past tense:

FINITE VERB PHRASE

He $\left\{ \begin{array}{l} \textit{studies/studied} \\ \textit{is/was studying} \end{array} \right\}$ English.

NON-FINITE VERB PHRASE

$\left\{ \begin{array}{l} \text{Studying English is useful.} \\ \text{It is useful to have studied English.} \end{array} \right.$

876

Finite verb phrases occur as the verb element of main clauses (*see* 826). There is usually also person and number concord between the subject and the finite verb. Concord is particularly clear with *be* (*see* 500, 541):

> I *am* / you *are*/he *is* here.

With most finite main verbs, there is no concord contrast except between the 3rd person singular present and all other persons:

> He *reads* (They *read*) the paper every morning.

Modal auxiliaries count as finite verbs, although they have no concord with the subject:

> I / you /he /they *can* play the piano.

877

The non-finite forms of the verb are the infinitive (*to call*), the *-ing* participle (*calling*), and the *-ed* participle (*called*). Non-finite verb phrases consist of one or more such items. Compare:

FINITE VERB PHRASES	NON-FINITE VERB PHRASES
He *smokes* heavily.	*To smoke* like that must be dangerous.
He *is working* hard.	I found him *working* hard.
After he *had left* the office, he went home by car.	After *having left* the office, he went home by car.

Combinations of verbs

878

When a verb phrase consists of more than one verb, there are certain rules for how they can be combined. We have four basic verb combinations:

(A) MODAL, a modal auxiliary followed by a verb in the infinitive:
      He *can type* quite well.

(B) PERFECTIVE, a form of *have* followed by a verb in the past participle form:
      He *had typed* several letters.

(C) PROGRESSIVE, a form of *be* followed by a verb in the *-ing* form:
      He *was typing* when the telephone rang.

(D) PASSIVE, a form of *be* followed by a verb in the past participle form:
      Several letters *were being typed* by him.

879

These four basic combinations may also combine with each other to make up longer strings of verbs in one single verb phrase. The order is then alphabetical (A)+(B)+(C)+(D), for example:

(A)+(B):	He *may have typed* the letter himself.
(A)+(C):	He *may be typing* at the moment.
(A)+(D):	The letters *may be typed* by Mrs Anderson.
(B)+(C):	He *has been typing* all morning.
(B)+(D):	The letters *have been typed* by Ann.
(C)+(D):	The letters *are being typed*, so please wait a moment.
(A)+(B)+(C):	He *must have been typing* the letters himself.
(A)+(B)+(D):	The letters *must have been typed* by the secretary.

As we can see, the verbs in the middle of the phrase serve both as the second part of the previous combination and as the first part of the following combination:

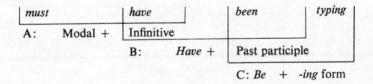

Tense and aspect

880

By TENSE we understand the correspondence between the form of the verb and our concept of time (past, present, or future). ASPECT concerns the manner in which a verbal action is experienced or regarded (for example as complete or in progress).

English has two simple tenses: the PRESENT TENSE (*see* 106–11) and the PAST TENSE (*see* 112–14).

THE PRESENT TENSE	Today Bill *is* in his office.
THE PAST TENSE	Yesterday Bill *was* at a conference.

881

English also has two marked aspects: the PROGRESSIVE ASPECT (*see* 116, 122) and the PERFECTIVE ASPECT (*see* 115–19).

THE PROGRESSIVE ASPECT	Bill *is/was* just *writing* a letter home.
THE PERFECTIVE ASPECT	Bill *has/had written* five letters.

882

The present and past tenses can form combinations with the progressive and perfective aspects (the letters in [square brackets] denote the basic combinations, *see* 879).

PRESENT TIME	THE SIMPLE PRESENT	He always *writes* long letters.
	THE PRESENT PROGRESSIVE [C]	He *is writing* one now to his wife.
PAST TIME	THE SIMPLE PAST	He also *wrote* to her yesterday.
	THE PAST PROGRESSIVE [C]	He *was writing* a letter when somebody came in.
	THE PRESENT PERFECT [B]	He *has written* several letters to her.
	THE PRESENT PERFECT PROGRESSIVE [B + C]	He *has been writing* letters all morning.
	THE PAST PERFECT [B]	He *had written* five letters by lunch-time.
	THE PAST PERFECT PROGRESSIVE [B + C]	He *had been writing* letters all morning and felt tired.

These are the ACTIVE tenses and aspects. The PASSIVE (*see* 676–82) is formed by adding combination type [D], for example:

THE PASSIVE SIMPLE PRESENT [D]	Nowadays long letters *are* rarely *written* by hand.
THE PASSIVE PRESENT PROGRESSIVE [C + D]	The letter *is* just *being written*.

There is no future tense in English corresponding to the time/tense relation for present and past (*but see* 128–37).

Contrasts in the verb phrase
883

In addition to the contrasts already mentioned of *a* tense, *b* aspect, and *c* the active-passive relation, there are other constructions in which the verb phrase plays an important part. For these constructions, the first auxiliary of the verb phrase has a special role as OPERATOR (*see* 672–5).

d Yes-no QUESTIONS (*see* 778) requiring movement of the subject involve the use of an auxiliary as operator:

John *sang*.   *Did* John *sing*?

e NEGATION WITH *not* (*see* 629–31) makes a similar use of operators:

John *sang*.   John *didn't sing*.

f EMPHASIS (*see* 272, 313) is frequently carried by the operator:

John *did* sing!

g IMPERATIVES (*see* 520–1):

Do be careful.

Word-classes (*see GCE* 2.12–16)

884
We distinguish between minor and major word-classes.

(A) Minor word-classes

AUXILIARY VERBS	*can, should, used to, etc* (*see* 497–503)
DETERMINERS	*the, a(n), this, every, such, etc* (*see* 550–67)
PRONOUNS	*he, they, anybody, one, which, etc* (*see* 747–9)
PREPOSITIONS	*of, at, without, in spite of, etc* (*see* 744–5)
CONJUNCTIONS	*and, that, when, although, etc* (*see* 542–7, 829–32)
INTERJECTIONS	*oh, ah, ugh, phew, etc* (*see* 309)

(B) Major word-classes

MAIN VERBS	*search, get, say, do, etc* (*see* 617–26)
NOUNS	*John, room, belief, etc* (*see* 45–56)
ADJECTIVES	*happy, steady, new, large, round, etc* (*see* 456–63)
ADVERBS	*steadily, completely, really, very, etc* (*see* 480–8)

It is quite common in English for words belonging to different word-classes to have the same written or spoken form. *Mary* is both a determiner and pronoun; *love* is both a verb and a noun; *since* is both a conjunction and a preposition, *etc*.

885
Members of the MINOR WORD-CLASSES are also called CLOSED-SYSTEM ITEMS. That is, the sets of items are *closed* in the sense that they cannot normally be extended by creating new members. The members in a closed system can be listed.

886
The MAJOR WORD-CLASSES are sometimes called OPEN CLASSES. Unlike minor word-classes, major word-classes are 'open' in the sense that they can be indefinitely extended. No one could, for example, make a complete inventory of all the nouns in contemporary English, because new nouns are continually being formed (*miniskirt, minicomputer, minimovie, minirecession, etc*). On the other hand, determiners, pronouns, or conjunctions form a fixed class of words which changes relatively little from one period of the language to another.

308

Table 8

THE MEANING OF THE NUMBERS USED IN VERB PATTERNS AFTER THE LETTERS **L, T, V, D, X,** AND **I**

NUMBER	**L** Linking	**T** Transitive (+Object)	**V** Object+ Verb	**D** Ditransitive (+Object +Object)	**X** Complex Transitive (+Object +Complement)	**I** Intransitive
∅	—	—	—	—	—	**I∅** VERB alone
1 +NOUN *or* +NOUN +NOUN	**L1** VERB+ NOUN *or* VERB+ (*to be*) NOUN	**T1** VERB+ NOUN	—	**D1** VERB+ NOUN +NOUN	**X1** VERB+ NOUN +NOUN *or* VERB+ NOUN+ (*to be*) NOUN	—
2 +BARE INFINI-TIVE	—	**T2** VERB+ BARE INFINITIVE	**V2** VERB+ OBJECT+ BARE INFINITIVE	—	—	—
3 +*to*-INFINI-TIVE	—	**T3** VERB+ *to*-INFINITIVE	**V3** VERB+ OBJECT+ *to*-INFINITIVE	—	—	**I3** VERB+*to*-INFINITIVE
4 +*ing*-FORM	—	**T4** VERB+ *-ing*-FORM	**V4** VERB+ OBJECT+ *-ing*-FORM	—	—	**I4** VERB+ *-ing*-FORM
5 +*that*-CLAUSE	—	**T5** VERB+ *that*-CLAUSE	—	**D5** VERB+ OBJECT+ *that*-CLAUSE	—	—
6 +*wh*-WORD	—	**T6** VERB+ *wh*-WORD	—	**D6** VERB+ OBJECT+ *wh*-WORD	—	—
7 +ADJEC-TIVE	**L7** VERB+ ADJECTIVE *or* VERB+ (*to be*) ADJECTIVE	—	—	—	**X7** VERB+ NOUN+ ADJECTIVE *or* VERB+ NOUN+ (*to be*) ADJECTIVE	—
8 +*-ed*-FORM	—	—	**V8** VERB+ OBJECT+ *-ed*-FORM	—	—	—
9 +ADVER-BIAL	**L9** VERB+ NECESSARY ADVERBIAL	—	—	—	**X9** VERB+ OBJECT+ NECESSARY ADVERBIAL	—

Index

References are to section numbers

Grammatical terms are entered in SMALL CAPITALS (*eg* ABSTRACT NOUNS). Other subjects and notions appear in ordinary type (*eg* ability). Individual words treated in the Grammar are printed in *italics* (eg *able*.)